The Confucian Transformation of Korea

HARVARD-YENCHING INSTITUTE MONOGRAPH SERIES

36

The Confucian Transformation of Korea
A Study of Society and Ideology

Martina Deuchler

Published by the COUNCIL ON EAST ASIAN STUDIES, HARVARD
UNIVERSITY and distributed by HARVARD UNIVERSITY PRESS,
Cambridge (Massachusetts) and London   1992

10 9 8 7 6 5 4

The Harvard-Yenching Institute, founded in 1928 and headquartered at Harvard University, is a foundation dedicated to the advancement of higher education in the humanities and social sciences in East and Southeast Asia. The Institute supports advanced research at Harvard by faculty members of certain Asian universities, and doctoral studies at Harvard and other universities by junior faculty at the same universities. It also supports East Asian studies at Harvard through contributions to the Harvard-Yenching Library and publication of the *Harvard Journal of Asiatic Studies* and books on the premodern East Asian history and literature.

Library of Congress Cataloging-in-Publication Data
Deuchler, Martina, 1935–
    The Confucian transformation of Korea : a study of society and
  ideology / Martina Deuchler.
       p.   cm.—(Harvard-Yenching Institute monograph series ; 36)
    Includes bibliographical references (p.   ) and index.
    ISBN 0-674-16089-4
    1. Korea—Social life and customs—1392-1910.   2. Korea—
  Civilization—Confucian influences.   3. Neo-Confucianism—Korea—
  History.   I. Title   II. Series.
  DS913.27.D48   1992
  951.9—dc20   92-18507
                                       CIP

Index by Martina Deuchler

To the memory of my parents

Acknowledgments

This book has been in the making for a long time. I first explored the topic when I studied as a special student at the Institute of Social Anthropology, Oxford University, for six months in 1972. I had then the good fortune to find in the late Maurice Freedman an enthusiastic and inspiring mentor. I owe him an immense debt of gratitude. At that time, practically no secondary sources in any language dealing with the structure of Korean society were available to guide my first steps. When I ventured into the essentially uncharted territory of Korea's rich recorded past, many times I lost my way or got entangled in thorny theoretical issues. Unfailingly, Professor Freedman came to my rescue and gave me the benefit of his vast knowledge of Chinese society. His insightful comments and constant encouragement spurred my research along. The outline of this work was just emerging by the time of Professor Freedman's untimely death in 1975.

My study of ancestor worship was first presented to the Conference on Korean Religion and Society sponsored by the Social Science Research Council, New York, on Mackinac Island, Michigan, in August 1980. I was fortunate to meet there Arthur P. Wolf, who took an interest in my work for the contrast it provided to his own studies of Chinese society. For the last ten years, he has inspired my research with his astute comments and unstintingly discussed problems of analysis and presentation. Without his continued support, my work on Koryŏ society in particular would not have reached a presentable stage. I owe him therefore an immense measure of thanks.

I should also like to give thanks to Roger L. Janelli and Robert C. Provine, who assisted me in the preparation of this work and read and commented upon parts of the manuscript at an earlier stage of its preparation. The penultimate version was read by Laurel Kendall, JaHyun Kim Haboush, and Hill Gates. I gratefully acknowledge their perceptive and helpful comments. James B. Palais subjected the manuscript to his usual critical scrutiny, and I owe him thanks for encouraging me to reformulate some major points. Edward W. Wagner generously gave me the benefit of his profound knowledge of Chosŏn dynasty social history. He also made innumerable editorial suggestions that substantially improved the manuscript. I should like to express my heartfelt thanks to him. In Korea, I benefitted from the unselfish help and stimulation I have received over many years from my Korean teachers and colleagues, in particular Yi Hye-gu, Song June-ho, Yi Ki-mun, Yi Man-gap, Ko Yŏng-gŭn, Yi Sŏng-mu, Han Yŏng-u, Yi T'ae-jin, and Hŏ Hŭng-sik. My archival studies in the Kyujanggak Archives of Seoul National University were always pleasant, thanks to the assistance I received from Yi Sang-ŭn. Sandra Mattielli has been unfailing in giving editorial assistance on many occasions. Nobody other than I myself, of course, must be held responsible for any errors or misinterpretations that might have remained undetected.

Last but not least, I should like to thank Mr Cho Ik-ho and his family who over many years have provided me with a second home in Korea. Their care and encouragement, always generously given, have in many ways contributed to the development and completion of this work.

From 1972 to 1988 my research was generously supported by the Swiss National Science Foundation, Berne. This unusual support came at a time when Korean Studies had no secure institutional abode in Switzerland. I hope that with the publication of this work I can redeem to some extent the expectations and trust the Foundation put in my research for such a long period of time. I have no other way to express my thanks to the Foundation. I also gratefully acknowledge a grant from the Jubiläumsspende für die Universität Zürich for a research trip to Korea in the summer of 1986.

Earlier versions of some of the chapters were published as "The Tradition: Women during the Yi Dynasty," in Sandra Mattielli, ed., *Virtues in Conflict: Tradition and the Korean Woman Today* (Seoul: Royal Asiatic Society, 1977); "Neo-Confucianism: The Impulse for Social Action in Early Yi Korea," in *Journal of Korean Studies* 2 (1980); and "Neo-Confucianism in Action: Agnation and Ancestor Worship in Early Yi Korea," in Laurel Kendall and Griffin Dix, eds., *Religion and Ritual in Korean Society,* Korean Research Monograph number 12 (Berkeley: Institute of East Asian Studies, University of California, 1987; copyright 1987 by The Regents of the University of California). I am grateful for the permission to reuse these copyrighted materials.

Contents

Diagrams

Table

The Confucian Transformation of Korea

Introduction: Society and Ideology

This study started out with a simple observation: during the first century after the Chosŏn dynasty (1392–1910) was founded, the volume of legislation that was concerned with social issues was unusually high. It far surpassed the scope of legislative activities ordinarily to be expected at the outset of a new dynasty. Moreover, not only the quantity, but the quality of that legislation was remarkable. It soon became clear that the early legislators attempted to introduce into Korean society notions and concepts which ran counter to established tradition and therefore gave rise to conflict. What were the motives that stimulated such legislative ventures? It was certainly not a new insight to link the spirit of that time to Confucianism, the declared "state religion" of the new dynasty. There the conventional wisdom seemed to end, and a multitude of questions and problems emerged. What, for example, were the elements in Confucianism that became the levers of social legislation? Which institutions of society were earmarked for change? What was the overall purpose of such endeavors? The general direction and the first results of this legislative campaign pointed to a general rationalization of social structure and organization on the basis of a patrilineal ideology. But had Korean society not always been a patrilineal society? This became one of the most challenging questions and necessitated research beyond the originally envisaged time limit of early Chosŏn into the relatively unknown terrain of Koryŏ (918–1392).

The scope of the study at hand thus widened when it became clear that the developments at the beginning of Chosŏn could not be revealed without reference to Koryŏ society. Very little substantial research about Koryŏ society, however, had been done. Available information concentrated mainly on institutional, economic, and political history. A relatively small number of scattered articles treated aspects of Koryŏ's social history. An overall view of Koryŏ's social tradition that could have been used as background for evaluating early Chosŏn was altogether lacking. This explains the lengthy first part on Koryŏ in this book.

Throughout—this is true for Koryŏ as well as for Chosŏn—the data could not have been sorted merely in a historical framework. As I. M. Lewis pointed out years ago,[1] history has little or no theory, and therefore the social historian is fortunate to have at his disposal a vast body of theory developed by the social anthropologists. In the meantime, the insight that the historian and the social anthropologist tackle the same problems and questions and benefit from each other's methodology to resolve them has become commonplace.[2] It will become evident that the conception and the analytical framework of this study are greatly indebted to a combination of these two disciplines. The materials concerning Koryŏ social organization in particular are fragmentary. They are scattered over a long period of time and therefore do not reveal their meaning when merely put into a time sequence. Social anthropology provides the instruments that help unlock their meaning, relate it to other phenomena, and finally create an overall explanatory pattern. Such a procedure also avoids the hitherto all too prevalent danger of looking at Koryŏ data from the well-established interpretative framework of "Confucian" tradition.

Whatever the method, it cannot do more than concentrate on and arrange the data available in historical sources. The historian has no access to informants who would be able to fill the gaps in information and provide a "native" view. Therefore much of the day-to-day life remains in obscurity, and the reconstructions the historian comes up with at best present the outer or normative limits within which life in historical times was lived. Where information is fragmentary, it is dangerous to argue a case on the basis of theory. On the other hand, without the advantage of comparative knowledge many a piece of intelligence would not yield its significance. This is again particularly true for Koryŏ. The dearth of materials allows glimpses rather than a panoramic view of Koryŏ's social life. The picture improves for early Chosŏn when many facets of life were discussed and singled out as target areas of reformatory policy.

This study is not a social history of Korea. Rather, it focuses on the process of change during the transition period from late Koryŏ to mid Chosŏn. To highlight the process of change, a few major topics were selected for discussion—ancestor worship and funerary rites, succession and inheritance, the position of women and the marriage institution, and the formation of descent groups. In the concluding chapter an attempt has been made to relate the significance of change in these areas of social life to the broader questions of status assertion and lineage formation.

The exploration of the above topics over a period of approximately seven hundred years has greatly benefitted from previous research undertaken within the last three decades by Korean and Japanese scholars of diverse persuasions. To be sure, in comparison with political, institutional, and economic history, social history has generally been a relatively neglected field of inquiry. Nevertheless, the number of Korean scholarly works treating specific social institutions or addressing particular questions of Korea's social past is rapidly increasing. In an underdeveloped research area, concentrating on single topics may at times unavoidably obstruct a researcher's comprehension and appreciation of connective links. Moreover, when researchers adhere to traditional periodization that follows dynastic cycles, they often overlook transition periods. There also are as yet few signs in Korea of cooperation between historians and social scientists, although such interdisciplinary cooperation will undoubtedly become more important in the future. In addition, the field has drawn much inspiration from the enviably rich studies of

Chinese society, which have set high standards by combining factual description with new theoretical approaches.

The purpose of this study, then, is to test two major hypotheses. First, the picture of Korean society as it emerged in the second half of Chosŏn (roughly from the second half of the seventeenth century) contrasts strikingly with the picture that can be drawn, however sketchily, of Korean society of the Koryŏ period. This conspicuous difference must have resulted from a fundamental transformation that Korean society underwent during the transition period from late Koryŏ to mid Chosŏn. Second, the driving force that initiated and directed this transformation was not so much generated by political or economic factors—in both these realms there was a great degree of continuity—than provided by Neo-Confucianism. Chinese Neo-Confucianism, which from late Koryŏ became the major intellectual force in Korea, inspired a new class of Korean scholar-officials with a particular vision of social organization and gave them the necessary guidelines to implant it in their own environment. The reorganization of Korean society thus inaugurated reached a scope and depth that were rarely attained by social action anywhere else. Although undated and nameless because it is not linked to a single datable event, the Confucian transformation of Korea ushered in a period of epochal change in Korean history.

THE CONTOURS OF KOREAN SOCIETY IN LATE CHOSŎN. To illustrate the immensity of this reorganization, a brief sketch of the salient features of Korean society, as they emerged in the course of the seventeenth century and survived into the twentieth century, may be in order. It is this picture that has become the standard view of "traditional Korean society" and has thus often obscured the extraordinary development of which it was the final result.

The hallmark of Korean society in late Chosŏn was a kinship system that rested on highly structured patrilineal descent groups. These patrilineages[3] comprised groups of agnates who derived their common descent from a real or putative apical ancestor *(sijo)* and identified themselves with a common surname *(sŏng)* and a common ancestral seat *(pon'gwan)*,[4] for example the Kim of Andong or the

Yi of Chŏnju. Lineages (and families) clearly distinguished between main lines formed by the firstborn sons of primary wives, branch lines formed by sons born after the first son by the same mother, and secondary sons, who, as offspring of secondary wives, were of secondary status and therefore not full-fledged lineage members.[5] Lineage perpetuation thus was secured through primogeniture, and strict lineage exogamy was observed. The size of such groups varied in accordance with the relative prestige of the ancestor from whom they claimed descent. Recapture of ancestral prestige—the prestige of a high government official *(hyŏnjo)*, for example—was a primary motivation for forming a new lineage or a lineage segment.[6] Lineage organization could therefore be quite complex, although Korean lineages generally were subject to lesser internal segmentation than their Chinese counterparts. A higher-order lineage could comprise thousands of members who lived in localized sub-lineages spread over the whole peninsula.[7] What held these kin structures together was the memory of common descent and a common geographical focus, the original ancestral seat (although the latter might be neither the place of birth nor residence for most of the kinsmen concerned).[8]

Important charters of common descent were the genealogies *(chokpo)* that began to appear in great numbers from roughly 1600 and were in the early 1930s still the most frequently printed publications.[9] The compilation of a genealogy usually was initiated by the members of a descent group residing in the capital who became aware of the importance of demonstrated common descent—for example, for attaining government office or for forging marriage alliances. They were therefore interested in displaying their influence and power in the political world by fostering the common ancestral bond with close relatives. Even though some of the latter may have lived in the countryside, geographical dispersal did not necessarily lead to a break in the consciousness of common identity. Lines within a larger descent group that for some time did not produce a prominent member (i.e., an examination passer and government officeholder), however, were eventually dropped from the records. Daughters were listed only when they married, if at all, and then by the name of their husbands. Genealogies were thus from time to time amended and supplemented and, for large descent groups, grew into compendia of considerable volume and complexity. The impossibility of including all members of a descent group in one single genealogy could give rise to lineage segmentation. The inclusion of people with spurious backgrounds, moreover, at times caused disputes that induced certain lineage members to separate themselves and start their own genealogical records. Only properly certified lineage membership could ensure access to social, political, and economic prominence.[10]

The most intimate ritual expression of kinship was ancestor worship. Called *tangnae,* the worshipping group usually consisted of those agnatic kinsmen who traced their descent from a common great-great-grandfather and consequently wore mourning for each other according to the five mourning grades *(obok).* Such a group thus included third cousins. Chief officiant at the ancestral ceremonies was the primogeniture descendant of the most senior line *(chongga* or *pon'ga),* the "lineage grandson" *(chongson).* He was assisted by his counterparts of the collateral junior lines *(chi'ga* or *pun'ga).*[11] The foci of ritual action were lineage-owned graves and an ancestral hall *(sadang)* in which the wooden tablets of the ancestors were housed. Not only did the gatherings of these agnates at fixed dates during the year serve the purpose of presenting offerings to the common ancestors, but such demonstrations of common descent also enhanced kin solidarity and cooperation. At least a delegation, if not all, of these kinsmen was expected to be in attendance at the seasonal ancestral services for remoter antecedants conducted by members of more comprehensive lineage segments. The economic basis of ancestor worship was corporately held land that usually was administered by the primogeniture descendant. Besides these lineage rituals, individual ancestors were remembered on their death anniversaries with rites held in the households of their immediate descendants. While women were excluded from lineage rites, they participated at the domestic rites on the sidelines. Their principal function was the preparing of the sacrificial foods.[12]

Locality was one of the most salient principles of kinship organization in Korea. Ideally, agnates who descended from a common ancestor lived together in immediate geographic proximity and formed what was called "single-lineage villages" *(tongjok purak)*.[13] Such villages were most often founded by the descendants of an ancestor who had migrated to the locality. In the 1930s, some 15,000 such villages dotted the map of Korea, with a heavy concentration in the central and southern regions. Most of these villages were less than three hundred years old and seldom comprised more than sixty households.[14] In such settlements, the largest compound containing the most impressive tiled buildings and the ancestral hall usually belonged to the main line represented, the "big house" *(k'ŭn chip)*. It was surrounded by the smaller compounds of the various kinsmen who constituted the "small houses" *(chagŭn chip)*. The architectural design of these walled compounds complied with the Confucian dictum that the men's and the women's quarters had to be strictly separated: the master's domain *(sarang)* was situated close to the main gate *(taemun)*, whereas the inner rooms of the women were hidden behind a second gate *(chungmun)*. Nearby pavilions were common property.[15]

While the ritual head of the lineage *(chongson)* owed his prestige to his genealogical status, the "lineage elder" *(chongjang or munjang)*, chosen from among the lineage members on the basis of age and experience, wielded the greatest authority within the lineage. Although he had no exclusive power over lineage finances and property, he could appoint various lineage officials *(yusa)* to assist him and convene the "lineage council" *(chonghoe)* in which the different households were represented by their respective heads. Council meetings were usually held in conjunction with the ancestral services; and matters discussed pertained to lineage finances, lineage graves, help to destitute lineage members, compilation and emendation of the genealogical records. Decisions were based upon majority opinion. Besides the lineage council, there were other lineage organizations, often endowed with their own property, that concerned themselves with lineage welfare, education, solidarity, and cooperation. The economic basis of a lineage was corporately held property in the form of slaves, land, woods, and buildings. The amount of land, variously called "lineage land" *(chongt'o),* "exalted land" *(wit'o),* "ancestral service land" *(chejŏn),* or "grave land" *(myo-jŏn),* in principle increased in every generation because a certain proportion of each lineage member's estate would be set aside for defraying the costs of his funeral, ancestral rites, and upkeep of his grave.[16]

Economic wealth and ritual leadership might be said to reinforce each other when the two happened to coincide, but the former did not seriously challenge the latter in case the ritual main line was destitute economically. On the contrary, an impoverished "big house" could count on the support of wealthier lineage members, and economic motives seldom led to lineage segmentation. Maintenance of the main line did not only demand economic measures. Because of its overwhelming importance for continuing the lineage's ritual obligations, the main line had to be perpetuated, even at the cost of collateral lines. When it lacked a male heir, elaborate adoption procedures were invoked to secure an appropriate substitute. The ideal solution was the taking in of an agnatic nephew; but if none was available, the search extended, on the basis of genealogical records, to more remote collaterals. Even the giving up of an only son for the benefit of the main line was not considered an undue sacrifice.[17] Exclusive emphasis on male succession prevented a daughter from acquiring status in lineage affairs. Upon marriage, she joined her husband's group; and the door of her natal home closed behind her for good, even though she paid infrequent visits later on. In case she became widowed and, for economic reasons, returned to her own kin, she remained a member of her husband's lineage no matter how long she stayed away; and, after she died, it was the duty of her affines (her husband's kin) to perform ancestral rites for her.

Korean lineages were not only social and economic entities exerting paramount influence in local communities, they also constituted the reservoir from which the members of the officialdom were recruited. In other words, lineage organization was directly connected with the political process. This was, for example, stated in a scathing remark made by a middle-rank official, Kim Ching (1623–1676): "When the officials of the Board of Personnel recommend someone to the throne, they always mention that he is worthy to be appointed or promoted because he is a son, brother, or a lineage member of so and so. They do not question whether he is wise or ignorant."[18] Lineage background, thus, was a critical determinant of a man's political career, and it was carefully checked when someone wanted to be admitted to the government examinations. Significantly, during the Chosŏn period the majority of the passers of the higher civil service examinations *(munkwa)* originated from a small number of prominent descent groups.

Usually only certain lines within lineage segments became politically well established in the capital, the sociopolitical hub of the kingdom, or its environs, yet the aura of eminence reflected on all lineage members, even those remaining in the countryside. The capital representatives of the various segments, however, did not necessarily pursue the same political goals, so that in the intermittent struggles for political power some survived, while others perished—without destroying the fame and fortunes of the lineage as a whole.[19] The more prominent a kin group, the greater were its chances to acquire land in even remote areas of the country, causing the dispersal of some of its members. Geographic overextension then could lead to weakened ties to the capital and consequent loss of political momentum, with the result that successful examination candidates were no longer produced. Distance from central power was, however, often compensated by local influence. The emergence of regional elite culture during the mid sixteenth century was a distinct and important facet of the overall political landscape of the Chosŏn dynasty.[20]

Lineage culture was closely related to Confucianism, the ideology that provided the moral foundation for both private and public life. Whether in the capital or in the countryside, a life of scholarship, ritual purity, and conspicuous consumption was required. A great number of lineages were directly connected with private academies *(sŏwŏn)*—centers of learning and local power that from the mid sixteenth century on not only trained prospective examination candidates for the central bureaucracy, but also grew into bastions of local self-sufficiency. At the core of these academies stood the shrines in which exalted lineage members known for their learning and achievements were remembered at regular intervals. Controlling large amounts of tax-free land, these academies, and through them the lineages attached to them, exerted influence far beyond local boundaries.[21]

Lineages represented the social organization of the Korean upper class. Called *yangban*,[22] the elite of Chosŏn Korea constituted a relatively small segment, perhaps not more than ten percent, of the total population; but, drawing on descent and heredity, it monopolized the political process, economic wealth, and Confucian learning. Because yangban status was never clearly delineated legally, there is no sure guide to determine who deserved to be counted among the elite. Nevertheless, some criteria seem to have been indispensable: a clear line of descent, a "distinguished ancestor" *(hyŏnjo)*—"distinguished" meant, above all, scholarly reputation—from whom ancestry was traced and generally acknowledged, a clear geographic area within which such status was recognized, close marriage ties with other reputable lineages, and a special way of life.[23] It was thus largely the social environment, over which the government had little or no control, that set the rules of status ascription. Yangban status was clearly a relative concept and therefore could have quite different connotations of social and political prestige depending on whether it was claimed on the national or local level. Whatever their claim, established yangban were scarcely threatened by the inflation of "yangban ranks" toward the end of the dynasty, especially during the nineteenth century, by social upstarts who used yangban titles and purchased official ranks from the government, because the criteria mentioned above were lacking. Unlike the Chinese gentry, then, the Korean yangban showed the characteristics of a hereditary aristocracy that effectively controlled access to political power by defining eligibility for the examinations and occupied the upper echelons in government, possessed large landed wealth, and generally enjoyed the prestige and culture Confucian education conferred upon them.

How did the rest of the population organize itself? From of old, Korean society rested upon a strict social hierarchy which was topped by a hereditary aristocracy, for most of the Chosŏn period known as yangban. The next lower status group was that of the "good people" (*yangin* or *sangmin*), usually termed "commoners," that is to say, those who did not belong to the ruling class. It was this group that had to bear the burden of taxation, military service,[24] and corvée labor. Its majority consisted of peasants who lived in scattered villages and tilled either their own land or, as tenants, that of others. Some were landless. From the late seventeenth century on, with the rise of commerce, a small number of commoners began to acquire some economic prominence in urban centers.

At the beginning of the dynasty, the demarcation line between yangban and commoners may not yet have been inflexibly drawn. No legal restrictions prevented commoners from taking the civil service examinations and occasionally holding minor government posts.[25] As the dynasty moved into its second century, however, the distinction between yangban and commoners as two separate status groups was marked; and in the extant household registers (*hojŏk*) of the seventeenth century, the terminology designating commoner householders clearly differed from that used for yangban.[26] Because commoners did not form lineages, their kinship system was less complex and less ritualized.[27]

Moreover, commoners did not keep genealogies and thus lacked recognized charters of descent. Intermarriage between yangban and commoners was rare for primary marriages, although commoner women entered yangban houses as secondary or minor wives (*ch'ŏp*). Visually, the commoners were distinguished from yangban by different dress and by their simpler mode of life.

In turn, commoners set themselves off against the lower class of "base people" (*ch'ŏnmin*), who consisted mostly of slaves but included those with base occupations, such as butchers, leatherworkers, and shamans. Membership in all these status groups was ascribed by birth rather than acquired by achievement, and the law as well as social custom guarded against infringement of social boundaries. Consciousness of social status, deeply rooted in Korean society, has lingered on until recent times.

This, in outline, is a generalized picture of Korean society as it presented itself during the second half of the Chosŏn dynasty. Lineage organization was typical only for the elite segment of society—the product of a developmental process that at the beginning of the dynasty was set in motion by social reforms inspired by Neo-Confucianism. Because the Confucianization of Korean society is an upper-class phenomenon, the ensuing discussion will heavily concentrate on this upper class, well aware of the fact that an upper class does not constitute the whole of a society. Yet, in the Korean case (and this is not unique to Korea), the written record available was written by and for the elite and thus touches upon the lower classes only in special instances. Moreover, although Confucianism filtered down and provided cultural guidelines for the lives of commoners and slaves alike, it was a multivalent instrument that only when wielded in the hands of the upper class could reach its full sociopolitical and moral potential. It is therefore necessary to trace next the history of Confucianism in Korea.

THE TRANSMISSION OF CONFUCIANISM TO KOREA. As a part of Chinese culture, Confucianism reached the Korean peninsula at various stages of its development. Initial knowledge of Confucian tenets may have been transmitted through the Chinese commanderies that dominated the northern part of Korea during the first three centuries A.D. In 372, a Confucian academy reportedly was established in the native kingdom of Koguryŏ. With the rise of Paekche and Silla, Confucianism began to penetrate the southern half of the peninsula; and in 682, a Confucian academy was built in Kyŏngju, Silla's capital. Because the spiritual milieu in both kingdoms was dominated by Buddhism, the role of Confucianism was limited to some state functions, most notably the education of officials. This didactic duty gained importance during United Silla when in 788, in imitation of the T'ang, a kind of examination system was instituted, and the Confucian classics became the basic study materials of examination aspirants. But presumably more important for deepening and expanding the knowledge of Confucianism in Korea were the Korean students who returned home after spending some time in T'ang China. An outstanding example is Ch'oe Ch'i-wŏn (857–

?), who sojourned seventeen years in T'ang China, passed the civil service examination in 874, and after his return propagated Confucian values as reasonable criteria for conducting state affairs. At that time, Confucian studies were principally pursued by men who belonged to the middle echelon, head-rank six *(yuktup'um)*, of the general Silla aristocracy—men who, on the basis of their birth, were denied access to the top decision-making positions in government. Confucianism was then and later intimately connected with the search for rational standards that would weaken, if not sever, the indigenous link between the prerogatives of birth and political participation and would condition advancement to high office on achievement.[28]

T'ang influence remained decisive in Koryŏ. The dynastic founder, Wang Kŏn (877–943), surrounded himself with Confucian advisers and acknowledged Confucianism as the ideology of a centrally organized state, although at that time Koryŏ was anything but centralized. In 958, an examination system was established with Chinese assistance.[29] The basic Confucian literature was studied with the commentaries by K'ung Ying-ta (574–648), and this training generally served the purpose of providing the state with capable officials. More important than the government-sponsored school system for the development of Confucianism were the private schools which flourished from the second half of the eleventh century. These contributed significantly to the deepening of Confucian learning when the government-operated schools showed signs of decline. The most famous private school was that of Ch'oe Ch'ung (984–1068), who was later celebrated as the "Confucius of the Land East of the Sea." Ch'oe seems to have been preoccupied with such texts as the *Chung-yung* (Doctrine of the Mean), but it is uncertain whether he had knowledge of the revival of Confucianism in late T'ang and early Sung.[30]

There are various reasons why Korea was initially cut off from the intellectual developments in China known as Neo-Confucianism. Neo-Confucianism was principally a phenomenon of Southern Sung (1127–1279). Therefore, when the Jurchen overran and occupied North China in the early twelfth century, Korea's direct contacts with South China were severed. Moreover, the establishment of military regimes in Korea from 1170 negatively affected the development of Confucianism. While some Confucian-trained bureaucrats continued to serve the military rulers, other Confucians fled from the center of power. They retreated into the mountains and, in symbiotic existence with the Buddhists, continued their studies. As refugees in Buddhist monasteries, they lived in inner and outer isolation, a circumstance that put a lasting imprint on Koryŏ Confucianism.

With the rise of the Mongol empire in the middle of the thirteenth century, an entirely new chapter in Korea's intellectual history was opened. Subjected to Mongol rule, Korea became part of a vast multinational system, and manifold human and material connections tied Korea to Peking. Although this integration imposed great sacrifices upon Korea, for the Korean Confucians it meant the opening of new intellectual horizons. Yüan China (1271–1368) provided an efficient network that facilitated the exchange of ideas, books, and men.

It was a gradual and rather precarious process through which Neo-Confucianism was transmitted from the south to North China— a process that began only after Khubilai (r. 1260–1294; after 1279 as Shih-tsu) had become convinced that it was more advantageous to recruit the Confucians of the occupied territories into government service than to kill them. The captive Neo-Confucian scholar, Chao Fu (c. 1206–c. 1299), in person brought the Neo-Confucian works north and started a successful teaching career at the Mongol court. His most prominent disciple was Hsü Heng (1209–1281) who with the zeal of a convert absorbed the teachings of the Ch'eng-Chu school and made them the basis of Confucianism in Yüan China.[31]

For Korea, first contact with this new world of thought was facilitated by the close marital relationships that existed between the Mongol imperial house and the royal family of Koryŏ. King Ch'ungnyŏl (r. 1274–1308) married one of Khubilai's daughters; and their son, the later King Ch'ungsŏn (r. 1308–1313), felt more at home in Peking than in Kaesŏng. One of his frequent trips between the two capitals became particularly momentous for Koryŏ Confucianism. When he returned to Peking in 1289, An Hyang (1243–1306) was a member of his retinue. Having passed the higher civil service examinations in 1260, An held some minor posts before he devoted himself to educational tasks in Kaesŏng. In 1289, he was appointed to the newly established Koryŏguk yuhak chegŏsa (Office for the Promotion of Confucian Studies in Korea), which was a subdivision of the Chŏngdong haengsŏng (Eastern Expedition Field Headquarters), an instrument of Mongol interference in Korean affairs.[32] It must have been because he was recognized as a mature Confucian scholar that An was selected to go to Peking. And this trip turned out to be a revelatory experience. His biography notes, "At that time the works of Master Chu [Chu Hsi] were newly circulating in Peking. When An first got to see them, he absorbed himself in them and respected them greatly. He recognized that they represented the true tradition of Confucius and Mencius, whereupon he copied them by hand, drew [Chu Hsi's] likeness, and brought everything back home."[33] After his return to Korea, An Hyang reportedly advanced to high office, but his main concern was the desolate state of scholarship. Therefore, in 1304, he established a scholarship fund and also sent a certain Kim Munjŏng to southern China to purchase portraits of Confucius and his disciples, some ritual implements, the classics, works by Confucian scholars, and the "new books" by Chu Hsi (1130–1200). An himself is said to have built behind his house a kind of memorial shrine in which he venerated the portraits of Confucius and Chu Hsi. In his words: "Chu Hsi's merits equal those of Confucius. If one wants to study Confucius, one ought to study Chu Hsi first!" Out of respect for his newly found master, An included in his pen name *(ho)*, Hoehŏn, one character (Chin. *hui;* Kor. *hoe*) of Chu Hsi's pen name, Hui-an. When An went to Peking for a second time, he visited the Shrine of Confucius and was asked by some officials whether there was such a shrine in Korea. An reportedly answered promptly, "Our country's culture and rituals completely follow those of China. Why should there be no Shrine of Confucius?" His discussions of Neo-Confucian thought, moreover, agreed so closely with Chu Hsi's views that his Chinese interlocuteurs exclaimed in admiration, "This is the Chu Hsi of the East!"[34]

Although such stories undoubtedly are apocryphal embellishment, they nevertheless underline the momentousness of An Hyang's first encounter with Neo-Confucianism. An's recognition of the Ch'eng-Chu school's unique contribution to Confucianism was the vital spark that set off new interest in Confucian studies at a time when the Korean Confucians were enthralled by Buddhist ideas. An's first concern, therefore, was the revitalization of the decayed school system. With the reconstruction of the Confucian Academy and the recruitment of some able teachers, "the Confucian atmosphere greatly improved, and those who wanted to study flocked together like clouds, for everyone realized for the first time that there was [something like] Neo-Confucianism *(tohak)*."[35] Among An's disciples were all those who contributed to the Confucian revival in the first half of the fourteenth century: Kwŏn Pu (1262–1346), U T'ak (1263–1342), Yi Chin (1244–1321), Yi Cho-nyŏn (1269–1343), Paek I-jŏng (n.d.), and Sin Ch'ŏn (?–1339).[36]

While An Hyang's efforts as an initiator and teacher were certainly important, continued stimulation received from firsthand contacts with Chinese scholars in Peking must have been crucial to sustain the initial enthusiasm. Especially Paek I-jŏng is credited with devoting himself with special fervor to Neo-Confucian studies. After spending some ten years in Peking, Paek reportedly returned home with many books and spurred widespread interest by demonstrating that Confucianism meant more than merely polishing literary styles.[37] To satisfy the demand for reading materials, in 1314 two officers of the Confucian Academy were dispatched to South China to purchase books. In the same year, the Mongol ruler himself sent a large gift of books, which apparently had belonged to the former imperial library of the Sung, to Kaesŏng. They were catalogued by Kwŏn Pu, Yi Chin, and others.[38] The following passage from U T'ak's biography may reflect the scholarly excitement of that time: "When the Neo-Confucian literature [lit., the commentaries of the Ch'eng] first arrived in the East, there was nobody who could understand it. [U] T'ak closed his door and studied it for over a month. When he comprehended it, he taught it to students, whereby Neo-Confucianism began to flourish."[39]

An early product of such teaching efforts was Yi Che-hyŏn (1287–1367). Belonging to a family of scholars—his father, Yi Chin, was a classics scholar and his father-in-law, Kwŏn Pu, reportedly was the first who urged the printing of the Four Books in Korea[40]—Yi enjoyed a thoroughly "modern" education. His principal teacher apparently was Paek I-jŏng. He thus was well-versed in Neo-Confucian studies when he went to Peking in 1314 at the age of twenty-eight. There he was closely associated with King Ch'ungsŏn, who a year earlier had abdicated in favor of his son, King Ch'ungsuk (r. 1313–1329; 1332–1339). Ch'ungsŏn retired to the Mongol capital, where he founded the famous library, "Hall of the Ten Thousand Scrolls" (Man'gwŏndang). This library became an ideal meeting place for Chinese and Korean scholars to discuss Neo-Confucianism.[41]

The Chinese personalities with whom Yi Che-hyŏn had frequent contact in the Man'gwŏndang were all well-known scholars of their time.[42] Perhaps the most conspicuous name was that of Yao Sui (1238–1313), who was the nephew of the eminent Yao Shu (1203–1280), the man responsible for persuading Chao Fu to go north and introduce Neo-Confucianism to the Mongol court.[43] Yao Sui was one of Hsü Heng's most promising disciples and was close to Yüan Ming-shan (1269–1322), who in turn was a disciple of famous Wu Ch'eng (1249–1333). Educated in a southern academy that was connected with some of Chu Hsi's direct successors, Wu became a respected representative of the Ch'eng-Chu tradition in the north. Another of Wu Ch'eng's disciples, Yü Chi (1272–1348), a great literatus, was also an often-seen visitor in the Man'gwŏndang. From this brief list of names—it could easily be extended—it is clear that the men with whom Yi Che-hyŏn associated in the Man'gwŏndang belonged to the intellectual elite of the Mongol capital. All of them were directly connected with the Ch'eng-Chu school of thought and were instrumental in elevating Neo-Confucianism to the position of

state doctrine of the Yüan and in propagating Chu Hsi's works as
the basic study canon for the civil service examinations revitalized
in 1313.[44]

During the early fourteenth century, then, many personal contacts between Korean and Chinese scholars stimulated the growth
of Neo-Confucian studies in Korea. The effect of this early dissem-
ination may be reflected in the increasing number of Korean students who passed the higher civil service examinations in Peking.[45]
One of the first passers was An Chin (?–1360), who after his success
in 1318 had an active literary and historiographical career.[46] He
was followed in 1321 by Ch'oe Hae (1287–1340), one of Yi Che-
hyŏn's friends, who came from a scholarly milieu where Confucian
studies were pursued with particular fervor.[47] One of Yi Che-hyŏn's
most prominent disciples, Yi Kok (1298–1351), successfully passed
the examinations in 1333 and subsequently was given various posts
at the Mongol court. His son, Yi Saek (1328–1396), gained top
honors in the examinations of 1354 and became the influential teacher
of all those who helped build the intellectual foundation of the
Chosŏn dynasty. Examination success in Peking not only honored
scholarly excellence but also inspired a kind of professionalism which
became the hallmark of the newly rising Confucian elite.

THE EARLY FORMATION OF KOREAN NEO-CONFUCIANISM. What was the
nature of Yüan Neo-Confucianism that the Koreans absorbed in
Peking and later disseminated in Korea? Unfortunately, only very
few sources are left to tell the Korean side of this story, and therefore it is useful to approach the question first from the Chinese side.
Yüan Neo-Confucianism was firmly grounded in the teachings of
Chu Hsi and the Ch'eng brothers, Ch'eng Hao (1032–1085) and
Ch'eng I (1033–1107), and took the Four Books as its scriptural
foundation. Chu Hsi had grouped the Four Books —*Lun-yü* (Analects of Confucius), *Meng-tzu* (Works of Mencius), *Ta-hsüeh* (Great
Learning), and *Chung-yung*—together for the first time and had elucidated them with extensive commentaries. Yüan Confucians chiefly
occupied themselves with practical matters and shunned metaphys-
ical speculations. Hsü Heng who came to dominate the philosoph-

ical scene particularly emphasized that "in ancient times, the rise of order and peace necessarily depended on elementary education and great learning."[48] Teaching in an essentially non-Chinese milieu, Hsü Heng stressed moral education and therefore made the *Hsiao-hsüeh* (Elementary Learning), a primer compiled by Chu Hsi in 1189, his basic text. It contained the elementary rules of personal conduct and interpersonal relationships. Being a simple text, it served as an introduction to the Four Books, especially the *Ta-hsüeh*, which took the moral issues up to the higher level of society, state, and world. The *Ta-hsüeh* was read mainly in the edition prepared by Chen Te-hsiu (1178–1235), the *Ta-hsüeh yen-i* (Extended Meaning of the Great Learning).[49] The Four Books were held in such high esteem that in 1313 they were decreed to become, with the Five Classics,[50] the core materials required for the civil service examinations. While Hsü Heng was concerned with extending Confucian learning beyond the elite, his foremost task was the education of the ruler. The ruler, Hsü believed, had first, in conformity with the precepts laid out in the *Ta-hsüeh,* to rectify his own mind and then become an example in the process of renovating the conduct of those below, leading them to moral lives. Hsü's teachings were pragmatic and action-oriented. His aim was to build a solid Confucian foundation upon which state and society could rest.[51]

Some major themes addressed by Hsü Heng and others are clearly reflected in the thinking of early Korean students of Neo-Confucianism. Yi Che-hyŏn characterized the new creed as "concrete (or solid) learning" *(sirhak),* and practicality was the tenor of his advice to Ch'ungsŏn. The king once pondered the reason why in Korea, long familiar with Chinese culture, the scholars were all adhering to Buddhism and occupied themselves with trivialities of writing style. Where were the learned men who understood the classics and polished their conduct? For this desolate state of scholarship Yi squarely held the king responsible. If he had extended the educational facilities, paid due respect to the Six Classics, and illuminated the Way of former kings, Yi preached, nobody would turn his back on "pure Confucianism" *(chinyu)* and follow the Buddhists; nobody would abandon "concrete learning" *(sirhak)* for trivialities

of writing style. Yi's message was clear: a king's first task was education.[52] In a memorial submitted on the occasion of Ch'ungmok's
(r. 1344–1348) accession to the throne in 1344, Yi Che-hyŏn became more specific. Unmistakably referring to two key concepts of
the *Ta-hsüeh,* Yi made the realization of "reverence" *(kyŏng)* and
"watchfulness" *(sin)*—preconditions of kingly rule—dependent on
the king's polishing his own virtue first. For doing so, the best
method was instruction, and Yi recommended as study materials
the *Hsiao-ching* (Classic of Filial Piety) and the Four Books. The aim
was to practice the way of the "investigation of things" and the
"perfection of knowledge," the "sincerity of the will" and the "rectification of the mind"—the four basic steps of self-cultivation. Once
the Four Books were mastered, the next stage of instruction was the
Six Classics.[53] Yi Che-hyŏn's pedagogical philosophy clearly rested
on Yüan concepts and became the basis of all educational programs
in late Koryŏ.

Yi Che-hyŏn's disciple, Yi Saek, articulated similar concerns. He
called Confucianism "the source of the civilizatory process" and
connected it with the workings of government. Human qualities
form the foundation of government. If they are not cultivated, he
said, the foundation is not firm. If they are not enlightened, the
source is not clear. This was the state of things he observed in his
own time and attributed it to the decay of the school system. "Of
old, the scholars strove to become sages. Nowadays, remuneration
is all the scholars are after." He sharply censured what he thought
was meaningless scholarship and pleaded for the reconstruction of
schools, both in the capital and in the provinces. Yi Saek became
instrumental for the revival of the Confucian Academy (Sŏnggyun'gwan) in 1367, where he became one of the most inspiring
teachers of Neo-Confucianism.[54]

At the center of early Korean Neo-Confucianism, thus, stood the
revitalization of the education system, a precondition for spreading
the teachings of the Ch'eng-Chu school in Korea. The curriculum
was modelled after the precepts received from the Yüan teachers,
and the whole educational venture rested on the optimistic assump-

tion that if the "learning of the sages" (sŏnghak) was sufficiently absorbed by the ruler and his officials, state and society would regain their vitality and harmony. There also was the notion that those called to assist this revitalization process should be recruited on the basis of their talents rather than their family backgrounds.[55]

The spiritual milieu in which the Neo-Confucians began to assert themselves was molded by Buddhism. Although a man like An Hyang had deplored that grass was growing in the Confucius Shrine, while everywhere else incense was burned in reverence for Buddha,[56] anti-Buddhist feelings at first were not strong. After all, Buddhist temples had protected the Confucians during the Military Period (1170–1270). The Koreans who studied in Peking under the Yüan also were not exposed to radical anti-Buddhism. On the contrary, the co-existence of the "Three Teachings" (Confucianism, Buddhism, Taoism) had a long tradition in China.[57] It is understandable therefore that scholars like Yi Che-hyŏn or Yi Saek did not make their commitment to Neo-Confucianism contingent on a critical attitude toward Buddhism. Paek Mun-bo (1303–1374) must thus have been one of the first to write a memorial entitled "In Rejection of Buddhism" (Ch'ŏkpulso). But he, too, did not use doctrinal grounds for contrasting Confucianism with Buddhism. Rather, quoting Shao Yung's (1011–1077) complex cosmological chronology,[58] he pointed out that in Korea the age had come "to revere Yao and Shun and the Six Classics and to discontinue the [Buddhist] theories of merit and fate." If this were done, Paek maintained, the fate of the country would be secure for a long time as Heaven would be pure and protective and yin and yang in harmony with the time.[59]

The tone of the Confucians changed, however, under King Kongmin (r. 1351–1374). With waning Mongol domination and interference, an opportunity for national reassertion seemed to have arrived, and the Confucians began to clamor for a reform program far beyond the reconstruction of the school system. Lingering domination of pro-Mongol forces and the meteoric rise of a Buddhist monk, Sin Ton (?–1371), to the pinnacle of decision-making power

radicalized the Confucians' demands for renovation. Their laxity
toward the Buddhists ended, and they began to envisage a new age
in which Confucian norms and values would shape state and society.

NEO-CONFUCIANISM AS AN IDEOLOGY OF CHANGE. The transmission of
Neo-Confucianism to Korea poses various important questions. How
did the Koreans see themselves as inheritors of the Confucian heritage? What drew them to Neo-Confucianism? What were the elements within Neo-Confucianism that they could adopt as a sociopolitical ideology? Here some general aspects of these questions will
be outlined, while the discussion of their practical application in
early Chosŏn will form the subject of Chapter Two.

The Koreans seem never to have doubted their belonging to the
civilized, that is, Confucian world. As Pyŏn Kye-ryang (1369–1430)
put it: "Since antiquity Korea has revered rites *(ye)* and etiquette
(ŭi) and submitted to Kija's teachings."[60] Having in the person of
the legendary Kija a presumed direct link to Chinese antiquity,
Korea had a natural claim to the heritage of "the Way" *(sado)* and
was proud of it. "Was this not Heaven's special favor vis-à-vis Chosŏn?" Although the Koreans at times invoked the Mencian formula
of "using Chinese doctrines to transform the barbarians" *(yung-Hsia
pien-i)*[61] to justify and enforce the adoption of Chinese institutions,
they were convinced of their natural propensity to become Confucians. This was the optimistic spirit of the Confucian scholars that
prevailed throughout late Koryŏ and early Chosŏn.

What elements in Neo-Confucianism justified this optimism not
only for a small elite but also for society at large? At the center of
an answer to this question undoubtedly stands the Confucian conviction that human nature can be perfected from without, regardless
of whether this nature is originally good or bad. Although the early
Korean Neo-Confucians have left no clear pronouncements about
this problem, circumstantial evidence suggests that they were aware
of its overwhelming importance. How, for example, does one go
about transforming corrupt Buddhist habits? Does one start from
the feelings, that is, from within, or from the ritual details, that is,
from without? For Chŏng To-jŏn (?1337–1398), false ritual prac-

tices could lead a son's feelings toward his parents astray, and therefore he insisted that reforms had to start with giving people suitable models for correcting their feelings.[62] Chŏng was not alone with this insight. At the beginning of Chosŏn, the opinion prevailed that, through stimulation from without, men's human properties not only could be guided but also profoundly changed. This belief in the perfectability of man demanded the creation of an appropriate environment in which human nature would be realized to its fullest. Such an environment could be achieved only through legislation that took the vagaries of human nature into account, that is, through Confucian legislation.[63]

A key role in this transformatory process was accorded to rites and rituals. Rites are "correct" acts in the outer realm that exert a profound impact on the inner disposition of man. In ancestor worship, for example, they not only demonstrate how things have to be done correctly but also are a crucial method for creating harmony among the participants. Rites thus address, beyond the individual, the collectivity of kin and, in a wider sense, society at large. They are principles that grow out of human relationships and form part of the entire normative sociopolitical order.[64] The Neo-Confucians of early Chosŏn clearly recognized the significance of rites as devices for ordering society; and for formulating their social policies, they heavily relied on the ritual literature of ancient China transmitted by the Sung Neo-Confucians.

Models for perfect ritual behavior and a sound sociopolitical order are contained in ancient China's canonical works that constituted the inexhaustible source of inspiration for generations of Confucians. In Korea, these works had been known for centuries and had served as the educational basis for examination candidates and instructional materials for kings. They gained critical relevance, however, as handbooks of change and reform through the commentaries of the Sung Neo-Confucians, especially Chu Hsi. It was these commentaries that unlocked their potential as guidebooks of social renovation. The canonical literature, in particular the *Li-chi* (Book of Rites), the *I-li* (Book of Etiquette and Ceremonies), and the *Chou-li* (The Rites of Chou), depicted in great detail an ideal society created by the sage-kings of ancient China. Through the idealization of the Sung Neo-Confucians, the institutions of this "historical" age gained normative power, and it was this power that persuasively called for a re-creation of these institutions in the contemporary situation (Chin. *fu-ku;* Kor. *pokko*). This was a creative recourse to Chinese antiquity.[65] The Korean Neo-Confucians came under the spell of this canonical literature and interpreted it in the most literal sense. They were receptive to the call for renovation and understood it as a commitment to transforming their own society into a Confucian society. Their reenactment of ancient institutions at the beginning of Chosŏn was motivated as much by their sense of responsibility toward the classics as by their will to rectify the evils of their time. Nowhere in East Asia, therefore, was the re-creation of the institutions of Chinese antiquity more compelling than in Korea.

The sheer weight of its canonical literature makes Neo-Confucianism an elitist enterprise. It addresses the moral as well as the scholarly qualifications of its practicioners, the *ju* (Kor. *yu*), vaguely to be translated as "Confucians." Often used synonymously with *shih* (Kor. *sa*)—this term contains the notion of professionalism— the *ju* were men who made the studying and teaching of the Confucian classics their profession and at times, by passing the examinations, entered the officialdom. But the *ju* were more than merely learned scholars turned bureaucrats. A group apart and above general society, the *ju* adduced their special moral qualities as justification for taking on a leadership role within and without the government. In the widest sense of the word, they were professionals who with their moral endowment, learning, and skills were indispensable functionaries of state and society.[66]

In Korea, the nature of the *yu* as a professional group in the Koryŏ-Chosŏn transition was bound to considerations of social status. Neo-Confucian learning provided an important new method for asserting elite status. To be sure, the aforementioned men of head-rank six *(yuktup'um)* at the end of Silla and perhaps even the civil administrators *(nŭngmun nŭngni)* during the Military Period formed professional groups with distinct social overtones. But at the end of Koryŏ and the beginning of Chosŏn, Neo-Confucian training became the professional ethos of a body of men who from within the established aristocratic order sought to increase their power by exploiting their special knowledge. This notion of superiority based on Neo-Confucian education thus did not transcend traditional considerations of heredity and upper-class privileges. Rather, it reinforced the social criteria of status ascription. In other words, the Neo-Confucians of early Chosŏn, in contrast to the *shih* of early Ming China, claimed social as well as professional eminence in their quest for power.

With the advent of Neo-Confucianism in Korea, an ideology[67] emerged that was addressing itself in a comprehensive and compelling way to social problems. It stimulated an unprecedented political discourse on man and society. Neo-Confucianism contained clear precepts of sociopolitical renovation and anchored the guarantee of their workability in the exemplary world of the sage-kings of Chinese antiquity. Moreover, the reformatory thrust of Neo-Confucianism turned its practitioners into activists and demanded their full commitment to its program of social change. The Neo-Confucians of early Chosŏn became infected with this call to action and strove to determine and implement a reform program that would Confucianize Korean society. After the failure of Wang An-shih's (1021–1086) reforms in eleventh-century China, their program was to become the most ambitious and creative reform experiment in the East Asian world.

ONE

The Pre-Confucian Past: A Reconstruction
of Koryŏ Society

When Koryŏ (918–1392) emerged during the first decades of the tenth century, unifying the Korean peninsula once more, the T'ang empire (618–906) had disintegrated, and China was witnessing a succession of short-lived dynasties that fragmented its territory. While T'ang's political fortunes had come to an end, its institutional and cultural achievements endured; they provided basic elements for the foundation of a new dynastic venture in Korea. Wang Kŏn, the founder of Koryŏ, posthumously known as T'aejo (r. 918–943), expressed his admiration for T'ang China in his political testament (hunyo). He declared, "We in the East have long admired T'ang ways. In culture, ritual, and music we are entirely following its model."[1]

During the formative period of Koryŏ, the early kings relied heavily on the institutional patterns of the T'ang.[2] The close contacts they sought to establish with some of the Chinese kingdoms during the Five Dynasties (907–960) and later with Northern Sung China (960–1126) were strongly motivated by their desire to copy the well-tested institutions of the Chinese and to give their own nascent dynasty the trappings of imperial rule.[3]

Yet, however strong and persuasive T'ang culture was, its adaptation to Korean circumstances was not unquestioned. Indeed, even as fervent an admirer of things Chinese as Ch'oe Sŭng-no (927–989) was ready to admit that the submission to Chinese influence should not lead to the obliteration of local customs. He said, "The customs and manners of the four directions are all following local characteristics, and it seems difficult to change them completely [according to Chinese usage]. As far as the teachings of rituals, music, poetry, and writing, and the ways of ruler and subject, of father and son, are concerned, it is apt to take China as a model in order to reform the inferior and vulgar. As far as other institutions such as carriages and horses, and clothing are concerned, it is permissible to follow local usage."[4] In fact, Ch'oe Sŭng-no was echoing a thought that T'aejo had already expressed earlier: it was not necessary that everyone strive toward uncritical conformity.[5]

The ambivalence of the Koreans toward China's overwhelming influence seems to have been only superficially reconciled by tolerating local diversity in material culture. The problem was far more complex than adopting Chinese "rituals" and leaving Korean fashion untouched. The crux lay in the fact that Korea and China had two fundamentally different social traditions. Chinese terms and idioms that were introduced into Korea through legal and ritual institutions and writings, most notably the T'ang code, found easy acceptance in the Korean vocabulary, but they did not necessarily come to correspond to Korean social realities. Chinese ideographs were inadequate to write the Korean language, as Chinese social concepts and terms were imperfect to represent Koryŏ's social features.[6] This basic incompatibility between Chinese terminology and Korean social reality has often been overlooked and has consequently led to a distorted view of Koryŏ society—in the past as well as in the present.

The study of Koryŏ society has been hampered by a dearth of available documents. The main sources are the *Koryŏsa* (History of Koryŏ), the *Koryŏsa chŏryo* (Condensed History of Koryŏ), some private writings *(munjip)*, scattered funerary inscriptions, genealogical and census fragments, and the first few volumes of the *Chosŏn wangjo sillok* (Veritable Records of the Chosŏn Dynasty). The historical materials compiled during and especially toward the end of Koryŏ nc longer exist. They must have been consulted, however, for the composition of the *Koryŏsa,* which was started almost immediately after the inception of the Chosŏn dynasty (1392–1910) and completed after several revisions in 1451.[7] Its organization was based on examples of Chinese historical writing, and the Chinese model may have influenced its contents to a certain extent.

The assessment of Koryŏ social institutions is made problematic not only by the shortage of documents but also by the infelicitous circumstance that the official history of Koryŏ was compiled and edited by a group of Neo-Confucian scholars who had little taste for the social conditions of Koryŏ—in their eyes a decadent age. Information on society, especially family and kinship, is consequently scant. The Confucian compilers occasionally admit that they did not understand certain features, for example the wedding rite.[8] Not surprisingly, the marriage institution is not discussed, and the social position of women is generally ignored. The monographic chapters *(chi)* rely heavily on Chinese legal patterns; and it is often not clear how these rules, in particular those concerned with household and marriage, were handled and applied in specific instances.

The Confucian-trained chroniclers of Koryŏ history found it difficult to see and describe Koryŏ society other than in comparison with the new social system they intended to institute at the beginning of the Chosŏn dynasty. While they shunned describing Koryŏ society in their writing of the official history, they were outspoken in their criticism of Koryŏ social institutions when they propagated Confucian-style legislation. What they so fervently condemned must have been practiced. Thus, the early parts of the *Chosŏn wangjo sillok* represent a valuable source for Koryŏ social history.

Besides the Korean materials, two contemporary Chinese reports command credibility. The *Kao-li t'u-ching* (Report on Koryŏ) was written by Chinese envoy Hsü Ching (1091–1153), who stayed in the Koryŏ capital of Kaegyŏng (Kaesŏng) for about a month in 1123. Coming from a different social milieu, Hsü was keenly aware of Koryŏ's social peculiarities. His descriptions of Koryŏ society are therefore revealing and in fact tally rather well with testimony presented at the beginning of the Chosŏn dynasty. Another, nearly contemporary source is the *Chi-lin lei-shih* (Kor. *Kyerim yusa;* Classified Facts about Korea), which was compiled by a member of an imperial Sung embassy, Sun Mu (dates unknown), and is commonly dated between 1102 and 1106.[9]

Koryŏ society was a highly stratified society, consisting of aristocrats, commoners, and slaves. Social status was principally based on genealogical considerations and, at least at the beginning of the dynasty, could not be easily changed. The ruling elite, the aristocrats *(kwijok),*[10] was a status group characterized by a number of privileges, which included intermarriage with the royal house, officeholding as *munban* (that is, civil officials), protection privilege *(ŭm, ŭmsŏ),* intermarriage within the group, and landed property. The aristocrats were known as "those who wear cap and gown and have the official tablet stuck in their girdle" or "who on their body wear cap and gown and in the their mouths [have words of] humanity and righteousness"[11]—a sure indication of the close relationship between aristocratic status and officeholding.

The aristocratic group was not static and, in the course of Koryŏ, continuously absorbed newcomers. The aristocrats of the founding period, among them the merit subjects of T'aejo—those who were especially rewarded for their merits in the dynastic founding *(kŏn'guk kongsin)*—were a mixed group incorporating people of diverse social background: Silla aristocrats (including members of the former royal house), military leaders, and local strongmen *(hojok)*. The latter possessed their own economic and often also military bases in the countryside and posed a formidable threat to the nascent dynasty. It was therefore a major concern of the early Koryŏ kings to integrate these local forces into a centralized government located in Kaesŏng and to create an officialdom that would be subject to strong royal rule. King Kwangjong (r. 949–975) was the first who attempted to break the power of the original elite by purges and by introducing several bureaucratic measures copied from the Chinese, most notably the civil service examination system in 958. Some twenty years later, in 976, the "graded portions of land and firewood" *(chŏnsikwa)* were instituted as a remunerative system for those who rendered service to the state. Under King Sŏngjong (r. 981–

997) the initial bureaucratization of the Koryŏ state reached a first climax with the civil element clearly in command. Therefore, when in 995 the officialdom was generally divided into civil and military officials, *munban* and *muban*, the "two lines of officials," called *yangban*, were not on an equal footing. Because *pan (-ban)* boundaries could not be easily crossed, the military found themselves in an inferior position. The three top ranks of the officialdom were closed to them, since there was no examination system for them to reach the top. Moreover, the highest military posts were held by civilians.[12]

The supremacy of civil aristocratic rule and the consequent imbalance between the two categories of officials led to the military revolt of 1170—the first major hiatus in Koryŏ history, which set an end to a period of great cultural and artistic achievements and heralded in a century-long internal conflict under military domination. During the Military Period, the original civil concept of aristocracy began to deteriorate, although the old aristocracy was not destroyed. Men of military background, however, advanced into the highest civil posts and claimed aristocratic status. This resulted in a certain equalization between the two *pan*. Moreover, during this time officials rose to prominence solely by successfully passing the civil service examinations *(nŭngmun nŭngni)*. Ability tested in examinations became an increasingly important criterion for upward mobility. This was also exemplified by the so-called "powerful families" *(kwŏnmun sega)* who emerged under the Mongols from the last quarter of the thirteenth century. Some of them attained the highest offices as professionals with Mongol backing.[13]

Throughout the dynasty, the acquisition and maintenance of high social status were conditioned on a balance between ascription and achievement. At first, birth and heredity alone were the principal conditions for belonging to the aristocracy. With the increasing bureaucratization of the state apparatus, ability and knowledge demonstrated in the examinations came to be superimposed upon purely social considerations, and officeholding turned into an important source of prestige. Although the criteria of aristocratic status thus changed and expanded over time, the top group itself remained remarkably exclusive. This is reflected in the list issued by King Ch'ungsŏn in 1308 that designated the "ministerial families" *(chaesang chi chong)* with whom the royal house was encouraged to exchange marriage partners. This list contained only fifteen surnames.[14] Although not all of the aristocratic families prominent at that time were included, it is clear that the aristocratic element of society was numerically small throughout Koryŏ. Equally clear is its continuity. Four names mentioned in the 1308 list had survived from the early period—the Kyŏngju Kim, the Kyŏngwŏn (Inju) Yi, the Ansan Kim, and the P'ap'yŏng Yun. The late Koryŏ aristocracy differed, however, from that of the early period insofar as members with military backgrounds served in the highest government positions alongside civilian aristocrats.[15]

The official life of the Koryŏ aristocracy was molded by Confucian education, and reciting Chinese poetry and adherence to Confucian moral principles were the attributes of a cultured gentleman. Confucianism was given due recognition as a practical way to handle state affairs, in particular the recruitment of officials; but it never penetrated deep into everyday existence. Koryŏ was Korea's Buddhist age, and it was Buddhism that permeated every facet of social and religious life. Buddhist temples and monasteries flourished because they were lavishly supported by the royal house and the aristocracy alike. Buddhist state festivals were the most important events in everyone's calendar; and the most intimate rituals, especially those connected with death, were entrusted to the monks' care. An enduring expression of faith in Buddha's protective power against northern invaders—first the Khitan and then the Mongols—was the carving of the entire Buddhist canon on woodblocks, known as the Koryŏ Tripitaka.

Koryŏ was a long-lived "dynasty." It rose when the T'ang empire collapsed and outlasted both the Sung and Yüan dynasties to witness the rise of the Ming (1368–1644). Perhaps on account of its longevity, Koryŏ hardly has the characteristics of a coherent dynasty. Rather, it was a sequence of distinct periods, each marked by extraordinary internal and external events. Any attempt, therefore, to reconstruct the structure and organization of Koryŏ society is in danger of telescoping the distant past into the near past and of generalizing the data of one period for the whole dynasty. Development and change are not easily traced. Moreover, "Koryŏ society" is here understood in a narrow sense. The kind of documents available make the focus on the aristocratic upper class unavoidable. Although commoners and slaves constituted the numerical majority of Koryŏ society, almost nothing is known about their kin structure. They play therefore only a marginal role in the considerations which follow.

Any reconstruction must remain tentative, but the aim of this study will be achieved if it succeeds in demonstrating convincingly that Koryŏ elite society was fundamentally different from that of the subsequent Chosŏn period.

KINSHIP AND DESCENT. No extant Korean source provides a comprehensive picture of Koryŏ kinship. Some revealing terminological details emerge from the glossary of Korean native words contained in the *Kyerim-yusa* (Classified Facts about Korea).[16] Transcribed by the phonetic use of Chinese characters, this list of native kin terms allows the reconstruction of a kin group over five consecutive generations (see Diagram 1).[17] Its center is constituted by a married son (ego), his parents, and his children. Laterally ego's older and younger siblings of both sexes are included. Each member is clearly differentiated from the others by terms that indicate sex and sequence of birth. The generations are separated, the second ascending and second descending generations designated by derivative terms. While in ego's generation the female siblings are terminologically differentiated from the women who married in, in the parents' generation all women, whether consanguineously or affinally related, are lumped together with the same term. Collaterality is evident and especially emphasized in the parents' generation: the parents are isolated vis-à-vis their siblings who in turn are differentiated. The terms for a mother's male siblings, denoting sequence of birth, differ from the single term used for all of the father's brothers. (The terms for cousins are unfortunately missing.) This collateral bifurcation on a mother's side, which contrasts with the treatment of a

Diagram 1. Koryŏ Kinship Terminology Based on *Kyerim yusa*

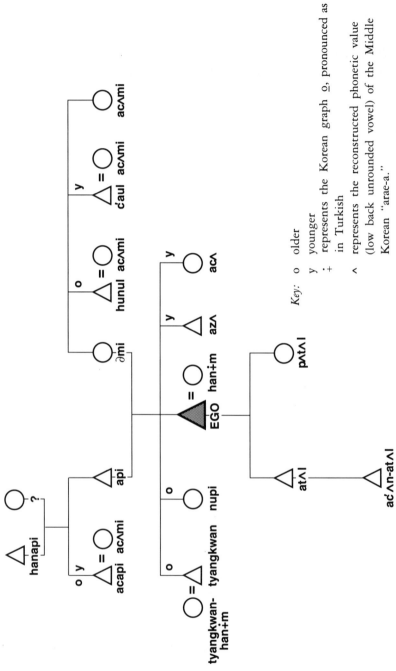

Source: This figure is based on Yi Ki-mun, "Koryŏ sidae ŭi kugŏ ŭi t'ŭkching," *Tongyanghak* 6:299–305 (1976), and personal communication from Professor Yi.

father's brothers as a category is a remarkable feature. It may be the vestige of an older, perhaps matrilineal system—kinship terminology tends to be conservative and resistant to change—and definitely points to a uxorilocal residence rule.

Conspicuous emphasis on matrilateral kin clearly demonstrated in the kinship vocabulary with separate terms for the mother's brothers is also discernible in the Koryŏ version of the mourning chart (Chin. *wu-fu;* Kor. *obok*). The mourning system,[18] the most important instrument of kinship affairs in T'ang China,[19] provided the Koreans with a reservoir of Chinese technical terms, the mourning grades. They could delineate the perimeter of near relatives with them and rank their respective ritual weight. Although the Koreans copied the system punctiliously, they felt, nevertheless, compelled to counterbalance the asymmetrical emphasis on patrilateral kin of the T'ang model with a marked revaluation of mourning for maternal kin. The maternal grandparents were given a one-year mourning period (in T'ang five months) and thus enjoyed the same ritual respect as the paternal grandparents. Consequently, the mother's brothers and sisters were also assigned higher grades than prescribed in the T'ang model, although this did not make them equal with their patrilateral counterparts. Moreover, by pointedly adding the mother's first cousins, the Korean mourning chart recognized at least tacitly the maternal great-grandparents (for whom, however, there were no mourning grades).[20] A similar matrilateral slant is evident in the Korean adaptation of the Chinese "law of avoidance" *(sangp'i).*[21] It differed from the Chinese pattern by showing an almost complete balance between patrilateral and matrilateral kin.

The manner in which these two Chinese kin categories were assimilated in Korea sheds important light on the kin composition of Koryŏ. Following their own social concepts, the Koreans deemphasized the Chinese patrilineal bias by giving more prominence to maternal and affinal kin. This was done more easily in the law of avoidance, an administrative regulation, than in the rigidly conceptualized mourning system. The correspondence between the range of kin in the law of avoidance and that described in the *Kyerim yusa* is thus striking and leads to the tentative conclusion that, by focus-

ing on a particular individual, Koryŏ kinship recognized a cognatic
group of kinsmen. The focal person's closest kin were taken from
his kindred, which seems to have usually extended to first or second
cousinship. The Chinese models, to be sure, equally centered on a
given person, but surrounded him principally with patrilineally related relatives. The difference between the Chinese rules and their
Korean adaptation was thus a fundamental one. It originated from
divergent conceptualizations of kinship and highlighted the Koreans' recognition of the fact that cognatic kin formed an individual's
societal perimeter.

A person's kin in the widest sense were designated by the Chinese
term *chok* or, at times, *ssijok*. *Chok* was probably the Sino-Korean
rendering of the pure Korean word *kyŏre*, meaning "kin," "persons
of the same ancestry."[22] Appearing first in scattered documents of
Silla, *chok* does not seem to have been a precise conceptualization of
kin. Rather, anyone who was related to a person through either a
parent or an affine belonged to that person's *chok*.[23] When the term
chok was, in accordance with Chinese practice, used in legal and
ritual texts, it was often subdivided into the "three *chok*" (*samjok*):
paternal *chok* (*ponjok*), maternal *chok* (*oejok*), and affinal *chok* (*ch'ŏ-
jok*).[24] But, as numerous examples show, such a distinct internal
division of *chok* was clearly of Chinese origin and not common in
the everyday context of Koryŏ. A vivid illustration of this concept
is given in the report that after Yi Ŭi-min (?–1196) was killed in
1196, his "three *chok*" were exterminated. This specific reference to
Yi's patrilateral, matrilateral, and affinal relatives attests to the fact
that a man's kin was thought to embrace a multilaterally connected
body of people. Only the destruction of all three kin groups could
break for good an adversary's power. For all practical purposes, then,
chok was used as an imprecise and elastic term for any kind of kin,
overlapping several surnames *(sŏng)*.[25]

Occasionally the term *ch'inch'ŏk*, "relatives," appears in the sources.
In contrast to *chok*, it seems to denote the circle of kin with which
an individual interacted most closely, for example fraternal kinsmen
(hyŏngje ch'inch'ŏk).[26] *Ch'inch'ŏk* seems to be a narrower and less formal term than *chok*. It was likely synonymous with *ch'indang* and

choktang in the meaning of kindred. It was from this pool of people
that occasional action groups were recruited. A striking example is
the composition of Yi Cha-gyŏm's (?–1126) faction active in the
first quarter of the twelfth century. Yi's kinsmen *(ch'indang)* were
clearly distinguished from mere partisans *(tangyŏ)* and comprised
sons, sons-in-law, younger brother, agnatic and non-agnatic nephews, patrilateral and matrilateral cousins, and affines. The majority
of Yi's henchmen in fact were matrilaterally and affinally related
relatives.[27] Koryŏ history provides numerous further examples that
testify to the importance of mobilizing kindred for extra-domestic
activities.[28]

   Chok thus rested on a flexible and inclusive kinship concept. Such
flexibility was also apparent when *chok* was used in the loose meaning of "descent group." As will become abundantly clear, a group
traced its descent through both male and female links, not just one
or the other, because genealogical thinking did not follow unilinear
principles. Rather, both matrilateral and patrilateral connections
were used to include in a descent group as many members as possible. Because of this bilateral strategy, the group was equally interested in retaining its male and female members. Whatever its
genealogical depth, such a descent group was a compact body of
people. The larger the group was, the greater its potential for holding property, for providing social status, and for exerting political
influence.

   In the hierarchically structured Koryŏ society, certified descent
meant attested membership in a descent group that looked back to
an illustrious ancestry. It was a Koryŏ aristocrat's key to elevated
politico-jural status. High social standing, articulated and maintained over generations, functioned as the platform for his advancement in the political world. It also assured him an adequate economic basis. Significantly, proof of membership in a (recognized)
descent group was first demanded for any examination candidate as
early as 1055.[29] But how was such membership certified? This could
be done practically only through systematic genealogical recordings. At the beginning of the dynasty it was reportedly not customary to keep family records *(po);* therefore the names of the anteced-

ents *(kisŏn)* got lost and only their origin from Silla was vaguely remembered.[30] Judging from funerary inscriptions of the elite,[31] around the middle of the twelfth century genealogical recordings became more precise, and two or even three generations of agnatic antecedents began to be listed. It is not certain from what time the so-called "four ancestors" *(sajo)* served as minimal genealogical formula for identifying the immediate ancestors: father, paternal grandfather, paternal great-grandfather, and maternal grandfather. Although undoubtedly inspired by a Chinese genealogical pattern, with its inclusion of the maternal grandfather this scheme was uniquely Korean.[32] Toward the end of the thirteenth century, certification of the "four ancestors" became a requirement for registering as an examination candidate.[33] Clearly, proof of descent as a crucial means of social identification became more detailed in the course of the first centuries of the dynasty.

The actual tracing of ancestral lines undoubtedly ran counter to native genealogical consciousness, but it became a prerequisite for the capital elite that monopolized political office. As the equation between well-established social status and political participation came to be variously challenged by social newcomers during the second half of the dynasty, ancestral reckoning became even more important and consequently grew more elaborate. To depict an individual's ancestry, a sophisticated construct was developed: the elementary pattern of *sajo* was extended by calculating the "four ancestors" of the paternal grandparents, the paternal great-grandparents, and the maternal grandparents, thus pushing the ancestral reckoning back to the sixth ascending generation. Such a construct produced for a male at birth a maximum of six lines of descent: one for each member of the two grandparental pairs, one for the paternal great-grandmother, and one for the paternal great-great-grandmother. These six lines of descent were joined to two lines of descent, the paternal and the maternal, on the wife's side to form what came to be known as "the eight ancestral lines" *(p'alcho)* (see Diagrams 2 and 3).[34]

This method of demonstrating descent along fixed lines obviously introduced a patrilineal bias. Symmetry between the sexes was

Diagram 2. EGO's Six Ancestral Lines

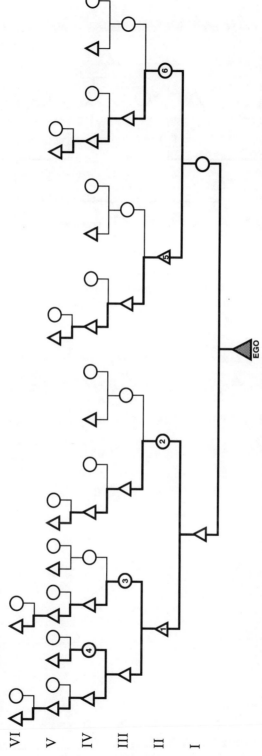

Note: Arabic numbers indicate the patrilateral and matrilateral grandparents, the patrilateral great-grandmother, and the patrilateral great-great-grandmother from whom ancestral lines extended. Roman numerals indicate the generations above EGO.

Diagram 3. EGO's Wife's Two Ancestral Lines

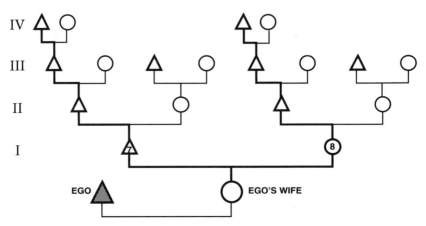

Note: Arabic 7 and 8 indicate the ancestral lines extending from EGO's wife's parents. Together with EGO's six ancestral lines, shown in Diagram 2, they constituted the so-called "eight ancestral lines" (*p'alcho*). Roman numerals indicate the generations above EGO's wife.

maintained only in the first and second ascending generations. Although two lines—one in the third, and one in the fourth generation—originated from ancestresses, these two women seem merely to have represented their respective patrilines (women remained members of their natal groups); they did not stand as independent ancestral links. The underlying philosophy of the *p'alcho* chart was evidently patrilineal, even though its basic *sajo* elements typically had a matrilateral offshoot.

The eight descent lines a Koryŏ male thus could in theory draw upon were connected to clearly marked territorial bases, the so-called "eight homelands" *(p'arhyang)*.[35] "Homeland" *(hyang)* as a technical term in the meaning of native ancestral place had been in use since early Koryŏ.[36] The landed resources connected with these homelands formed in their totality the patrimony, often referred to collectively as "ancestral property" *(choŏp)*, to a share of which each individual with the proper descent credentials was entitled.

The conceptualization of the "eight ancestral lines" and "eight homelands" undoubtedly signifies a late stage in Koryŏ's adaptation of Chinese patrilineal thinking. This is suggested by the fact that no extant Koryŏ source, except a few household registers dating from the fourteenth century, illustrate a possible application of this system. Called "household registers with eight ancestors" *(p'alcho hogu)*,[37] these census documents were such elaborate versions of household registers *(hojŏk)*[38] that they could have been typically compiled only by the aristocracy. They usually listed the household head's and his wife's "four ancestors" *(sajo)* and, in addition, the household head's paternal grandmother, paternal great-grandmother, and maternal grandmother. In the surviving examples the paternal great-great-grandmother was never listed, and the wife's parents were often omitted.[39] Clearly, there was a good deal of confusion and tension between the rigid conceptualization of kin and actual practice. Occasional gaps and irregularities do imply some degree of choice: only those connections that under certain circumstances such as the acquisition of political office promised to be advantageous were recorded.

The extravagant tracing of actual and putative ancestral links to remote generations may have often been a meaningless attempt to demonstrate high social status and was of doubtful usefulness for registering households. Certain limitations were therefore imposed by law, first apparently in late Koryŏ. But only the stipulations of similar restrictions issued in early Chosŏn period are known. Accordingly, officials of second rank and above alone were supposed to prove all eight ancestral lines, whereas the information demanded from the officialdom of rank three and below was less extensive, diminishing with lower ranks. This came to exclude maternal and affinal links.[40] These restrictive measures apparently resulted from the governmental authorities' frustration with too complex a notation of social status that rendered household registration "troublesome and confusing and of little benefit for the state."[41]

Vertical kin calculations only loosely bound an individual to the kindred with whom he interacted closely, perhaps even in the same residential unit. A residential compound may have consisted of one or more households (*hogu*). According to the law, each household head (*hoju*)—usually, but not always, the oldest male member (women also at times functioned as heads of households)—was required to register with the authorities the following persons co-residing in his household: sons, older and younger brothers, nephews, and sons-in-law. Resident slaves who were attached to the household as servants and laborers also had to be included.[42] Households were thus units of varying complexity. The simplest household consisted of one nuclear family, but commonly a household was variously extended, comprising stem or joint families. In the generation of the household head, such extension was lateral, including older and younger brothers and sisters. In the first ascending and the first descending generations—household registers usually covered three living generations—extension could be in the male as well as, through marriage, in the female line. Frequent household members were the wife's parents and the daughter's uxorilocally residing husband. The household ranged from four to twenty members (the average size being 7.4 persons)[43] who resided in closely adjoining quarters, presumably grouped around different hearths. One of the more common and effective methods to ruin an enemy during the Military

Period was to brutally demolish such a compound, the existential basis of the Koryŏ household.[44]

SUCCESSION AND INHERITANCE. During most of the Koryŏ period, then, descent was clearly not traced unilineally, and an individual's social status was established by bilateral considerations. A Koryŏ kinship group was inclusive: all members, male and female, of the same generation enjoyed equal rights and duties. This tradition of basic equality among siblings had important consequences for succession to office and inheritance of property. Because the transfer of high office, in particular the kingship, was not predetermined by clear rules of descent, succession was not automatic, and claimants over the throne emerged from among the incumbent's brothers as well as sons. Lest the royal power and domain be divided up among all heirs, succession to the throne had to be indivisible. Recognition of this fact—it was never really disputed—gave rise to stiff competition among the potentially equal collaterals whose claims had natural precedence over those of the next generation. In early Koryŏ, therefore, fraternal strife surrounded each change of reign.

Realizing the danger of this tradition to the dynasty he had founded, King T'aejo attempted in 943, shortly before his death, to regulate dynastic succession. To prevent fraternal strife among his numerous sons by various wives, he wanted to institute the patrilineal principle contained in the T'ang succession rules.[45] In his instructions to his successors *(T'aejo hunyo)* T'aejo therefore emphasized "direct lineal descent" *(chŏk)* as a fundamental law. In view of historical precedence, however, he added that if the firstborn son *(wŏnja)* was incapacitated, the next son or the most able among the sons should be chosen to continue the royal line.[46] Early succession practices suggest that T'aejo's affirmation of lineal succession had little practical effect. During the first half of the dynasty, the throne was handed on in erratic fashion among brothers, sons, and nephews, often in disregard of generational sequence. In no instance did fraternal succession result from incapacity. Rather, fraternal succession stood in contradiction to lineal descent.[47]

This contradiction is vividly illustrated by the problems that arose when the royal spirit tablets were to be enshrined in the Royal Shrines (Omyo). First introduced in Silla for enhancing royal prestige, the Royal Shrines of Koryŏ were laid out during the reign of King Sŏngjong. The basis for the arrangement of the tablets was the *chao-mu* (Kor. *somok*) order according to which the tablet of the dynastic founder was installed in the west facing east and those of his agnatic successors were placed to its left *(chao)* facing south and to its right *(mu)* facing north in such a way that two consecutive generations could not be enshrined side by side. Because a combination of lineal and generational considerations was fundamental to the *chao-mu* order, its adoption in Korea where both these considerations were of little importance led to continued controversies. The workings of the *chao-mu* system itself were difficult to understand. Moreover, because the Royal Shrines were limited to five, in accordance with Koryŏ's accepted lower status of "feudal lord" *(chehu)*, occasional rearrangements of the tablets were necessary. This demanded a change in the *chao-mu* sequence. Without going into the details of these controversies, it is clear that the system was unworkable; for if brothers were lumped into one generational group, the sequence of reign was destroyed, and if the tablets were arranged according to the ruling sequence, the generational principle was violated. In short, fraternal succession and disregard for generation could not be forced into a lineal system.[48]

The issue of succession was no less important for the aristocracy. Succession was the key mechanism for maintaining, through generations, high social status. Its automatic validation, however, was threatened by the civil service examination system, introduced in 958, that subjected recognition of social status to certain qualifications tested and confirmed by the state. Although the aristocrats initially resisted the centripetal pull of the examination-based bureaucracy, they nevertheless came to acknowledge the importance of office-holding for the continued maintenance of high social status. Complete severance of social status from heredity could be prevented by the "protection privilege" *(ŭmjik, ŭmsŏ)* that guaranteed free access to office to at least one member of the junior generation. Throughout the Koryŏ period, a protection appointment was as prestigious as a regular appointment attained by examination success, but it often functioned only as a preliminary safeguard and did not exclude the possibility of later taking the civil service examinations.[49]

The privilege of entering officialdom on the strength of a father's or an ancestor's high social status (and concomitant holding of important government offices) and meritorious achievements was granted to the descendants of T'aejo and his brothers, to descendants of merit subjects *(kongsin)* (especially of the founding period), and to descendants of officials of the fifth rank and above.[50] While for the royal offspring practically no generational considerations limited this privilege, the cutoff line for descendants of merit subjects and of high officials was, on paper, the generation of the grandson. In the case of merit subjects, however, this limit was at times considerably extended, invoking the merits of a great-great-grandfather in claiming the right to office. Significantly, such protection appointments could be bestowed in acknowledgment of either a paternal or a maternal ancestor (especially the maternal grandfather).

In the light of jural equality of brothers, succession to aristocratic status by means of the protection privilege was not confined to one son. Several sons could enjoy such privilege, and for the members of the highest officialdom (third rank and above) this privilege extended, in the absence of sons, to agnatic and non-agnatic nephews, to sons-in-law, adopted sons, and to agnatic and non-agnatic descendants *(nae-oe son).*[51] Succession to aristocratic status significantly was not tied to unilineal descent as royal succession was, for high social status was divisible, while the royal prerogatives were not. Although sons were the preferred heirs, collateral agnates possessed potentially the same credentials, and even non-agnatic and affinal kinsmen were recognized as acceptable successors. Kinship status, thus, retained its high value as a key element for keeping up an exalted position in society.

Succession was flexible and non-lineal. Primogeniture was absent; it would not have been accepted easily, for it would have unduly discriminated against the other heirs. Collaterals could thus function as substitute heirs. To be sure, even in Koryŏ male issue was highly valued and desired, as some biographies testify;[52] and an only son *(tokcha)* enjoyed preferential treatment in military service.[53] Nevertheless, a large number of biographies end with the laconic remark, "He had no [male] offspring *(muja)*." The inherent flexibility of succession practices meant, however, that sonlessness was not a social catastrophe. The legal "establishment of an heir" *(iphu, ipsa)* was therefore a rather alien concept, but in imitation of T'ang law,[54] an exact fixation of succession was nevertheless instituted in 1046. It read, "In general, the people, following legal stipulation, establish as their heir *(ipsa)* the firstborn son *(chŏk)*. If the firstborn son has died, [they establish as heir] the firstborn grandson *(chŏkson)*; if there is none, a younger brother by the same mother; if there is none, a grandson. In case there is no agnatic descendant, it is also permitted [to establish as heir] a non-agnatic grandson."[55] In its Koryŏ guise, this law was a curious mixture of Chinese and native elements. Whereas the emphasis on linearity was borrowed from the T'ang model, the addition of non-agnatic grandsons reaffirmed Koryŏ practice. Although in this instance *chŏk* must be rendered as "firstborn son," from other textual evidence it is clear that the Koryŏ Koreans used this term in the meaning of "lineal" in contrast to horizontal or lateral.[56] The law of 1046—a further application will be discussed later—certainly contradicted the rules operable for the handing on of the protection privilege; and, because establishing an heir was structurally unnecessary, it can in this context have meant nothing more than a legal nicety.

Similarly, the taking in of an abandoned child under three years of age *(suyang)* for continuing a childless line was not a social necessity. A law of 1068 permitted such an act, again in imitation of a T'ang model, if there were no direct or collateral descendants (agnatic nephews). But the few known cases show that the majority of the children taken in were non-agnatic kin, even though an (undated) Chinese-inspired legal stipulation prohibited under punishment non-agnatic adoption.[57] Moreover, as will be discussed later, "adoptions," which apparently increased toward the end of the dynasty, were frequently economically motivated and thus had nothing to do with the continuation of a descent line. In Koryŏ, then, succession easily shifted to a collateral line, or an incoming son-in-law could take on the role of an "adopted" son. The lack of a natural heir did not demand the extraordinary measure of adoption.

The state was particularly interested in regulating succession when land over which it claimed authority was involved.[58] In early Koryŏ, the as yet weak and little centralized state made a pretentious attempt to demonstrate full control over the country's landed resources by instituting, in 976, the *chŏnsikwa* system, "graded portions of land and firewood."[59] Emulating the administrative model of the T'ang, this system aimed at making the officialdom economically dependent on the state.[60] Twenty years earlier, in 958, similar ambition to transform the aristocrats into bureaucrats had led to the introduction of an examination system. The *chŏnsikwa* system seems to have been a logical complement for strengthening the nascent bureaucracy. There is reason, however, to believe that this institution had a high ideational rather than an important economic value, for private ownership of land is now thought to have existed from the beginning of the dynasty. Moreover, it is hard to imagine how such a complex system could have been administered without elaborate local administrative machinery with which the state could have extended its authority over all land, a necessary precondition for the functioning of *chŏnsikwa*.

Under this presumably fictional system, the state would grant to its functionaries, as compensation for their services, the right to collect from specified lots of land a certain percentage of the crop (allegedly fifty percent). The beneficiary would not become the owner of such land, and after his death the prebend was to revert back to the state. This mechanism hinged upon the state's ability to keep this land, called "private land" *(sajŏn)*,[61] under its supervision and to prevent its alienation from state control.

The danger of alienation was real because some functions that were compensated with such land (or prebendal) grants *(chŏnjŏng)*[62] apparently were automatically handed on to a younger substitute when the incumbent died, became sick, or reached the age of seventy.[63] It was in the interest of the state, therefore, to regulate such transfers, and the aforementioned law of 1046 which defined succession may have in fact been principally applicable to the transfer of prebendal rights.[64] By singling out lineal descendants as a man's successors, it fixed the transfer of *chŏnjŏng* vertically. The flexibility of traditional collateral succession might have sidetracked the prebends horizontally and alienated them from state control. Subsequent laws issued in 1069 and 1080 reconfirmed this vertical sequence,[65] but only a few decades later prebends seem to have been legally transferred to a functionary's paternal or maternal kin. A rare source, a grave inscription of 1123, even records that a man obtained a prebend from his wife's adoptive father.[66] If there was no appropriate successor, a prebend could be handed on to someone outside the designated range of kin; but, because it was bound to certain offices, the transfer usually occurred within the same status group.[67]

The purpose of the *chŏnjŏng* grants and their automatic transmission to a successor of possibly the next generation was to secure for the state an uninterrupted flow of recruits for specific services. If a kin group was no longer able to provide such service, the function and the land attached to it passed beyond kin boundaries, or perhaps even back to the state. Hereditary aspects were involved, but it was clearly a matter of succession rather than of inheritance. This is also suggested by the terms *ch'erip* or *yŏllip,* "to transmit," that designated such state-supervised transfers from one holder to the next.[68]

In contrast to *chŏnjŏng* grants, the state awarded land to merit subjects and protection appointees in perpetuity. This "merit and protected farmland and woodland" (*kongŭm chŏnsi*) was to guarantee to its recipients, members of the highest officialdom, an adequate income for sustaining a proper standard of living over generations.[69] The land, however, did not completely pass into the private management of the beneficiaries, as is indicated by the rules the state devised for its transmission from one generation to the next. In 1021, a ruling stipulated that if the direct successor (*chikcha*)[70] had committed a crime—revolt and rebellion excluded—the land was to be transferred (*i'gŭp*) to his grandson.[71] This law was made more specific in 1073 when, in the absence of sons, the line of succession was fixed as follows: son-in-law, nephews (both agnatic and non-agnatic), adopted son (meaningless in Koryŏ), and the wife's son by a previous marriage (ŭija).[72] Significantly, this order of succession closely paralleled the passing on of the protection privilege.

The different transfer mechanisms of chŏnjŏng and kongŭm chŏnsi reflect the dilemma of the state in the face of the irreconcilable principles of vertical and horizontal succession (although the latter could not in the long run, of course, prevent the former). The state tried to implant the lineal and male-oriented T'ang rules in a tradition that always kept the sideways option open and, at least indirectly, even recognized women. Women could not receive kongŭm chŏnsi, but through their husbands and sons they nevertheless had a stake in such land. A husband could, in his capacity as son-in-law, function as a "proxy" heir for his wife and his father-in-law's non-agnatic grandsons and reap for them the appropriate economic benefits.[73] The state, thus, was forced to compromise in its attempt to regulate succession and was unable to prevent state land from turning into private property. With the rapid expansion of privately owned landed estates around the middle of the dynasty, the rules of transfer (yŏllip) lost whatever significance they may initially have had, and kongŭm chŏnsi melted into the patrimony its original recipient bequeathed to his heirs.

Inheritance differs critically from succession. Succession in Koryŏ was a state-controlled mechanism that governed the transferral from one generation to the next of service land over which the state claimed authority, even if only nominal, and that benefitted specified individuals. In contrast, inheritance refers to the mode by which a man devolved his private property upon his heirs. For an individual recipient, an allocation under the chŏnsikwa system may have been of only marginal economic importance. Much more essential for his existence, it must be presumed, was the land which he owned privately. There is sufficient reason to believe that right from the beginning of the dynasty, despite the declared ideal of state ownership of all land, most land in fact was in private hands. Called "people's land" (minjŏn),[74] private land was owned by aristocrats, commoner peasants, monks, and even slaves and was usually cultivated directly by its owner with or without the help of slaves. Private ownership included the right to buy and sell this kind of land, to give it away as a gift, and, significantly, to hand it on to heirs without state interference.[75]

Inheritance of private property followed its own customary procedure which clearly contrasted with the state-imposed succession rules. In principle, all of an owner's heirs, male and female, could expect a share of the "patrimonial land" (*choŏpchŏn, pujojŏn*)—land that accumulated over generations. This transaction was called "dividing the property" (*punjae*) and presumably most often took place when the household divided up (*pun'ga*). Typically, the equal allotment of such property among sons and daughters was not regulated by law—the state had no power over it.

This customary division of property molded the characteristic structure of the Koryŏ household. Brothers and sisters were co-heirs in a double sense: they each inherited a share of the patrimony and, under certain circumstances, they could expect to inherit from one another. Such expectations must have strongly motivated the siblings to hold together as long as possible, thus creating complex households. As mentioned earlier, the household was a residential unit that typically comprised, besides the household head and his wife, one or more other married couples either in lateral or vertical extension or both. In the still extant household registers, the average age of the household head exceeded fifty years. This indicates that the majority of households included legally adult sons, and often, in addition, married daughters with their husbands.[76] To be sure, the law prohibited, under penalty of two years' forced labor, the establishment of separate households and the division of property as long as the grandparents or parents were alive, if such an act deprived the older generation of its livelihood.[77] But for large domestic units the motivation to stay together rather than to split up cannot have derived solely from legal constraint. The common bond, then, must have lain in the economic realm.

The Koryŏ household was not only a residential but also an economic unit. Data on Koryŏ are entirely lacking; but, as in other agrarian societies,[78] the complexity of the Koryŏ household composition must have been connected with landholding patterns, general productivity of the land, and any other economic activity that could be pursued more profitably by a larger rather than a smaller group. This is illustrated by the report of the "eight sons and one son-in-law who lived together in a deep mountain valley and made their living by fishing and hunting."[79] If it is assumed (on the basis of evidence from the early Chosŏn period) that land productivity was relatively low—productive years were followed by long fallow periods—larger tracts of land meant higher income that could sustain sizable households. Larger households had the necessary manpower to keep more land under cultivation and to undertake large-scale land reclamation projects. There must have been a dynamic relationship between the number of household members and the amount of land under cultivation: people were scarcer than land, and therefore the household made every effort to keep its original members and to recruit new ones. A major incentive as well as reward for staying together was the prospect of inheritance.[80]

All descendants, and not one preferentially treated heir, were, according to the law, collectively responsible for the upkeep of the older generation. Consequently, after the death of all seniors, when a general adjustment of the property became necessary, all descendants could claim a share of the patrimony. Although such claims by the younger generation may have been automatic, a considerable amount of discretion in disposing of the property was apparently left to the older generation. This is suggested by the great importance of the will *(mun'gye)* in assigning individual shares. Wills could be instruments of preference, contingent upon certain conditions—for example filial behavior. More important, they indicate that property was not considered as a corporate entity, and that ownership of the patrimony was vested in individuals. The household head thus had the say over the disposal of what he owned. The handing on of the patrimony involved, therefore, strategic decisions that gave expression to individual choice, but at the same time had to forestall undue competition among the co-heirs. This is, for example, illustrated by the biography of Yun Sŏn-jwa (1265–1343). When Yun was taken ill in 1343, he called together his children

by his two wives, admonished them to keep peace among themselves in order to be exemplary for future generations, and ordered
his eldest son to write up a will according to which the patrimony
(*kaŏp*) would be divided into equal shares.[81]

In the absence of a will, quarrels among heirs apparently were
frequent, and the only legal stipulation concerning the inheritance
of private property was related to the situation when no will had
been left. A law of 1122 provided that if no will concerning the
patrimonial fields (*pujojŏn*) existed, the eldest son (*chŏkchang*) should
have the prerogative to apportion the shares.[82] The responsibility of
managing the division of the patrimony was thus vested in the eldest son. Even though he may have had first choice of shares, his
primary task was to ease contention among the siblings.[83]

Despite the suggested discretionary nature of the will, customary
pressure to treat offspring evenhandedly seems to have been strong.
When wills were unjustifiably partial, they could be disputed. This
is vividly illustrated by a case Son Pyŏn (?–1251) arbitrated. A
conflict had broken out between an elder sister and her younger
brother because their father's will had assigned the major portion of
the patrimony to the sister and had left the brother only such trivia
as a formal dress, a cap, a pair of shoes, and a roll of paper. At the
time of the father's death, the sister was already married and, because the mother had died earlier, the younger brother had grown
up under her care. Called upon to end the discord, Son's ruling
articulated the social mores of his time. The parents' devotion, he
argued, is impartial toward all their children, and therefore it could
not have been their intention to be generous toward the daughter
and stingy toward the son. Rather, because the son, a child, was
completely dependent on his married sister, the father feared that
equal division of the property would ease the sister's responsibility,
making her negligent toward her younger brother. The father left
his son the four items so that, when he grew up, he would be able
to hand in a petition for the final settlement of the inheritance
dressed in proper attire. This wise judgment caused an immediate
reconciliation of brother and sister.[84] The equal allotment of the
patrimony is also suggested by the example of Yi Chi-jŏ (1092–

1145) who, upon the death of his father, out of stinginess did not want to share the inheritance with his five younger brothers and two sisters. He therefore drew contempt from his contemporaries.[85]

The patrimony was composed of the property each parent had obtained through inheritance and of possessions acquired during their married life. The consciousness of the separate origin of paternal and maternal shares, coming from different "homelands" *(hyang)*, was always kept alive—the slaves, for example, were clearly marked as "received from father's side" or "received from mother's side"— and even after the parents' death, their contributions to the patrimony were not merged in a general pool but were kept apart. Every one of the heirs had a rightful claim to a part of each portion of the patrimony. Such division, if consistently undertaken for the properties of the parental and perhaps even further removed ancestral generations, resulted in individual shares that consisted of a number of distinct parts. Evidence for the high divisibility of the patrimony may be the fact that landed property was often widely scattered. The famous scholar-official Yi Kyu-bo (1168–1241), for example, owned land at two places, at least, and Yi Saek's landed holdings were dispersed over ten different places.[86] Even though some of these parcels were acquired by purchase, the rest must have resulted from patrimonial division. This system of exact apportionment of shares provides an additional explanation for the apparent indispensability of the will. Besides being an instrument of preference, the will also served a distributive function. In view of the complexity of the patrimony, it had to stipulate the composition of the individual allotments.

The most precious part of the patrimony was land. But it also included movable property *(chaemul)* such as cloth, household utensils, and work animals. These items were subject by law to equal division among the heirs.[87] The most valuable "movable property" was the slaves *(nobi)* who, attached to a household for generations, worked in the house and in the fields. Although no legal stipulations regulated the inheritance of slaves, there is sufficient evidence to suggest their equal distribution among their master's heirs. The story of Na Ik-hŭi's (?–1344) modesty and righteousness gives an example. When Na's mother divided her property during her lifetime, she intended to give her only son an extra share of forty slaves. Na protested: "You have one son and five daughters. How dare I take them [the extra slaves] and thereby solicit your special favor?" Na's mother had to respect her son's argument.[88] Chŏng To-jŏn (?1337–1398) is known for similar selflessness. After the death of his parents, in a demonstration of filial piety and brotherly generosity, he reportedly gave all the strong slaves to his younger brothers and sisters and kept the weak and old ones for himself.[89]

Equal inheritance created a strong bond among the siblings and prompted them to keep the common household intact as long as possible. Even marriage does not seem to have been a major breaking point in a household's life cycle. A sister did not receive her share in the form of a dowry, but delayed her claim until after the parents' death. Whether she left the household at marriage or continued to live there with her husband, she could always count on being welcomed back or on continuously drawing on its economic resources. Marriage, then, did not disrupt a household and accelerate its division. Rather, a household tried to keep its married women, with or without uxorilocally residing husbands. This provided women with a high degree of economic security.

Claiming a share of the inheritance may not have depended on continued active membership in the natal group, at least not for a woman who may have left the household at marriage. But her coheirs kept a close watch over her portion of the property. If she died without issue, her portion was not allowed to pass into the hands of affines and was promptly demanded back.[90] For a man, the expectation of a meager inheritance may have been a major incentive to leave his group and to marry uxorilocally in the hope of a brighter economic future. As a member of his wife's household, he not only had for himself usufructuary rights over his spouse's property, but he also established his children as potential heirs of her group. The size of the economic reward, then, must have significantly influenced the cohesion and thus the size of a household.

MARRIAGE IN KORYŎ: SOCIOPOLITICAL ASPECTS. Koryŏ marriage customs were early recognized as peculiar. The compilers of the *Koryŏsa* wrote in the preface to the biographies of the queens *(hubi):* "T'aejo took [Chinese] antiquity as his model and intended to transform [his country's] mores. Bound, however, to local custom, he married sons to daughters [by different mothers] and concealed this by using the surnames of their mothers. His descendants regarded this as a 'house rule' and did not think it strange. Alas!"[91]

Linking close kin through marriage was one of T'aejo's most effective measures in his effort to consolidate his power. When he established himself as dynastic founder, he lacked a large supportive kin group. He therefore created an intricate network of marriage alliances with his closest allies, the merit subjects, loyal local strongmen *(t'oho),* and trustworthy aristocrats. With his twenty-nine queens, T'aejo had twenty-five sons and nine daughters, a progeny large enough to form an exclusive royal group. To underscore the superiority of the king's line, T'aejo did not exchange his daughters with his allies. Except for the first and ninth daughters, whom he married to Kim Pu, the last king of Silla and socially his equal, he kept his daughters within the family by marrying them to half brothers.[92]

T'aejo's social strategy of concentrating on close kin was continued and strengthened by his successors. Disregarding generational considerations, two of T'aejo's sons, Hyejong (r. 943–945) and Chŏngjong (r. 945–949), accepted daughters from men who had previously given brides to T'aejo. An aristocrat from Hu-Paekche, Pak Yŏng-gyu (no dates), provided T'aejo's seventeenth queen and later gave two daughters in marriage to Chŏngjong. Two daughters of a merit subject, Wang Kyu (?–945), became T'aejo's fifteenth and sixteenth queens, and one daughter became Hyejong's second queen. Hyejong and Chŏngjong, moreover, took wives from among the daughters of the same father, Kim Kŭng-nyul (no dates).

Hyejong married his oldest daughter to his own half brother, Kwangjong (r. 949–975), in an unsuccessful attempt to strengthen his own position as T'aejo's successor.[93] Kwangjong's only other

queen was his half sister on whom he begot his successor,
Kyŏngjong (r. 975–981). Kyŏngjong in turn married a daughter
of Silla's last king, Kim Pu, two cousins, and two daughters of his
mother's brother, who was also his father's half brother. With one
of the latter wives he had a son who became King Mokchong (r.
998–1009). T'aejo's fourth son, Uk (posthumously called Chaejong), also married a half sister; the offspring of this union was King
Sŏngjong (r. 981–997), Mokchong's predecessor. Hyŏnjong (r.
1009–1031) married across generations two daughters of his cousin,
Sŏngjong. Both his first son, Tŏkchong (r. 1031–1034), and third
son, Munjong (r. 1046–1083), married half sisters. Through multiple marriages among T'aejo's descendants during the first 150 years
of the dynasty, the royal house became a solid kin group.[94]

The royal house generally kept its own women for itself; but it
also took in aristocratic women from the outside, a situation which
opened the palace to external influence. Throughout the dynasty,
"presenting a consort" *(nappi)* was one of the hallmarks of aristocratic status. Forging affinal ties with the royal house guaranteed
the bride-givers preferential treatment and in turn advanced their
own attractiveness as prestigious bride-receivers. Social acceptability was typically correlated with a high degree of political influence,
attributes which remained valid over generations. Linked in affinity
to the royal line, some aristocrats were tempted to manipulate
succession. During the first succession struggle in 945, Wang Kyu
turned against Hyejong—his son-in-law, who lacked a power base
of his own—and unsuccessfully tried to put his royal grandson (i.e.,
T'aejo's son by his sixteenth queen) on the throne.[95]

An even more complex situation arose four generations later when
members of the powerful Kyŏngwŏn (Inju) Yi family attempted to
seize royal power. Of *hojok* background in the Inch'ŏn area, the Yi
owed their rise to their affinal relationship with the Ansan Kim
whose most illustrious representative was Kim Ŭn-bu (?–1017).
Kim had demonstrated his considerable strength by providing King
Hyŏnjong with three queens, one of whom became the mother of
the future Tŏkchong and Chŏngjong (r. 1034–1046), and one the
mother of the future Munjong. Kim Ŭn-bu had few direct descen-

dants to reap the profit from these matches; but his wife's relatives, the Kyŏngwŏn Yi, especially Yi Cha-yŏn (?–1086), used the close connections with the royal house for their own advancement. Yi Cha-yŏn gave three daughters in marriage to Munjong. One of them became the mother of three future kings, Sunjong (r. 1083), Sŏnjong (r. 1083–1094), and Sukchong (r. 1095–1105). In the next generation, three granddaughters were matched with two of the royal grandsons, Sŏnjong and Sunjong. The daughter of a grandson, Yi Cha-gyŏm (?–1126), moreover, became the wife of Sukchong's son, Yejong (r. 1105–1122). Yejong's son, Injong (r. 1122–1146), was forced to marry two maternal aunts. This intricate involvement with the royal house brought the Kyŏngwŏn Yi to the apogee of their political power, but also to the brink of self-destruction. In 1095 Yi Cha-ŭi (?–1095), Cha-gyŏm's first cousin, and in 1126 Cha-gyŏm himself, driven by magical prophecies, attempted to gain royal power. Both revolts failed, and the political fortunes of the family declined. Kyŏngwŏn Yi continued, however, to be recognized as one of the outstanding families until the end of the dynasty.[96]

During the Military Period, Koryŏ kingship was degraded and disgraced: kings were deposed or even killed at will by the military strongmen. A certain estrangement between the royal house and its political environment may be seen in the fact that Myŏngjong (r. 1170–1197), Sinjong (r. 1197–1204), and Hŭijong (r. 1204–1211) each had only one queen, a relative, and Hŭijong, Kangjong (r. 1211–1213), and Wŏnjong (r. 1259–1274) were products of close marriages within the royal family. Perhaps the royal house made a deliberate attempt to keep aloof from daily politics, or it may have been the intention of the military overlords to prevent hostile alliances between the royal house and the aristocracy. Nevertheless, Ch'oe Ch'ung-hŏn (1149–1219) secured for himself access to the inner chambers of the royal palace. Through his second wife, Lady Im, whom he married after he seized power in 1196, he was connected with the Chŏngan Im, a prominent family which had provided Injong's third queen, the mother of Ŭijong (r. 1146–1170), Myŏngjong, and Sinjong. His third wife was a secondary

daughter *(sŏnyŏ)* of Kangjong. The Ch'oe's relationship to the royal
house was continued in the next generation when two of Ch'oe's
sons became royal in-laws.[97]

During the last quarter of the thirteenth century, when the Mongols began to dominate Korean affairs, the Korean royal house suffered unprecedented outside interference. The Mongols repeatedly
criticized Koryŏ marriage practices,[98] and the royal house was forced
to abandon its traditional policy of marrying women of royal blood
to their own kinsmen and to begin exchanging princesses with the
Mongol rulers. In Ch'ungsŏn (r. 1308–1313), the grandson of the
great Khubilai, founder of the Yüan dynasty in China,[99] the Mongols had a cooperative ally. Backed by an admonitory decree he had
received from his late grandfather, Ch'ungsŏn declared upon his
accession to the Korean throne in 1308 that marriage with someone
of the same surname as well as with matrilateral cousins would
henceforth be prohibited. He made this a binding rule for the royal
house and the higher officialdom. To accentuate this break with the
past, he issued in the same year a list of fifteen select aristocratic
families, "ministerial kin groups" *(chaesang chi chong),* with whom
the royal house was to exchange brides.[100] This assault on one of
the most distinct features of Koryŏ kingship—consanguineous marriage—did not result only from Mongol coercion. It may have been
equally connected with structural changes in the composition of
Koryŏ's upper class.[101] Despite this forced "opening," however,
marriages among royal kin continued to be contracted until the end
of the dynasty.

At the beginning of the dynasty, consanguineous marriages were
not only typical for the royal house, but were widely practiced among
the upper class and presumably the commoners. Unions with patrilateral and matrilateral cousins were frequent, and marriages among
half brother and half sister (siblings with different mothers) may
not have been uncommon.[102] To be sure, no rules prescribed marriage among near kin;[103] but during the uncertain times of a dynastic beginning, the linking of close relatives by marriage was politically prudent and economically beneficial. It provided regional
strongmen and aristocrats with an indispensable degree of distinc-

tiveness and of kin solidarity. Beyond these individual concerns, however, a certain amount of regional integration was an equally necessary condition for survival. The exchange of marriage partners with other local families was the best means for establishing and maintaining alliances. In the northern part of Kyŏngsang, for example, the locally influential Andong Kim connected affinal ties with other representative kin groups of that region such as the Andong Kwŏn, the Andong Cho, the P'ungsan Yu, and the Hamch'ang Kim.[104] During the founding phase of Koryŏ, marriage was thus characterized by choosing a spouse from among either close kin or certain families within a limited geographical area.

With the increasing consolidation of power in the capital and the consequent absorption of local families into the central bureaucracy, marriage strategy had to answer to political competition as well as to social pressures. The right connections were a condition for advancement and often also for survival. Coming from a poor family, Mun Kong-in (?–1137) "endeavored to become powerful and rich" by marrying the daughter of Ch'oe Sa-ch'u (1034–1115), at that time the most influential representative of the Haeju Ch'oe.[105] Mun Kŭk-kyŏm (1122–1189), on the other hand, survived the aborted countercoup that Kim Po-dang (?–1173) attempted in 1173 against the rising military only because his daughter had married strongman Yi Ŭi-bang's (?–1174) younger brother.[106]

Over generations, such marriages to social equals or superiors were decisive vehicles of upward social mobility. The Andong Kim gradually moved into the ranks of the officeholding elite in the capital by marrying their daughters into socially more prominent yangban families.[107] The critical turning point in the social and political advancement of the Chiksan Ch'oe from the lower military into the higher civil aristocracy occurred when Ch'oe Hong-jae's (?–1135) son, Tan, married the daughter of Im Wŏn-hu (1089–1156), a mighty member of the Chŏngan Im, who was in turn closely related to the royal house. Later, Ch'oe Tan's daughter became Ŭijong's second wife.[108] The skillful arrangement of affinal ties was an art that demanded cultivation. The degree of its mastery determined a family's success in Koryŏ's social and political life. Region-

alism had eventually to be abandoned for a more cosmopolitan outlook, and marriage networks grew more complex. The capital elite,
variously composed throughout the dynasty, underscored its exclusiveness by repeatedly exchanging sons and daughters among barely
two dozen family names.[109] The ultimate triumph was to present a
consort to the royal house. In sum, the qualifications for receiving
or offering the "right" partner in marriage were the result of an
intricate interplay of social and political considerations.

Marriage was never solely a private matter, even less so in a young
state that strove to emulate the institutional features of the T'ang
dynasty and to incorporate some of the basic Confucian values about
state and society. In 976, in the course of building a centralized
bureaucracy, a "marriage system for civil and military yangban"
(*honin chi che*) was reportedly fixed,[110] but no details are known.
During the eleventh century, in particular in the reign of King
Munjong, the bureaucratic groundwork of the dynasty was further
strengthened; and, in this process, Munjong was admonished by
one of his own sons to reform "the old customs (*sǔp*) according to
[Chinese] rites (*ye*)."[111] In 1058, he took a first hesitant step: sons
of marriages with patrilateral parallel cousins (daughters of one's
father's brothers; third mourning grade, *taegong*) were henceforth
barred from an official career.[112] Toward the end of his reign, however, in 1081, Munjong refused to exclude the offspring of such a
union from office and, upon the protest of a Confucian-minded state
councillor, conceded only the lowering of his rank.[113]

Munjong's second successor, Sŏnjong, reinforced his father's law
by closing government offices to sons whose parents were half siblings (same father, different mothers).[114] Under Sukchong, in 1096,
the law was extended to include the offspring of marriages between
relatives of the fourth mourning grade (*sogong*). This presumably
meant only marriages with a sister's daughters, as the prohibition
may not yet have been extended to patrilateral second cousins.[115]
Only five years later, in 1101, all previous laws were rescinded, and
even sons born of "wrong" marriages were again admitted to the
lower ranks of the officialdom.[116] In 1116, the law turned, for the
first time, directly against those who contracted marriages with rel-

atives of the third or fourth mourning grades and barred them from office.[117] After the ruling of 1101 was reversed in 1134,[118] the most comprehensive legislation so far was promulgated by King Ŭijong. In 1146, a law defined the meaning of relatives within the range of third and fourth mourning grades as including patrilateral first (parallel) and patrilateral second cousins. This law in effect prohibited not only intermarriage with collaterals within the range of second cousins, but also across generations. Moreover, from 1147 offspring of such marriages were definitely stopped from entering the officialdom.[119] These proscriptive rules (see Diagram 4), decreed during the first half of the dynasty, step by step removed hitherto marriageable relatives within the patrilateral kin group from a man's choice of partners—matrilateral cousins came under discussion only toward the end of the dynasty.[120]

Significantly, all these laws were administrative measures—they were listed under the heading "selection of officials" (*sŏn'gŏ*)—and were therefore binding only for the officeholding elite. With the exception of the law of 1116, they did not outlaw marriages among close kin as such, but introduced sanctions against their progeny. This reluctance to focus legislation more directly on the marriage institution itself as well as the repeated retractions suggest the difficulty of limiting customary marriage practices with legal concepts that were borrowed from a different social context. T'ang law punished intra-lineage marriage and marriage across generations.[121] In contrast to its adaptation in Koryŏ, T'ang marriage law was not principally directed at the bureaucratic class, but was part of the legal category "household and marriage" (Chin. *hu-hun*) and was backed by drastic punishments. Unions with patrilateral cross-cousins (daughters of one's father's sister) and closer kin were even more severely punished as "adultery" (Chin. *chien*).[122] The Koreans seem to have been aware of these differences because the laws of 1096 and 1146 also appeared, slightly reformulated, under the heading "adultery" (*kanbi*),[123] presumably with the intention to give them wider applicability.

It is difficult to assess the impact of these legislative measures on Koryŏ marriage customs. The higher officialdom, both the initiator

Diagram 4. Successive Stages of Excluding Marriageable Kin

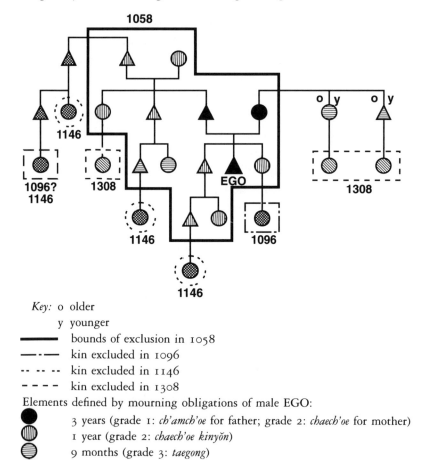

Key: o older

y younger

━━━━━ bounds of exclusion in 1058

—·— kin excluded in 1096

·· ·· ·· kin excluded in 1146

- - - - kin excluded in 1308

Elements defined by mourning obligations of male EGO:

● 3 years (grade 1: *ch'amch'oe* for father; grade 2: *chaech'oe* for mother)

◍ 1 year (grade 2: *chaech'oe kinyŏn*)

◒ 9 months (grade 3: *taegong*)

◓ 5 months (grade 4: *sogong*)

◯ 3 months (grade 5: *sima*)

NB: Mourning grades ascribed to female agnates and matrilateral cousins apply only as long as these persons remained unmarried.

and the target of the laws, learned from political expediency the advantage, and from its Confucian education the propriety, of out-marriages. Its motivation to avoid unions with close patrilateral kin would therefore seem to have been especially strong. The statement in a funerary inscription that Kim Hwi-nam (n.d.), who married Kim Yun's (1277–1348) daughter, did not belong to the same kin group was clearly intended to dispel possible later doubts about the legality of the match.[124] There is, however, sufficient evidence to suggest that not all members of the ruling class, and even less society at large, felt apprehensive about the law. Until the end of the dynasty, marriages with near kin, across generations, and with a dead wife's sister continued to be contracted—the frequency perhaps in proportion to the social and geographical distance from the center of power.[125]

Throughout Koryŏ, then, marriages with close cognates were customary. Although unions with patrilateral kin were eventually, at least on paper, outlawed, those with matrilateral relatives remained largely unaffected until late in the dynasty. The complexity of multiple ties, even across generations, between a relatively small number of persons related consanguineously or affinally or both—a process that may have continued over a number of generations—must have given a kin group special cohesiveness. In many cases, it may have been difficult to differentiate clearly between paternal and maternal kin; and therefore kin consciousness presumably was exclusively concentrated neither on the father's nor the mother's side, but encompassed the whole kin bloc.

MARRIAGE IN KORYŎ: INSTITUTIONAL ASPECTS. No extant source describes the Koryŏ wedding ceremony in any detail. Circumstantial evidence suggests that it was performed in the house of the bride.[126] Negotiations preceding the wedding were handled by a go-between. Bride as well as bridegroom were usually in their late teens—members of the elite married earlier than commoners—and the groom tended to be slightly older than his prospective spouse.[127] At the wedding itself the couple reportedly exchanged some gifts, but the main act seems to have been a banquet that marked the final settlement.[128] This was an occasion for displaying personal wealth, fine silk fabrics of foreign origin, and precious utensils. Many a wedding apparently was postponed to save up for the necessary fineries. If "poverty" prevented an official from preparing a feast for his daughters appropriate to his status, as is reported of Kim Chi-suk (1237– 1310), the daughters had no alternative but to enter a nunnery.[129]

The most characteristic residence pattern—although certainly not the only one—in Koryŏ was uxorilocal: the bridegroom moved into the bride's house, and their children and often even their grandchildren were born and raised in the mother's house.[130] Whether this arrangement was always permanent, lasting for a lifetime, or whether the wife eventually moved into her husband's house cannot be determined with any certainty.[131] Both these possibilities are feasible and documented in household registers. Uxorilocal marriage could be advantageous to the bridegroom as well as to the bride. It was therefore not only frequent, it may often have been preferred. The motivation for establishing uxorilocal residence was not necessarily the lack of sons in the bride's house. Rather, the overwhelming attractiveness of the arrangement was based on the favorable economic status Koryŏ women enjoyed.

The source of the Koryŏ woman's economic strength was the right of inheritance she shared with her male siblings. As endowed women, daughters were valuable members of their natal families as well as attractive brides. Giving away a property-owning daughter or sister in marriage was not in the natal family's interest; and yet the acquisition of a son-in-law or brother-in-law was not only necessary, but also desirable. These diverse interests—apparently often negotiated by a matchmaker—could be reconciled by arranging uxorilocal residence for the new couple: the daughter/sister was thus not lost, and the household obtained the economic and/or political benefit of an additional male member. Such a living arrangement was obviously even more appropriate when the match involved closely related partners, for example cousins. Kin ties then were reinforced by common economic interests.

There is no indication that at the time of the wedding a major economic transaction in either direction took place. No bridewealth was sent to the bride's family, and the daughter did not receive her portion of the inheritance in the form of a dowry. Consequently no conjugal fund formed a separate economic basis for the newly wedded couple. On the contrary, the couple obtained its livelihood from the household of which it had become a part.[132] This is consistent with the uxorilocal living arrangement, which made sense only if the daughter's stake in the inheritance could be retained for the general benefit of the household as long as possible, that is at least until the parents' death.[133] Under certain economic circumstances—for example, when productivity would have been threatened by the division of land—a uxorilocally residing couple may have agreed to postpone indefinitely the dissolution of the common household.

At times a son-in-law *(sŏ, yŏsŏ)* took the place of a son in a household that lacked a male heir. In such a case, he may have been taken in as a son-in-law *in spe (yesŏ)* at an early age and raised by his future parents-in-law.[134] More often a son-in-law joined a group of brothers-in-law upon marrying their sister. The intimate bond between a son-in-law and his in-law family is illustrated by the fact that his fate was closely linked to the ups and downs in the life of his affinal kin. His advancement in the political world—often under the protective aegis of his father-in-law *(puong)*[135]—was frequently proudly mentioned as a special asset in his father-in-law's biography.[136] Both the sons and the sons-in-law of Chi Nog-yŏn (?–1126), who had lost his life in an unsuccessful attempt to remove Yi Cha-gyŏm from power, were rewarded with ranks of nobility after Yi's final defeat in 1126.[137] On the other hand, the sons-in-law of Yi Hyŏn (n.d.), who was executed for his collaboration with the Mongols in 1253, were exiled to a remote island.[138] This close relationship between son-in-law and father-in-law was not a mere public convention. It was anchored in a deep feeling of loyalty. This is tellingly expressed in the anxious exclamation of a son-in-law who unexpectedly found himself in the opposite military camp: "Human feeling cannot bear that a son-in-law would attack his father-in-law!"[139]

A daughter of the elite could not, along with her brothers, claim the privilege of a protection appointment, but her husband could.

Her jural inequality vis-à-vis her brothers was alleviated by her husband's position as potential heir. Through him she could secure for her children the social and economic prerogatives appropriate to her status. A son-in-law himself stood a chance to become his father-in-law's successor, and at the same time he mediated between his wife's father and the latter's non-agnatic descendants.[140] A son-in-law's remarkable position was also underscored by his mourning responsibilities: he had to observe (after 1184) a full year of mourning for his parents-in-law; they in turn mourned an exceptional five months for him.[141]

Uxorilocal living affected the children. Growing up in their mother's house, they developed close emotional ties to their maternal kin.[142] The affection they received from their grandparents, they reciprocated with a long mourning period of one full year. The locality of the mother's residence often became a man's place of origin. Im Yŏn's (?–1270) father, for example, whose natal background is unknown, had moved to Chinju where he married the daughter of a local *hyangni*. His son, Yŏn, later used Chinju as his place of origin.[143] In sum, then, a son-in-law, especially when he was residing uxorilocally, was a prominent member of his in-law family. He himself profited from its social and economic standing and also enhanced his wife's potential as an heir.

In Koryŏ, a man could have several wives. Plural marriage *(chunghon)* was a typical feature of the royal house. There is sufficient evidence to suggest that it may also have been a common feature of aristocratic marriage throughout the dynasty. The Chinese envoy, Hsü Ching, who visited Kaesŏng in 1123 reported: "In a wealthy house the man might marry three or four wives *(ch'ŏ)*."[144] Documentary examples are especially numerous for the Mongol period, but it is not always clear whether plural or serial marriages are meant.[145] For the same reason, a representative number of examples from funerary inscriptions of all periods of the dynasty does not seem to provide unequivocal proof of plural marriages.[146] The most credible and authoritative confirmation of this form of marriage is undoubtedly provided by the testimony of the censorial agencies at the beginning of the Chosŏn dynasty. In unmistakable language they fulminated against the social implications of this Koryŏ custom. [147]

A man's maintenance of more than one wife was possible because married women were not, at least not solely, dependent economically on their husbands. The wives seem to have resided separately, presumably most often with their natal families. Their husbands must have lived with them on a visiting basis. [148] Evidence from the extant census registers of late Koryŏ seems to support this solution. The amazing number of apparently unattached, yet marriage-aged daughters recorded in these documents may be interpreted as indication that the "visiting husbands" were absent when the registers were compiled. [149] A man may have started out with an uxorilocal living arrangement, but after becoming successful he may have broken off to establish his own group. The motivation for taking additional wives may then have derived less from considerations of economic gain than from calculations of political advantage. This strategy worked well in the royal house; there is no reason why it should not have worked equally well in aristocratic houses.

The various wives apparently came from similar social and economic backgrounds [150] and were therefore not differentiated according to a ranking order. This fact is underscored by the reported similarity of their hair and dress styles. [151] The impartial treatment these women enjoyed was decisive for their children: all were their father's rightful heirs and thus could expect to inherit equal shares of his property. [152]

Was there, besides the regular wife (wives), who were designated as *ch'ŏ,* a category of women of inferior standing, "secondary wives," as the occasional appearance of the term *ch'ŏp* might suggest? Plural marriage does not exclude the existence of such women in the same household. They would naturally be relegated to the domestic periphery. Nevertheless, where *ch'ŏp* appears in the biographies, it is almost always clear that it does not mean a secondary wife in the sense used later in the Chosŏn period, but a person who functioned as a servant. At times these servants had special skills, were exceptionally beautiful, and were used as sexual partners. They were "light" women, as no property was attached to them. A word "to marry" (e.g., *ch'wi*) is never used in combination with *ch'ŏp*.[153] It is therefore quite safe to assume that there were no secondary wives in Koryŏ. Only toward the end of that period, terms such as *ch'ŭksil*, "adjoining room," or *oesil*, "outer room," began to appear.[154] They seem to point to a nascent classificatory system under Confucian influence.

The assertion of plural marriage in Koryŏ seems to be called in question by a memorial submitted by a certain Pak Yu (no dates) who served in the higher bureaucracy during the reign of King Ch'ungnyŏl (r. 1274–1308). Pak wrote, "In our country men are few and women numerous. Nowadays both the high and the low officials confine themselves to a single wife *(ch'ŏ)*. Even those who lack a son do not dare keep *(ch'uk)* a concubine *(ch'ŏp)*. Aliens [i.e., the Mongols] come and marry [our women] without restraint. I fear a human exodus northward. I [therefore] request that the high and low officials be permitted to marry *(ch'wi)* commoner women *(sŏ-ch'ŏ)*[155] [as concubines], the number diminishing according to their rank down to someone without rank who could marry *(ch'wi)* one wife *(ch'ŏ)* and one concubine *(ch'ŏp)*." Pak further suggested that the offspring of such women should, like the main wife's sons *(chŏk-cha)*, be admitted to the bureaucracy. The memorial ended with an expression of the hope that "by doing so, the widows and widowers would decrease and the households increase." Pak's proposal reportedly was greeted by commoner women with a storm of indignation, and no action was taken.

What was the purpose of Pak's memorial? Obviously writing under the pressure of the Mongols' insistent demand for Korean, mostly aristocratic, women, Pak was concerned about the shrinking household size of the aristocracy. The remedy he proposed was congruous with the social situation: because the members of the official class were principally marrying among themselves, they would therefore take commoner women only as concubines. It was against this degradation to become subordinate members of yangban households—denoted by the term *ch'ŏp*—that the women in the street protested. Pak's memorial should not be interpreted as proof against the existence of plural marriage, as some scholars take it,[156] but rather as an indication that concubines of lower social origin were not institutionalized in Koryŏ. Pak, however, seems to have worried about demographic, not institutional problems.[157]

Marriage in Koryŏ seems to have been a rather loose institution which was not restricted by a multitude of rules and regulations. This at least was the impression contemporary Chinese observers received.[158] Was this an accurate impression? The most persuasive evidence for its accuracy is the strong economic position married women enjoyed. Whether the residential arrangement was virilocal or uxorilocal, the wife retained her rights as heir in her natal family, a fact which gave her the liberty to leave an incompatible husband without jeopardizing her livelihood. But the same was true for the husband. Even if he moved into his wife's house and was accepted there like a son, he kept a firm hold upon his own inheritance. Economic backgrounds being similar, both partners were subject to conflicting loyalties between natal family and affinal family, a fact that might, under certain circumstances—for example, the breaking-up of an alliance between two families—have hastened the dissolution of the conjugal bond. A case in point is the expulsion from the royal palace in 1126 of Yi Cha-gyŏm's two daughters whom Yi had forcibly given Injong in marriage.[159] Or, the motives for discarding a wife may have been purely economic. After a man advanced in office, he might have been tempted to "change his [poor] wife" (*yŏkch'ŏ*) and seek a more prosperous spouse.[160]

Separation may not have been as common in uxorilocal marriages. Although uxorilocal marriage is judged by modern anthropologists to be more brittle than virilocal marriage,[161] in Koryŏ it was clearly an important vehicle of political and economic advancement for a significant number of men. It is likely that such marriages, which guaranteed a man and his descendants definite advantages, were relatively stable. In contrast, plural marriages often may have been only temporary arrangements. As the Chinese chronicler reported: "[In case of plural marriage] the slightest incompatibility [of the partners] resulted in separation."[162]

It is a telling fact that the semi-legal Confucian "seven instances of extreme wifely disobedience" (*ch'ilch'ul*) were not adopted from the T'ang code as reasons for expelling a wife in Koryŏ, although such rhetoric is evident in a number of biographies in the *Ko-ryŏsa*.[163] A Koryŏ wife could not easily be threatened with expulsion. She could afford to leave her husband at her own discretion because she and her children were always welcomed back by her natal family. There was, however, a legal provision, taken from the T'ang code, that made a wife's leaving her husband without the latter's consent a punishable act![164] Yet, it was not honorable for a woman to break and reestablish marital ties too often. Promiscuous behavior earned her the reputation of being "licentious," and her name was entered in the Register of Licentious Women (*Chan-yŏrok*).[165] Koryŏ society, however, was not prudish, and the generally free and easy contact between the sexes amazed the Chinese observers.[166]

Widowhood did not stigmatize a woman as an undesirable marriage partner, and remarriage after the husband's death was common and did not entail a loss of social status. In fact, remarriage was easy because the widow had no function or authority in her husband's family. To be sure, a law of 999 promised widows of high officials ennoblement as reward for "keeping their chastity" (*sujŏl*), and cases of "virtuous widows" who abstained from remarriage, at times even under difficult economic circumstances, won honorable mention on funerary steles.[167] These were undoubtedly exceptions. Widows were even accepted as queens in the royal palace,[168] and they were also welcomed in aristocratic houses, especially when they held property of their own or their dead husband's.[169] Remarriage with undue haste, however, was a social offense, and at least the mourning period for the dead spouse had to be observed before remarriage was considered.[170] Upon entering the house of a second husband, a woman usually brought the children she had borne during her previous marriage with her—they did not belong to her dead husband's family. This could create tense family relationships as she, known as "succeeding mother" (*kyemo*), was often accused of favoring her own children over those her second husband may have had from a previous wife.[171] Remarriage, even though fully sanctioned socially, was not quite like a first marriage.

It was exposed to greater intrafamilial pressures, and more human skills were needed to make it a success.

MOURNING AND FUNERARY RITES. The *obok* system was introduced to Koryŏ in 985 in the course of King Sŏngjong's ambitious sinicization of major cultural institutions.[172] This was not the first formalized mourning system in Korea. In 504, King Chijŭng (r. 500– 514) of early Silla reportedly instituted and propagated mourning laws *(sangbokpŏp),* the details of which are not known.[173] For Silla and later for Koryŏ, the adoption of such mourning rules was clearly an attribute of a civilized state, however ill-suited the rules may have been to native custom. Koryŏ's model was the T'ang *wu-fu* that had been codified in 732. Significantly, the Koreans of Koryŏ were forced to make some major changes in order to adapt Chinese theory to Korean social realities. The difficulty of this adaptation is suggested by the fact that these imported mourning prescriptions were at best considered normative for the officeholding elite in the capital, while society at large adhered to native practice.[174]

An analysis of some of the differences between T'ang *wu-fu* and Koryŏ *obok* highlights peculiarities of Koryŏ society (see Diagram 5).[175] The woman's strong position within the family rendered inapplicable the ancient Chinese rule according to which the mourning period for the mother had to be reduced while the father was still alive. This ritual prescription was therefore ignored, and both the father as well as the mother were mourned for three years (effectively twenty-five months), even though the mourning garments differed. If, after the death of his first wife, the father had a second wife, called "succeeding mother" *(kyemo),* she was mourned for only one year. This short period indicated the *kyemo's* relative unimportance for the son of the father's first wife who had to mourn her. For a mother who remarried after her husband's death *(kamo),* no mourning was provided on the original chart. In a ruling of 1068 this omission was regretted, and an irregular mourning period of one hundred days was devised. Remarriage was obviously too common an event to be ignored in ritual life.[176]

As might be expected, the contrast between the T'ang model and

Diagram 5. Select Koryŏ Mourning Grades

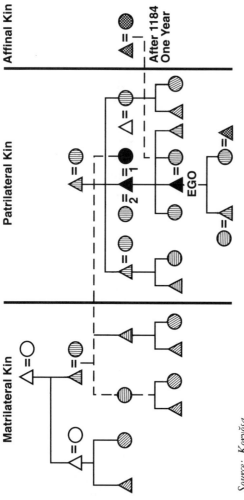

Source: Koryŏsa

Key (defined by mourning obligations of male EGO):

3 years (grade 1: *ch'amch'oe* for father; grade 2: *chaech'oe* for mother)

1 year (grade 2: *chaech'oe kinyŏn*)

9 months (grade 3: *taegong*)

5 months (grade 4: *sogong*)

3 months (grade 5: *sima*)

NB: After 1184, EGO mourned his wife's parents for 1 year.

its Koryŏ adaptation was most marked for the matrilateral relatives. Whereas the mourning obligations toward patrilateral kin closely followed the T'ang pattern, those toward the mother's family were enhanced. The maternal grandparents were assigned a one-year mourning period (in T'ang five months) and thus enjoyed the same ritual attention as the paternal grandparents. Consequently, the mother's brothers and sisters also were given higher grades (*taegong,* nine months) than provided for in the T'ang model (*sogong,* five months), although this did not bring them up to par with their patrilateral counterparts whose grade was *chaech'oe*—one year. In a noteworthy deviation from the T'ang model, the Koryŏ system also irregularly prescribed a three-month mourning period for the mother's first cousins, a provision that at least tacitly recognized the maternal great-grandparents (for whom, however, there were no mourning grades). Matrilateral first cousins were not given such preferential treatment. In agreement with T'ang usage, they were accorded a mere three months *(sima).*

Because the daughter's husband often assumed the role of a real son, especially when he resided uxorilocally in the wife's house, his ties to his in-laws were particularly strong. This was recognized by upgraded mourning obligations of five months for the wife's parents (T'ang had only three months). This was reciprocated with the equally unusual five months of mourning for the son-in-law. In 1184, a ruling increased the length of mourning for the wife's parents still more to one full year (*chaech'oe*—one year).[177] The law also took into account that a man could have several wives and thus different sets of parents-in-law: for each one he was granted a leave of absence from office to fulfill his mourning duties.[178] In contrast, there is no mention of any ritual responsibilities of the wife toward her husband's kin—a significant indication that the wife was not recognized as a full-fledged member of her husband's family, but instead was treated like an outsider.[179]

The Koryŏ adaptation of the Chinese mourning system clearly reveals a conscious attempt to incorporate the main characteristics of Koryŏ society. By expressing the social weight of matrilateral and affinal kin, the Koryŏ mourning chart acquired unique features.

The Chinese *obok* system was inherently inadequate to accommodate Koryŏ kinship because it was constrained by some structural principles, most notably its patrilineal preference, and by its traditional rigor—mourning grades could be modified, but not newly "invented."

Throughout Koryŏ, the *obok* system remained a basically alien institution. While some of its terminology was used in legal context, its main ritual function to provide guidelines for correct mourning among close kin was jeopardized by the impractical length of mourning for the parents as well as by the predominantly Buddhist atmosphere of the time. To be sure, official historiography and a number of grave inscriptions record the ritually proper behavior of exemplary sons who spent the full time in a lightly built mourning shed *(yŏmyo)* at their parents' graves. Such acts were rewarded with the attribute of filiality and at times with the erection of a commemorative arch *(chŏngmun)*. The special attention paid to these events underscores their uniqueness—their deviation from the usual conduct of mourning.[180]

In official circles, a one-hundred-day mourning period apparently was normal. Because of the close connection of mourning legislation with the officeholding elite, the shortened mourning was rationalized as a measure that took into account the exigencies of national affairs and thus harnessed filial piety to loyalty toward the state.[181] This sentiment seems to have been embodied in the rules that regulated an official's mourning leave. One hundred days of absence from office were granted to a son who mourned for either one of his parents. The number of free days was scaled down according to the decreasing degree of mourning. Leave was also given to observe all major ceremonies during the remaining mourning period and seasonal celebrations.[182] It was not possible for an official, therefore, to complete full mourning according to the ritual prescriptions without resigning from office. He was urged to return to duty after one hundred days, and at times of national emergencies he could expect to be recalled to office at short notice *(kibok)*. He marked this circumstance by wearing special dress.[183] Examination candidates were occasionally exempted from mourning.[184] The death of the parents and the mourning for them—mourning for other kin was never discussed in practical terms—were obviously difficult to deal with during an official career, and it would seem that legislation favored the official above the mourner.

Among the officeholding aristocracy, the *obok* system, although respected as an ideal, was variously bent by practical needs. Among the rural elite and the commoners, it seems to have been but vaguely known. For them, mourning rarely extended beyond one hundred days. Soldiers, who were the only commoners who had statutory mourning guidelines, were granted a leave of one hundred days, later cut to fifty days.[185] Even such periods were often too long and apparently were shortened by the simple method of "converting months to days" (*iil yŏgwŏl*).[186] By expressing the length of the mourning period in terms of days equivalent to the original number of months, this left only twenty-five days of mourning for a parent.[187] Such economy did not allow for ritual elaboration and, toward the end of the dynasty, was criticized as regrettably "superficial."

The funerary customs of Koryŏ are not described in detail in the historical records. The evidence suggests that burial practices of aristocrats and commoners differed more on paper than in reality. For both, Buddhist funeral procedures and concepts of afterlife provided the ritual framework within which they dealt with death and its aftermath.

Select members of the influential capital elite were granted "state funerals" (*kukchang, yejang, kwanjang*) with all concomitant honors such as posthumous name and title and funerary provisions.[188] The construction of the tombs of civil and military officials were subject to fixed rules;[189] and the coffin, apparently richly decorated and at times even covered with gold sheathing—a luxury later officially prohibited[190]—was placed into a stone vault (*sŏksil*).[191] Because of this solid tomb construction, a great number of Koryŏ's famous celadon ware, given to the dead as a last sign of respect, was preserved until recent times. Wives of high officials, at death, were often interred in the same grave as their husbands (*hapchang, kwi-*

jang, pujang).[192] The grave site of the powerful was marked with a tombstone, an offering table, and various stone figures—the visible trappings of high social status.[193]

The evidence is insufficient to draw firm conclusions, but it may be surmised that, as the central bureaucracy increased, the officials residing in Kaesŏng were buried in the mountains surrounding the capital. The west and north sides apparently offered favored burial sites. Although taking up residence in the capital tended to loosen the ties to the place of origin, at times the deceased was returned to ancestral burial grounds *(sŏnyŏng)* in the countryside.[194]

Funeral rituals were profoundly influenced by Buddhist traditions. Besides containing conventional Buddhist rhetoric, grave inscriptions convey the impression that even high-standing personalities—the carriers of Confucian culture—saw the deeper meaning of their existence in Buddhist terms. It was not uncommon to await death in a Buddhist temple. The famous Ch'oe Sa-ch'u, for example, died in Chaunsa, east of the royal palace. And even the prominent Confucian scholar, Yi Saek, ended his life in Sillŭksa, east of Seoul. Some women, when they felt their death was near, cut their hair and died as nuns.[195]

The way to the final resting place was often a long one. The funeral procedures at times extended over months and even years, although it apparently became a widely observed practice—in disregard of all ritual prescriptions—to inter the dead on the third day.[196] Prompt burial presumably was the rule when the dead was encoffined and deposited in the earth *(t'ojang).* When the corpse was cremated *(hwajang)* in the precincts of a temple—a custom of Buddhist origin practiced by elite and commoners alike—burial was delayed for varying spans of time. Cremation, it was believed, expedited the continuation of life in Heaven and the entrance into the Western Region.[197] The cremated remains *(yugol)* usually were temporarily entrusted to a Buddhist temple and buried considerably later on an auspicious day. At times, temples were used as indefinite repositories of parents' remains, relieving the descendants of burial arrangements—an abuse that a government ruling of 1133 no longer tolerated.[198] The first grave was rarely the final resting place. Changes of the burial site *(ijang, kaejang)* were so common that a leave from office of thirty days was granted on such an occasion.[199] The proper accommodation of the dead was a serious matter that affected not only the repose of the departed soul but equally the fortunes of the descendants.[200]

In the funeral rites of the common people, Buddhist and shamanist notions mixed. The death of a parent, it was believed, gave rise to adverse forces that would destroy the house. Therefore, the dying parent was moved out of the house into an outer building to die. Once the danger of pollution was over, the funeral was a gay affair in which even the pallbearers *(hyangdo)* joined. Alcohol was consumed and music played.[201] The dead were not always buried: reportedly, their bones were sometimes scattered in the streets of the capital and in open fields. The government tried to cope with this neglect of propriety by promising to cover the funeral expenses of the needy.[202]

CONCLUSIONS: *KORYŎ SOCIETY RECONSIDERED.* The data presented in this study are heterogeneous and fragmentary. The documents are scattered over almost five hundred years, and for no one period are they sufficient to allow comparisons or to see major developments. Moreover, the majority of the records extant deal with the aristocratic upper class—a numerically small social elite that cannot be taken as representative of the entire Koryŏ society. In view of these limitations, it is not possible to draw a definitive picture of Koryŏ society. Nevertheless, certain features stand out clearly enough to permit the following generalizations.

The most likely social environment in which a Koryŏ man grew up was his mother's natal group. His father, upon marriage, had chosen to move into his bride's house for political or economic reasons. Uxorilocal residence was common in Koryŏ. There were no apparent restrictions on the choice of residence. Parental residence, whether uxorilocal or virilocal, may not have determined a child's status. In his mother's house, he was surrounded by maternal kin; and his mother's brothers, differentiated by separate kin terms denoting sequence of birth, were likely to be important persons in his early life—one of them, perhaps, even his future father-in-law. Marriage with matrilateral cross-cousins was, at least in the early part of the dynasty, not uncommon and perhaps even preferred. The seniors in the household were the maternal grandparents whose love and indulgence were reciprocated with an impressive one-year mourning period.

Life in the maternal home may have ended when the father decided to return with his family to his own natal group. The motives for doing so varied. The most important one was to claim his share of his parents' inheritance. Or he might have succeeded his father in political office. It appears that at midlife a man had to make a choice between the three kin groups—paternal, maternal, affinal (the two latter may have coincided)—of which he was a potential member. Political and economic considerations must have determined his eventual recruitment into one of these groups.

A Koryŏ man was surrounded by a bilateral kindred, and from this pool of consanguines his partners and allies in life—often even his bride—emerged. One kinsman could be easily substituted for another: a first or second cousin was as good as a brother. Thinking in cognatic terms, a Koryŏ Korean was disposed to claim a privilege on the basis of either a patrilateral or matrilateral ancestor's prestige. When he considered his chances as an heir, his calculations ran vertically as well as sideways, even crossing sex and generational boundaries. There can be no doubt that competition among siblings, perhaps even extending to cousins, for political and economic advantages was severe. Such a system excluded the possibility of primogeniture, and the Chinese-inspired legislative efforts to establish a fixed line of succession for certain functions conflicted with native laterality. While in the public realm an established order of succession made sense—political office or function was, after all, indivisible—in the private realm such rules were meaningless and thus were never applied.

Most of what has been said is also relevant to the Koryŏ woman. The basis of her strength was her economic, if not jural, equality with her brothers. She competed with them for land, while her sons competed with their uncles for land as well as office. It is apparent that as an heir a woman was "courted" by her brothers more than by her husband, and that tension over property was apt to arise between a woman and her male siblings rather than between her and her spouse. From the latter she could separate herself, while her fate was tied to that of her brothers. A wife's property passed to her husband's family only through her children. If she did not have children, her property reverted back to her natal group. A woman, thus, never became a member of her husband's house, but despite her marriage remained a permanent outsider.

This picture of social life in Koryŏ shows typical cognatic traits. Siblings enjoyed equal status regardless of sex, and the sibling bond stood in opposition to the conjugal bond. Moreover, high interchangeability of lineal kin with collateral cognates is evident. Siblings could easily be replaced by cousins, and cousins of either patrilateral or matrilateral extraction were marriageable. Bilateral kindred played an overriding role in any individual's life. This cognatic interpretation is supported by a cursory look at Silla society. Without going here into the complexities of the different interpretations of the evolution of Silla society,[203] there is evidence of Silla precursors for many characteristic features of Koryŏ, most notably close-kin marriages, uxorilocal residence, and succession to royal office by sons, sons-in-law, agnatic and non-agnatic descendants.[204] If at least late Silla is characterized as a society that rested on cognatic organization, this leaves unexplained the social context from which the different kin terms designating the mother's brothers, noted at the beginning of this chapter as indicators of an earlier, possibly matrilineal past, originated. Data on descent and marriage of early Silla are obscure through later manipulation of historical evidence, and therefore it is uncertain whether Silla ever passed through a matrilineal stage. Double descent has been suggested for early Silla;[205] but it is not only worldwide a rare phenomenon, it is unlikely to be the structural forerunner of a cognatic system.[206] There is thus as yet no easy explanation for the differential terms for mother's brothers. They surely were a concomitant of uxorilocal

residence. While uxorilocal residence persisted into the fifteenth
century and beyond, the terms in question finally disappeared from
the kinship vocabulary of early Chosŏn.[207]

There are striking similarities between Koryŏ tradition and the
social institutions of Heian Japan (tenth to twelfth centuries). The
rich literary and historical documents of this period show that Japan, too, had a kind of "pre-Confucian" past before society moved
to its feudal and strictly patrilineal stage under the subsequent Ka-
makura regime (thirteenth and fourteenth centuries). During the
Heian period, the status of women was high, based on their economic independence. Daughters were able to inherit, besides other
property, their parents' house (this was commonly passed on from
mother to daughter); and this property remained theirs even after
marriage, as a married women retained membership in her own
descent group. Because a woman's property played an important
role in a marriage's economy, a husband had almost always an economic stake in the marriage. The various wives of a Heian courtier
lived thus separately and were not subject to ranking (although the
first wife married commonly became the major wife). Marital residence could be duolocal, uxorilocal, and neolocal. The *Kagero nikki,*
the diary of one of Fujiwara Kaneie's (929–990) wives, written in
the second half of the tenth century, describes in great detail how a
relationship with a visiting husband that lasted for her whole married life functioned.[208] The dissolution of a marriage was simple
and informal; the wife retained custody over her children who, however, kept their father's name. As in Koryŏ, therefore, the maternal
grandparents played a preponderant role in the upbringing of their
non-agnatic grandchildren. Heian marriages were contracted among
a relatively small circle of families that were permitted to hold court
rank and office. These Heian data are briefly mentioned here because
the women's literature of that time—unfortunately entirely lacking
in Koryŏ—provides invaluable illustration of a very special way of
life that was to a significant extent also typical for Koryŏ. A possible
generic explanation of these similarities must await further research.[209]

If, in conclusion, Koryŏ society were simply termed a cognatic society, such an interpretation would fail to take notice of a phenomenon that clearly set Koryŏ society on a course of change: the impact of the patrilineally oriented legislation imported from T'ang and, to a lesser degree, Sung China. The patrilineal intrusion into Korean society began as early as Silla—leaving Koguryŏ and Paekche out of consideration—and continued and gained momentum during the first two hundred years of Koryŏ. With the expansion of a bureaucratic system modelled on that of the T'ang, norms and rules were adopted that not only jeopardized the continued validity of kinship in the public realm, but also forced upon the existing structure certain new ordering principles. To be sure, more than the public realm the state could not touch. But household registration, the nomenclature of the mourning system, and the laws regulating succession and marriage became important channels through which patrilineal thinking was injected into everyday life, despite obvious efforts to accommodate native social tradition in the newly borrowed institutions. The shift toward patrilineal thinking first occurred in legislation and was naturally much slower to take practical effect, a fact that explains the coexistence of a number of apparently disparate social practices. But if the "cognatic beginnings" of Koryŏ are taken as a baseline and the "household registers with eight ancestors" as an example of kin conceptualization of late Koryŏ, the extent to which Koryŏ society absorbed patrilineal influence must indeed be termed as marked. It was not simply a matter of shifting emphasis. It meant the laying out of foundation stones upon which a truly patrilineal social structure could later arise.

Whereas the importation of the T'ang model had enormous consequences for the development of Koryŏ society,[210] the almost one hundred years of Mongol domination of Korean affairs between the thirteenth and fourteenth centuries seem to have left but a light imprint. The Mongols were admired for their military organization and prowess; but apart from some fancy fashions, they seem to have furnished little of substance for imitation. While there was close interaction between the Koryŏ royal house, the Yüan emperors, and their Korean supporters, there was little direct contact between the Mongols and the Koreans at large. None of the outstanding Mongol social practices—levirate, bride-price, virilocal residence of married women, heirship of the youngest son—were taken over in contemporary Korea.[211] As in China, no force was used to make the customs of the weaker conform to the legal sense of the stronger.[212] Only one social institution of Koryŏ, plural marriage, is frequently attributed by Korean scholars to Mongol influence.[213] This would make plural marriage an innovation of late Koryŏ. Although the Mongol elite indeed was polygamous (women were acquired by purchase, capture, or inheritance),[214] it is clear from evidence of the early twelfth century that plural marriage in Koryŏ antedated Mongol domination and was qualitatively quite different from the Mongol form. The Mongols, then, cannot be credited with acting as social innovators in Koryŏ.

What, then, did the key term *chok* mean? In the Koryŏ context, it designated a descent group that held on to its ancestors as well as to their descendants. Ancestry was traced back through both male and female links. At the beginning of the dynasty, in particular, the various descent lines may have gotten tangled up through close kin marriages, or remembered only as far back as a famous truncal ancestor on whose prestige the descendants were still living. Some of the famous descent groups may have been able to survive over a long period of time for the important reason that they could replenish their ranks and shore up their prestige by recruiting new members from the large pool of cognatic kin. The flexibility of succession may in many cases also have played a crucial role: when a descent group was near extinction because of lack of agnates, it could rejuvenate itself with in-coming sons-in-law and their offspring.

These descent groups were identified by Chinese-style surnames (Chin. *hsing;* Kor. *sŏng*) that were originally introduced to Silla in the course of the sixth century when the emerging kingdom sought diplomatic contact with China. The royal families of Silla, the Kim and the Pak, apparently were among the first to use surnames; but they were soon followed by the Silla aristocrats, and the adoption of surnames proliferated during United Silla.[215] How the surnames were chosen is not clear, but a number of them were bestowed *(sasŏng)* by the T'ang emperor upon Korean envoys. The founding ancestor *(sijo)* of the Kyŏngwŏn (Inju) Yi-ssi, Yi-Hŏ Ki (no dates), for example, is said to have received the imperial surname Yi as a gift from Hsüan-tsung (r. 712–756). This honorable label, however, clearly did not fully match the genealogical sense of the recipient's descendants, for it is reported that down to the seventh generation they used the double surname Yi-Hŏ.[216] Such genealogical duplication seems to point to the fact that a descent group was hard pressed to identify itself with one single surname. Significantly, early Korean historical sources, too, often were at a loss to record a person's "correct" surname. Thus, the famous martyr Ich'adon (506–527) is referred to by the *Samguk yusa* (Memorabilia of the Three Kingdoms) with three different surnames, Pak, Sŏk, and Kim.[217] Even though the T'ang term *hsing* seems to have connoted a descent group rather than simply a surname,[218] it is evident that this Chinese term put the Korean descent group into a conceptual straitjacket that gave it a patrilineal twist obscuring its true nature.

A surname was further identified by an "ancestral seat" *(pon-gwan)* that usually was the name of the administrative unit where the descendants of the original settler had established themselves as local power-holders at the end of Silla or in early Koryŏ.[219] Many of the "great families" that became part of the central aristocracy *(kwijok)* in the new capital, Kaegyŏng (Kaesŏng), originated from these regionally powerful descent groups *(hojok)*. Regional ties remained an important asset as the *pon'gwan* system turned into a legal institution.[220] Although the designation of a man's *pon'gwan* eventually may no longer have had anything to do with his place of birth or residence, it continued to certify his high status.

What, then, besides surname and ancestral seat name, made a Koryŏ descent group "great" *(taejok)*, "famous" *(myŏngjok)*, or "respected" *(mangjok)?* There seem to be a number of conditions which all aristocratic descent groups, regardless of whether they belonged to the dynastic founding establishment or emerged to prominence at a later time, had to fulfill to build up and maintain their reputation. One of the conditions was holding high rank and concomitant high office in the central bureaucracy over a number of generations. "High" meant the attainment of at least rank five. Another condition was economic wealth; and a third one was proper marriage connections, preferably with the royal house. But the most crucial, if largely intangible, element of high status was descent. Descent represented the foremost component of a patrimony and was more important than merit. By descent the rights and obligations concerning property, inheritance, jural and political privilege, and social status in the widest sense were transmitted. Genealogy and heredity permeated the political structure, conspicuously exemplified by the institution of the "protection privilege." Descent, then, not only determined an individual's membership in a famous descent group, but at the same time gave him a head start in Koryŏ society.

No national list of prominent descent groups seems to have been compiled in Koryŏ, although the existence of such registers in T'ang China was known in Korea.[221] The only, albeit exclusive, numerical estimate available is King Ch'ungsŏn's list of 1308. It enumerates fifteen aristocratic descent groups (of some, however, only one line) with which the royal house at that time was allowed to intermarry. From among these, only four descent groups—the royal Kyŏngju Kim, the Kyŏngwŏn Yi, the Ansan Kim, and the P'apyŏng Yun—were able to maintain their elite status from the early days throughout the dynasty. The dominance of these descent groups rested above all on kin solidarity. Even though they occasionally brought forth outstanding personalities who rose to high office, it was the social connectedness and marital ties that were instrumental in achieving and preserving descent group power and influence over a long period of time. Only a surprisingly small number of descent groups, however, seems to have been able to make this work for them.[222]

Prominence as well as cohesion of a Koryŏ descent group rested on the principle of descent, but such a descent group was not as homogeneous a body as the neat surname, which was patrilineally transmitted, might suggest. On the contrary, as has been argued before, *chok* was a flexible and inclusive concept. *Chok* was thus definitely not coterminous with *sŏng* or *tongsŏng* (same surname), two terms that connote exclusion and that, significantly, rarely appear in the sources. Moreover, *chok* cannot be regarded as synonymous with the Chinese *tsu* (written with the same character), which meant in T'ang times a branch of a patrilineal descent group *(tsung)*.[223] Toward the end of Koryŏ, however, even the concept of *chok* seems to have been affected by patrilineal considerations, for it was often replaced by the clearly narrower term "descent line" *(chong)* that connoted a vertical string of agnates.[224]

In the course of centuries, Koryŏ's society gradually changed character. Under the pervasive influence of China, a patrilineal philosophy subtly superimposed itself upon the originally cognatic Korean system. The result was not a massive shift away from tradition. Rather, it was a slow reduction of the range of choices that the traditional social system had granted to an individual and his group. Flexibility and strategy inherent in Koryŏ's social organization were narrowed by patrilineally calculated rules that left little room for options. This development, promoted from the top, principally affected the public realm of the government-bound elite layer of society. It hardly penetrated the aristocrats' private life. Even less did it percolate into the lower social strata. Nevertheless, it prepared the ground for the advent of Neo-Confucianism at the end of the dynasty. It was the thrust of this ideology that in time completed the patrilineal transformation of Korean society.

TWO

Neo-Confucianism: The Ideological Foundation of Social Legislation in Early Chosŏn

When Yi T'aejo (Yi Sŏng-gye, 1335—1408) ascended the throne in 1392, the existing sociopolitical order was not a moral polity in the Confucian sense. Reform programs, begun a quarter century earlier during the reign of King Kongmin of Koryŏ, were ineffective in revitalizing the country after almost a century of Mongol domination. Royal authority was eroded, and the fate of the country was largely in the hands of well-established aristocrats who occupied the highest positions in the central government and maintained large landed estates. They opposed reforms that aimed at strengthening the king's rule and strongly supported the Buddhist establishment. Recurrent invasions by the Red Turbans in the north, devastating raids by Japanese pirates *(Wakō)* along the coasts, and repeated attempts by the Mongols to maintain a dominant voice in Koryŏ internal politics were events that favored the reemergence of military forces. Moreover, Kongmin's prestige as a reformer was irreparably damaged when he placed an obscure Buddhist monk, Sin Ton, in command of government affairs.[1] Although some reforms, especially in education, were moderately successful, Sin Ton failed to break the aristocracy's grip on power and to create a climate conducive to social renewal.

Dynastic change in China with the rise of the Ming in 1368, Sin

Ton's fall from power in 1371, and King Kongmin's assassination three years later opened the possibility of a far-reaching realignment of political forces. The last kings of Koryŏ lost their credibility as rulers through questionable succession practices. Supreme power eventually shifted to the military, who propelled themselves into commanding positions during the declining years of Koryŏ. The triumph of the alliance between Yi Sŏng-gye, the military hero, and the Neo-Confucian scholar-officials was the founding of the Chosŏn dynasty.

The new rulers faced formidable tasks: consolidation of the country's territory, reconstruction of the bureaucracy, reorganization of local administration, extensive land reforms, increasing agricultural productivity, and social regeneration. The solution of the problems besetting Korean society would be instrumental not only in striking a new balance between land and people, but also in introducing a new sense of order and security into society. The transition from Koryŏ to early Chosŏn did not bring about abrupt institutional changes. Koryŏ political institutions were taken over as the organizational basis of the new government. Their framework was tightened by increasing bureaucratization and centralization. Royal power, concentrated in the capital, was strengthened and represented in the countryside by officials dispatched by the king.

The Koryŏ-Chosŏn transition was multifaceted, and it would be difficult to isolate any one cause as bringing about the founding of a new dynasty. Rather, it was the extraordinary interaction of events and personalities during the waning years of Koryŏ that ultimately made dynastic change inevitable. The underlying theme—recurrent in Korean history—was the struggle between throne and aristocracy that escalated after the collapse of Mongol domination as each strove for a redistribution of power and influence. This deepened factional strife and its concomitant dismissals from office, purges, and banishment, in the course of which the military reasserted itself as a power in politics.

The increasingly embittered political scene in Kaesŏng was overshadowed by the international situation. The retreating Mongols still had followers in Korea, and the rising Ming posed a formidable threat to Korean territory. Loyalties were split; but in the end the pro-Ming forces, led by Yi Sŏng-gye, won out. The assessment of Korea's chances in an open conflict with the Ming had led him and his advisers to realize that the country's economic situation would not sustain prolonged military action. Yi Sŏng-gye's pro-Ming stance was therefore informed above all by a timely realpolitik. Rather than subject Korea to a military venture with uncertain outcome, he started his offensive at the home front. Foremost on his agenda was a reordering of economic resources.

Toward the end of Koryŏ, as its power declined, the state's economic condition was depressed because it had lost tax rights over large portions of land. Despite the frequently pronounced ideal of state ownership of all land, from the beginning of Koryŏ there had been privately owned land. As the dynasty moved into the fourteenth century, privatization of land accelerated. The vast landholdings of the Buddhist establishment and the cancerous growth of private estates deprived the state of revenues and forced many previously free tillers into tenancy (*chŏn'gaek*). The state, itself in the grip of the representatives of landed interests, was powerless to check these developments and drifted into insolvency. Calls for land reform gave rise to heated political debates during the waning years of the dynasty.[2]

As early as 1352, Yi Saek pleaded in a programmatic memorial for reforms of the land system,[3] but it was in the summer of 1388 that Cho Chun (1346–1405), backed by Yi Sŏng-gye, submitted the first of three proposals which together mapped out an irreversible course of reform. The reformers believed that in antiquity the state had held all the land, distributed it to the people for cultivation, and collected rent from them. This system eliminated not only the difference between rich and poor, but also provided the state with necessary revenues. Those who rendered service directly to the state were given the right to collect rent from specially allocated land in return for their services. This was believed to be the essence of Koryŏ's original land system (*chŏnsikwa*). Both Cho Chun and his partner in spirit, Chŏng To-jŏn, urged its revival in order to break the economic power of the landed Koryŏ aristocracy and to put the country on a new economic basis. Their call was echoed in a number of partisan memorials. Cho's program pitted the reform-minded against the guardians of vested interests, and this polarization of the political forces over economic issues eventually provided a major impulse to found a new dynasty. The Koryŏ scheme indeed became the basis of the new "rank-land system" (*kwajŏnpŏp;* see below, p. 203.) that was proclaimed in 1391, but put into effect only after the change of dynasties.[4]

A complex religious situation surrounded the dynastic change. Buddhism and shamanism governed the country's religious life, especially the cult of the dead and belief in life after death. At the royal court as well as in the rest of society, both Buddhist and shamanistic rituals were performed. While shamanism was an all-pervasive folk phenomenon, Buddhism was a well-organized religion with a coherent doctrine. Designated as the protective spiritual power of the state by the founder of Koryŏ, Buddhism also had developed powerful economic institutions. Moreover, the egalitarian thrust of Buddhism and its promise of spiritual liberation had induced many to leave worldly troubles behind and enter monkhood. Indeed, Buddhism had given rise to social mobility as exemplified by the rise of Sin Ton. The Buddhist question, then, was another issue that awaited urgent solution.

Above all, however, the establishment of the Chosŏn dynasty was a moral and intellectual venture that set out to prove itself by articulating a sociopolitical program that would give the new dynasty a firm Confucian basis. It signified a felicitous conjunction between the ideological orientation of progressive reformers on the one hand, and the pragmatic aims of the military on the other. In a true sense, it was the Korean rendition of the celebrated Confucian concept of "renovation" (*yusin*).

THE RISE OF NEW DYNASTIC FORCES. Who were the men who assisted Yi Sŏng-gye in the founding of the Chosŏn dynasty? The names on the three lists of merit subjects created at the inception of the dynasty (in 1392, 1398, and 1401)[5] suggest that Yi Sŏng-gye was surrounded by a mixed group of supporters. The majority comprised civilians, most of whom had passed the higher civil service examinations during and just after King Kongmin's reign, held middle- and high-level positions under the last Koryŏ kings, and teamed up with Yi Sŏng-gye at the latest after the dramatic turnabout of 1388. The social background of these civilians was not uniform. A good number of them, like Cho Chun, belonged to established descent groups which formed the ruling aristocracy, while almost twice as many had less distinguished ancestries. Their places of origin were widely scattered over the peninsula, although Kyŏngsang province seems to have brought forth a significant number of them. None of these civilians is reported to have personally possessed large landed property. On the contrary, complaints about poor economic circumstances—undoubtedly often exaggerated—abounded.

The next important segment of Yi Sŏng-gye's partisans was the military. The lack of information about their social and economic origin seems to be indicative of the relative obscurity from which they emerged. Only a few held commanding positions and even fewer could have passed the military examinations (which were instituted only in 1390). Yi Sŏng-gye himself rose to power from rather modest beginnings in the Northeast to where a forefather had migrated. It was in that area that he started to recruit his private army. He owed his gradual advancement to commanding posts to his victorious campaigns against the Japanese pirates along the coasts and the Jurchen intruders in the north. Because his connections were predominantly regional, he was able to gain some foothold in the central government only after 1383. Yi Sŏng-gye's slow advancement—most of his appointments were only short-term—seems to be generally representative of the career limitations the military outside the capital had to endure. The decisive moment in his career came when in 1388, true to his pro-Ming orientation, he refused to lead his troops across the Yalu against the Ming and instead turned them around to seize de facto power in Kaesŏng.

The smallest group of merit subjects was formed by members and in-laws of the royal family of the Chŏnju Yi. Their share of honors was conspicuously large in 1398 after the first succession struggle. Yi Hwa (?–1407), Sŏng-gye's younger half brother, who was instrumental during the consolidation phase of the new dynasty, was honored all three times. Others were rewarded for either siding with the winning party or staying neutral in the ongoing competition among Yi Sŏng-gye's sons for the throne.[6]

Those, then, who were elevated as merit subjects of the early Chosŏn dynasty rose from diverse social and economic backgrounds; they received titles and sizable grants of land and slaves in return for their contributions to the founding of the new dynasty.[7] It was a small elite group that was forged together not only by political and military activities but also by marital ties.[8] The civilian element clearly predominated, and it was personalities like Chŏng To-jŏn, Cho Chun, Ha Yun (1347–1416), and Kwŏn Kŭn (1352–1409) who became the true architects of the Chosŏn dynasty.

Chŏng To-jŏn belonged to a minor kin group, the Ponghwa Chŏng, and thus lacked the prestige of illustrious forebears. His grandfather was the first to attain a minor post in the central bureaucracy, and his father was an examination passer in the early fourteenth century under King Ch'ungsuk. Chŏng To-jŏn is said to have grown up in modest circumstances; but he had enough leisure to prepare himself for the higher civil service examinations, which he passed in 1362. After some years of service in the Confucian Academy (Sŏnggyun-gwan), where he first came in contact with Neo-Confucian thought, he was banned from the capital in 1375 and during the next eight years led a life of deprivation and isolation in the countryside. It was, however, a period of intense intellectual preoccupation with Neo-Confucianism from which his first philosophical works resulted. Chŏng was perhaps not a very deep thinker, but he certainly commanded an impressively wide range of knowledge—from military science to medicine, from calendrical science to mathematics. When he joined Yi Sŏng-gye in 1383, he was therefore well-equipped to become one of the general's closest advisers.[9] It was Chŏng To-jŏn who intellectually paved Yi Sŏng-gye's road to power in 1392 and largely determined the reform course during the first few years of the new dynasty.

In contrast to Chŏng To-jŏn, Cho Chun was a scion of the powerful P'yŏngyang Cho who had risen to prominence under the Mongols and had marital relations with the Koryŏ royal house as well as with the most powerful surname groups of that time.[10] Cho Chun thus belonged to the Koryŏ establishment. He passed the higher civil service examinations in 1374 and afterward held a number of minor posts. Because of differences with the dominant faction of Yi In-im (?–1388) under King U (r. 1374–1388), he retired from government service in 1384 and devoted the next four years to intensive historical and philosophical studies. He maintained close friendship with Yun So-jong (1345–1393), an early Neo-Confucian adept. In 1388, he entered Yi Sŏng-gye's camp. Cho Chun teamed up with Chŏng To-jŏn; but this initially fruitful collaboration eventually foundered on policy differences, the most dramatic and fateful of which was that over the choice of T'aejo's successor. Cho Chun opted for Yi Pang-wŏn, the later T'aejong (r. 1400–1418), whereas Chŏng To-jŏn was killed in 1398 for supporting the latter's half brother, Yi Pang-sŏk, T'aejo's youngest son. Cho Chun not only was a skillful politician, but also a thoughtful and resourceful legislator whose legal conceptions shaped much of the new dynasty's future course.

Both Chŏng To-jŏn and Cho Chun were surrounded by inner circles of followers some of whom had themselves been placed on one of the merit-subject lists. Not among these intimates were Ha Yun and Kwŏn Kŭn, both of whom left indelible marks on the legislative and intellectual history of early Chosŏn. Ha Yun was a newcomer from the south about whose ancestry nothing much is known. He passed the higher civil service examinations in 1365. Because he was connected by marriage with Yi In-im's faction, he was sent into exile when Yi was toppled. While he saw the necessity of reforms, he apparently opposed Chŏng To-jŏn's and Cho Chun's plans of establishing a new dynasty. Once this feat was achieved, however, Ha Yun adapted himself rather easily to the new political circumstances. What services won him merit-subject status twice (in 1398 and 1401), however, is unknown. During the first two decades of Chosŏn his name was prominently connected with important legal and social legislation.[11]

Unlike Ha Yun, Kwŏn Kŭn was the descendant of the well-established and distinguished Andong Kwŏn, who had a long tradition of civil service in the central bureaucracy. Moreover, he inherited from his great-grandfather, Kwŏn Pu, a firm commitment to Neo-Confucian studies. After passing the higher civil service examinations in 1369, he occupied a number of educational offices. During the last years of Koryŏ, he held a decisively pro-Ming attitude, and it was because of his involvement in a diplomatic exchange with the Ming in 1389 that he fell into disgrace and was banished from the capital. While in solitude, Kwŏn Kŭn devoted himself to scholarship and wrote his first philosophical and exegetical works. Banished to the countryside, he failed to take active part in the dynastic change in 1392, the prospect of which he had viewed with reservations—a stance he later apparently regretted.

T'aejo himself called him back to active duty; and he dedicated his superb writing skills to various official tasks, among them the diplomatic correspondence with the Ming court. A controversy over stylistic form decided in his favor incurred him Chŏng To-jŏn's open antipathy—their relationship had always been rather strained—but also won him belated merit-subject status.[12] He maintained a close personal relationship with T'aejo; but because of the animosity between him and Chŏng To-jŏn, he could move into the political foreground only after Chŏng's death in 1398. Kwŏn Kŭn's contributions to the early Chosŏn dynasty were varied: with his annotations and exegeses of Chinese classical works, he opened to his contemporaries an entirely new vista on the Chinese canon; and as a devoted teacher, he built a solid basis for Korea's own Neo-Confucian development.[13]

There can be no doubt that these merit subjects—in particular the civilian segment—exercised commanding influence over the course of events during the first few decades of the new dynasty. They constituted the first generation of occupants of high office[14] and thus laid the dynasty's legislative foundation. It is less certain, however, how long such influence could be maintained by the merit subjects' descendants. To be sure, a merit subject's appanage was hereditary and tax-exempt; but in an increasingly sophisticated bureaucracy that came to prize achievement tested in the examination system as much as ascribed status, economic comfort alone did not for long guarantee social and political prominence. Distinction won in the founding days had to be justified in later generations by going through the regular channels of advancement. [15]

It would be a mistake, however, to accord the merit subjects exclusive recognition as dynastic builders. Among the latter must also be counted personalities who for unknown reasons—they may have just been a little too young—did not receive merit-subject status, but who were prominently involved in the initial legislative process. One such personality was Hwang Hŭi (1363–1452). He passed the civil service examinations in 1389 and thereafter held an educational post. The final days of Koryŏ he spent in retirement from which he was recalled by T'aejo to one of the most remarkable careers in the higher officialdom. A similarly influential official was Maeng Sa-sŏng (1360–1438), who passed the examinations in 1386. After holding some minor posts in late Koryŏ, he started climbing the official ladder during the first decades of the Chosŏn dynasty and left his imprint on the social and cultural history of his day. Another prominent name was that of Pyŏn Kye-ryang, who was successful in the higher civil service examinations in 1385. Besides using his famous writing talents for the new dynasty, he was a principal formulator of early social legislation. He often teamed up with Hŏ Cho (1369–1439), who, himself an examination passer of 1390, became one of the leading ritualists of the early Yi kings. All of these four men belonged to descent groups that had not distinguished themselves in late Koryŏ. [16]

In sum, then, the men who helped bring about the dynastic change of 1392 and seized the new dynasty's command posts were, in their social and economic backgrounds, very much the sort of men who had always held power and filled government posts. To be sure, some of them may have harbored economic grievances because they had no part in the vast landed estates (*nongjang*) of the ruling Koryŏ elite and may at times even have led impoverished lives. But it would be difficult to discern purely economic motives for their participation in the new dynastic venture. With very few exceptions—some commoners apparently infiltrated the military segment—they all belonged to the aristocratic upper class, even if in some cases at its bottom fringes; and they did possess sufficient wealth to support themselves during the long preparations for the civil service examinations. The numerical proportion of examination passers among them is certainly conspicuous: success in the examinations, often combined with illustrious family background, gave them access to the central bureaucracy. Their advancement, however, was slow and frequently even blocked by the adverse political conditions of the time. The bureaucracy was overstaffed and political life was rent by factional strife. This was most probably a real source of personal frustration that drove them to seek alignment with the winning military forces around Yi Sŏng-gye.

The evidence that among the merit subjects of early Chosŏn, with the exception of a few military, there apparently were no social elements that would have indicated the rise of a strikingly new ruling class seems to be corroborated by a study of the social origin of the high officeholders in the general officialdom. For approximately half the officials of early Chosŏn whose names were recorded, descent group affiliation is known. Altogether some 158 different descent groups were represented. Of these, thirty-two provided close to half of the officials whose social background is known. Two-thirds of these kin groups had brought forth members who occupied high government offices since the middle of the twelfth century; that is to say, they belonged to the core of the Koryŏ aristocracy. It is equally clear that the number of newly emerging descent groups was insignificant, and that only a few Koryŏ descent groups ceased to be politically active at the beginning of Chosŏn. In short, the evidence points unmistakably to the fact that there were no new social forces which assumed power in the new dynasty, and that the highest offices continued to be staffed by descendants of well-established aristocratic kin groups.[17]

If it is clear that the founding fathers of Chosŏn were the descendants of Koryŏ aristocrats and not rebellious peasants stirred to insurrection by calamitous economic conditions as in Ming China, from where, then, did that dynamism originate which made the establishment of the Chosŏn dynasty an epochal event in Korea's social history? It must have been produced by the materials the intellectual founders of the new dynasty studied: the Neo-Confucian canon. It was this literature that opened up to them the vision of a new sociopolitical order grounded on moral principles and that committed them to re-create this order in their own time.

THE INTELLECTUAL FORMATION OF THE NEW ELITE. The center of learning during the last decades of Koryŏ was the Confucian Academy, which was reestablished under King Kongmin in 1367 after a long period of decay. Connected with the reemergence of the government-operated Academy was the introduction of the three-stage civil service examination system two years later. In conformity with the Mongol model, the examination subjects were entirely drawn from the classics; and the relationship between examiner and examinee, in Koryŏ times determined by personal ties, was put on a more professional basis. That the introduction of this new, more impersonal selection of officials was an important innovation is evidenced by the fact that it was strongly opposed by the established ruling circles and abolished in 1376. This conflict between those who were interested in upholding the old order and those who sought to exploit the emergent institution to their own advantage ended when King Kongyang (r. 1389–1392) was put on the throne as Yi Sŏnggye's puppet, and the new examination system was reestablished.[18]

The best known Confucians of the time were appointed teachers at the Confucian Academy; and after the daily teaching sessions, teachers and students gathered to debate outstanding problems of Neo-Confucian thought. This was an intellectual exchange that differed markedly from the earlier mechanical internalization of the classical wisdom. The leader of these disputations was Yi Saek who presided over the first large-scale debates about Chu Hsi's Four Books. He is credited with having chaired the sessions skillfully because he "was analytical and was able to reconcile [differing opinions]."[19] Yi Saek thus helped shape an intellectual milieu from which the most inspiring thought of the time emerged.

One of the most fervent debaters was Chŏng Mong-ju (1337–

1392). Calling literary composition a "peripheral art," he believed the "teachings of body and mind" *(sinsim chi hak)* to be all embodied in the *Ta-hsüeh* and the *Chung-yung*. With a friend, he is said to have retreated to a Buddhist hermitage to study these books. At the Confucian Academy, he expounded the meaning of the Four Books; and legend has it that his interpretations were found to match those of Hu Ping-wen's (1250–1333) *Ssu-shu t'ung* (Interpretations of the Four Books) so closely that, when the latter work was brought to Korea, Chŏng's colleagues' respect for him increased rapidly. Because his works, except for some poetry, were lost in the turmoil surrounding his death in 1392, an assessment of Chŏng's thought is not possible, and one must rely on a brief entry in his biography: "He widely read a lot of books and daily recited the *Ta-hsüeh* and the *Chung-yung*. He investigated principle *(i)* and thereby perfected his knowledge; he searched in himself to give it practical expression. He truly exerted himself for a long time and thus, unaided, resolved the mysteries [the solution of which] the Sung Confucians had not transmitted." Yi Saek worded his admiration for Chŏng thus: "When Mong-ju discusses principle, none of his theories misses it." It was Yi Saek who called Chŏng the "ancestor of the Eastern [Korean] school of principle *(ihak)*."[20]

No other book of the Confucian canon suited the early pursuers of the Neo-Confucian Way better than the *Ta-hsüeh*. This small treatise, by tradition considered to be the product of the immediate post-Confucian period and selected by Chu Hsi as one of the Four Books, set forth a systematic and pragmatic program that combined the imperative of moral education with the urgent appeal to political action. The *Ta-hsüeh* sustained the Neo-Confucians' claim to complete mastery over the totality of public and private life. Moreover, by referring to the sage-kings of Chinese antiquity, it lent credibility to the manner in which the Korean Confucians went about their tasks. The edition of the *Ta-hsüeh* most widely used was Chen Te-hsiu's *Ta-hsüeh yen-i*.

For Yi Saek and Chŏng Mong-ju and others with whom they shared the rostrum at the reestablished Confucian Academy—Kim Ku-yong (1338–1384), Pak Sang-ch'ung (1332–1375), and Yi Sung-in (1349–1392)[21]—the discovery and disputation of Neo-Confucian thought were an intellectual adventure that liberated them from the dull routine of traditional scholarship. Their teachings contained the elements of a moral and political plan of action; but in the waning years of Koryŏ, disrupted by party strife and marked by the Buddhist heritage, neither Yi nor Chŏng could or would draw the ultimate consequences from the Confucian message. Yi was later stigmatized as a compromiser with Buddhism, and Chŏng died as a Koryŏ loyalist in his vain attempt to prevent the establishment of the new dynasty in 1392.

Yet Yi Saek and Chŏng Mong-ju inspired a sense of mission in others—men who had no scruples about joining Yi Sŏng-gye in founding the Chosŏn dynasty. Certainly their most prominent disciple was Chŏng To-jŏn. Combining broad scholarship with political acumen and ambition, Chŏng "made the elucidation of the Learning of the Way and the repulsion of heterodox teachings [i.e., Buddhism] his own responsibility."[22] His contemporary and commentator, Kwŏn Kŭn, connected Chŏng directly to the Mencian tradition. As Mencius (371–289 B.C.?) had to put an end to heterodox doctrines to carry on the work of the three sages (Yü, the Duke of Chou, and Confucius),[23] so Chŏng was compelled to wipe out Buddhism to succeed Mencius. By teaming up with an enlightened ruler (i.e., Yi Sŏng-gye), Chŏng was able, Kwŏn stated, to restore the kingly influence (*wanghwa*) and to build a political order (*ch'i*) for the present age.[24] Undoubtedly, Chŏng To-jŏn was a most remarkable personality, the prototype of the omniscient scholar-official whose extensive erudition and large oeuvre seem to eclipse the works of his contemporaries. His philosophical treatises were written with the aim of delineating the Confucian point of view vis-à-vis the Buddhist challenge and thus carried a decidedly militant overtone; they were not intended as introductory texts to Neo-Confucianism.

Kwŏn Kŭn spoke of learning as the instrument for bringing people under control (*ch'i*) by activating their moral nature. For him, this "concrete learning" (*sirhak*), which stood in contrast to a mechanical internalization of the classics that had no practical application, had two closely related dimensions: it stimulated the process of self-realization with the ultimate aim of finding the Way in oneself; and it developed the proper human relations between ruler and subject, father and son, older and younger, and friends so that everyone would come to know his proper station in life. Both the search for the Way and the enrichment of human morality had to concentrate on the teachings of the Three Dynasties (Hsia, Shang, and Chou) and on the classics.[25] Kwŏn Kŭn's thinking was clearly guided by the *Ta-hsüeh* to which he devoted a chapter in his *Iphak tosŏl* (Illustrated Treatises for the Beginner) of 1390. This booklet, which essentially consisted of diagrams with commentaries, was immensely influential as a convenient guide through the maze of Neo-Confucian philosophy. It was reproduced a number of times during the first centuries of the Chosŏn dynasty.[26]

The new elite that was trained during the last decades of Koryŏ and participated in the founding of the Chosŏn dynasty received from the Neo-Confucian literature the impulse to define, in an essentially non-Confucian milieu, the norms for the building of a Confucian state. It also had to commit itself to the propagation of the Way in Korea. Under the pressure of this dual mission, it was forced to set priorities: the majority opted for participation in the political process; a few kept to the books.[27] For the political activists, Neo-Confucianism was more than the intellectual basis for testing their abilities for civil service careers. They took Neo-Confucianism as the universal basis upon which the state itself would have to rest. The establishment of a new dynasty was thus equal to the renewal of society through the articulation and implementation of Neo-Confucian principles. In their view, Neo-Confucianism was "concrete," pragmatic learning,[28] providing the key to a new understanding of the classical Confucian literature. In contrast to earlier Confucian studies, it made such understanding pertinent to the contemporary situation. The Neo-Confucian scholar-officials of the early Chosŏn dynasty were inspired with confidence both in the workability of their precepts and in their ability to translate them into action.

THE DISINTEGRATION OF KORYŎ SOCIETY AND THE BUDDHIST QUESTION.
The establishment of a new dynasty under Yi T'aejo provided the
Confucians with a vantage point from which they could view Koryŏ
society, evaluate its quality in Confucian terms, and demand change.
To the Confucians, Koryŏ society had lost its basic order and had
ceased to function properly. They blamed this breakdown on the
pervading influence of Buddhism: it had eroded the primary con-
trols of society; social status had become meaningless because of
social mobility; human relationships had collapsed because of detrimental customs; and correct social behavior *(ye)* clearly had disappeared.[29] To the new Confucian elite, Buddhism lacked the pragmatic standards necessary for social control and had caused the
disintegration of Koryŏ society.

During Koryŏ, Confucianism and Buddhism were credited with
fulfilling two complementary functions. Buddhism served the people's spiritual needs, while Confucianism provided the fundamentals of statesmanship. Ch'oe Sŭng-no in the tenth century was among
the first Confucians to compare the two systems critically and extol
the advantages of Confucianism. He pointed out that self-cultivation *(susin)* as practiced by the Buddhists was directed toward gaining rewards in a future life, whereas Confucianism was concerned
with managing the state in a contemporary situation. Would it not
be an error, he suggested, to abandon what is of immediate relevance for what is removed in time?[30]

The introduction of Neo-Confucianism in the late thirteenth century initially did not disturb the peaceful coexistence of Buddhism
and Confucianism. An early Neo-Confucian, Yi Che-hyŏn, even
attempted to find Buddhist equivalents for Neo-Confucian concepts: he related Buddhist compassion *(chabi)* to Confucian hu-
maneness *(in)*, and charity *(hŭisa)* to moral responsibility *(ŭi)*.[31] His
famous disciple, Yi Saek, was criticized by later Neo-Confucians for
his lax stand toward Buddhism. Although he had taken issue with
the Buddhists' economic excesses, he had avoided philosophical
criticism.[32] Toward the end of Koryŏ, Confucianism was still
embedded in the Buddhist environment and most Confucians did
not consider Buddhism a social menace.

Under King Kongmin, the Confucians' tolerance of Buddhism faltered. Sin Ton's meteoric rise and fall made it evident that Buddhism had extensively invaded the government apparatus, the traditional domain of the Confucians. In particular, the monk frustrated the young Confucian scholars and radicalized their demand for a new political order. Moreover, Buddhist institutions became targets of Confucian censure. Chŏng Mong-ju became a harsh critic of Buddhist monks and proposed legislation that would counteract Buddhist rites by encouraging the establishment of ancestral shrines. Confucians, he claimed, engaged in such normal activities as eating, drinking, and sex; even Yao and Shun's lives had not deviated from these rational standards. But the Buddhists broke with these patterns: they left their relatives, severed marital relationships, sat alone in caves staring into space, wore garments made of grass, and ate roots. This was not an ordinary way of life.[33] Although Chŏng Mong-ju's legislative proposals were the first serious attempt to take a stand against Buddhism by relating Confucian ritual precepts to everyday life, he did not envisage the establishment of a new social order on Confucian terms.

With the founding of the Chosŏn dynasty, the attacks on Buddhism both as a religion and an institution became more intense and sophisticated. Criticism focused on two main points: the Buddhists' emphasis on life after death, which rendered the present irrelevant; and their cultivation of self, which isolated the individual from family and state. Chŏng To-jŏn attempted a wide-ranging analysis of the philosophical differences between Confucianism and Buddhism. His treatise *Pulssi chappyŏn* (Various Arguments Concerning Buddhism) broke with the earlier Confucians' concessions to Buddhism and advanced doctrinal arguments against it. Chŏng To-jŏn stressed the Confucian endeavor to come to a full understanding of human nature by active self-cultivation, and he condemned the contemplative and passive methods of Buddhism for reaching the same goal. He turned against the major Buddhist doctrines on reincarnation, cause and effect, the underworld, the vicissitudes of life, and mercy.[34] Chŏng's scathing, if not always reasoned, criticism of Buddhist teachings helped to formulate the Confucians' demand for establishing a Confucian social order.

In 1400, Ha Yun stated that Buddhist doctrine *(pulbŏp)* was not the right way to rule a country and keep the people at peace. Dismissing their explanation of the human life span in terms of cause and effect, luck and misfortune, Ha argued that longevity depended entirely on fate. "How can the Buddhists prolong or shorten life?" Buddhist doctrine, Ha concluded, was of no use to statesmanship. Ha's argument was supported by Kwŏn Kŭn, who remarked that human life was formed on the principle of the five elements *(ohaeng),* the quality of which determined the fate of an individual. The Buddhists' theory about life being formed by earth, water, fire, and wind, Kwŏn contended, was false.[35]

The argument that the Buddhists were misleading the people with their vague speculations on life and death and by promising them instant rewards without the effort of serious moral training became a constant theme in the Confucian demands for harsher measures against the Buddhists. Calling Buddhism the worst of heresies *(idan),* the Confucians deplored the Buddhists' destruction of the basic human relationships between father and son and ruler and subject. They also accused the Buddhists of goading believers into squandering their possessions, especially at times of bereavement, in the vain hope of gaining the Buddha's special favor. The monks, the Confucian critics further stated, were frightening people with their false beliefs about the punishments of hell and the rewards of heaven.[36]

Students of the Confucian Academy demanded that Buddhist monks be secularized and inducted into military service, their books burned, their landed property used for military purposes, their slaves distributed among the various government agencies, the metal of Buddhist statues be used to mint coins, the printing blocks reused for publishing Confucian literature, and the temples and shrines converted into government storehouses, postal stations, or local schools.[37]

Personal confrontations with Buddhist malpractices furnished the

Confucians of the transition period with ample material for building
their case against the Buddhists. Historical studies helped put their
experiences into a wider framework: the dynasties of Chinese antiquity prospered and lasted for so long because they were entirely
free of Buddhism. The introduction of Buddhism into China during
the later Han (second half of the first century A.D.) was followed by
a chain of disasters, proving that the new creed was harmful to the
state and its people. The Sung Confucians, the Korean memorialists
pointed out, understood the clear connection between adherence to
Buddhism and misrule.[38]

The first kings of the Chosŏn dynasty were guarded in their reaction to pressure from the Confucians to replace the traditional
content of the people's religious life with Confucian principles. They
did take harsh measures against the vast landholdings and human
resources of the Buddhist monasteries. To prosper, the new dynasty
had to strengthen the economy by increasing its own landholdings
and by recruiting people from the monasteries into its military and
public work forces. Although these rehabilitation projects were a
severe blow against Buddhism, the dynastic founders did not easily
accept their advisers' demands to link the political-economic realm
with the religious-philosophical one, and to conclude that Confucianism and Buddhism were mutually exclusive in both. Yi T'aejo,
and to a lesser degree his immediate successors, tended to regard
them as two different issues that could not be dealt with simultaneously. The royal house repeatedly antagonized Confucian officialdom by continuing Buddhist rituals. King Sejong (r. 1418–1450)
summed up the extent of the dilemma: acknowledging that the
Confucians' arguments were reasonable, he nevertheless reminded
them that Buddhism had been part of the people's spiritual life for
a long time, and that it would be impossible to suppress it abruptly.[39]

The Buddhist question at the beginning of the Chosŏn dynasty,
then, was fashioned by the Confucians into an ideological tool. By
exposing the defects and inadequacies of Buddhism as a religion as
well as an institution, the scholar-officials were able to enhance, by
contrast, the qualities of Confucianism. Their insistence on identifying Koryŏ as a "Buddhist age" drew a historical dividing line that

marked the beginning of a new age committed to the establishment of a Confucian social order.

IN SEARCH OF A NEW SOCIETAL MODEL. The Neo-Confucians saw the demise of Koryŏ society as a lesson in history. They found an analogy between their own time and the Sung Neo-Confucians when they had had to deal with the heritage left to them by the T'ang, a Buddhist age that they felt had ended in disaster. Following the lead of Chu Hsi, the early Korean Neo-Confucians discovered in the classical literature of ancient China an ideal societal order that could serve as a model for rebuilding their own society. Through his interpretations and commentaries, Chu Hsi reopened an approach to the complex world of China's antiquity and revealed a social organization that had ensured stability and longevity to the dynasties of ancient China. The Koreans saw their primary task as recreating in the contemporary situation those well-tested social institutions of the past.

The Koreans believed that the authority of the "ancient institutions" *(koje)* was grounded in the creation of these institutions by the Chinese sage-kings, Yao and Shun, and the founders of the Three Dynasties, Hsia, Shang, and Chou. The institutions and rituals of antiquity were compelling as models because their originators established them after closely evaluating human nature and matching social institutions to human needs, thereby putting people's minds at ease and ensuring their compliance without coercion. The institutionalization of society's functions thus was not an imposition upon human nature, and it guaranteed the durability of the ancient kings' reigns.[40]

To the social architects of early Chosŏn, the adoption of ancient Chinese institutions was not an arbitary measure to restore law and order, but the revitalization of a link with the past in which Korea itself had had a prominent part. The figure that was thought to connect Korean history with Chinese antiquity was Kija, the second outstanding ruler of ancient Korea. Kija, who was credited with the authorship of the *Hung-fan* (The Great Rule) that became the basis of his later *P'alcho* (Eight Rules), was enfeoffed by the founder of the

Chou Dynasty, King Wu, as the feudal lord *(chehu)* of Chosŏn.[41] Kija, Chŏng To-jŏn stated, made Chosŏn known throughout the world by his exemplary management of state affairs. For Chŏng, who was the principal promoter of this historical connection, the establishment of the Chosŏn dynasty signified the restoration of Kija's Chosŏn.[42] He urged King T'aejo to recreate Kija's good government by translating Kija's teachings into the contemporary situation.[43]

This discovery of an ideal past led the Koreans to trust the authority of the texts that described the institutions of antiquity. The "ancient institutions" of the Three Dynasties of ancient China were found to be comprehensive and expedient blueprints for the reorganization of Korean society, and were studied whenever a new social policy had to be devised. When it was impossible to find suitable evidence in the classical literature, the making of decisions was greatly hampered and at times delayed for years. Always watchful that the ancient models were not impaired by a convenient yet unorthodox policy, the Confucians insisted that nothing could be added to or subtracted from the traditional wisdom of the Chinese sage-rulers. Chŏng To-jŏn saw the ancient system as a powerful instrument for eradicating the decadent mores of the previous ages, and he frequently admonished King T'aejo to pattern his rule after that of the all-knowing rulers of antiquity.[44]

THE REORGANIZATION OF SOCIETY. The legislators of early Chosŏn demanded that the restorative process begin with the structural principles of society *(kanggi)* that were the state's lifelines.[45] Comparing them to the body's blood vessels, Cho Chun warned that a state could not function properly without them; they were the channels through which the government's ordinances *(yŏng)* circulated.[46] Pyŏn Kye-ryang declared that the king's most urgent task was to establish firm structural principles, for which the ruler himself must have three major qualities: perfect virtue *(in)*, right insight *(myŏng)*, and dedication *(kŭn)*. Perfect virtue, Pyŏn argued, was the ruler's all-embracing benevolence that united heaven, earth, and the ten thousand things and that could bring everything within the radius of his civilizing influence *(tŏkhwa)*. Pyŏn thus reiterated Mencius' statement that the rulers of the Three Dynasties had brought the world under control by the force of perfect virtue. Pyŏn interpreted right insight as the ruler's understanding of the operation of government and his ability to set the proper priorities and choose the right advisers. The third element, dedication, was the ruler's capability to be constantly alert and dedicated to his task.[47]

The pivotal position of the ruler in the governing process was put into historical perspective by Chŏng To-jŏn. Describing the lives and deeds of earlier rulers from Yao and Shun down to the kings of Koryŏ, he carefully delivered judgment on their merits and demerits. Just as heaven was the "ancestor of the ten thousand things," Chŏng stated, the king was the "head of the ten thousand states." He should approach his inferiors with sincerity as well as authority so that they would stand in awe of him.[48] Chŏng's extolling of kingly responsibilities was directed at King T'aejo, who, because of his strong Buddhist inclinations, did not emerge as an unequivocal Confucian leader.

The king had to display exemplary behavior and an irresistible civilizing influence on his subjects, and he had to avail himself of the right assistants to fulfill his mission. No state, Sŏng Hyŏn (1439–1504) noted, could exist without Confucian practitioners *(yu)*[49] to guard the proper way of government. Chŏng To-jŏn characterized the ideal *yu* as a man who had the capacity to generate morality *(todŏk)* and apply it to government—a versatile man who delved into the natural sciences, morality, history, philosophy, education, and literature. Selected through the examination system, he was a scholar as well as a bureaucrat—a man who edified the people and at the same time advised his sovereign.[50] Because both the ruler and his subjects were guided by the moral way, the Confucian Way, the government should reach the highest standard without any effort, as exemplified by Yao and Shun. The scholar-official fulfilled a prominent role as a morally superior man *(hyŏn)* who was called upon to lead the ignorant masses.[51] The scholar-officials set themselves apart from the rest of society as a special social group that was, on the basis of its merits in government service, vested with extraordinary privileges.

Governing was essentially an educative and regulatory process by which the unruly nature of the people was subjected to state control and brought into harmony with the universe. It was a matter of "renovating the people" *(sinmin)*[52] by invigorating society's basic relationships *(kanggi),* which were expressed in its customs *(p'ung-sok).* P'ungsok represented the basic moral energy of the state. The quality of the customs its people practiced was an unmistakable indicator of the state's health and strength and was directly related to its rise and fall. The term *p'ungsok* denoted the interdependence of the ruler and his subjects: *p'ung* was interpreted as the civilizing influence of the ruler, whereas *sok* meant the people's habits. The ruler's first care had to be to win over the people's hearts by the rectitude and integrity of his own mind. The people's compliance thus was intimately linked to the ruler's moral leadership. Nurturing *p'ungsok* into becoming "good and rich" was the state's most urgent duty.[53]

The essence of *p'ungsok* was contained in the three cardinal human relationships *(samgang)* that provided human society with a fundamental and unchangeable structure: the relationships between ruler and subject, father and son, and husband and wife. They were reinforced by the five moral imperatives *(illyun* or *oryun)* that guided interpersonal relationships: righteousness *(ŭi)* between sovereign and subject; proper rapport *(ch'in)* between father and son; separation of functions *(pyŏl)* between husband and wife; proper recognition of sequence of birth *(sŏ)* between elder and younger brothers; and faithfulness *(sin)* between friends.

These relationships were maintained by the concept of *ye,* proper ritual behavior, which was at the very core of the educative process; its cultivation made the people's minds firm and receptive to order. There were four rites by which the development of *ye* was fostered: capping, wedding, mourning, and ancestor worship. The four rites *(sarye)* were instituted by the sage-kings of antiquity to bring human passions under control and make the people amenable to proper government. Through its interconnection with the cosmic forces of *yin* and *yang,* the conjugal bond furnished the three relationships with a strong and correct foundation. The four rites, as the norms of social behavior, stabilized the order of government functions.[54]

Social organization was tied together by a threefold mechanism: the domestic sphere, represented by the wife, was subordinated to the public sphere, represented by the father and son; they in turn were the sovereign's subjects. *Samgang* objectified the hierarchical order of human society and at the same time stressed the interdependence between domestic and public spheres *(nae-oe).* Ideally, this order was maintained by the force of *ye* as expressed in the *sarye.* The four rites were social ordering devices that kept society in balance and guaranteed the prosperity of the state.

Ye, the ideal instrument with which society could be brought into harmony with the universe, was the moral concept of ruling *(chŏng).* It could be fully activated only if the common people were deterred by sanctions from straying away from it, because its loss would endanger the society as well as the state. Since the common people did not naturally understand its true meaning and therefore failed to observe it, the ancient sage-kings devised laws and regulations *(pŏpche)* as necessary concomitants of *ye.* Laws were not simply means for controlling *(ch'i)* the people. They were supplementary devices that assisted governing by helping people to develop their innate moral potentialities. Laws were the force that regulated the people's customs. Men and law were interdependent: men were controlled by law; law was observed by men. Whereas *ye* was a heavenly property that took human nature into account, law was a man-made rational instrument.[55] The concept of law had two facets. It was conceived of as a deterrent in the form of criminal law and it also had an exhortatory side. Punishment was likened to a bridle that helped keep people in check; but it was to be carefully counterbalanced by rewards; and the ruler was to exercise complete impartiality in the application of both.[56]

THE NEO-CONFUCIANS' RESEARCH SOURCES AND INSTITUTIONS. After conceptualizing the ideal human order on the basis of the model conceived by the sage-kings of Chinese antiquity, the Neo-Confucians had to fill in the ideological contours with content. The principles embodied in ideology had to be reduced to practicable precepts that would guide daily social conduct. For this task the Neo-Confucians used two Chinese literary sources: books that described the workings of the ideal society of antiquity, and books that presented definitions and interpretations for translating ideology into everyday practice.

The two works that gave the Korean Neo-Confucians the most authoritative approach to ancient society were the *Li-chi,* and the *I-li.* Together with the *Chou-li,* these books,[57] which contain a vast amount of pre-Confucian lore and present a detailed description of ancient life, had been known to the Koreans in T'ang editions from early Koryŏ.[58] These texts developed their potential as ritual sourcebooks only through Chu Hsi's commentaries. At the beginning of Chosŏn, they gained significance during the Koreans' search for social blueprints and were studied and quoted whenever a basic decision of social significance had to be formulated. "The ritual classics *(yegyŏng)* are the great records through which the Sage [Confucius] established his teachings, and they are pertinent to the everyday application of the human imperatives." Thus wrote Ha Yun in his preface to Kwŏn Kŭn's *Yegi ch'ŏn'gyŏllok* (Annotations to the Book of Rites), a work that was praised for its clarifying qualities.[59] The edition of the *I-li* the Koreans commonly used was the text prepared by Chu Hsi and published posthumously, the *I-li ching-chuan t'ungchieh* (Complete Explanation of the Book of Etiquette and Ceremonies and Its Commentaries).[60] The *Li-chi* and the *I-li* exerted a deep and lasting influence on Chosŏn society—most notably through the concepts of patrilineal descent groups, ancestor worship, the differentiation of wives, and the mourning system *(obok).* The description of the ancient system *(koje)* contained in these handbooks set absolute standards which the Koreans interpreted in a literal and fundamentalist way that imposed considerable limitations on the legislative process at the beginning of the new dynasty.

The most representative work of definition and interpretation was the *Chu Tzu chia-li* (House Rules of Master Chu). Said to have been

Chu Hsi's last work and finished by his disciples, this short, definitive description of the four rites *(sarye)* provided the most effective
means to restore order and stability to society. In 1403, officials
entering the bureaucracy and incumbent officials below the seventh
rank were required to pass an examination on the *Chia-li.*[61] The
Koreans thought this book was important because Chu Hsi bridged
the gap between antiquity and the contemporary situation, struck
a balance between ritual and law, embodied the principle of heaven
and earth in it, and was in harmony with human nature.[62] Chu Hsi
thus provided an ideal program of ritual through which the people
could be freed from Buddhist tradition and led toward a life of
morality. In particular, Chu Hsi's regulations for funerals and ancestor
worship were recommended as useful antidotes to Buddhist abuses.
The edition of the *Chia-li* most widely used at the beginning of
the dynasty was a text prepared and annotated by Kwŏn Kŭn, the
Sangjŏl karye (Annotated Chia-li).[63] Later amended and supplemented many times, the *Chia-li* became best known in the edition
prepared by Yi Chae (1680–1746) in the early eighteenth century
and entitled *Sarye pyŏllam* (Easy Manual of the Four Rites).[64]

While the *Li-chi,* the *I-li,* and the *Chia-li* were consulted most
often, at times they were found to be lacking in the minute details
necessary for fixing the ritual procedure for an exemplary event—
for example, the wedding of a member of the royal house. Further
advice had to be sought in encyclopedic works such as the *Ta-T'ang
k'ai-yüan li* (Rites of the *K'ai-yüan* Period [713–741] of the Great
T'ang) and the *T'ung-tien* (Encyclopedia of Rites).[65] The latter work
in particular was highly esteemed for its rich information on ritual,
and it was often used for answering questions about major court
ceremonies. An important supplementary source used during the
T'aejong and Sejong periods was the *Wen-hsien t'ung-k'ao,* which was
an expansion of the *T'ung-tien* that updated it to 1224.[66] It was
found valuable for its richness and interpretation of factual data.

Only much later, from the beginning of the sixteenth century,
the Koreans also sought advice from contemporary Ming sources.
They found references to Ming institutions in the *Ta-Ming hui-tien*
(Statutes of the Great Ming), which was compiled between 1488

and 1505 and brought to Korea by a Korean envoy in the summer of 1518. The work stirred up excitement at court because it contained misinformation about Yi Sŏng-gye's ancestry.[67] Although this work was printed in Korea only some fifty years later—after imperial approval for revising the questionable passages was received—during the reigns of King Chungjong (r. 1506–1544) and King Myŏngjong (r. 1545–1567) it was frequently consulted as a ritual handbook in conjunction with the *T'ung-tien*. Its particular usefulness lay in its descriptions of ancient rites, relating them at the same time to the contemporary situation, and thus providing detailed and balanced models of ritual institutions.[68] The *Ta-ming hui-tien* replaced two shorter works, the *Chen-kuan cheng-yao* (Essentials of Government of the *Chen-kuan* Period) and the *Chih-cheng t'iao-ke* (*Chih-cheng* Code), which contained deliberations on government policy of the *chen-kuan* period (627–649) and the *chih-cheng* period (1341–1367), respectively. The *Chen-kuan cheng-yao* seems to have been an important reference work from the beginning of the dynasty, and it was carefully annotated during the Sejo (r. 1455–1468) period. It was considered a significant supplement of the *I-li*.[69]

Although different in nature and content from the above works, the *T'ung-chien kang-mu* (Abridged View of the *Comprehensive Mirror*), given an introduction by Chu Hsi in 1172, was highly valued as a work of reference that put the success and failure of social policies into historical perspective. It warned against aberrations from the right path of government and exhorted the ruler to re-create in the present the ideal order of the past.[70]

While this ritual and historical literature indeed constituted a vast inspirational reservoir for sociopolitical legislation, it represented but the functional component of the Neo-Confucian reform program. This functional component necessarily had to rest upon the ideological foundations of the classics, the Five Classics and the Four Books. The classics articulated the fundamentals of good rulership. Only good rulership could create the environment that would render social and political reforms successful. The study of the classical literature by the ruler as well as by his officialdom therefore was a necessary precondition for any reform plan. A thorough knowledge of the classics, it was said, led to an understanding of the ways of the sage-kings, and this resulted in turn in the achievement of "happiness for this age and this people."[71]

The Four Books with the annotations and commentaries by Chu Hsi were considered to contain the clearest formulations of the Neo-Confucian vision. In 1398, Cho Chun, Ha Yun, and others presented to King T'aejo a shortened version entitled *Sasŏ chŏryo* (Essentials of the Four Books), which the king had apparently ordered to familiarize himself with the fundamentals of the learning of the mind-and-heart *(simhak)*.[72] That learning had to be the point of departure for good rulership was the short, but urgent message of the *Ta-hsüeh*. This programmatic treatise in particular became the favored textbook of the early Chosŏn rulers. King T'aejo is said to have enjoyed it in Chen Te-hsiu's version, the *Ta-hsüeh yen-i*. As an inspirational work it was praised by King T'aejong, who read it avidly and ordered it to be written in large characters on the palace walls for the benefit of all officials. He also rewarded the workmen after they completed the first Korean printing in movable type in 1412.[73] The *Ta-hsüeh yen-i* continued to be revered as a principle text of the Neo-Confucian canon throughout the first part of the Chosŏn dynasty.

An important addition to and supplement of the Four Books and Five Classics was the famous symposium of Sung philosophy, the *Hsing-li ta-ch'üan* (Great Compendium on Human Nature and Principle), which contained selected texts of the Sung masters on metaphysics, moral cultivation, and ritual matters.[74] Together with the Four Books and Five Classics it was presented to King Sejong by the Ming emperor in the early 1420s. In a postface dated 1427, Pyŏn Kye-ryang hailed what must have been their first complete printing in Korea as a major breakthrough because Korean scholars had hitherto lacked proper study materials.[75] Although the *Hsing-li ta-ch'üan* served as an authoritative source for ritual matters at the beginning of the dynasty, it seems to have reached its full significance for the development of Neo-Confucian thought in Korea only after it was excerpted by Kim Chŏng-guk (1485–1541) as *Sŏngni taejŏnsŏ chŏryo* (Essentials of the *Hsing-li ta-ch'üan*).[76]

The Four Books were regarded as forming one coherent body of literature with Chu Hsi's *Chin-ssu lu* (Reflections on Things at Hand) and the *Hsiao-hsüeh*. Containing the essence of Neo-Confucian thinking, the *Chin-ssu lu* came to have special significance for social legislation in the second half of the fifteenth century. It concisely related philosophical concepts to the concerns of daily life, elaborated on the practice of the moral imperatives, and put emphasis on clarifying descent groups and institutionalizing ancestor worship. The book also explored the several stages from cultivation of self to putting the state on a solid moral basis. It therefore was considered an essential text and a helpful manual for solving policy questions.[77] The *Hsiao-hsüeh*, a primer for the young, was highly acclaimed for its educative value. In 1407, Kwŏn Kŭn recommended it be made the required introductory text for all students; no examination candidate should be admitted without demonstrating full comprehension of this book. Its importance as a basic tool of moral transformation was frequently emphasized. It was reprinted repeatedly after its first printing in 1429, and its rendering into the Korean vernacular was demanded.[78]

During the early years of policy formulation, King T'aejo was assisted by a small group of personal advisers, among them most notably Chŏng To-jŏn and Kwŏn Kŭn. After the turn of the century, the Confucians who had risen at the end of Koryŏ and had earned special merit in founding the new dynasty, began to disappear. Under T'aejo's successors, policy making gradually became more institutionalized because of the intensive research necessary for determining social policies. In 1410, the Ŭirye sangjŏngso (Office for the Establishment of Ceremonies) was created with Ha Yun, Pyŏn Kye-ryang, and Yi Cho as its first directors *(chejo)*.[79] Although it was a continuation of an institution that had been established in the first half of Koryŏ,[80] under T'aejong it functioned as an ad hoc advisory office, usually in cooperation with other government agencies, most notably the Department of Rites. After drafting most of the ritual programs of the young dynasty, it had fulfilled its purpose and was abolished in 1435.[81]

After 1428, a new consultative body, the Chiphyŏnjŏn (Hall of Worthies), founded in 1420, gained stature as a research institution and reference library. It was staffed with young and promising men who, without exception, passed the highest civil service examinations at an early age and belonged to the social and political elite. They constituted a new generation of scholars who grew up under Sejong's tutelage. Because of long tenure and absence of concurrent appointments, they could devote themselves entirely to their Confucian studies and as royal lecturers (*kyŏngyŏn'gwan*) enjoyed easy access to the king. Among them were Chŏng In-ji (1396–1478), Ch'oe Hang (1409–1474), Sin Suk-chu (1417–1475), Yang Sŏng-ji (1415–1482), Sŏ Kŏ-jŏng (1420–1488), and Kang Hŭi-maeng (1424–1483)—outstanding personalities who in the second half of the fifteenth century, under Sejo and Sŏngjong (r. 1469–1494), were repeatedly awarded merit-subject status and eventually rose to the most influential positions in the central government. All of them were intimately involved in the compilation of the dynasty's first comprehensive law code, the *Kyŏngguk taejŏn* (Great Code of Administration), and thus were instrumental in shaping the dynasty's fundamental law.[82]

One of the most important functions of the members of the Chiphyŏnjŏn was the close scrutiny of "ancient institutions," a task that involved painstaking studies of the Chinese classical literature. From these studies resulted edited and annotated Korean versions of the Chinese classics, most notably the Four Books. Moreover, such historical sources as the *Tzu-chih t'ung-chien* and the *Chen-kuan cheng-yao* were prepared for use as governmental guidebooks. The Chiphyŏnjŏn scholars possessed no legislative powers, and the final settlement of details and the formulation of policies were left to the ministers of the Department of Rites and the state councillors.

From the very beginning of the dynasty, the fixing and execution of social policies were influenced and closely supervised by the censorial agencies—the Sahŏnbu (Office of the Inspector-General) and the Saganwŏn (Office of the Censor-General). Many former Chiphyŏnjŏn scholars received their first appointments in these offices. Although initially not directly involved in policy formulation, both offices assumed within the government structure a powerful position through their assignments as guardians, investigators, and enforcers of social policy.[83]

THE RELEVANCE OF ANCIENT MODELS. To enact the "ancient institutions" in Korea was a commitment as well as an obligation. The Korean king was put in a position equal to that of feudal lord *(chehu)* vis-à-vis the Chinese emperor. He was subjected to well-defined social rules that both underlined his special position as the successor to Kija's legacy and compelled his exemplary conduct. T'aejo and his successors were constantly reminded that they were exponents of the ideal principles of rule set forth by Yao and Shun. The Korean royal house was, in terms of ritual, clearly separated from the rest of society because it was the apex of the state. It represented Korea to the outside world, especially China, and was responsible for maintaining Korea's ritual image. While the royal house was urged to strive for ritual purity, the scholar-officials allowed themselves to deviate from ideal norms whenever they thought it necessary.

Royal ritual was gradually developed during T'aejong's reign. The first major ritual event at the royal court was the funeral rites for King T'aejo who died in 1408. Although Chu Hsi's *Chia-li* was to be used for programming the arrangements, T'aejong's Buddhist inclinations and the officialdom's ritual inexperience gave the occasion a Buddhist rather than a Confucian appearance.[84] T'aejong did, however, make efforts to determine royal ritual protocol by ordering Hŏ Cho, who held high positions in both the Department of Rites and the Ŭirye sangjŏngso, to study and compile the sequence and ceremonial details of the Auspicious and Sacrificial Rites *(killye)*. The task was completed in 1415.[85] Research and compilation were accelerated under King Sejong who, after developing the proper procedures for the wedding of the crown prince, gave orders in 1444 to Chŏng Ch'ŏk (1390–1475) and Pyŏn Hyo-mun (1396–?) to compile the remaining four of the Five State Rites. It is clear that King Sejong supervised the compilation personally and had his own ideas incorporated into the final version. The Five Rites *(Orye)* of King Sejong[86] were finished in 1451 and appended to the *Sejong sillok*. They provided the basis for the first official manual of state rituals, the *Kukcho oryeŭi* (Manual of the Five State Rites), which was completed under the supervision of Sin Suk-chu in 1474.[87] As Kang Hŭi-maeng stated in his preface to this work, its principle source was the *T'ung-tien,* presumably in particular the *Ta-T'ang k'ai-yüan li* contained therein. When found lacking in specific details, the *Kukcho oryeŭi* was often supplemented by the *T'ung-tien* and the *Ta-Ming hui-tien.*[88]

The scholar-official class of the Chosŏn dynasty assumed the role of "great and common officers" *(sadaebu),*[89] the "proper assistants" the king needed to help him govern the country. Endowed with a special share of virtue and innate wisdom, they were the *yu* who embodied the ideal Confucian gentlemen (Chin. *chün-tzu;* Kor. *kunja*). In Confucianism, this ideal was originally attained by achievement; but in Korea, gentlemanly status was acquired by being born into the right status group. Correlated with *sadaebu* status were specific rights and privileges (for example, exemption from corvée labor and, later in the dynasty, from military service or tax) and economic compensations.[90]

On the model of ancient precedent, the *sadaebu* eventually formed highly structured patrilineal descent groups that distinguished between genuine members (those born of primary wives) and marginal members (those born of secondary wives). A person's position within the group was rigorously defined on the basis of his or her sex (which determined roles), age, and relationship to the group's past and future generations through the mourning system. Power within the group was distributed according to the "social offices" of grandfather, father, and son. The emergence of well-defined descent groups, however, was not only a moral venture. It was closely linked to the *sadaebu*'s ambition to define the terms of political participation in the new dynasty. The clear structure of a patriliny functioned, in a narrow sense, as a rational ordering device of its membership. In a wider perspective, it was equally suited for limiting access to the ranks of the elite. It thus also defined social status. Descent and

political participation therefore came to be inextricably inter-
twined.

The *sadaebu* set themselves off from the rest of Korean society by
a distinct ritual program based on Chu Hsi's *Chia-li* that was launched
in the summer of 1392 "to enrich human morality and to rectify
customs."[91] The general officialdom was exhorted to engage in Confucian-style self-cultivation and prepare for its role as the intellec-
tuals and bureaucrats of the new dynasty.[92] The *Chia-li,* regarded
as the foundation of ritual behavior, was supported by a number of
ideological devices that elucidated the binding force that Confucian
teachings exercised on society through proper ritual behavior.[93]

The process of social control was first of all the task of the descent
group, and it was based on the assumption that man had to be
constantly encouraged to strive for moral perfection. A practical
application of this assumption was the domestic rules *(kahun),* an
idealized code of conduct through which the civilizing influence of
Confucian doctrine could be realized in the domestic sphere and
intrafamily affairs. These rules emphasized the Confucian dictum
that self-cultivation was the starting point of putting one's house in
order; they took the individual person as the center of concentric
circles of obligation that began with the exercise of moral integrity
and economic austerity, widened to harmonious relations with family and kin, and finally linked the domestic sphere directly to peace
and stability in the public realm. The *kahun,* as the link between
the individual and the state, contained the essence of Confucian
society's moral capabilities that, if properly developed, were the
mainstay of the Confucian state.[94] They were intimate domestic
laws, creating the correct family atmosphere for training a privileged young man in the moral order of his society and enabling him
eventually to assume an appropriate position—that of scholar-official.

The *sadaebu,* drawing structure from the "ancient institutions"
and inner cohesion from the Confucian classics, were from the early
years of the dynasty preoccupied with blending the two into one
coherent, unalterable, and normative system. A programmatic attempt in this direction was Chŏng To-jŏn's *Chosŏn kyŏnggukchŏn* (Code

of Administration of the Chosŏn Dynasty) of 1394. Although it did not fully develop the concept of the descent group as a mediatory device between individual and state, Chŏng recognized the significance of elementary social actions (for example, wedding and mourning) in the well-being and stability of the state. He also stressed the importance of ritual as a general standard by which authority and status were delineated and differentiated.[95]

The idea that morality was a latent form of law and of institutions and, conversely, that laws and institutions were a visible manifestation of morality was a recurrent theme. Since laws, together with ritual, formed the great "societal bulwark" *(taebang)*, the strength of which determined the quality of government, they could not be conceived and enacted in a hurry.[96] On the contrary, social legislation had to be pursued in such a way that forthcoming laws would retain their validity and usefulness for future generations. Trusting in the workability of Mencius' dictum that nobody ever erred by honoring the laws of the ancient kings, the legislators under T'aejong thought the "ancient institutions" guaranteed the durability of their laws. Their legal concepts were expressed in such works as Cho Chun's *Kyŏngje yukchŏn* (The Six Codes of Administration) of 1397 and Ha Yun's *Sok yukchŏn* (Amended Six Codes) of 1413 (revised and amended in 1426 and 1433), preserved today only in fragmentary quotations.[97] Earlier, in 1395, the Ming criminal code was rendered into the clerks' writing system *(idu)* under the title of *Tae Myŏngnyul chikhae* (Literal Explanation of the Ming Code).[98] By Sejong's time these legislative writings were regarded as a kind of dynastic constitution that could be supplemented, but not changed. Although under Sejong some legal adjustments were made to take into account certain social peculiarities of Koryŏ times (for example, plural marriage), such compromises were regarded as temporary measures and were not intended for transmission to future generations.[99]

A certain tension, however, existed between the concept of social order, which by virtue of its ideal constancy did not need legislation, and the laws, which had to be adaptable to the actual social situation. This tension characterized the legislative process during the initial period of experimentation and may have been at least partly responsible for the delay in the compilation of the first comprehensive law code, the *Kyŏngguk taejŏn* (Great Code of Administration) of 1471.[100] The social stipulations of this code provided a legal framework within which society could function, as far as that function was directly relevant to the state. It was the law that underpinned morality as expressed in the ritual handbooks and was binding for those who occupied the ranked positions in the government, that is, the *sadaebu*.[101]

ASSIMILATION AND CONFLICT. The desire to give new stability and order to Korean society was motivated by idealism as well as by pragmatic considerations. If the models and rules found in China's classical literature were instituted in Korea, it was believed, Korean society would eventually be transformed into an ideal Confucian society. The "ancient institutions" would replace native customs that had led to the distintegration of society.

The strongest demand for complete assimilation of the institutions of Chinese antiquity in Korea was made at the beginning of the dynasty by Chŏng To-jŏn, who insisted that the corrupt native customs and the vestiges of Mongol rule be discarded and the new institutions be given permanency "for a full age." For Chŏng, the rationalization was simple: Kija originally laid the foundation of Korea's fame as a country of "ritual and etiquette"; yet even though the Koryŏ dynasty modelled some of its institutions after Chinese patterns, there remained some unadjusted native customs. T'aejo's accession to the throne provided, in Chŏng's opinion, a unique opportunity to complete the mission Kija had begun.[102] The Confucianization of Korea's social institutions was for Chŏng the expression of a double commitment; it was an essential condition for his Neo-Confucian thinking, and the final realization of an obligation toward Kija's heritage. T'aejo's task, Chŏng argued, was to create the political milieu in which the legacy of the past could finally come to fruition.[103] Chŏng's idea of reform was to close the gap between the ideal past and the contemporary situation by removing the last vestiges of indigenous, that is non-Kija customs, and replacing them with institutions that would guarantee the continuation and eventual full integration of Kija's teachings in Korean society. By insisting so strongly on restoration at the expense of native idiosyncrasies, Chŏng typified Neo-Confucian preoccupation with recapturing the utopian past.

Chŏng To-jŏn's attitude may have been supported in essence by early Neo-Confucians such as Kwŏn Kŭn and Ha Yun, but others questioned his heavy dependence on China. Pyŏn Kye-ryang's position presumably was somewhere in the middle. While he favored a literal interpretation of the classics and an exact reenactment of their precepts, he advocated that the Korean king show his independence by carrying out sacrifices to Heaven, a privilege normally reserved for the Chinese emperor.[104] But even a sovereign as committed to restructuring Korean society on the basis of ancient models as was King Sejong believed that local custom (*t'op'ung*) should not be disturbed by too hasty an introduction of Chinese rites. The past and the present, he remarked, are different; it is therefore necessary to accommodate oneself to the exigencies of the times. "How can we be bound by what the people of the past did?"[105]

In mid fifteenth century, the dilemma of assimilating Chinese values and preserving native customs was articulated more sharply by Yang Sŏng-ji. Stressing the necessity of following the examples of early rulers in establishing kingly rule, Yang argued that Yao, Shun, and the rulers of the Three Dynasties should not be the only examples. Even the later dynasties had good institutions that could be of use. Moreover, Korean history also should be taken into account. Yang thought it deplorable that the Koreans knew only China's prosperous ages and ignored Korean history.[106] Yang Sŏng-ji expressed not only the growing reassertion of a national consciousness, which had been threatened by close imitation of Chinese-style institutions, but also the awareness that more than half a century of legislation had not transformed Korea into a model Confucian state. Some memorialists ascribed this failure to the king's neglect in improving the people's customs (*p'ungsok*),[107] while an increasing number of scholar-officials expressed the opinion that the Chinese rites were not entirely compatible with Korean tradition (*t'osok*).

The unease with the inadequate results of the legislative process that set in as soon as the first euphoria about the discovery of antiquity began to wear off was thus nurtured by conflicting feelings. Clearly, no one had anticipated the strength of Koryŏ tradition and the consequent time lag that would separate the introduction of legislation from its actual implementation. Even among the general officialdom, which was supposed to blaze with a pioneering spirit the renovative trail, there were too many forces that impeded the acceptance and enforcement of new social concepts. The clearest result of such reluctance was the *Kyŏngguk taejŏn.* It reflected an almost century-long attempt to restructure Koryŏ tradition on the basis of "ancient institutions," but its reformatory thrust was weakened in crucial areas of social life, for example inheritance matters, by compromise between tradition and innovation. It was therefore later at times challenged and even surpassed by the authority of the ritual handbooks. Nevertheless, it gave society an instrument that was often used successfully as an explanation of and a justification for Korea's singular social order.

The debate gained momentum during the sixteenth century. By that time, the practical aspects of patrilineal organization as outlined in the *Chia-li* were given ever more careful attention for descent group formation. In particular, the clear distinction between sons of primary and secondary wives was emphasized as a crucial element for streamlining the descent group. It could also serve for introducing sharper criteria for defining social status and, ultimately, access to political power. The Koreans recognized that by articulating this distinction so succinctly they differed from the Ming Chinese who, they noted, tolerated blurred descent lines and even admitted slaves to the officialdom. But it was not only a matter of dissimilarity between Korea and Ming China. The social practices of both countries differed in certain respects from the models of ancient China. [108]

This difference between Ming China and Chosŏn Korea was not considered surprising: in comparison to China, Korea was a small country with its own particular geographical and climatic circumstances. Customs could not be the same. [109] The assertion of a distinct regional identity came to be expressed in the concept of *kuk-sok,* "national practice," which meant in essence that Korea had developed its own characteristic version of social organization. This *kuksok,* a distinct blend of assimilated Confucian values and indigenous tradition, was, by the middle of the sixteenth century, emerging as a coherent system.

This awareness of unique native characteristics was supported and confirmed by rationalizations that justified Korea's selective adaptation of ancient institutions and also provided a framework within which the acculturation process could be understood. The key concept in these calculations was *ye,* "proper ritual behavior." In Neo-Confucian terms, *ye* was a manifestation of principle *(i)* that together with *ki,* matter, was the salient component of Neo-Confucian metaphysics. *Ye* was thus one facet of the heavenly principle and often became interchangeable with it. Standing above the human world, it was a moral principle, the normative character of which was based on its superhuman origin. It was embodied in the five interpersonal relationships.[110] The heavenly *ye* that provided human society with an unchanging fundamental structure stood in contrast to the narrower *ye* that found expression in rituals. This variable *ye* had been different in each of the Three Dynasties; and even in a contemporary situation, this *ye* was not the same in all countries. It was thus impossible to conceptualize *ye* into one consistent pattern applicable to all times and places.[111]

This analysis of the interrelationship between *ye* and *p'ungsok* reveals the flexibility that the Korean Neo-Confucians of the sixteenth century developed to explain Korean idiosyncrasies. In this light even Chu Hsi's *Chia-li* was submitted to a reevaluation. To be sure, the fundamental assumptions on which the *Chia-li* rested, most notably the patrilineal layout of descent groups, were supported by such classics as the *Li-chi* and the *I-li* and were therefore beyond dispute. On the contrary, with the eventual enactment of primogeniture, they reached in Korea a degree of acceptance unparalleled in China. But some details of rites, for example in the wedding ceremony, were debatable. In this respect, the *Chia-li* was believed to describe the variable component of *ye* and therefore was itself subject to alterations and amendments. What was applicable to Chu Hsi's times, it was argued, was not necessarily meaningful for Chosŏn Korea.[112] The flexibility of the term *ye* as expressed in the adjustability of *p'ungsok* thus furnished the Neo-Confucians of the mid sixteenth century their major argument for justifying the Korean blend of Confucian precepts with native elements.

ELITISM AND IDEOLOGY. Regardless of how its results were evaluated and judged later on, the Confucian transformation of Korean society originated from a powerful and persuasive vision that was held by the founding elite of the new dynasty. This elite was not new in terms of its social background—it was rooted in the traditional aristocracy—but it was new as far as its ideological training was concerned. Through their studies, the initially small number of Neo-Confucian adepts acquired a professionalism that prepared them for far more than careers as docile bureaucrats. Such studies gave them an exclusive, closely knit identity as a group (that was further strengthened by multiple marital ties) and instilled in them a sense of mission that could not be brought to success in the sociopolitical environment of late Koryŏ. They felt compelled to enter into their unusual alliance with the military. To a significant extent, then, the dynastic change of 1392 must be understood in connection with the rise of this professional elite.[113]

   To be sure, Yi Sŏng-gye might have been able to solve some of the economic and political problems plaguing Korea at the end of Koryŏ within the existing political order with policies inspired by earlier reform measures. But from the outset he surrounded himself with articulate Confucian-trained advisers who superimposed their normative framework upon the contemporary scene. They demanded the founding of a new dynasty. Yi Sŏng-gye was not a Ming T'ai-tsu (r. 1368–1398), who during his long reign relied on the military and laid the basis of despotic rule by suppressing the admonishing voices of the Confucians.[114] In Korea, the civil element dominated. Yi's advisers couched the question of power in moral and not military terms. They left the basis of Korea's traditional political structure—monarchy versus aristocracy—intact; they themselves were part of this establishment. But they redefined its inner workings and balancing mechanisms in terms of Confucian political philosophy: the ritualization of Korean society would re-store the "natural order" of the Three Dynasties as the moral order of Chosŏn—an order that they thought would gain nourishment through the dialectic relationship between the dynamism of self-cultivation and the stability of tested social institutions.

As the initiators of this transformatory process, the Neo-Confu-cians found themselves confronted with a bureaucracy that in the early years of the new dynasty was dominated by officials whose outlook on life and daily conduct of social relations naturally were deeply rooted in Koryŏ traditions. For them, the Neo-Confucian solution to the problems of man in contemporary society may not have had the same compelling plausibility. Social change inevitably aroused competition and conflict. Many, therefore, at first resisted the rapid pace of social legislation and were slow in being molded into exemplary *sadaebu*. After all, even the royal house often failed to comply with the Neo-Confucian directives. The transformatory process therefore depended on the initiative of the small elite group of Neo-Confucians that established itself as the vanguard of the new dynastic venture.

The Neo-Confucian program of action was a grandiose construct that developed its own momentum by addressing the diverse social, political, and economic issues that arose as the dynasty moved on. At first, when a pragmatic alternative to the existing societal dis-order was sought, the message of the classics was translated into social policies. Next, the conception of the Confucian mission be-came increasingly differentiated. Finally, the Confucians took into full account the persistent importance of native tradition. This pro-cess ranged from an initial commitment that concentrated on the close imitation of Chinese social institutions to the development of a concept that integrated Confucianism into Korea's social circum-stances. It culminated in the formulation of a distinct notion of cultural identity, contained in the expression "national practice" *(kuksok).* It was this expanded form of Neo-Confucian thinking that eventually provided the framework within which Korea's version of social Confucianism could be explained.

The Chosŏn dynasty, thus, saw the rise of a reconstituted scholar-official class that on the one hand claimed its leadership role on the basis of descent and heredity and on the other hand wielded its Neo-Confucian learning as an ideological tool. With this tool, the scholar-officials succeeded in reshaping the sociopolitical environment to an extent the Sung Neo-Confucians would never have dreamed possible.

THREE

Agnation and Ancestor Worship

For establishing a Confucian-style society, a first crucial step was the implantation of the agnatic principle in the social matrix and the activation of an agnatic consciousness within a descent group. No mechanism was better suited to accomplish this than ancestor worship. Ancestor worship is more than a mere part of the cult of the dead. It is a religious domain in which kinship relations are indispensable. In its Confucian configuration, it ritually puts the principle of agnation into practice and thus is equally concerned with the living and dead members of an agnatic descent group.[1] Ancestor worship, above all, provides structure that is significant for both the domestic and the public realms. A place in the ritual hierarchy of agnates determines an individual's rights and duties within the descent group and allocates to him a corresponding standing in the political sphere. As an instrument for imposing a patrilineal pattern on Korean society, then, ancestor worship became a major agent of change at the beginning of the Chosŏn dynasty.

THE NEO-CONFUCIAN VIEW OF SOCIETY. Neo-Confucian sociopolitical theory makes agnatic lineal descent groups the basic element of society. Such descent groups have a double function: they structure society and, at the same time, guarantee the uninterrupted continuation of the political process. The *Hsing-li ta-ch'üan* puts the key term "agnatic principle" (Chin. *tsung-fa;* Kor. *chongppŏp*) under the heading of "political methodology" (Chin. *chih-tao;* Kor. *ch'ido*). Several Neo-Confucian thinkers of the Sung (960–1279) discuss this principle in the following terms: if there is no law governing the selection of the lineal heir (Chin. *tsung-tzu;* Kor. *chongja*), the court cannot depend on having officials from one generation to the next (Chin. *shih-ch'en;* Kor. *sesin*). This is so because, without agnatic law, a descent group (Chin. *tsu;* Kor. *chok*) disintegrates at the death of the lineal heir, and the house is not transmitted to the next generation. If the agnatic principle is established and the high officials of the land preserve their houses, they develop loyalty and righteousness, and the state's foundation is firm.[2]

Chu Hsi had equally explicit ideas about the benefit the state draws from the lineal-agnatic principle. In his *Chin-ssu lu* he quoted Ch'eng I: "In order to control the minds of the people, unify one's kin, and enrich social customs so that people will not forget their origin, it is necessary to clarify genealogy, group members of the clan together, and institute a system of heads of descent." Or again: "Since there are no heads of descent today, there are no ministers at court who have come from families noted for generations. If the system of heads of descent is established, people will know how to honor their ancestors and take their origins seriously. As they take their origins seriously, the power of the court will naturally be highly respected. . . . Furthermore, it is according to the Principle of Nature that there should be a system of the head of descent. It is like a tree. There must be the main trunk which shoots straight up from the root, and there must also be branches."[3] Clearly, Chu Hsi endorsed clarifying the line of descent, establishing the head of the descent group, and institutionalizing ancestor worship. These three he considered the main pillars upon which social, and therefore political, stability rests.

Chu Hsi and Ch'eng I unearthed the "ideal type" of descent group from China's classical literature, most notably the *Li-chi* and the *Po-hu t'ung* (The Comprehensive Discussions in the White Tiger Hall); and Chu Hsi made it the basic concept of his *Chu Tzu chia-li* (see Diagram 6). According to the rule of primogeniture operative in

Diagram 6. The Neo-Confucian Concept of "Five Descent Groups"

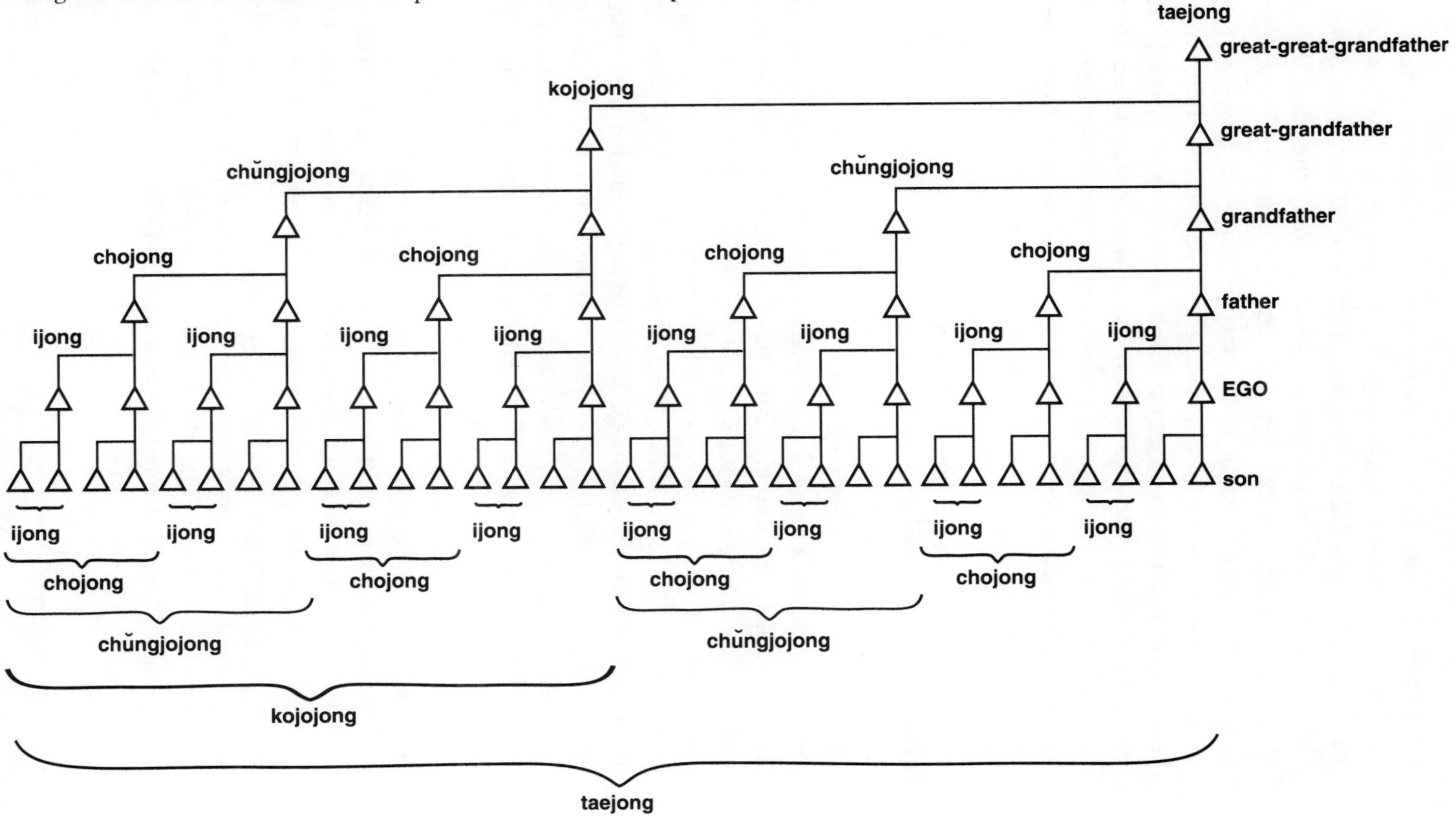

China's feudal past, only the eldest son by the primary wife could succeed his father (who was known as "separate son"; Chin. *piehtzu;* Kor. *pyŏlcha*). Called "major ritual heir" (Chin. *ta-tsung-tzu;* Kor. *taejongja*), this eldest son inherited not only the ritual obligations but also his father's fief and rank. In contrast, his younger brothers were called "minor ritual heirs" (Chin. *hsiao-tsung-tzu;* Kor. *sojongja*). The major ritual heir continued the ancestral line which, as a superordinate descent group (Chin. *ta-tsung;* Kor. *taejong*), developed unlimited genealogical depth, since its ancestor tablets "were not removed for one hundred generations." His younger brothers founded subordinate descent groups (Chin. *hsiao-tsung;* Kor. *sojong*) that were replicas of the superordinate groups, but with lesser genealogical depth; they developed only to the generation of great-great-grandson and split up in the next generation. In other words, whereas the superordinate group continued the ancestral sacrifices for the original founder of the descent group, there were four subordinate groups with varying spans: the first (Chin. *ni-tsung;* Kor. *ijong*) consisted of a man's direct agnatic descendants, who sacrificed to their father; the second (Chin. *tsu-tsung;* Kor. *chojong*) included collateral agnatic descendants of the first degree, that is, the first cousins of the *ijong,* who together held sacrifices for their common grandfather. The third (Chin. *tseng-tsu-tsung;* Kor. *chŭngjojong*) and the fourth (Chin. *kao-tsu-tsung;* Kor. *kojojong*) included the second and third cousins, respectively, who continued the ancestral services for their common great-grandfather and great-great-grandfather, respectively. Thus, whenever a generation disappeared, the relationship between the members changed according to the formula: "the ancestor's tablet (Chin. *tsu;* Kor. *cho*) moves upwards, whereas the line (Chin. *tsung;* Kor. *chong*) moves downwards."[4]

The superordinate group and the four successive generations of subordinate groups together constituted the "five lines of descent" (Chin. *wu-tsung;* Kor. *ojong*). In each successive generation, the eldest son by the primary wife in the superordinate line continued the *taejong,* and his younger brothers each established his own new subordinate line *(sojong).* The eldest son of the primary wife of the founder of a *sojong* continued the new line by becoming the head of that *sojong* upon the father's death, while each of his younger brothers founded a "second generation" *sojong*. Thus the branching-out of subordinate descent lines was a continuous process. In short, each member of a descent group first belonged, in varying genealogical positions, to every one of the four subordinate lines and ultimately to a superordinate line, however remote his position from the main stem of the total descent structure might be.[5]

Chu Hsi based his social philosophy on the ritual mobilization of the five worshipping groups. *Tsung,* the "agnatic descent line," was equated by the *Po-hu t'ung* with the verb "to honor" *(tsun).* Such a descent line was "in charge of the sacrifices to the ancestors and is honored by the kinsmen."[6] Chu Hsi treated ancestor worship as one of the basic four rites (Chin. *szu-li;* Kor. *sarye*) in his *Chia-li.* The ritualized communion with the ancestors pervades every man's life. The ancestors and their descendants, Chu Hsi remarked, consist of the same mind-matter (Chin. *ch'i;* Kor. *ki*). Although a man's *ki* dissipates upon his death, its substance is preserved in his descendants. If they exert their utmost sincerity and reverence, they can call back their ancestors' *ki* during the ritual (Chin. *chi-szu;* Kor. *chesa*). Therefore people unrelated by blood to the dead cannot perform ancestral sacrifice for them. Chu Hsi likened the succession of generations to the relentless forming and breaking-up of waves; although no one wave is the same as the one that came before or will come afterward, all waves consist of the same water. Similarly, the same *ki* unites the ancestors and their descendants in the ritual process.[7]

The Chinese Neo-Confucian thinkers thus formulated a strong agnatic ideology that found its practical expression in a tightly organized unilineal descent group. The one common action that provided this group with a kind of corporateness was ancestor worship. Through ancestor worship the group's *ki* was activated and descent thereby ritually reinforced. The focus on the ancestors gave structure to their descendants, who were united by the common ancestral substance *(ki).* While this group developed its inner dynamics by the natural principle of changing generations, it was a stable unit toward the outside world. The Sung Neo-Confucians' conception was an ideal system that never as such existed in Chinese antiquity,[8] and that they did not succeed in implanting in their own time.

THE INTRODUCTION OF ANCESTOR WORSHIP. During the last decades of Koryŏ, some Confucians began to demand the implementation of Confucian-style ancestor worship. Taking Chu Hsi's advice that "each family should have an ancestral shrine,"[9] they urged the construction of such shrines. Chŏng Mong-ju was the first Neo-Confucian scholar in late Koryŏ to propose that nobles and commoners be advised to establish shrines and conduct ancestral services.[10] Chŏng's concern was shared by Cho Chun. Deploring that in Korea the "system of domestic shrines had been in decay for a long time," Cho demanded that a ritual system on the model of Chu Hsi's *Chia-li* be introduced.[11] It was presumably Cho who initiated the wave of ritual legislation during the very last years of Koryŏ.

In early 1390, a new law was enacted to renovate the ritual behavior of the officialdom: officials from *taebu* status upward (i.e., from the fourth rank and above) were ordered to perform ancestral services for three generations of ancestors; officials of the sixth rank and above, for two; and officials of the seventh rank and below and rankless persons *(sŏin)*, for only one. A few months later, a detailed ritual program entitled "Ancestor Ceremonies for *sadaebu* Households" *(sadaebuga cheŭi)* was issued. It required the officeholding officials *(sadaebu)* to commemorate the great-grandfather, the grandfather, and the father during the second month *(chungwŏl)* of every season. The direct lineal descendant *(chŏkchangja)* was to officiate at the rites, assisted by his younger brothers and his first and second cousins. The latter were reminded that they were to establish separate spirit tablets for their own fathers and grandfathers in their houses. No collective ancestral services could be held. If the direct lineal descendant had no direct agnatic descendants, the responsibility for holding the services shifted to the oldest of his brothers or nephews. Further details on social and ritual aspects were added, and the ritual procedure was spelled out at length. Although the *Chia-li* was used as the source of inspiration, some modifications were tolerated to suit specific social requirements, and even some concessions concerning the tending of the graves in the traditional, that is Buddhist, way were made. In the summer of 1391, this program was supplemented by the "System of Domestic Shrines" (*kamyo chi che*).[12]

The impact of these laws cannot have been very great, although sporadic reports mentioned filial sons who held rites for their parents. One such case was even rewarded with a commemorative tablet.[13] Others seem to have abused the new order by illegally seizing land as "land for ancestral services" (*choŏp chi chŏn*) on the pretext of fulfilling their filial duties.[14]

These pieces of legislation were enacted on the eve of the founding of the Chosŏn dynasty and repeated in the new dynasty's first law code (no longer extant), the *Kyŏngje yukchŏn* (The Six Codes of Administration) of 1397, edited by Cho Chun. They opened a new era of ritual thinking and ritual behavior. The proper observance of these new ritual prescriptions, on the surface so deceptively simple, implied basic adjustments of the social structure. The introduction of Confucian-style ancestor worship was, therefore, more than the mere adoption of new rituals; it acted as the catalyst of fundamental social change. And this change, against social and religious tradition, came painfully slow.

The legislators of the early Chosŏn period put all their zeal into getting the official class to show compliance with the new laws by erecting at least the outer manifestation of ancestor worship, the ancestral hall (*sadang*). Special incentives were devised to hasten cooperation. The Brewing Office, for example, was instructed to sell wine—the consumption of which was normally prohibited—to those who wished to conduct ancestral services. Extraordinary filial behavior was royally rewarded. Violators of the laws were threatened with harsh punishment.[15]

Under King T'aejong, when the general pace of Confucianization quickened, the increasingly impatient censorial agencies set deadlines: the officials in the capital were to complete their halls by the first month of 1402; the officials in the countryside were given one more month.[16] These deadlines were, however, ignored by the majority of officials for "lack of filial feelings," as one critic put it, and had to be extended to the end of 1407. Moreover, officials below the third rank who were poor and did not have the necessary land to build a hall were allowed to "select a purified room to conduct the seasonal sacrifices for the ancestors."[17] Further extensions (the last until 1428 for officials above the second rank and 1433 for lower officials) and concessions are clear evidence that legal pressure was an insufficient instrument for forcing compliance with measures that were basically alien to native tradition.[18] Although in 1431 an official confidently told King Sejong that all the shrines had been built, it turned out that many did not have spirit tablets.[19] A year later, in 1432, the Department of Rites still was demanding sterner censorial action against recalcitrants but also had to grant some building concessions to less well-off officials.[20]

THE FIRST CONTOURS OF A LINEAL CONCEPT. When Cho Chun deplored the "long decay of the agnatic principle" *(chongppŏp)* in Korea, he must have referred to a mythical age when this system was supposed to have been operative. Cho presumably drew from this nostalgic statement a sense of mission to restore agnatic law in his own time. For guidance he relied on Chu Hsi's *Chia-li* and, significantly, he chose ancestor worship as his focus of action. He obviously perceived the fundamental value of ancestor worship for the making of a lineal society. But, sharing the status consciousness of his society, he made some major allowances to the hierarchical social structure of Koryŏ. The most consequential one was the gradation of the sacrificial obligations toward the ancestors on the basis of office-holding. Cho must have been aware that his concept deviated from the *Chia-li,* which prescribed four ancestral generations, as well as from contemporary Ming practices. He may have been less aware, however, of the potential danger its practical execution posed to the very lineal concept itself.

During the Sejong period, in 1428, the problems that had arisen in connection with the generational gradation of ancestral services were thoroughly discussed for the first time. The most pressing question, it turned out, was the distribution of ritual obligations among brothers who held offices of different ranks. As long as the most senior brother, who was the ritual heir *(chongja)*, held high enough office to continue the ancestral rites in the same manner as his father had done, the transfer of ritual obligations was clear and simple. If a younger brother climbed the official ladder higher than his elder brother, conflict between the brothers over ritual rights was inevitable. The resolution of such conflict was critically important because it was directly related to the clear delineation and separation of superordinate and subordinate descent lines.

Such prominent ritual and legal experts as Hŏ Cho, Pyŏn Kyeryang, Yi Chik (1362–1431), and Hwang Hŭi searched through the *Li-chi* and found confirming evidence for their view that the ritual heir's rights and obligations toward the ancestors were inviolable, regardless of his official station in life. Admitting that in Korea the system of superordinate and subordinate descent lines was unknown, they pleaded that the differentiation between the ritual heir and his brothers *(ch'aja)* be henceforth enforced on the basis of Chu Hsi's "Diagram of Superordinate and Subordinate Descent Lines" *(Ta-tsung hsiao-tsung t'u)*. This would, they maintained, prevent the usurpation of the main line by a branch line. For the actual distribution of ritual obligations, they recommended the solution found in the *Li-chi:* so long as the eldest brother was too poor to establish a shrine and to fulfill his ritual duties, his more affluent younger brother was permitted to conduct ancestral rites temporarily on behalf of the ritual heir; under no circumstances should the government tolerate the younger brother's taking ritual prerogatives away from the older brother.[21]

If the ritual heir's obligations toward the ancestors were unchallengeable, nevertheless a number of tricky procedural problems arose. If the ritual heir did not attain the same official rank as his father and thus could not worship the same number of ancestral generations, the spirit tablets of the ancestors who could not be worshipped had to be either buried or wrapped up and stored away until the day when the ritual heir attained the proper office to worship them. Several memorialists found such a procedure degrading for the ancestors concerned, but the Department of Rites ruled that since the ritual position of the eldest son was sacrosanct, the tablets of those ancestors he could not worship had to be stored away until his advancement in office.[22] A short time later the department amended this ruling and, basing the change on the *Li-chi* and on the opinions of earlier Confucians, allowed the number of ancestral generations to be worshipped to conform to the higher rank of the younger brother. The rites were nevertheless to be conducted in the house of the ritual heir.[23]

This rule was also applicable across generations, as the settlement of a controversy in 1437 confirmed. The agnatic grandson of Yi Sa-hu (n.d.), one Chang-saeng, who should have taken care of the ancestral hall in place of his deceased father, was still a child and did not have an official rank. Sa-hu's second son, Chang-saeng's uncle, felt obliged to assume the ritual responsibilities. The discrepancy between the social standing of the two was striking. Chang-saeng was rankless *(sŏin)* and, thus, would have been legally allowed to worship only his father. His uncle, a high official, could have worshipped three generations. Alert to the danger that the main line might get split between uncle and nephew, the officials in charge of the case ruled on the basis of an appropriate passage in the *Hsing-li ta-ch'üan* that Chang-saeng, as the lineal heir, should be authorized to conduct the services for as many generations of ances-tors as his uncle would have been entitled to worship.[24] The rule that the number of generations of ancestors to be worshipped should be determined by the highest official rank attained by any one of several brothers was eventually written into the *Kyŏnggguk taejŏn.*[25]

The easiest solution to the problem of how to observe this poten-tially conflict-laden law would have been to replace it with a gen-erational cutoff rule uniform for all worshippers regardless of rank. Such a suggestion was submitted and touched off a heated debate in 1428. The chief proponent of a uniform four-generation cutoff line, Chŏng Ch'o (?–1434), quoted Ch'eng I's well-known argu-ment that because mourning was worn for the great-great-grandfa-ther, he should also be worshipped. He further adduced the *Chia-li* and the *Ming hui-yao* (Ming Statutes) as pertinent evidence that Sung ritual as well as contemporary Ming usage prescribed the wor-ship of four generations of ancestors.

The dissenting opinion was presented by Pyŏn Kye-ryang. He was adamant in his insistence that the law of the dynastic founders should be respected and not tampered with. He had recourse to the *I-li*, which, he asserted, approved as heavenly principle the differentiation of ancestral generations that the Son of Heaven and the common man should worship.[26] Pyŏn not only found Chu Hsi's pronouncements on the issue unconvincing, but also thought his prescriptions impractical because they put too great a burden on those without rank. Pyŏn Kye-ryang's view was supported by the majority of the higher officialdom.[27] King Sejong himself was undecided but seemed to lean toward Pyŏn's argument. He feared that the introduction of a uniform rule might blur the lines between high and low officials.[28] Although the differential cutoff rule continued to pose problems, it was nevertheless reaffirmed in the *Kyŏngguk taejŏn*.[29]

Ancestor worship thus continued to be tied in with status consciousness, as already recognized by Cho Chun. A long ancestral cycle was the privilege of the sociopolitical elite. For those who had neither rank nor office, the remembrance of the ancestors was of less importance. A son could not inherit his father's rank; therefore the potential for attaining proper official status for remembering the ancestors had to be distributed among the several sons, a solution that in turn was possibly injurious to the lineal principle. The commitment, however, with which Sejong's ministers defended the agnatic principle against collateral attacks was remarkable. The affirmation of the lineal heir's ancestral rights within his generation was a crucial first step.

LINEAL SUCCESSION AND ANCESTOR WORSHIP. Not only was the lineal principle threatened by intragenerational pressure but, with temporal continuation as its most basic mechanism, linearity was even more seriously challenged across generations when, upon the death of the lineal heir, a successor had to be designated. The *Chu Tzu chia-li* regulated the transition from one generation to the next by primogeniture, while Koryŏ custom was based on fraternal succession. Here lay the most trying task of the legislators of the early

Chosŏn dynasty: to implant the vertical principle of primogeniture in a horizontally oriented society. They succeeded only by compromise.

A descent line, once established, was under pressure to perpetuate itself, if only for one reason: to continue the observance of rites for the ancestors of the line. As soon as a legitimate heir, a son by the primary wife, was born, lineal continuation was secure. If no direct lineal descendant existed, succession became a central issue of concern or even conflict because succession was closely tied in with the concept of descent. Several issues were involved. A substitute heir who was to guarantee the continuity of the group from within had to emulate the characteristics of a son as closely as possible. He therefore had to be a close relative of the deceased, ideally a nephew. An especially sensitive problem was the question of whether the son of a secondary wife (secondary son; *ch'ŏpcha*) was fully qualified to take the place of a primary son and precede his father's brothers and their sons. Heirship, moreover, entailed jural as well as ritual obligations. The latter included the discharge of ancestral rites not only for the deceased but also, in principle, for more distant generations of ancestors. The balanced consideration of all these issues was a precondition for choosing the "right" heir.

At the very beginning of the Chosŏn dynasty, the concept of lineal succession was vague because in Koryŏ a man's heir did not necessarily have to belong to the succeeding generation. Typically, Cho Chun had prescribed fraternal succession when the direct lineal heir was without issue. This rule was apparently repeated in the *Kyŏngje yukchŏn* and its amended later version, the *Sok yukchŏn,* and early cases of doubtful succession were settled accordingly.[30]

During the Sejong period, succession practices were closely scrutinized for the first time. Theoretical as well as practical issues motivated Sejong's high officials to give this subject a thorough review. Initial discussions reveal that the understanding of succession rules in a lineally structured society was rudimentary and the technical vocabulary was limited.[31] On the practical side, it is not surprising that succession problems first came up in families of merit subjects. Enjoying extraordinary social and economic privileges, this elite segment of officialdom was alert to the advantage tight regulation of the transmission of its hereditary rights would bring to its group. Although the evidence is not abundant, it is clear that as early as the 1430s, a law regulated succession of merit subjects by primogeniture.[32]

In 1437, the Council of State discussed succession practices in a lengthy memorial. The state councillors had become aware of the adverse effects that an incorrect choice of heir could have on family affairs. To gain better understanding of the mechanism of succession, they consulted a wide range of literature—the *I-li,* the *T'ung-tien,* and the *Hsing-li ta-ch'üan.* The final recommendation they presented to the king reflects their close adherence to the ancient model: if there was no direct heir *(sa),* a "branch son" *(chija),* that is, a nephew, was to be made heir; a nephew who was his own father's first son *(chŏkcha)* was unacceptable. The transfer was subject to the approval of both sides. The dead man's younger brothers as well as ascendants were to be excluded from such heirship.[33]

In this document the state councillors formulated for the first time the principle of lineal succession; the direct line had to be continued, if not by a real son, at least by a closely related kinsman of appropriate generation. To designate this procedure, they introduced the ancient Chinese term "to establish an heir" *(iphu),* a term that had hitherto not been used in Korea.[34] Henceforth glossed as "jural succession," *iphu* meant not only the jural transfer of household headship, titles, and property rights but also limited ritual obligation. A jural heir was, at least in principle, called upon to conduct ancestral rites only for the man he succeeded. The state councillors, however, omitted two issues: they did not discuss the position of secondary sons in this scheme; and, more important, they did not relate the ritual aspects of jural succession to the rules in the *Kyŏngje yukchŏn* that had originally fixed the transfer of ritual obligations. It was therefore the scope of a jural heir's ritual functions that gave rise to uncertainty and subsequent disputes.

Even though the law was made quite explicit, the principle upon which it was built was slow to take root. Moreover, the state was at times hard-pressed when it had to counterbalance the "constant rule" *(kyŏng)* with the "temporary convenience" *(kwŏn)*—as in the case of Cho Mal-saeng (1370–1447), for example. Cho, a high official, determined in his will that not his lineal grandson, Cho Yŏng, who was a cripple, but his third son *(ch'aja)*, Cho Kŭn, should be his heir *(iphu)* and perform the ancestral services. More than ten years after his death, in 1458, Cho Mal-saeng's will was scrutinized by the Council of State and the Department of Rites. The officials of the Department of Rites were adamant in their contention that even if the lineal heir (son or grandson) was, for economic or physical reasons, unable to perform the ancestral rites, a younger brother *(ch'aja)* was not entitled to establish a separate shrine; all he could do was support his elder brother in the fulfillment of his ritual duties. The same officials insisted that the "law of lineal heir" *(chongja chi pŏp)* was inviolable and that if a father were left to designate his heir on the basis of personal preference, the law of the land laid down in the *Kyŏngje yukchŏn* would be in jeopardy.

Those officials, on the other hand, who were ready to grant Cho's will did not dispute the principle of lineal descent but feared that if the patriarch's will were not upheld, the ancestral services might be discontinued. The king favored the flexible approach and endorsed Cho Kŭn as the rightful heir.[35] Cho's case, as well as many similar cases, illustrates that, despite the law, lineal descent could be endangered by collateral lines *(t'alchong)*. It also shows that the state was at times pressured into honoring an individual's last will and thus was not yet in complete control of succession matters.

Sooner or later the high officials who were so careful in implanting the lineal principle in Chosŏn society had to face the dilemma of reconciling jural succession with the first succession rule written into the law books of the young dynasty. That rule, hereafter glossed as "ritual succession" *(pongsa)*, was principally concerned with recruiting the most senior agnatic descendant as ritual heir in charge of ancestral services for more than one generation of ancestors. It seems to have continued the Koryŏ tradition of fraternal succession, and at the same time it fulfilled the dictum of the classics that ancestors enjoy a sacrifice only when it is offered by a close agnatic descendant.

Ritual succession seems to have been practiced less frequently for the obvious reason that ancestor worship was not yet fully developed.[36] Yet the legislators must have become aware of the basic incompatibility of these two succession rules. Stressing collaterality, ritual succession jeopardized jural succession, which emphasized linearity. A resolution of this conflict, however, was hampered by the strong commitment that was felt toward the legal heritage of the dynastic founders. Ritual succession could not be reformulated or simply scrapped for the benefit of strengthening the lineal principle. This must have been the reason that in the end both rules were written into the dynasty's first comprehensive law code, the *Kyŏngguk taejŏn* of 1471.[37]

The provision that regulated ritual heirship *(pongsa)* presumably repeated an earlier law. It fixed the transmission of ritual obligations toward the ancestors in the following order of succession: the direct lineal descendant *(chŏkchangja)*, the latter's son(s), younger brother(s) *(chungja)*[38] and their sons, and secondary son(s). Entirely new was the regulation that detailed jural succession *(iphu)*, that is, the establishment of an heir for a man who died without a primary or secondary son.[39] This was the first binding legal formulation of the lineal principle that had received its initial contours in 1437. In this version, it was expanded to include secondary sons. Only if the secondary wife, too, did not have sons could a collateral agnate of the appropriate generation *(tongjong chija)* be chosen, subject to official approval.[40]

The *Kyŏngguk taejŏn* established for the first time the principle of direct lineal descent as a means of perpetuating the main line—at the cost of collateral lines if necessary. On the model of the Confucian agnatic principle *(chongppŏp)*, it singled out the eldest son as preferred heir and thus implanted inequality in the relationship among brothers. The introduction of primogeniture in succession matters was a decisive first step in shifting Korean society away from Koryŏ tradition, and its codification in 1471 signaled a crucial advancement from ideological desideratum to legal instrument. But the *Kyŏngguk taejŏn*'s commitment to primogeniture was not yet complete. The two succession rules resulted from a compromise between tradition and innovation, and consequently their exact interpretation and practical application often were problematic. In other major areas of social legislation, most notably in inheritance and mourning rules, the code also retained Koryŏ features. More than one hundred additional years of trial and error had therefore to pass before primogeniture began to be firmly rooted in everyday practice.

The new laws regulating succession, to be effective, needed the backing of some sanctions against those *sadaebu* who preferred to flout it. Motivated by personal likes and dislikes—heirship entailed economic benefits (see below)—such recalcitrants bypassed their eldest sons and by testament entrusted the ancestral task to one of their junior sons. In 1473, the Department of Rites demanded that such arbitrary displacements of first sons (*p'yejŏkcha* or *t'alchŏkcha*) be punished, according to the Ming code, with eighty strokes of the heavy bamboo. This request was granted.[41] But because the two succession rules of the *Kyŏngguk taejŏn* were not congruous, the designation of an heir remained a problem. The higher officialdom, in particular the Department of Rites and the censorial agencies, carefully watched over possible infringements of the direct lineal heir's jural and ritual prerogatives. It was intent on enforcing the lineal principle, as is clear from two celebrated cases repeatedly debated in Sŏngjong's reign (1469–1494).

In 1475, the will of a distinguished official, Kim Yŏn-ji (1396–1471), was contested by his daughter-in-law, Song-ssi,[42] who was the wife of Yŏn-ji's eldest son, Ik-su. Yŏn-ji had designated his third son, Kyŏn-su, as ritual heir because he apparently considered his first son unfit for the ancestral responsibilities. Yŏn-ji had written his will, it turned out, after consulting with his sons and sons-in-law and thus was not considered guilty of violating the lineal principle. The authorities, therefore, were unwilling to rescind it and rather accused Song-ssi of tarnishing womanly mores by going against her father-in-law's will. But Song-ssi complained again in 1489. Although the Department of Rites did not want to reopen the case, this time, with the help of a royal order, Song-ssi got a more extensive hearing. When her husband died in 1467, Song-ssi reported, their son, Tŏk-hŭng, was a mere infant, and Yŏn-ji consequently chose Kyŏn-su as ritual heir. In the meantime, however, Kyŏn-su had died and Tŏk-hŭng had grown up. The ritual heirship, Song-ssi correctly insisted, should therefore now be transferred to Tŏk-hŭng.

The ensuing debate evidenced overwhelming support for direct lineal descent. Two-thirds of the debaters endorsed Tŏk-hŭng as the rightful lineal heir *(chongja)* and denounced Kim Yŏn-ji's will as unlawful because it so clearly disregarded the agnatic principle. Even those few voices that favored upholding Yŏn-ji's will did not question the lineal principle, but feared that if Yŏn-ji's will were nullified, this would give rise to disputes over previous settlements of similar cases, for example Cho Mal-saeng's case. The general loud endorsement of the lineal principle was dampened by only one thing: Song-ssi's daring complaint against her father-in-law. Her act was judged to be worse than Yŏn-ji's failing, and this may have convinced King Sŏngjong to uphold Kyŏn-su's heirship.[43]

A similar, yet more complicated case was that concerning the continuation of the main line of Sin Hyo-ch'ang (n.d.) (see Diagram 7). Because Sin Hyo-ch'ang's eldest son, Cha-gŭn, was sonless, Cha-gŭn designated his secondary son, Kye-dong, for eventually performing ancestral services for himself and his father, Hyo-ch'ang. Yet Sŭng-min, a grandson of Cha-gŭn's second brother, Cha-su, had apparently already been put in charge of ritual responsibilities for the main line. An edict in 1470 ruled that Kye-dong should hold services for Cha-gŭn, Sŭng-min for Hyo-ch'ang.

The case was reopened in 1479, and Sŭng-min's ritual position scrutinized. It turned out that Hyo-ch'ang himself, in a last will, had first favored his third son's line, but then changed his mind and made Yun-dong, the only son of his second son, Cha-gyŏng, his heir. When Yun-dong died, Hyo-ch'ang merely stipulated that the "morally fittest" *(hyŏn)* among his grandsons should succeed him. Sŏngjong's high ministers were thus again confronted with a will and a very complex ritual situation. The fittest grandson apparently had been Cha-su's third son, Yun-gwan. When he died, his son, Sŭng-min, Hyo-ch'ang's great-grandson, took over the ritual charge.

Diagram 7. The Case of Sin Hyo-ch'ang

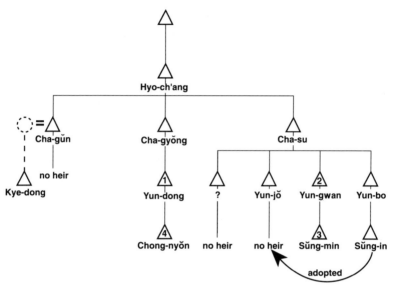

Key:
- - - - secondary line
/1\ sequence of assigned heirship

Source: Mansŏng taedongbo, II, 43b.

Notes: The Mansŏng taedongbo, P'yŏngsan Sin-ssi, gives Cha-gyŏng's line as the main line.

The ancestral rites for Cha-gŭn were performed by his secondary son, Kye-dong. The main line shifted, therefore, to Hyo-ch'ang's second son's line.

P'yŏngsan Sin-ssi kyebo (1976), pp. 77–84, does not mention Kye-dong as a secondary son. It lists Yun-bo as Cha-su's first son, as does the Munhwa Yu-ssi sebo (1565) 2:64. There are thus considerable discrepancies between the information given in the Sillok and that given in the various genealogies.

There were, however, several serious objections to Sŭng-min's heirship. The proper candidate, the ministers found, was not Sŭngmin, but Chong-nyŏn, Cha-gyŏng's grandson. Sŭng-min not only infringed upon the most direct lineal descendant's rights, he also was generationally not in a proper relationship to Hyo-ch'ang. Neither was Chong-nyŏn, but he belonged to the most senior line because Cha-gŭn's secondary son was unfit to continue the main line. The ministers unanimously concluded that therefore Chong-nyŏn had to become the heir taking charge of the ancestral responsibilities. Despite his ministers' decisive support of the lineal principle, the king did not dare invalidate Hyo-ch'ang's will because similar such cases, like Cho Kŭn's and Kim Ik-su's, would certainly be reopened again. Nevertheless, at this point some of the ritual property seems to have been divided up between Chong-nyŏn and Sŭngmin.

Sin Hyo-ch'ang's case had an aftermath in 1483 when Sŭng-min, smarting from the challenge to his prerogatives as Hyo-ch'ang's successor, claimed that the document establishing his cousin, Sŭngin, as heir of his uncle, Yun-jŏ, was falsified. This arrangement, making Sŭng-in his senior in line, would also have deposed Sŭngmin as ritual heir of his grandfather, Cha-su. No fault could be found with Sŭng-in's heirship, however, and no legal stipulation provided for the performance of ritual duties by Sŭng-min. Because Sŏngjong agreed that Sŭng-in as jural heir should continue the ancestral services of Cha-su's line, Sŭng-min in the end lost by royal edict all his ritual claims.[44]

In the above cases, the tendency to close the gap between jural and ritual heirship by emphasizing the most senior descent line was evident, but the jural heir's ritual position remained a problem. King Chungjong himself presented the following hypothetical question to the Department of Rites: if a man's first and second sons do not have agnatic issue but the second son has an established heir *(kyehuja),* should the latter take care of the ancestral rites or should the third son's son? The king admitted that there was no serious problem as long as the second son's heir was a nephew and thus related to the ancestors in the same way as the third son's first son

(actually they might have been brothers). Yet, if the heir were chosen from among some more distant kinsmen, his attitude toward
the ancestors would be indifference. Could the real grandson be
deprived of his privileges under such circumstances?[45] In answer,
the Department of Rites interpreted the law to the letter: if the
established heir were a nephew, he would be in a proper position to
hold services for the ancestors (who would be his grandparents); if
he were a more distant relative, he would be entitled to hold services only for the parents whom he had been designated to succeed.
The real grandson would have to take care of the grandparents.[46]
To alleviate the uncertainty that arose from the legal complexities,
the *Taejŏn husongnok* (Later Expansion of the *Kyŏngguk taejŏn*) of 1543
was more specific. It stipulated that the sonless direct lineal descendant had to establish as heir a *close* collateral agnate *(tongjong kŭnsok)*.
If he wanted to set up a separate line, that is, if he were willing to
give up claim to direct descent, he was allowed to choose a more
distant kinsman.[47]

   This ruling was obviously not sufficient to stop the arbitrary choice
of an heir. In 1552, the Department of Rites frankly pointed out
that jural succession and ritual heirship were not congruous. The
revised formulation of the *Husongnok,* it deplored, was not serving
as clarification; and the unfortunate addition of a clause mentioning
a possible more distant kinsman was misleading "ignorant widows"
into making wrong choices. The department therefore urged a general debate.[48] A year later, in 1553, the Censorate tried once more
to give a binding interpretation. Ritual heirship meant the performance of services for three generations of ancestors—even if no nephew
were available as heir, the son of the first cousin would be acceptable
because he would at least be a lineal descendant of the grandfather.
Jural succession, in contrast, meant the establishment of an heir for
only one man. The Censorate regretted that the law was still little
understood.[49]

   The Council of State seconded the Censorate's demand for further
clarification.[50] The result of this continued search was the expanded
explanation of "jural succession" in the *Taejŏn chuhae* (Annotations
to the *Kyŏngguk taejŏn*) of 1555. The original sentence of the *Kyŏng-*

guk taejŏn read, "One establishes as heir a 'branch son' *(chija)* of the same descent group *(tongjong)*." This was reinterpreted as meaning that "if the direct lineal descendant has neither a primary nor a secondary son, the son of a younger brother must be made heir; he then can worship the grandfather as well as the more distant ancestors. A collateral agnate of appropriate generation *(tongjong chija)* is acceptable, but he cannot perform services for the grandfather and remoter ancestors. This is so because the ancestors cannot abandon their own descendants and yet enjoy collateral descendants. Those who have no nephew are not bound by this rule."[51] Clearly, the concept of jural succession was tightened, and the jural heir had to be qualified to conduct services for a wider circle of ancestors. This seems to have been a not entirely successful attempt to force the "ideal" choice through legislation. The law code enacted at the middle of the dynasty, the *Sok taejŏn* of 1746, seems to have again watered it down. It only mentions "a close relative of the same descent group" *(tongjong kŭnsok)*.[52]

The establishment of a jural heir was often regarded only as a temporary safety measure. As soon as a real son was born, the jural heir was terminated *(p'agye)* or "degraded" to the status of "second son." This practice was based on a clause in the Ming code that allowed the real son to perform the ancestral services, whereas the adopted heir *(kyehuja)* was made his junior. The issue came to the attention of the Censorate in 1553 after the Department of Rites had accepted the termination of a *kyehuja* arrangement on the basis of unacceptable evidence. Upon the Censorate's protests, a royal edict was issued that in effect reiterated the Ming stipulation, but added a prohibition of unjustified terminations. Because, besides ritual considerations, economic interests were involved—even as "second son" a *kyehuja* could expect a share of his adoptive parents' property—numerous quarrels between *kyehuja* and their later born rivals were brought before the authorities.[53]

While the higher officialdom apparently tended to follow the Ming regulation, concerned Confucians like Yi I (1536–1584) deplored the weakening regulatory force of ritual prescriptions over human feelings. For Yi I, a father's relationship with an established son should be emotionally and ritually not different from that with a real son. Therefore, how could a father be allowed to break these ties at will? Such arbitrariness, Yi feared, would introduce double standards into the father-son relationship and be detrimental to moral values. He pleaded for sterner legal measures. Yi I's concerns were later supported by Ch'oe Myŏng-gil (1586–1647) who wanted to have his *kyehuja* recognized as eldest son *(changja)*, even though he later had a son of his own. Ritually motivated by a Sung precedent, Ch'oe's bold act was approved by King Injo (r. 1623–1649) and signalled the eventual rescission of the earlier royal edict of 1553. The *Sok taejŏn* followed the ritualists and ruled that if a son was born after the official establishment of a jural heir, such a son was to be ranked as a second son; the jural heir was to continue the ancestral services.[54]

The formulation of satisfactory succession laws was fundamental to the continued existence of a lineal descent group. Yet such laws had to be "retrospective" in character. The choice of a particular person, however acceptable to the living, could be totally ineffectual if that person lacked the necessary rapport with the ancestors. Heightened awareness of succession practices was the expression of a deepened understanding of the agnatic principle—itself the result of greater familiarity with the Confucian literature. During the reign of King Chungjong, from the beginning of the sixteenth century, official attention turned with ever greater interest to the concept of "line" *(chong)* and its implications for the working of a moral society.[55] It is therefore not surprising that during that time the state strove to get the final say in succession matters, and succession laws were reformulated. Enhanced "lineal consciousness" resulted in the emergence of bolder lineage contours and a more prominent position for the eldest son. This development had a negative effect on secondary sons and women.

ANCESTOR WORSHIP AND SECONDARY SONS. Secondary sons *(ch'ŏpcha* or *sŏja)* were a phenomenon that arose at the beginning of the Chosŏn dynasty on account of the strict differentiation between a man's primary *(ch'ŏ)* and secondary *(ch'ŏp)* wives legalized in 1413. According to the ritual literature of ancient China, a high court official had one primary wife and two secondary wives in order to assure for himself the birth of an appropriate heir.[56] On the basis of this evidence, it seemed clear that a secondary son could become his father's ritual heir. But the issue nevertheless created a social and legal puzzle. Were the sons of secondary wives bona fide sons who could, if there was no son by the primary wife, carry on the ancestral services, or did their marginal status within the descent group prevent them from doing so? There can be no doubt that in the early years of the Chosŏn dynasty a secondary son, especially a son of a commoner mother *(yangch'ŏp)*, was often preferred as heir to a more distant relative, even a brother's son. A secondary son who took care of the ancestral services of his father's line became a more important person socially, enjoyed some economic benefits, and in a way even received state recognition insofar as he could advance to certain offices from which he would otherwise have been barred.[57]

Because of the social stigma, however, that was cast on the issue of secondary unions, respected families were nevertheless reluctant to entrust a secondary son with the ritual prerogatives. Moreover, attempts by a second son to deprive a first son's secondary son who had been established as heir during the father's lifetime of his ritual rights after the father's death was a common source of intralineage feuds.[58] The designation of a secondary son as the ritual heir of a descent group *(sŭngjungja)* therefore involved moral, legal, economic, and social considerations.

It is not surprising that one of the first discussions on the status of secondary sons concerned a merit subject. T'aejo's younger half brother, Yi Hwa, who had been richly rewarded for his contributions to the founding of the dynasty, did not have a lineal grandson *(chongson)*, but only a secondary grandson by a commoner mother *(yang ch'ŏpcha)*. A debate in 1435 resulted in the ruling that because Yi Hwa had other sons and grandsons, a secondary grandson could not become his heir.[59]

The first attempt to regulate the order of succession in the *Kyŏngguk taejŏn* did not significantly clarify the problem. Both the rule of jural succession *(iphu)* and the rule of ritual heirship *(pongsa)* mentioned secondary sons. The establishment of a jural heir was permitted only if both the primary and the secondary wives did not have sons. In contrast, for ritual heirship, the lineal descendant's brothers were preferred to the secondary son.[60] These two rules, not congruous and therefore often juggled at will, put secondary sons at a disadvantage; they stood last in line of succession and often were disregarded completely.

In 1473, the pros and cons of the secondary son's ritual function were discussed in detail among the most influential government officials. The reason for this debate was the case of Cho Pang-nim (n.d.), a high official of the early days of the dynasty who, lacking a son by his primary wife, had designated his secondary son, Pok-hae, as his jural heir. After Cho's death his younger brother, Pu-rim, disputed this choice and, quoting the rule in the *Kyŏngguk taejŏn* concerning ritual heirship, prevented Pok-hae from fulfilling his ritual duties.

The widely divergent opinions held by the various discussants testify to the inconsistent and therefore controversial stipulations of the *Kyŏngguk taejŏn*. The Department of Rites took the phrase "if the direct lineal descendant does not have a successor" in the stipulation on ritual heirship to have the same meaning as the initial phrase in the stipulation on jural succession. It thus confirmed Pok-hae's right to be Cho's legitimate heir. The dissenters, among them compilers of the *Kyŏngguk taejŏn* like Ch'oe Hang and Chŏng In-ji, contended that the distinction of primary son and secondary son was as "Heaven is high and Earth low." Thus, from a legal as well as a moral point of view, it would be absurd to let a secondary son perform the services for the ancestors as long as there was a younger brother. A secondary son was, however, free to perform services for his own parents; in such a case his father's spirit tablet had to be removed from the ancestral shrine.

This last point, which amounted to the shifting of the main line to a branch line, became the central argument of a third group. If, in theory, a secondary son could be deprived of his ancestral obligations by the lineal descendant (even a grandson) of his father's younger brother, the principle of generations (the *Kyŏngguk taejŏn* spoke only of the son's generation) would be rendered meaningless. The opinion, however, that a secondary son was unfit for continuing the main line was shared by the majority. With this support, the king ruled that Pu-rim, instead of Pok-hae, should continue the ancestral rites.[61]

Cho Pang-nim's case was not an isolated example. Toward the end of the first century of the dynasty, similar complaints became more frequent. Often the choice of a secondary son as heir was disputed by other family members. Sonless primary wives resented having to entrust their husband's ritual affairs to the son of one of their rivals in the domestic sphere. They particularly questioned the secondary son's ability to worship more than one generation of ancestors because, as a person without an official rank, a secondary son was legally entitled to worship only one generation. Primary wives therefore flooded the authorities with appeals to rescind their late husbands' choices of heirs and to be allowed to select their own candidates, usually collateral agnates. Such appeals apparently were routinely granted, so that opponents of this development deplored that having a secondary son was the same as having no son.[62] Even the renowned ritualist, Yi Ŏn-jŏk (1491–1553), who had only a secondary son, made his cousin's son his heir.[63]

Toward the middle of the sixteenth century, the stipulation on jural heirship was more and more read in the light of ritual succession and thus expanded in meaning to encompass the descent group as a whole and not just the heirless man's line. Consequently, if a direct lineal heir without descendants could not make his younger brother's son his heir, his next choice came to be the son of a cousin (*sach'on*) who connected with his line at the grandfather's generation. Clearly, this expanding scope of the descent group worked to the disadvantage of secondary sons.[64] And in fact, the *Taejŏn husongnok* of 1543 no longer mentioned secondary sons as possible candidates for succession.[65]

A decade later, the state councillors found this rule to be in violation of the original stipulation of jural succession in the *Kyŏngguk taejŏn* and expressed their fear that it might become the source of innumerable disputes. The result of their deliberations was a rather narrowly worded royal edict: a direct lineal descendant who had a secondary son would not be allowed to establish an heir, except a son of a younger brother *(tongsaengje)*.[66] This ruling, although not made retroactive, did not satisfy anybody. To give it more weight, the assurance that secondary sons, as ritual heirs of their fathers, could conduct ancestral services for as many generations of ancestors as their father's rank would allow was added in the *Taejŏn chuhae* of 1555.[67]

From a legal point of view, thus, ritual succession by a secondary son of commoner status—those of base origin were never discussed—continued to be acceptable and was even found compatible with ancient ritual prescriptions that rated a secondary son's physical connection with his patrilineal ancestors as more important than the social position society accorded him. Korean ritual handbooks—Chu Hsi had nothing to say about secondary sons[68]—acknowledged therefore the secondary sons' legal and ritual acceptability as ritual heirs. Even the respected Confucian, Yi I, who did not have a primary son, made the eldest of his two secondary sons his ritual heir.[69]

Despite these efforts to reactivate some of the legal thinking of the early years of the dynasty, the growing trend of forcing secondary sons out of family affairs seems to have been irreversible. The mid-dynasty code, the *Sok taejŏn* of 1746, no longer mentioned secondary sons.[70]

The ritual heirship of secondary sons was indeed problematic because it ran counter to the clear establishing of descent lines. Succession by secondary sons meant the discontinuation of the main line and the consequent shifting of ancestral prerogatives to a branch line. Moreover, the preference for a secondary son came dangerously close to disregarding or even discarding the criteria of high and low social status, thus possibly giving rise to social mobility. In view of the broad social implications secondary-son status had, it is amazing that the *Kyŏngguk taejŏn* would have mentioned secondary sons as possible jural and ritual heirs. The early legislators may have intended to soften the secondary wives' lot by giving their sons some recognition. It may have been a compromise between human sentiment and legal rationality, a compromise that did not survive into the second half of the dynasty.

ANCESTOR WORSHIP AND WOMEN. The legislators of the early Chosŏn dynasty found it difficult to deal with women and to define their proper position in a Confucian society. Yet they recognized that women were key figures in transmitting the rights of membership in the lineal descent group, and therefore their ritual roles during their lifetimes as well as after their deaths had to be carefully delineated. The law of 1413 that clearly distinguished between primary wife and secondary wife resulted in the secondary wife's exclusion from the ritual life of society: while she was alive, she could not participate in the ancestral services; after her death, she did not become a recognized ancestor and therefore was denied a spirit tablet in the descent group's ancestral shrine. In contrast, the primary wife played a limited role in the ancestral rituals; and when she died, she was enshrined beside her husband in the ancestral hall, thereby receiving the ultimate recognition of her social status.

There were two major problems that required special attention: the enshrinement of a second primary wife and the ritual obligations of the lineal heir's wife after her husband's death. The settlement of both these problems significantly contributed to the strengthening of the lineal concept.

Called *kyemo,* "succeeding mother," or *humo,* "later mother," the second wife was accorded during her lifetime the full privileges of a primary wife. After her death, problems arose. Could the spirit tablet of a *kyemo* be enshrined beside that of the original primary wife? And what was the duration of the mourning period her husband's son by the first wife, that is, the direct lineal successor, had to observe for his stepmother?

The answers to these ritual questions would provide the ultimate judgment of a *kyemo*'s position within the descent group. The issue of whether the *kyemo* should be enshrined with the first primary wife in the same ancestral hall was related to the prohibition against "honoring two wives in the same room."[71] Confucian opinion differed widely on this issue, but the Koreans based their final decision on the interpretations of Wei Kung-su, a ritualist of the time of the Hsien-tsung emperor (early ninth century), and Chu Hsi—both of whom had spoken in favor of enshrining both primary wives together. A request by the Department of Rites in 1429 to this effect received the royal endorsement and was eventually codified in the *Kyŏngguk taejŏn.*[72]

The decision on the enshrinement had direct bearing on the degree to which the *kyemo* would be mourned by the lineal heir, her ritual stepson *(pongsa ŭija)*. Although the dynasty's earliest code, the *Kyŏngje yukchŏn,* apparently had prescribed a mourning period of three years, in close analogy to the mourning precepts of the *I-li,*[73] such a long mourning period reportedly was only rarely observed. The reason for this neglect must have been the fact that a man could have several wives of equal status at the very beginning of the dynasty. Because the *kyemo* was to be enshrined in the same way as the first primary wife, the officials of the Department of Rites argued, she should also be mourned for an equal period—that is, three years *(chaech'oe)*. A reduction of this period, it was felt, would be tantamount to slighting the father's second wife. Although Chu Hsi had made the three-year mourning period optional, the Department of Rites pleaded for adherence to the *Kyŏngje yukchŏn* and the Ming law. A royal edict of 1434 granted this request; it was later reaffirmed in the *Kyŏngguk taejŏn.*[74]

The significance of this piece of legislation lies in the fact that the elementary relationship between mother and son was transferable to that between stepmother and stepson. By treating the stepmother in the same way as his own mother, the lineal heir reaffirmed his own position as eldest son and excluded his half brothers (that is, the sons the stepmother might have from his father) from competing for his position. The bestowal of full ritual honors upon the stepmother was a way not only to express esteem for the father's second wife but also to grade her sons as younger brothers. The *kyemo*'s recognition was thus, at least in principle, a regulatory device for reserving lineal succession for the offspring by the first primary wife. In this respect, the ritual honors conferred after death may have worked negatively during the *kyemo*'s lifetime; if she was honored as mother by the stepson, her own sons stood little chance of acquiring prominence within the descent group. The *kyemo*, therefore, must be regarded as a primary wife of some lesser degree.

The stipulations of the *Kyŏngguk taejŏn* clearly prescribed agnatic succession and thus excluded women—daughters and daughters-in-law—from jural succession as well as from ritual heirship. During the first two hundred years of the Chosŏn dynasty, however, women profited from several factors that ensured them an important voice in ritual matters. The women's customary strong standing in domestic affairs, a remnant of Koryŏ times, was not easily changed by law. Moreover, lineal structure and consciousness were not yet well developed, and marriage continued to be predominantly uxorilocal. Daughters, furthermore, still enjoyed inheritance rights. Although not acknowledged by, and even in violation of the lawbooks, women retained a great measure of independence of action even in ritual matters.

According to early Chosŏn custom, the wife of an eldest son who died without male issue was called *ch'ongbu*, "eldest daughter-in-law," regardless of whether or not her husband ever had acted as ritual heir. In this capacity, she had two important prerogatives: she succeeded to the line's ritual heirship, and she had the right to designate an heir to her late husband. Succession to the ritual heirship brought economic benefits to the widow. She usually moved into the descent group's main house (*taejongga*), to which the ancestral shrine was attached, and took possession of the land and slaves that had been specially set aside to sustain the ancestral services.[75] *Ch'ongbu* status could be passed on to the second son's wife upon the death of the original *ch'ongbu*.

In ritual succession, the *ch'ongbu* had precedence even over the sons of her husband's brothers. She may have gained this extraordinary position because, at the beginning of the Chosŏn dynasty, daughters-in-law were generally regarded as daughters. During this early period, daughters and sons often shared in the performance of the ancestral services on a rotation basis. The evidence suggests that because of fear that the family property would pass into the hands of other relatives when there were no sons, the existence of daughters was often used as a pretext not to establish a collateral agnate as heir. A *ch'ongbu* obviously fulfilled the same role; she could prevent the dispersion of her parents-in-law's family property.

The *ch'ongbu*'s privileges could give rise to severe tension among the descent group's members. Enjoying the ancestors' worldly possessions more than the obligation to satisfy them with periodic sacrifices, the *ch'ongbu* at times squandered the family fortunes by leading a sumptuous life or even by selling the ancestral fields. This independent existence made the *ch'ongbu* reluctant to designate an heir for her late husband, especially when she had daughters. Her tardiness could bring her into conflict with the still-living mother-in-law, who was concerned with securing the continuation of the ancestral rites. Moreover, the *ch'ongbu* usually hated to establish one of her husband's secondary sons as his heir and often seems to have disregarded her spouse's last will.

More serious, the *ch'ongbu* blocked the fraternal succession of the ritual heirship. Conflict between the *ch'ongbu* and her husband's younger brothers was therefore unavoidable. Numerous accounts point out the ramifications of such conflict. If a *ch'ongbu* did allow a brother-in-law to conduct the services for the family's ancestors, the brother-in-law at times refused to hold services for his older brother and thus forced the *ch'ongbu* to select an heir for her late husband. Moreover, younger brothers were often unkind to their widowed sisters-in-law and expelled them from their secure positions. All this suggests that it was in the *ch'ongbu*'s best interests to insist on and cling to her customary rights as tenaciously as possible.

The *ch'ongbu*'s position seems to have been relatively secure and undisputed until the first years of King Chungjong's reign. King Chungjong was concerned with the concept of lineal organization as a structural element of Confucian government, and official debate inevitably came to focus on the problem of lineal succession. Although it was acknowledged that the rule of ritual succession in Korea did not adhere to the prescriptions of the original texts on rites, the difficulties that had been created by the incongruous rules of ritual succession and jural succession were becoming an issue of serious concern. In the ongoing debates, the role of the *ch'ongbu* also came under close scrutiny. Ideally, the difficulties of succession could be mitigated if the oldest son of the younger brother who had become ritual heir also was appointed heir of his late uncle. This would preserve the direct agnatic descent line as closely as possible and concentrate ancestral property within a well-defined kin group. This ideal solution was often jeopardized by the *ch'ongbu*'s decision to select the son of a more distant relative as heir for her husband. By doing this, she split the descent line into two branches and scattered the line's ancestral property.

The question of the *ch'ongbu*'s ritual competence also was raised. That her name could not be written on the invocation (*ch'ungmun*) seemed to indicate that she was not in an appropriate position to offer the ancestors sacrifices. Doubt was also cast on the eldest daughter-in-law's right to be called *ch'ongbu* when her mother-in-law was still alive.

All these problems were pointed up by the struggle surrounding the succession to King Sŏngjong's twelfth son, Musan-gun, which occurred during King Chungjong's reign (see Diagram 8). Musan-gun's eldest son, Ku-su, died without male offspring. Ignoring the customary rights of Ku-su's widow, An-ssi, who was the *ch'ongbu*, Musan-gun's second son, Mi-su, with the help of his mother, Sin-ssi, usurped his elder brother's hereditary titles and office and performed the ancestral rites. An-ssi later selected the second son of Ku-su's youngest brother, Sŏk-su, as Ku-su's heir. This case strengthened the demands for introducing some uniformity into succession procedures.

Although King Chungjong acquiesced in Mi-su's rash act, he reviewed several instances of irregular selection of ritual heirs and, admonished by the censorial agencies, upheld the *ch'ongbu*'s customary privileges. In his effort to narrow down the choice of jural heirs to the "closest relatives of the same line,"[76] he not only diminished the discrepancy between the original stipulations for jural and ritual succession, but also limited the *ch'ongbu*'s alternatives.

Under Chungjong's second successor, King Myŏngjong (r. 1545–1567), the case of Musan-gun's succession was revived by an attack of the Inspectorate against Mi-su's infringement of An-ssi's rights

Diagram 8. The Case of Musan-gun

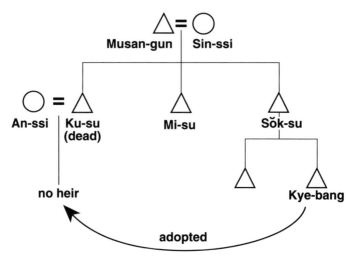

as *ch'ongbu*. The censors also demanded that Mi-su be stripped of his illegally acquired titles. It was found impractical, however, to rescind an earlier king's authorization, and the case was not pursued further. The debates among the king and his ministers nevertheless singled out the *ch'ongbu*'s ritual prerogatives as a practice that stood in the way of successful implementation of lineal principles. Despite persistent censorial protests, the state councillors eventually convinced the king that the *ch'ongbu* had to be deprived of her traditional powers.[77] Quoting a somewhat obscure passage from the *Li-chi*[78] to provide supporting historical testimony, and referring to the many abuses custom permitted the *ch'ongbu* to commit, a royal edict of tenth month, 1554, clearly defined the term *ch'ongbu* and at the same time carefully limited her previously sweeping ritual competence. As long as her parents-in-law were alive, the edict ruled, the wife of a dead oldest son was not allowed to perform the ancestral services. Only if her husband had actually become the ritual heir before his death was she granted the right to continue the services for the rest of her life.

The edict qualified the definition of *ch'ongbu* and narrowly circumscribed her ritual role, but it did not abrogate her right to have the decisive say in choosing her husband's jural heir. Subsequent official interpretation of jural heirship, however, forced the *ch'ongbu* to make the "right" choice. This much reduced ritual authority had also economic consequences for the *ch'ongbu*. She could no longer lay claim on land and slaves, and the ancestral property was divided among her late husband's brothers. The house to which the ancestral hall was attached passed to the one who was put in charge of the ancestral services and was not to be sold. Clearly, the campaign against the *ch'ongbu*'s ritual and economic prerogatives in mid sixteenth century gained momentum at a time when, as will be discussed further in Chapter Five, lineal consciousness came to focus on an increasingly specific group of agnates, and when growing scarcity turned land into part of an inviolable ancestral trust. The *Sok taejŏn* of 1746 merely confirmed the demise of the *ch'ongbu*.[79]

NON-AGNATIC SUCCESSION. The perpetuation of a direct agnatic descent line was endangered as soon as no direct lineal heir existed.

The manipulations necessary to rescue it from extinction and to continue the rites for its ancestors inevitably caused discord or even open conflict between closest kin. The legal guidelines laid down in the *Kyŏngguk taejŏn* lacked clarity and thus often failed to direct agitated human feelings toward the legally and ritually proper solution.

If lineal agnatic descent could be sidetracked by agnatic collaterals, it faced sure termination when its ritual concerns were put into the hands of a non-agnatic descendant—a daughter's son *(oeson)*. Nevertheless, during the first half of the dynasty, non-agnatic succession was widely practiced—often in preference of collaterals—because it corresponded to traditional familial values. In the absence of sons, a daughter and her often uxorilocally residing husband tended to assume wide-ranging responsibilities in the daughter's parental household, and it was therefore only natural that their children who grew up with their matrilateral grandparents *(oe chobumo)* would have particularly strong affinities for them. Such human bonds were taken into consideration when the *Kyŏngje yukchŏn* of 1397 apparently stipulated that the ancestral rites for sonless matrilateral grandparents should, according to "local usage" *(sogŭi)*, be entrusted to a non-agnatic grandson.[80]

The label "local usage" seems to indicate that the early legislators were well aware that the practice of non-agnatic ritual succession ran counter to their emphasis on direct lineal descent, and that its permission was a concession to tradition. In 1425, the non-agnatic grandsons of merit subjects lost their right to inherit merit-subject land *(kongsinjŏn)* on the ground that they did not continue the original recipient's family name. This loss of economic support surely discouraged many from performing ancestral rites for their maternal grandparents.[81]

While the merit subjects were especially conscious of agnatic concepts, nevertheless non-agnatic grandsons continued to be favored candidates for ritual heirship. When in 1442 King Sejong tried to find an heir for a meritorious military official, Kim Tŏksaeng (n.d.), who had died without male issue, several of his high ministers urged him to follow established custom *(sesok)* and to select the son of Tŏk-saeng's daughter. If he were given some land, this would ensure the unbroken performance of ancestral services for generations. Although the ministers realized that this would be an exceptional arrangement, they were certain that Tŏk-saeng's loyal soul would be better served by a real, albeit non-agnatic, grandson than by a nephew. Despite this plea, the king decided on the second son of Tŏk-saeng's younger brother. He was given six slaves and sixty *kyŏl* (or roughly 120 acres) of land to enable him to fulfill his ritual responsibilities.[82]

The predilection for non-agnatic ritual succession—not prohibited, but simply ignored by the compilers of the *Kyŏngguk taejŏn*—persevered into the sixteenth century. With ever-growing official insistence on the lineal principle, however, the ritual inappropriateness of the practice was increasingly revealed. Heaven, when creating things, gives them *one* root, Yi Hwang (1501–1570) exclaimed. The performance of rites for two different descent groups in one single shrine therefore was an offense against the natural order. Such an incorrect sacrifice would not be well accepted by the ancestral spirits. Yet, even Yi Hwang recognized the dilemma of heirless maternal ancestors whose spirit tablets did not have a secure abode. As a temporary measure, he recommended their installment in a special room where they could receive sacrificial food.[83] Later ritualists repeated Yi Hwang's point of view, which drew its authority from Chu Hsi, but none could ignore the continued existence of what was regarded as a particularly Korean custom. Under the heading "altered rites" *(pyŏllye)* non-agnatic descendants found in the ritual handbooks the necessary details for their irregular acts.[84]

The ritualists' clear rejection of non-agnatic heirship is echoed in official documents. When King Myŏngjong agreed to the establishment of a non-agnatic grandson, who even was a first son, for one of his half brothers, the *Sillok* historians deplored this irresponsible breach of law and rites for the benefit of one individual.[85] Under Sŏnjo, government policy seems to have become somewhat stricter in dealing with cases of non-agnatic succession.[86]

But ingrained customs die hard. Pak Sŭng-jong (1562–1623), a high official at the beginning of the seventeenth century, reportedly met with general approval when he bought his younger brother a house and gave him a gift of slaves and land to perform the ancestral rites for their heirless maternal grandparents. Official records, moreover, show that non-agnatic succession survived well into the eighteenth century.[87]

GENEALOGIES AS DESCENT GROUP CHARTS. The ideological construct that guided the formation of patrilineal worshipping groups was the "agnatic principle" *(chongppŏp),* a genealogical rule that activated what the *Li-chi* formulated thus: "The human way consists of recognizing one's relatives. If the relatives are recognized, the ancestors are honored. If the ancestors are honored, the line of descent is respected. If the line of descent is respected, the kin is in harmony."[88] Graphic illustration of how such genealogical dictates were implemented and became themselves persuasive elements in the formative process of the patriliny is provided by the written genealogies *(chokpo).* These records document in amazing detail the evolution of the patrilineal Chosŏn descent group over the first two hundred years of the dynasty.

The early genealogical records compiled during the fifteenth century clearly show that while the idea of starting such records derived from Confucian insights, the contents were dictated by the bilateral social realities of the time. A first problem was the selection of an apical ancestor *(sijo* or *pijo).* Many genealogies note an eminent public figure of late Silla or early Koryŏ as genealogical starting point. Up to about the mid thirteenth century, his posterity usually could be traced only through one representative per generation, any son or nephew remembered. Often, when records did not survive, intermittent generations were counted, but not documented.[89] Such lacunae *chokpo* compilers rightly attributed to the fact that in Koryŏ the Koreans knew "neither lineal principle nor genealogy" so that "after several generations the names of the ancestors in the four ascending generations were lost, and their descendants consequently became estranged from each other, looking at each other like strangers in the street."[90] Coverage becomes fuller for the approximately last one hundred and fifty years of Koryŏ because of available household registers *(hojŏk)*, which often spanned six generations and thus reached back to the mid thirteenth century, and other surviving family records. Finally on safer genealogical grounds, a personality of late Koryŏ or early Chosŏn was often designated "intermediate ancestor" *(chungjo)* to mark the fact that the recording of his posterity was no longer a haphazard reconstruction, but based on available documents and thus demanded credibility.

It remains indicative of early *chokpo* compilation that the compilers usually were able to record only one single descent line—the line deriving from their own immediate antecedents.[91] This may not have alone resulted from the early Confucians' preoccupation with fixing their personal line of descent according to the lineal principle. Presumably this format was also dictated by contemporary social convention that still included, in Koryŏ fashion, both agnatic and non-agnatic offspring among a man's descendants and thus made genealogical recording an extremely complex affair. The early *chokpo*[92] thus vividly reflect the "un-Confucian" social conditions prevailing at the beginning of the dynasty. One of the most conspicuous features in the Andong Kwŏn genealogy dated 1476— the oldest extant genealogy—is the attempt to record daughters fully (under their husbands' name) with their respective descendants. The non-agnates listed (some 9,000 names) are more numerous than the agnates (ca. 380).[93] Moreover, the listing of the children is by order of birth, the lack of an heir *(muhu)* is not remedied by adoption, and there is no indication of secondary sons. Second marriages of women are detailed, whereas marriage data for men can be found only under their wives' listings.[94]

Deeper understanding of what a Confucian descent group should look like is revealed in the *chokpo* prefaces written in the first half of the sixteenth century. In a variety of images—that of the tree with a single root and proliferating branches seems to be the most common—the rationale of fixing posterity on paper is expounded. "If the names [of the members of the descent group] are not recorded, there is no way of knowing who they are, and it is impossible to know the difference between distant and near, close and remote [relatives], and whence they originated."[95] Genealogical recordings thus helped to structure kin according to lineal and collateral, primary and secondary points of view so that "relatives who wear three-month mourning for each other *(sima)* [i.e., third cousins] would not treat each other as strangers."[96]

This growing awareness of and emphasis on the position and function of agnatic kin led the *chokpo* compilers in the seventeenth century to reconsider the appropriateness of the customary recording of non-agnatic descendants. The dilemma of excluding the daughters' offspring from the records finds at times passionate expression. Upon someone's question why those belonging to a different surname *(isŏng)* should be listed in as detailed a fashion as those belonging to the same surname *(tongsŏng)*, the famous statesman Kim Yuk (1580–1658) answered,

> A human being, upon being born, is initially only one single being, but it proliferates and [its descendants] reach thousands of people. Seen from their beginnings, they all came forth from the same origin. Therefore, the sons of sons are grandsons and have the same family name [as their ancestors], and the sons of daughters are also grandsons even though they have a different family name. Is someone's love for a daughter's sons different from the love for a son's sons? Although there is the differentiation between inside and outside [i.e., agnatic and non-agnatic], the natural affection is exactly the same for both. Seen from their ancestors, kin who now have a different surname are all equally beloved. How could I love exclusively my sons and grandsons and not those equally loved by their ancestors?[97]

Judging from the general tenor of contemporary *chokpo* prefaces and editorial rules, Kim Yuk's plea, although faintly echoed here and there, was not in tune with the growing trend to shorten the recording of non-agnates. Prominent scholar-officials who supervised the editing of their own genealogies justified abbreviated information on the daughters' descendants with the need to emphasize the agnatic lines. Whereas these have to be continued without generational limit, they declared, the recording of non-agnates should stop after three generations, except for an occasional eminent official who would have to be remembered even beyond such a limit. The distinguished scholar-official Pak Se-dang (1629–1703) demanded that a daughter's sons no longer be included in the main columns written in large characters in order "to rectify common mistakes and separate the different surnames." To highlight such separation, the genealogy of the Pannam Pak of 1683 entered a daughter's off-spring horizontally on the lefthand side of their father's name.[98] Other genealogies of that time used smaller characters for non-agnates, marked them by adding their different surnames, and broke their recording off after two or three generations. Moreover, generally, sons and daughters were no longer listed simply by order of birth, but by order of sex.

This acute interest in setting the patrilineal descent group in bold relief by reducing the information on non-agnates—admittedly also dictated by the graphic difficulty of recording all descendants indefinitely—equally affected secondary sons. Hitherto recorded together with primary offspring by order of birth, they were now separated into their own group and added at the very end of their generational entry.[99] This was "to clarify the differentiation between primary and secondary lines *(chŏkp'a-sŏp'a)*." Besides this visual clarification, subtle differences in the wording of the biographical information added to each name were introduced for the same purpose.[100] Secondary (male) offspring were often noted for one generation only, when indeed they were recorded at all. Some genealogies omitted reference to them entirely. When the lack of a primary son threatened a line with extinction, it was continued by an heir identified as "adopted" *(kye* or *kyeja)*.[101]

From this brief excursion into *chokpo* compilation, it is clear that these documents were an expression of a descent group's consciousness of one common root—historicism is an aspect inherent in the ancestral cult—and at the same time were a means to guide its development and internal organization, a function pointed out by the Sung Neo-Confucians and well recognized by the Korean compilers. An additional, frequently referred-to dimension of genealogies was the moral climate of filial piety and brotherly love, of etiquette and modesty they helped create. And, as manifestations of a heightened sense of identity and solidarity, these documents carefully circumscribed the descent groups' boundaries toward the outside world.

ANCESTRAL RITES: ECONOMIC ASPECTS. There can be no doubt that the legally recognized ritual heir of an agnatic descent group *(chongja)* enjoyed special economic benefits. He was entitled to receive the buildings to which the ancestral hall was attached *(chongga)*, and he was in charge of fields and slaves *(pongsa chŏnt'aek nobi)* that were set aside for financing and supporting ancestral services. A destitute lineal heir who could not afford the expenses of building a shrine and performing regular services was to receive economic aid from wealthier family members, especially his brothers. Although the evidence is scanty, it seems that at the beginning of the dynasty, when neither lineal descent nor ancestral services were fully developed, it was rare that special land was set aside to defray the costs of ritual obligations. If there was ancestral land, it often resembled private land. This is suggested by reports about disputes over such land and slaves among potential heirs. A father occasionally showed his favorite son special affection by turning the ancestral property over to him, and sometimes family members begrudged a ritual heir his full share of inheritance. The rotation of ancestral services among siblings *(yunhaeng)* may have taken into account the desire to let everybody share in the special benefits and, sometimes, the need to spread the economic burden of ancestral rites more equally.[102]

The technical term "sacrificial land" *(chejŏn)* rarely appears in the early period of the dynasty, and it is not clear how much land was set aside for the purpose of paying for the ancestral rites. It is unlikely that the prescription of the *Chu Tzu chia-li,* according to which one-twentieth of a deceased man's fields were to be designated for his services, was followed closely. A minimum of sacrificial land was guaranteed by law only for merit subjects for whom ancestral services were to be conducted in perpetuity. Even a ritual heir of slave status, the last in line of possible recipients, got at least thirty *kyŏl* of the hereditary merit-subject land as "sacrificial land" before the remaining land reverted back to the state.[103]

The ritual heir's economic position was first fully described in the *Kyŏngguk taejŏn*. He was to inherit the natal home that comprised the ancestral shrine; and, if he was the direct lineal descendant, he was entitled to receive one-fifth more of his parents' slaves than his siblings. They were called "lineal succession slaves" *(sŭngjung nobi)*. The same was true for land. The shares varied, however, greatly depending on the economic strength of the descent group. Even when the ritual heir was a secondary son of either commoner or slave origin, he was to receive an extra share of slaves from his father's primary wife.[104] The law thus acknowledged the economic burden ancestral rites entailed and recompensed the ritual heir for his duties. Although at the beginning of the dynasty such extra shares of land and slaves seem to have been more or less at the heir's disposal, they eventually became the corporate property of the descent group. From the late sixteenth century on, this ancestral trust was usually mentioned in inheritance documents as a distinct category of property *(pongsajo)*. Its stated purpose often was to end rotating services by strengthening the economic standing of the ritual heir. He was, however, forbidden to sell on his own initiative such property, which had to be handed on undivided to future generations.[105]

ANCESTRAL RITES: INSTITUTIONAL ASPECTS. In Confucian-style ancestor worship, the center of ritual action is the ancestral hall *(sadang)*. Beginning in late Koryŏ, when the Neo-Confucians propagated the Confucianization of Korean society, the building of an ancestral hall became the measurement of ritual conformity. Ideally, such halls were built apart from the main house, but most scholar-officials apparently found it difficult to follow ritual prescriptions to the letter. Cramped living quarters or economic destitution were often used as excuses for delayed compliance with the law. Some halls therefore were only the size of a "ritual room" *(chesil)*. At times, a "purified room" *(chŏngsil)* within the house was the only place that was available for rituals, a compromise that did not please ritual purists.[106]

Ancestral halls without spirit tablets *(sinju)*, however, were but "empty vessels," as King Sejong put it. Uncertainty about what

such tablets should look like was resolved when the Office for the
Establishment of Ceremonies (Ŭirye sangjŏngso), upon royal order,
ascertained that wooden spirit tablets rather than portraits con-
formed to ancient precedent. The exact measurements of the spirit
tablet were found in the *Chu Tzu chia-li*. [107] Although the ancient
Chinese ordering system of agnatic ancestors, the *chao-mu* order (which
will be discussed in Chapter Four below), was mentioned as a means
for clearly delineating generations, it was not used in Korea for
arranging the ancestral tablets in the ancestral hall. Instead, the
arrangement as given in the *Chia-li* was followed: the tablet of the
most senior ancestor worshipped was placed in the west, the direction of honor; the other tablets, in descending order, followed to
the right. At times, improperly, paper tablets *(chip'ae)* were used. [108]
The tablets of the original merit subjects were worshipped in perpetuity *(pulch'ŏnwi);* when their generational cutoff line was reached,
they were transferred to a special chamber of worship. [109] The Korean ancestral hall, then, accommodated only the spirit tablets of
the direct lineal ascendants. It had a simple, yet dignified, appearance.

Ideally, on the basis of the *Chia-li,* Confucian officials should
have held seasonal ancestral services *(sije)* on the first day of the
middle month of each of the four seasons and on the death anniversary of each ancestor *(kije* or *kiilche).* Judging from the numerous
censorial complaints throughout the fifteenth century, the officials
took their time in complying with these standards, although they
were eventually written into the lawbooks. The officials were given
two days off duty to fulfill their ritual obligations. [110] It is doubtful,
however, that the four seasonal sacrifices were observed carefully
even later. Rather, the Koreans kept to their customary holidays
(sokchŏl), especially Tano (the fifth day of the fifth lunar month) and
Ch'usŏk (the fifteenth day of the eighth lunar month), that were
linked to the agricultural cycle. When preparing for these festive
days, as a well-known scholar remarked, who would not remember
and feast the ancestors as well? As long as these local customs did
not impair righteousness, they were acknowledged even by such
outstanding ritualists as Yi Ŏn-jŏk and Yi Hwang. [111]

The chief officiant *(chujeja)* was the direct lineal heir or, if such a person did not exist, an appropriate substitute. His name was recorded on the spirit tablet because he was the socially recognized representative of the lineal continuum. Depending on the ancestor for whom the services were performed, he was assisted by varying groups of his closest agnatic kin. At the beginning of the dynasty, women, especially the wife of the direct lineal heir *(chubu)*, took part in the services, under certain circumstances even as chief officiants, although their names could not be written on the spirit tablets.[112]

In the early part of the dynasty, the performance of ancestral rites was rarely the task of the eldest son alone. The sons and grandsons, and often the sons-in-law, shared this task and rotated the services. Economic reasons may have accounted for such a division of responsibilities, but it may also have derived from the strong lateral tradition of Koryŏ that accorded all sons equal chances. When there were many siblings, each took charge of the services once every few years; or the ritual heir cared for the seasonal services and the grave-site rituals *(myoje)* while his younger brothers arranged the death anniversary rites *(kije)*. The possible division of the tasks varied greatly, of course. Ritualists did not, in principle, object to the rotating of ritual performance. They pointed out, however, that such a rotation system worked well only with grave-site rituals because these were likely to be performed in front of the ancestral graves and all the segments of descendants would attend. They deplored the fact that with rotating death anniversary rites, frequently only the one son in charge was in attendance and, if he was a younger son, he would often not bother to hold the rites in the ancestral hall. If, however, the ritual heir took charge of all the rites, his brothers might become negligent and forget ritual matters altogether.[113]

From the beginning of the dynasty, the number of ancestral generations that the official elite had to worship was fixed by law and later codified in the *Kyŏngguk taejŏn:* civil and military officials of the sixth rank and above were to worship three generations of ancestors, officials of the seventh rank and below, two generations, and persons without official rank *(sŏin)*[114] only one generation. Yet, as long as the lineal concept was not clear in the worshippers' minds, the ancestors were often indistinct entities, simply referred to as "objects of reverence" *(pongsa)*. The designation of the apical ancestor could be a problem. Under Sejong, it was suggested that the original merit subjects should be made the founders of descent groups, but this was considered impractical, presumably because many merit subjects traced their ancestry from Koryŏ forebears.[115]

Increased familiarity with ritual matters, especially from the sixteenth century on, heightened concern about the proper conduct of ancestral affairs, and there was a growing awareness that the legal norms did not correspond to the ritual prescriptions. The three ancestral generations in the lawbooks did not tally with the four generations in the ritual handbooks. Searching for an explanation, as well as a justification, for this discrepancy between legal and ritual norms, Yi Ŏn-jŏk, Yi Hwang, and other scholars decided that Chu Hsi had adopted Ch'eng I's view in the *Chia-li;* that is, because mourning was prescribed for the great-great-grandfather, he should also be worshipped.

The Koreans seem to have regarded Ch'eng I's concern as a ritual nicety rather than a necessity. Although they acknowledged that some scholars who were especially enthralled with ritual finesse were sacrificing to their great-great-grandfathers, they opined that the laws of the dynasty should not be changed. Yi Ŏn-jŏk suggested, however, that during the customary holidays in the spring and in the fall, a grave-site ritual might be held for the great-great-grandfather "so that the roots be not forgotten." Yi I, on the other hand, strictly observed the three-generation limit, a behavior that drew some puzzled questions from his contemporaries.[116] In Korea, then, no uniformity was established; but in the latter part of the dynasty, it seems to have become customary to include the great-great-grandfather and worship four generations of ancestors.[117]

RITUAL LITERATURE. Proper ritual knowledge and behavior, it was often emphasized, were the results of instruction; and the basis of this instruction was the ritual handbook. Since the late Koryŏ period, Chu Hsi's *Chia-li* had been esteemed as the most authoritative ritual book. Because it was a short and terse text, Korean Confucians saw the need for annotating and supplementing it.[118] At the beginning of the dynasty, the renowned Neo-Confucian scholar, Kwŏn Kŭn, prepared the *Sangjŏl karye* (Annotated *Chia-li;* no longer extant). More than a century later, Yi Ŏn-jŏk described the ancestral rituals in his *Pongsŏn chabŭi* (Various Ceremonies Concerning the Veneration of Ancestors). Others, like Yi I, drafted simplified ritual programs to assist ignorant performers.[119] Minimal ritual instruction for the *sadaebu* was also contained in the *Kukcho oryeŭi,* which was published as the ritual companion of the *Kyŏngguk taejŏn* in 1474.[120]

During the second half of the sixteenth century, as agnatic consciousness deepened, the attainment of knowledge about the correct enactment of rites became a central concern of the educated elite. Because, as one commentator remarked, neither the individual human being nor the state can afford to separate itself from the rites *(ye),* instruction and learning of ritual matters was a foremost task. It was easier to gain the necessary expertise in the capital—no doubt under the watchful eyes of the Department of Rites—than in the countryside. The difficulties with ritual matters, it was believed, lay not so much in the lack of emotional commitment as in the exact interpretation and execution of ritual texts.[121] These difficulties were eventually attenuated by a growing ritual literature.

The seventeenth century is often called "the century of ritual" because it witnessed an unprecedented preoccupation with "ritual learning" *(yehak)* and consequently a proliferation of ritual handbooks.[122] For all of them, the *Chu Tzu chia-li* remained the basic text. The study of this text undoubtedly received new impetus from the *Chia-li i-chieh* (Ceremonial Usages of the *Chia-li*), a work by the eminent Chu Hsi scholar of the Ming period, Ch'iu Chün (1420–1495). It was brought to Korea in 1518 by Kim An-guk (1478–1543) who praised it as being the "wings of Chu Hsi's *Chia-li,*" and recommended it for printing in Korea. The first Korean edition, however, apparently did not appear before 1626 when the work was printed under the supervision of Min Sŏng-hwi (1582–

1648), then governor of Chŏlla province.[123] During the first half of the seventeenth century, numerous profusely annotated and supplemented editions of the *Chia-li* were published. The most authoritative was the *Karye chimnam* (Collected Commentaries to the *Chia-li*)[124] by Kim Chang-saeng (1548–1631), who was generally recognized as the "brightest light" among the ritualists of his time. Collecting Chinese as well as Korean commentaries and opinions, Kim's work explores in minute detail the correct meaning of Chu Hsi's slim work.[125] The most widely used compact edition of the *Chia-li* came to be the early-eighteenth-century *Sarye pyŏllam* by Yi Chae. Besides these standard texts, there were a large number of popular renditions, for example Sin Sik's (1551–1623) *Karye ŏnhae* (Vernacular Edition of the *Chia-li*) published in 1632, and some written exclusively in the Korean script *(han'gŭl)*.

Although the blueprint for correct ritual behavior was Chinese— the ultimate touchstone for determining the purity of Korea's ritual life was the *I-li*[126]—the Korean ritualists were critically aware of the fact that there were genuinely Korean customs *(songnye)* which could not be ignored. Moreover, between Chinese prescriptions and their Korean adaptations there often existed considerable disparity that raised doubts in the performers' minds. Such uncertainties generated a number of works that in question-and-answer format provided indispensable guidelines. Widely used was Kim Chang-saeng's *Ŭirye munhae* (Questions and Answers on Doubtful Passages of the Rites). It highlights ritual concepts and actions that were not easily understood by the Koreans.[127] Equally influential works were Pak Se-ch'ae's (1631–1695) *Namgye yesŏl* (Namgye's Theories on Rites) and Yun Chŭng's (1629–1714) *Myŏngjae ŭirye mundap* (Questions and Answers on Rites by Myŏngjae [Yun Chŭng]). More specifically concerned with funerary rites was Sin Ŭi-gyŏng's (n.d.) *Sangnye piyo* (Essentials of Funerary Rites), which was prefaced by Kim Chang-saeng in 1620 and later supplemented several times.[128]

Despite this vast literature on Confucian rituals—a sure sign that "ritual matters" *(yesa)* were taken seriously—ritual behavior was never uniform, and a family might even pride itself on its own particular performance of ritual precepts. Confucian-style ancestor worship retained elitist traits; and, in accordance with the dictum of the *Li-chi* that "rituals do not go down to the commoners,"[129] the lower strata of society were not supposed to partake in a ritually pure life. Nevertheless, some formalistic features eventually filtered down into popular ritual, and commoners held simplified memorial services for their ancestors.

ANCESTRAL RITES: RELIGIOUS ASPECTS. Neo-Confucianism was established in Korea in a complex religious milieu. For centuries Buddhism and shamanism determined the beliefs and ritual behavior of the population. The cult of the dead, especially, was deeply molded by what the Confucians disdainfully termed "immoral rituals" (*ŭmsa*). People kept spirit shrines called "protection" (*wiho*) in their houses. Even members of the official class entrusted the care of their ancestral spirits to shamans (*mugyŏk*) and, under threat that the ancestors would otherwise punish their descendants with illness, paid up to four or five slaves for such services. Women in particular were devoted customers of shamans. Some families called in Buddhist monks to perform rites on death anniversaries, and a Buddhist altar was often the religious center of the house. It is clear that one reason the Confucians pushed so vigorously for building Confucian-style shrines was their determination to stamp out these beliefs, which they found contemptible, and to lead the upper class to a ritually pure life. Frequent reports by frustrated officials testify that the Confucian concepts were not readily accepted as satisfying alternatives to spirit worship.[130]

Confucian-style ancestor ritual was praised as the most filial act a son could perform for his parents. The textual basis of this proposition was a passage in the *Li-chi* that described the care of the dead parents as an extension of the son's serving them during their lives.[131] This was proof, as a censor remarked, that the departed parents could not really be regarded as dead—a remark with which he rejected the Buddhists' belief that the dead would disappear into the air.[132] For Confucians, the ancestor ritual was a medium through which the living could express filial piety by requiting the ancestors' favors (*pobon*) and keeping their memories alive (*ch'uwŏn*). This paraphrase from the *Lun-yü*[133] was often used to strengthen the Confucians' plea for prompt punishment of negligent sons. Indeed, the failure to perform ancestral rites was taken as evidence of insufficient filial piety and was punishable by law. Moreover, a son's show of extreme disrespect toward his living elders disqualified him from conducting services for them after they died. Worse, it also excluded him from a place in the ancestral shrine, because an unfilial son "cannot eat sacrificial food with his father."[134]

Clearly, the one who was called upon to carry on the heaviest of all human duties, the ritual heir, had to be a thoroughly moral man, a filial son. Filial piety, however, was not the only criterion for being ritually acceptable. The officiant had to be a full-fledged member of the descent group, a primary son. A secondary son, for example, was found unfit to conduct ancestral services for his ancestor who had been a merit subject.[135] To please the ancestors, moral and social qualifications were required, but social standing may, at times, have been the more important of the two.

TOWARD IMPLEMENTING RITUAL PRIMOGENITURE. Before ritual primogeniture, the essential feature of the Confucian agnatic principle, was fully implemented in Korean society, social legislation passed through several stages—each stage marked by critical policy decisions. In retrospect this process, however slow and arduous, shows a remarkable inner logic and dynamism such as no dynastic founder could have presaged. The paradigm that kept this process on course for over two hundred years was provided by Chu Hsi's "Diagram of Superordinate and Subordinate Descent Lines." This diagram not only opened the vision of a perfect society to which each generation of legislators committed itself anew, it also suggested the most effective means by which it could be translated into action: ancestor worship. Combining sociopolitical and religious-moral aspects, ancestor worship was an ideal instrument for initiating and controlling social change along the lines of Chu Hsi's concepts. Primogeniture, then, came to be institutionalized through ritual practice in the ancestral hall.

A brief recapitulation of the major legislative events during roughly the first two centuries of the dynasty shows a discernible progression from a vague notion of agnation and unilineal descent to a clear definition of the eldest son's particular position toward his father and the agnatic ancestors. A decisive first step was the categorization of a man's offspring in terms of "primary" sons, that is, his direct lineal heirs *(chŏkcha)* borne by the major wife, and "secondary" sons *(ch'ŏpcha)* borne by minor wives. This elevated the former set of sons—initially *chŏkcha* did not specifically point to the eldest son—above the latter and created within the descent group a fundamental difference between the various sons as far as their chances for succession and inheritance were concerned. It also came to denote differential social status in society at large.

The *Kyŏngguk taejŏn* of 1471 went one step further. It introduced for the first time inequality into the group of direct lineal heirs by raising the firstborn son *(chŏkchangja)* above his younger brothers *(chungja)*. It was not unequivocal, however, about the methods of continuing a descent line and serving the ancestors when there was no direct lineal heir. It legislated two conflicting rules: one regulated the succession to an heirless man's line *(iphu)*, whereas the other regulated the succession to that man's ancestors *(pongsa)*. The coexistence of these two rules had the potential of splitting the descent line, a danger that derived from the fact that jural succession *(iphu)*, in a narrow perspective, addressed only the problem of filiation, that is, the link between father and son, whereas ritual succession *(pongsa)*, in a wider perspective, was fixed on descent.[136]

It took legal debate and social experimentation far more than a century to establish the practice of designating as heir that member of the junior generation who most closely embodied the qualifications of both son and descendant, that is the most senior lineal candidate as defined by Confucian theory. Coupled with this trend was the growing emphasis on the continuation of the main line at the cost of the collateral minor lines. While the main line had to be perpetuated indefinitely by a ritual heir *(chongja* or *sŭngjungja)*, the fate of the minor lines was of lesser importance for the survival of the descent group as a whole. These calculations, moreover, excluded secondary sons from any considerations of descent and succession. The eldest son was put in a privileged position as the principal heir of his father and the principal officiant at the rites for his ancestors.

The eldest son's elevated status was discussed in great detail in the ritual handbooks of the seventeenth century. The essence was summarized in the brief formula: "The agnatic principle is the rite by which the primus *(chang)* is established without fail"—even against any last will. [137] This meant that even in the event the eldest son was in poor health and unable to perform the ancestral rites, his ritual tasks could not be transferred to his next younger brother *(ch'aja)*. If the eldest son had only secondary sons, it became common to adopt an appropriate heir *(kyehuja)* rather than to have a secondary son succeed—a solution which, as some ritualists observed, tallied with customary law, but not necessarily with ancient ritual prescription *(korye)*. [138]

The first son, then, connected to his father and his paternal ancestors in a very special way: he alone possessed that "correct substance" *(chŏngch'e)* that made him the exclusive heir of his antecedents and, in the name of posterity, the recipient of his father's rights and duties. [139] Representing the sibling group, the eldest son alone came to be recognized as the ideal link in the continuum of generations; and this determined his jural, ritual, and economic preeminence. His full emergence in the seventeenth century signifies the climax of agnatic thinking along the lines of Chu Hsi's conception of an ideal society.

FOUR

Mourning and Funerary Rites

Death sets in motion an elaborate ritual response in any society. Mourning rituals bid farewell to the dead and at the same time restructure the social constellation that was disrupted by death. The mortuary process is a rite of passage which, more powerfully than any other social ritual, activates certain feelings and behavior among kin. It is a sequence of social action that is cast in ritual terms, and its effect goes far beyond the actual fact of death. This social meaning has been variously expressed in China's ancient literature. The *Li-chi* states, "Funeral and sacrificial rites serve to inculcate benevolence and love. . . . [W]hen the mourning and sacrificial rites are clearly understood, the people are filial."[1] Confucius' disciple, Tseng Tzu, pointed a similar direction: "When proper respect towards the dead is shown at the End and continued after they are far away, the moral force *(te)* of a people has reached its highest point."[2] Both these texts emphasize the significance that the proper observance of rites for the dead has for the cultivation of moral stature in the living.

The ideal representation of the complex interaction of individual sentiments with the social environment is given in the system of the five mourning grades (Chin. *wu-fu;* Kor. *obok*).[3] Described in great detail in the *Erh-ya,*[4] the *Li-chi,* and the *I-li,* the system is best pictured as a chart with a given (male) individual at its center whose mourning obligations to certain categories of agnatic kin are graded on the basis of "social nearness or remoteness" according to five degrees of mourning. The mourning periods vary in length from three years (for the parents) to three months, and the material of the mourning garments ranges from coarse unhemmed cloth to fine hemp cloth. The circle of relatives for whom mourning dress was worn terminated at the fourth ascending and descending generations and at the fourth collateral line (i.e., third cousins). The system put heavy emphasis on agnatic kin and assigned non-agnatic relatives, the mother's kin and the wife's kin, peripheral positions.[5]

As a constructed schema, the mourning chart was not so much a depiction of the degrees of human attachment and feeling, as the Confucians claimed, as it was a paradigm of normative kin behavior that influenced, beyond mourning, almost every realm of social life.

PRELUDE TO REVISED MOURNING. In the course of the fourteenth century, the Korean intellectual atmosphere gradually changed. Some Confucians, the spiritual forerunners of the Neo-Confucian social transformation, demanded with increasing insistence that Buddhist mortuary procedures be replaced by the Confucian-style ritual program. The huge expenses lavished on superstitious practices as well as on the building of temples and pagodas, and the corrupting influence of the Buddhist clergy were held responsible for the precarious situation in state and society during the last decades of Koryŏ. "Who has ever seen any effect come forth from such expensive efforts?" asked an irreverent member of the Confucian Academy (Sŏnggyun'gwan), Kim Ch'o (n.d.), who even dared accuse the king of neglecting to take decisive measures against these abuses. Kim paid for his audacity with exile.[6] An equally forceful plea for substituting Confucianism for Buddhism came from Pak Ch'o (1367–1454) who, in 1391, demanded that King Kongyang espouse the Confucian cause.[7] The king's angry reaction—he wanted to punish Pak with death[8]—epitomizes the precarious position of the Confucians vis-à-vis a powerful and influential Buddhist establishment. Some Confucians therefore took a more prudent course of action: they propagated the establishment of domestic shrines *(kamyo)*. They intended to counter Buddhism with institutional innovations that would eventually shift the cult of the dead from the Buddhist temple to the Confucian shrine.

A further institutional change demanded at the end of Koryŏ was the extension of the mourning period from one hundred days to three years. The reason for the decay of the mourning system, as Yi Saek saw it, lay in the legal regulation that an official be called back to duty after one hundred days of mourning *(kibok)*. Although leave was subsequently provided to fulfill the periodic mourning obligations, the taking-off of the mourning dress really signified the end of mourning. This behavior was imitated, Yi regretted, by the rest of the people who no longer realized that this was a perversion of the original system.[9] Yi therefore requested in 1357 the formal enactment of a three-year mourning period, and this request was granted.[10]

The enforcement of the three-year mourning period during the stormy reign of King Kongmin was, however, less a ritual than a political and military issue. Its compulsory observation was a welcome method of keeping a political adversary out of office for a conveniently long time.[11] In 1359, the military situation necessitated that the order of 1357 be revoked for military personnel. Although in the summer of 1360 the officialdom was again instructed to adhere to three years of mourning, a few months later a counterorder was given because of a military emergency. This retraction was apparently facilitated by the realization that the old mourning customs were still prevalent, and three years were observed by only a few retired officials. The proclamation in 1391 of a new mourning system that would "follow completely" the mourning regulations of the Ming code opened a new chapter in Korea's ritual history.[12]

THE TRANSFORMATION OF THE MOURNING GRADES. The Neo-Confucian legislators of the early Chosŏn dynasty were well aware of their inability to reform quickly the mourning customs of Koryŏ which, they found, differed so significantly from the ritual prescriptions contained in the Chinese classical literature. They also realized that such reform had to start with trivialities, for instance with determining the quality of cloth for mourning garments; for a small error at the beginning could grow into a major abuse in the end.[13] Wrong practices and odd habits, Chŏng To-jŏn observed, could pervert a son's feelings toward his parents, even though such feelings were basically the same at all times. Legislation had to stop improper behavior and provide people with a correct model to guide their feelings.[14] Like no other rite, mourning was an intimate expression of human feelings—feelings that had to be channelled and activated by appropriate ritual prescriptions in order to give meaning to Confucius' often quoted exhortation: "While they [the parents] are alive, serve them according to ritual. When they die, bury them according to ritual."[15]

The first Confucian-style ritual handbook to equip the *sadaebu* mourner with basic information on mourning and burial was the *Chia-li*. This manual became the chief source of inspiration when Cho Chun drafted a ritual program of mourning and burial (*sangjang chi ye*) for his *Kyŏngje yukchŏn* of 1397. A mourning chart (*obok tosik*) was added. Cho did not break radically with Koryŏ tradition and preserved certain peculiarities of the former dynasty. Thus, his code differed in significant points from the *Chia-li,* a circumstance that gave rise to considerable confusion and demands for its revision. Only the promulgation of the *Kyŏngguk taejŏn* of 1471 created a reliable and authoritative basis for the mourning rites of the Chosŏn dynasty.[16]

The mourning chart, centered on the individual, could not become a major instrument for restructuring Koryŏ society into a Confucian-style society. For this purpose, the creation of ancestor-oriented worshipping groups was more suited. Nevertheless, the revision of the mourning chart was an important subsidiary measure for shifting "human feelings" into proper, that is, patrilineal channels (see Table and Diagram 9).[17]

The dynasty's early legislators repeatedly affirmed their commitment to the universality of a three-year mourning period for both parents. This was a "perfect system" devised on the basis of human feeling by the sages of antiquity and therefore binding for the *sadaebu*.[18] The message of the sages, however, was not unequivocal.

Table of Mourning Grades as Defined by Duration and Mourning Garment

Grade	Duration	Mourning garment	Person(s) mourned by a male mourner (selection)*
1a ch'amch'oe samnyŏn	3 years (effectively 27 months)**	Staff; coarse unhemmed sackcloth	Father
2a chaech'oe samnyŏn	3 years (effectively 27 months)	Staff; coarse hemmed sackcloth	Mother, if father deceased
2b chaech'oe changgi	1 year	Staff; somewhat finer, hemmed sackcloth	Mother, if father still alive; wife
2c chaech'oe kinyŏn	1 year	No staff; somewhat finer, hemmed sackcloth	Brother; unmarried sister; grandparents
2d chaech'oe sogong	5 months	Same as 2c	Great-grandparents
2e chaech'oe sima	3 months	Same as 2c	Great-great grandparents
3 taegong	9 months (effectively 8 full months)	Coarse cloth	Patrilateral first cousins
4 sogong	5 months (effectively 4 full months)	Fine cloth	Patrilateral second cousins; maternal grandparents
5 sima	3 months (effectively 2 full months)	Fine hemp	Patrilateral third cousins; wife's parents

Source: Chu Tzu chia-li.

Notes: *For a complete list of patrilateral, matrilateral, and affinal kin mourned, see the detailed charts in any edition of the Chia-li.

**There was no consensus about how long "three years" of mourning really was. Some ritualists argued for 25 months, whereas others insisted on 27 months. The calculation hinged on whether intercalary months were taken into consideration. The Chosŏn Koreans took 27 months as standard. See Kim Tu-hŏn, Han'guk kajok chedo yŏn'gu, pp. 566–567.

Diagram 9. The Transformation of the Mourning Grades in Early Chosŏn

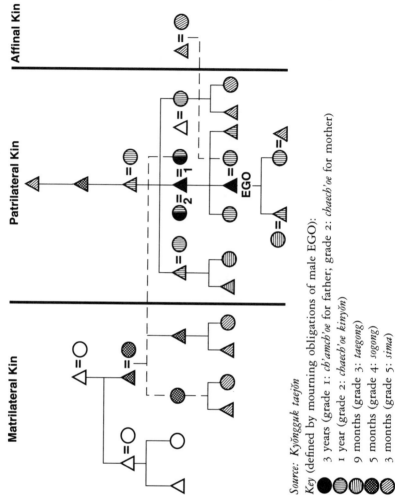

Source: Kyŏngguk taejŏn

Key (defined by mourning obligations of male EGO):

3 years (grade 1: *ch'amch'oe* for father; grade 2: *chaech'oe* for mother)
1 year (grade 2: *chaech'oe kimyŏn*)
9 months (grade 3: *taegong*)
5 months (grade 4: *sogong*)
3 months (grade 5: *sima*)

●◉◍◍◍

The basic argument in favor of a three-year mourning period derived from a saying by Confucius contained in the *Lun-yü:* "Only when a child is three years old does it leave its parents' arms. The three years' mourning is the universal mourning everywhere under Heaven."[19] This uniform rule, however, was, according to the *I-li,* applicable to the mother only when she died after the father. If she died before him, the *I-li* merely prescribed one year of mourning in hemmed sackcloth with staff *(chaech'oe changgi)* as "a sign of [her] inferiority." The commentary explained, "While the most honourable person in the marriage relationship is still alive, the son does not dare to exhibit to the full the respect he feels privately for his mother."[20] The *Li-chi* supported this view with the statement that "in the sky there are not two suns, nor in a land two kings, nor in a state two rulers, nor in a family two equally honourable."[21] These two texts, then, ruled that the mother, when she died before the father, could not enjoy her son's full ritual attention. It is clear that later in China this ancient precept was ignored. Chu Hsi as well as the Ming code stipulated an undifferentiated mourning period of three years for both parents.[22]

At first the Koreans unhesitatingly adopted the three-year rule. After all, this had also been, at least on paper, the rule in Koryŏ. And it reaffirmed the law of 1391 that had intended, on the authority of Ming law, to reform the short mourning period of one hundred days that was customary during Koryŏ. In his *Kyŏngje yuk-chŏn,* Cho Chun had followed Chu Hsi. The principle that reduced mourning for the mother while the father was still alive, as espoused in the *I-li,* apparently was first discovered when Sejong's mother died in 1420. Sejong's father, T'aejong, known for his predilection for "ancient institutions," was the first Yi king to pay close attention to royal ritual. He made his son, on the throne since 1418, mourn for only one year—an order Sejong reportedly obeyed with apprehension. This act was seized by the Department of Rites as precedent for making the prescription of the *I-li* a general rule for the *sadaebu.* Because this was an expression of reverence toward the father, but not a sign of contempt for the mother, the ministers insisted, three years of "mourning in heart" *(simsang)* had to follow formal mourning.[23]

The subsequent practice of this rule, supported by Sejong as T'aejong's unalterable legacy, proved difficult because of the conflict between its moral and political implications. Thoughtless officials, the censorial agencies pointed out, did not grasp the meaning of "mourning in heart" and, after taking off their formal mourning, led an unrestrained life reminiscent of Koryŏ times. Moreover, such unfilial behavior was even encouraged by orders to return to active duty. This amounted to slighting the mother and depreciating "mourning in heart." And why should the *I-li* be taken as more authoritative than the *Chia-li?* Sejong withstood the pressure to restore the three-year mourning period, and the "law of antiquity" was eventually enacted in the *Kyŏngguk taejŏn,* though with the express stipulation that an official was suspended from duty during "mourning in heart." This was taken over by later ritual manuals.[24]

Sejong's firm stand in this question must be understood within the framework of the ongoing debate about the social position of women. Mourning grades were yet another means for assigning a woman a distinctly lower rank in the new social order. An "elder" in her own rights during Koryŏ, a woman had to yield this honor to her husband in the early Chosŏn period. Because mourning most naturally engaged the younger generation, it was the son who had to adjust his mourning behavior as a consequence of his mother's lowered prestige. While his father was still alive, he could not reciprocate the affection he had received from his mother. This may also have facilitated his father's remarriage. This solution was peculiarly Korean; it had no counterpart in contemporary Ming China.

Closely related to the length of a son's mourning for his real mother were his ritual obligations toward his father's second wife, his stepmother *(kyemo).* The assignment of a three-year mourning period *(chaech'oe samnyŏn)* to the ritual stepson *(pongsa ŭija),* first laid down in the *Kyŏngje yukchŏn,* was justified with the argument that the father's second wife could not be treated less generously than his first wife. Therefore a *kyemo* had to be mourned like a real mother. This amazing upgrading of the stepmother's mourning grade was one of the most conspicuous changes on the mourning chart of the early Chosŏn dynasty. To be sure, this special recognition, it will be recalled, did not result from more esteem for the second wife, but from the necessity to rank her offspring as junior to that by the first primary wife.[25]

Like the *kyemo,* the foster mother *(yangmo)* who brought up an adopted child was regarded as a "real" mother and thus had to be mourned for three full years. Equal mourning was to be observed for the foster father *(yangbu)* as well.[26] Besides *kyemo* and *yangmo,* it was also important to assign mourning grades to mothers who lost their place in their husband's family: the remarried mother *(kamo)* and the expelled mother *(ch'ulmo).* In Koryŏ, when remarriage was not uncommon, the *kamo* was mourned for an exceptional one hundred days; but since the expulsion of a wife was a social impossibility, there was no mourning grade for *ch'ulmo.* In early Chosŏn, however, both types of mothers had to be brought into the Confucian scheme that treated women only in relation to men. *Kamo* as well as *ch'ulmo* had broken the conjugal bond and therefore were mourned for only a year with staff *(chaech'oe changgi)* with three years of "mourning in heart."[27] A primary wife, thus, was given full ritual recognition only if her life ended in her husband's house.

Different mourning grades were a convenient measure to distinguish between primary and secondary wives—a distinction that was first enacted by law in 1413. A secondary wife was mourned only if she was able to mark her presence by having a son. As *sŏmo,* she was at first mourned for one year with staff, a period which was considerably shortened later in the dynasty. Had she served as a wet nurse *(yumo),* mourning for her lasted three months *(sima).*[28] Mourning grades became, thus, a sure indicator of a woman's social status.

As never before, explicit mourning obligations toward the husband's family tied primary as well as secondary wives to their in-laws. The category of mourning for the husband's kin *(pujok)* was not mentioned in Koryŏ; it appears for the first time in the *Kyŏngguk taejŏn.*[29] As primary wife, a woman mourned her husband's parents for the same length of time as he did, whereas the mourning periods for the husband's other relatives were usually one degree shorter. A secondary wife was burdened with ritual duties toward her master, the master's primary wife, and the master's immediate lineal descendants. The married woman's absorption into her husband's family was accentuated by the fact that her mourning obligations toward her natal family were drastically lowered. She mourned her own parents for only one year.[30] Compared to Koryŏ tradition, then, it is clear that a woman's position as wife and mother was adjusted to the patrilineal principle by means of altered mourning grades.

It was also with the intention to rectify "unnatural" family relationships that the early Chosŏn legislators took a critical look at the mourning grades of maternal kin. This was an especially sensitive area that had been left untouched in 1391. At the beginning of the Chosŏn dynasty, the conflict between indigenous mourning customs and the prescriptions laid down in China's classical literature was acutely felt, and consequently drastic changes were avoided. The mourning grades for the maternal grandparents therefore were initially lowered only by one degree to nine months (*taegong*).[31] Sentiments nurtured by local irregularities, for example the customary uxorilocal residence pattern, could, however, no longer be tolerated and at last had to be sacrificed to "proper rites" (*chŏngnye*). In accordance with the *I-li* and *Chia-li*, mourning for the maternal grandparents was finally reduced to five months (*sogong*) in the *Kyŏngguk taejŏn*.[32] This depreciation of the maternal grandparents naturally affected other maternal kin. The mourning grades of the mother's brothers and sisters were cut by one degree to five months (*sogong*).[33] Matrilateral first cousins were particularly scrutinized. It was noticed that the *Kyŏngje yukchŏn* did not list a mourning grade for female cousins.[34] The Ming code also was silent on this point. This omission, it was feared, might facilitate intermarriage with such close kin. The Department of Rites, therefore, demanded an explicit three months (*sima*) as long as such cousins were unmarried—an effective law to exclude them from among eligible marriage partners.[35]

The Korean tradition of uxorilocal marriage had also determined the quality of mourning for the wife's parents. The son-in-law's sonlike relationship to his in-laws had required a higher degree of

mourning than prescribed in the ritual literature. The disparity between custom and etiquette was disquieting, and the debates at
court centered on the problem of whether the reform of customary
marriage practices would lead to proper mourning rites or whether
the enforcement of correct mourning grades would eventually transform deviant marriage traditions. In view of entrenched marriage
realities, compliance with right ritual norms was given priority.
The *Kyŏngje yukchŏn* apparently still followed Koryŏ usage as far as
the son-in-law's responsibilities were concerned (one year), but lowered the parents-in-law's mourning for him to three months. This
imbalance was partially corrected in 1411 by adjusting the mourning for the wife's parents to five months, but a royal decree of 1430
finally settled for the ritually proper three months.[36]

The mourning system, although principally focused on the ascending generations, also fixed mourning obligations toward the
younger generations. It is remarkable that the *Kyŏngguk taejŏn* here
did not differentiate between a major lineal heir, that is, the eldest
son, and junior sons and, by extension, nephews. For all, it prescribed mourning of one year *(kinyŏn)*. This issue, so central for
building a clear scheme of descent lines, does not seem even to have
been discussed. A possible explanation for the silence on this point
was the agreement of the *Kyŏngguk taejŏn* with the Ming code. More
important, however, may have been the fact that a man's sons were
not yet strictly categorized, although age and sequence of birth
must nevertheless have been crucial criteria. All sons, therefore,
would still be regarded as their father's potential heirs, a fact that
equal mourning grades for them underlined. Only one son could
eventually continue the line, however, and he was identified by the
mourning period of one year granted to his wife *(changjach'ŏ)*. The
wives of all other sons and nephews were mourned for only nine
months. In the generation of the grandsons, the heir *(chŏkson)* was
clearly designated. He was favored with a one-year mourning period, whereas the other grandsons got nine months.[37] Secondary
sons were, according to the *Kyŏngguk taejŏn*, mourned for only one
year by their respective mothers.[38]

The undifferentiated mourning grade of one year for all sons, codified in the *Kyŏngguk taejŏn,* was backed by the Ming code, but deviated from the *I-li* as well as from the *Chia-li,*[39] both of which prescribed the highest possible mourning of three years *(ch'amch'oe samnyŏn)* for the direct lineal heir, that is, the eldest son. At first apparently deliberately overlooked, this prescription gained relevance when, in the course of the seventeenth century, the position of the eldest son was raised above that of his younger brothers. The ritual handbooks were unanimous in their advocacy of a three-year mourning period and explained their position by arguing the first son's exceptional status vis-à-vis his father and his father's ancestors. This status was inalienable, and therefore the honor of three years of mourning could not be transferred to a possible substitute.[40] The first son's conspicuous ritual elevation was not reflected in the law-books—they remained unchanged; it derived solely from the prestige of the ritual handbooks that came to guide correct ritual behavior in seventeenth-century Korea.

In sum, then, at the beginning of the Chosŏn dynasty the mourning system underwent a major revision on the basis of the classical model contained in the *I-li* and *Li-chi.* This revision, motivated by the reformatory spirit of the Neo-Confucian legislators, was part of their overall endeavor to build a new social order. The system, perverted during Koryŏ, demanded rectification, and at the same time the rectification itself was expected to help create a new societal environment in which the old customs would become obsolete. By reconsidering the social weight of each mourning grade, conflicting family loyalties were disentangled, and close *(ch'in)* and distant *(so)* relatives were newly defined. The clearing away of Koryŏ irregularities, in particular the diminution of mourning for maternal kin, enabled the reemergence of the patrilineal structure inherent in the original *obok* system. Even though this clear shift to the patriliny ran counter to Korean sensitivities, it was fully justified, the Chosŏn legislators thought, by its corrective promise.[41]

The revised mourning chart of the Chosŏn dynasty not only restored to the mourning system its original patrilineal character, it also expanded the horizontal span to patrilateral third cousins. This meant placing on the chart immediate ascendants who in Koryŏ did not have clear mourning grades.[42] The most intimate category of kin for whom mourning was worn in the Chosŏn dynasty came to be known as *tangnae*. Among this group, mourning obligations were reciprocal *(pobok)*. The social distance between the one to be mourned and his mourner was, with a few exceptions—most notably the father-son relationship—expressed by the same mourning grades. Such reciprocal responsibilities made the tying of marital bonds impossible; the *tangnae* group was exogamous. Outside the boundary of *tangnae* kin remoter kinsmen, "fringe" relatives of the patriliny *(tanmun)*—they shared the grandfather of the fifth generation *(osejo)*—were recognized. Although not required to observe formal mourning, they marked the death of a kinsman with special attire.[43] In short, the *tangnae* kin group was built upon a well-balanced foundation of mourning obligations that was to become a mainstay of the agnatic principle.

RITUAL ASPECTS. Only a few years after the establishment of the new dynasty, the "Rites of Mourning and Burial" *(sangjang chi ye)* were laid down in the *Kyŏngje yukchŏn*. Although a sure sign of the young dynasty's changed ritual course, they must have been rather sketchy (and today are no longer known). It was under the vigilant and strong guidance of T'aejong and Sejong that the country's ceremonial life was gradually reformed along the guidelines contained in the *Li-chi* and the *Chia-li*. Revered by the Confucian legislators as the most complete textbooks of Confucian etiquette, these two works provided them with prescriptions for social change and the most effective arguments against the Buddhist tradition, especially in the area of mourning.[44]

The philosophy underlying the mourning behavior as demanded by the Confucians was succinctly expressed in the often quoted dictum of the Master: "While they [the parents] are alive, serve them according to ritual. When they die, bury them according to ritual and sacrifice to them according to ritual."[45] The son's devotion was thought to derive from the parents' function as "Heaven and Earth": through interaction they produce their offspring with always constant disposition; in return the children serve them with ritual acts

that equally demand constancy.[46] The parental grace *(ŭn)* of giving
life to and raising the children had to be counterpoised by filial
affection *(ŭi)* that found its highest expression in proper mourning.
This reciprocity also had a temporal aspect in the three-year mourning period that Confucius claimed was universal.[47]

Mourning entailed special behavior that accentuated the mourner's isolation from normal life. Death meant pollution, and mourning belonged therefore to the unlucky affairs *(hyung)* that had to be
kept apart from auspicious matters *(kil)*. The distance between these
two different spheres of life was conveyed by various rules observed
during mourning. The mourner dressed himself in coarse, colorless
mourning clothes—the coarseness of the material indicated the degree of mourning—and abstained from meat, alcohol, and spices.
He no longer visited the women's quarters and instead built himself
a lonely shed at the graveside *(yŏmyo)*. Loud and gay entertainments,
riding horseback, and sexual adventures were censured as grave offenses. During the mourning period weddings could not be conducted or examinations taken. The attempt to avoid the hardship
and privation of mourning by concealing a parent's death amounted
to a severe crime.[48]

The rules of mourning were exacting; and throughout the first
century of the new dynasty, numerous reports by the censorial agencies and the Department of Rites complained about their violation.
The most common offense was getting married while mourning for
a parent. This was a willful act—often apparently facilitated by the
bridegroom's taking up residence in the bride's house—that went
against filiality and the law. It was therefore heavily punished.[49]
Adultery was an equally intolerable misdeed that, if discovered, was
punished without mercy. A man who lost his wife was legally bound
to refrain from remarrying within three years.[50] Because the mourning periods for parents were so long, many a mourner was tempted
to take off his mourning clothes before the time was up. This temp-
tation was particularly strong during "mourning in heart" *(simsang)*
when the mourning son had to straddle the dark and light sides of
life. On the other hand, mourning was at times motivated by the

prospect of material gain so that mourning, for example, for a wealthy adoptive mother seemed a light burden.[51]

Deviant behavior stood in stark contrast to examples of sons, daughters, and wives who punctiliously carried out their mourning obligations and therefore were rewarded by the government. A son like that of Mun Ik-chŏm (1329–1398)[52] who observed full graveside mourning for both his parents was recommended for government employment. A son who became sick and emaciated by strict mourning, but who refused to eat meat and to drink wine to restore his health, was rewarded with a commemorative arch. There were special citations of young widows who, inspired by loyalty for their dead husbands, resisted attempts by relatives to remarry them and dutifully served their parents-in-law after their death as well as during their lifetime. Such exemplary cases were interpreted as hopeful signs of a gradually reforming ritual scene.[53]

Early Chosŏn times, however, were still permeated by Koryŏ traditions, and women, especially, kept to earlier customs and ignored ritual innovations. While the officials were under pressure to conform to the new laws and to observe mourning for three years, their wives maintained tradition and took off mourning after one hundred days. Such a discrepancy between male and female mourning behavior was equally evident in dress style. Upper-class women abhorred the coarse material of mourning clothes and, in late Koryŏ, used it only in their headgear. Even this token was occasionally replaced by fine fabrics. In 1403, Confucian purists demanded that the women be subjected to the new ritual program and be clad in the proper attire for three years.[54]

Even for men, the observance of the complete mourning period was difficult. Although all officials, regardless of rank and actual office-holding, were urged to adhere to the "common mourning of the world," those without office apparently did not regard it as mandatory and continued Koryŏ mourning customs. On the other hand, the state depended on the expertise and skills of its officials and therefore at times had to "deprive them of their feelings" and recall them to duty (*t'alchŏng kibok*). This was an emergency measure that lacked a textual basis in the classics and amounted to a dangerous mixture of the lucky and unlucky elements of life. This conflict between office-holding and mourning was particularly acute when a son "mourned in heart" for his mother while his father was alive. The mourner in heart, although subject to the same rules of dietary and sexual abstention as an ordinary mourner, had to divide his attention and loyalties between his ritual and profane obligations; and it was not unusual that the recall to office was taken as a welcome pretext to end mourning. Neglect of proper mourning, however, was also a state concern: an unfilial son was thought not to make a loyal official. The mourning behavior of the officialdom was not an entirely private matter.

Recall to office was legalized in the *Kyŏngje yukchŏn* and later incorporated in the *Kyŏngguk taejŏn*.[55] Presumably because of strong opposition by the censorial organs and the Department of Rites to unwarranted abbreviations of the three-year mourning period, the reappointment of a mourner became subject to royal approval. Even after resuming his duties, such an official was under certain restrictions. He was not allowed to attend royal audiences, and at home he had to change into mourning dress. For three years he was barred from all festivities and could not get married. Offenders who ended mourning too hastily in order to secure office had to expect punishment, but those who were recalled by royal command because of indispensable abilities often pleaded in vain to complete their filial obligations. An official, then, who was negligent in mourning not only severed himself from his parents' benevolence, but also exposed himself to the state's doubt concerning his qualities as a loyal servant. This intricate connection between the private and public spheres remained a hallmark of the Chosŏn dynasty.[56]

Even though the observance of three years of mourning for the parents was considered a common requirement for all members of the upper class, those without rank and office *(sŏin)* and military personnel *(kun'gwan)* were exempted from this rule from the beginning of the dynasty. Soldiers *(kunsa)* and guardsmen *(kapsa)*, in particular, were compelled to mourn their parents for only one hundred days because of the importance of their duties. This differential treatment was felt to violate basic human values and was often disputed. The *Sok yukchŏn* therefore added the stipulation that military personnel were allowed, upon request, to mourn for the full three years. Although this modification was for some critics insufficient to mollify the practical exclusion of some categories of people from the general ritual life, it was repeated in the *Kyŏngguk taejŏn*.[57]

The law did not mention slaves. In 1431, the minister of rites suggested that even private slaves and public slaves attached to government offices should be legally entitled to observe three years of mourning, if they wished, even though they would not be expected to keep vigil near the grave. Such ritual enthusiasm could not, however, be translated into generally acceptable terms and thus was not echoed in the law books.[58] One hundred days of mourning were prescribed only for the local functionaries *(hyangni)* who considered this rule discriminatory. Deep-seated antagonism against them seems to have dictated it. If they were allowed the full mourning period, the Department of Rites argued, they would either idle away their time or commit subversive acts. Those who indeed wanted to observe mourning for three years would have to be closely watched as to motive and behavior, the department demanded.[59]

While the option for a three-year mourning period had been meant as an encouragement for everyone to lead as full a ritual life as possible, at the beginning of the sixteenth century it was clear that few were striving for ritual purity and that even short mourning of one hundred days was often not observed. A broad debate on the problem in 1516 revealed that King Chungjong as well as his advisers were in principle in favor of permitting everyone, regardless of social status, to mourn for three years.[60] Yet, the danger that commoners *(sŏmin)* would abuse mourning as a pretext to avoid corvée labor, some officials opined, was real. Regretting the inconsistency of mourning between *sadaebu* and commoners, the king proposed the formulation of a new law that would guarantee full mourning to all commoners. The royal proposal, advanced with genuine commitment, was blocked by the counterargument that the *Kyŏngguk taejŏn* provided enough legal support for all sincere mourners, commoners included, to fulfill their filial duties.[61]

The three-year mourning period was acknowledged in principle as common ritual property belonging to all segments of society because filial piety, the emotional basis of mourning, pertained to each individual regardless of social status. Were filial devotion and concomitant mourning obligations, however, operable across social boundaries? This question was raised toward the end of the fifteenth century when the concept of adoption was scrutinized in the light of mourning. The *Kyŏngguk taejŏn* defined an adoptee as a child who was taken in before age three and brought up *(suyang)* by adoptive parents; such an adopted child incurred the same mourning debts as a natural child. But what if the adoptive parents were socially inferior *(ch'ŏn)?* The first version of the *Kyŏngguk taejŏn* of 1471 had obviously not taken into account this undoubtedly rather rare instance. The high officials who were ordered by the king to discuss the issue early in 1481 nearly unanimously agreed upon two points: adoption involved parental grace *(ŭn)* regardless of the adoptive parents' high or low social status *(kwich'ŏn);* despite this fact a *sadaebu* could not possibly humble himself by mourning for socially inferior adoptive parents. Even if mourning seemed warranted because, in addition to the human factor, property was involved, such behavior would lead to a dangerous mix-up of superior and inferior *(chonbi)* and upset social distinction. A royal edict confirmed this by stating that henceforth no *sadaebu* would mourn for someone socially inferior, and the request of the Department of Rites that *sadaebu* should no longer call their inferiors "adoptive parents" was granted. This resolute point of view was somewhat softened a month later when the king ordered a reconsideration of the subject. In case mourning for a socially inferior person was inevitable, the officials decided, it should last for not more than three months. This decision was added to the final version of the *Kyŏngguk taejŏn* of 1485.[62] Mourning, then, was in the Korean context bound to the hierarchical structure of society. "Noble" *(kwi)* could not bow to "base" *(ch'ŏn),* even though "human feelings" were thought to transcend social barriers. Mourning, too, had to be adjusted to Korea's overriding ordering principle—social distinction.

FUNERARY RITUALS AND GEOMANCY. Despite the legislative efforts of the early Chosŏn Confucians, Buddhism and shamanism continued to have a strong hold on the popular beliefs surrounding death and burial. There was a basic conflict between the Buddhist and Confucian concepts of the afterworld. The Buddhists cremated their dead in the hope that, released from their physical existence, they would reach paradise without delay. In contrast, the Confucians, paraphrasing a passage of the *Li-chi,* interpreted the term "to bury" *(chang)* as meaning "to preserve" *(chang).*[63] While the ashes of the Buddhist were scattered and became "the feed of fish and birds," the Confucian was buried in order to preserve his mind-matter *(ki)* that was thought to circulate between the living and the dead. If the ancestors found peace *(an)* in the ground, their descendants would find peace in the world. This interdependence was likened to a tree: if the tree's roots are burned, its branches and leaves wither away; they have no chance to prosper and to grow. Therefore the sages, it was argued, designed heavy inner and outer coffins for fear the corpse might rot too fast and dressed it in thick shrouds. But because they were still concerned that this might be inadequate, they put cereal in the coffin so that invading vermin would eat it instead of the body.[64]

For the Confucians, the importance of burial lay in preserving the link between the dead and the living: a properly prepared grave was the security for the well-being of both. This vital connection was elaborated upon by Yi Saek: "The grave is where the sentient spirit *(paek)* is preserved; the spiritual part of man *(hon)* is supported by the house. Therefore the sacrifice of repose *(uje)* is performed three times [in the house] to put it to rest. If the domestic shrine *(kamyo)* becomes dilapidated, the spirit wanders around, has nowhere to go and does not attach itself to the descendants."[65]

The Confucian care for the dead at the grave as well as in the ancestral hall was believed to emanate spontaneously from the most natural of all human feelings, filial piety. For the Confucians, it was an intolerable breach of filiality that Buddhists reported their dead parents as sinners to Buddha and the Ten Kings of the underworld and prayed for their rescue from punishment. Could such an act of grace be brought about by a single bowl of food? As absurd as such an expectation was, ignorant people—*sadaebu* and commoners alike—fearing punishment and hoping for redemption, squandered their property on the ceremonial seeing-off of the dead and praying for his happiness *(ch'uch'ŏn).*[66] Such lavishness early on became the target of the Confucian legislators. In 1413, a new law limited the mourners who were allowed to accompany a dead parent to the Buddhist temple to the relatives within the mourning circle. It also restricted the food offerings along the way.[67] This was undoubtedly a temporary compromise with the existing customs; for only a few years later, during the 1420s, the tone of the Confucian critics became shrill. The Buddhists' "misleading theories" *(sasŏl),* so perniciously effective at times of bereavement, presented the greatest threat to the Confucian Way *(sado)* and therefore, the Confucians demanded, the *Chia-li* should replace all Buddhist ceremonies and become the exclusive manual for the funerary and ancestral rites *(sangje chi ŭi).*[68]

In the Confucian view, the grave formed an essential connection between the bright world of the living *(myŏng)* and the dark world of the dead *(yu),* and its selection and construction were matters of the greatest importance in the funerary arrangements. It was a difficult task to reform existing customs and to establish legal norms that would eventually embody in the people's mind the Confucian notions of dealing with the dead. A first step in this direction was the prohibition of Buddhist-style cremation in 1395. Equally abominable was the abandonment of corpses in city streets and open fields. In 1410, a special Burial Office (Maech'iwŏn) was erected in the capital with the order to trace and punish offenders and to clean up the streets.[69] At the same time the censors demanded the enactment of regulations that would guide the funerals of *sadaebu (sadaebu changbun chi che)* and check their conspicuous spending.[70]

A special problem was fixing the time limit within which the dead had to be buried. Traditionally, this varied from three days to several years. Great delays were caused by taboo considerations: the year, the month, or the day of a son's or grandson's birthday were avoided as burial dates; and if the progeny was large, the selection of a suitable date was difficult. Meanwhile, the deceased was "buried provisionally" *(kajang)*, usually laid out in an open field. In a discussion of 1417, such aberrations were regretted; and the Office of Astronomy and Geomancy (Sŏun'gwan) was ordered to burn the "strange" books on *yin* and *yang* and prophecy that were the source of such unfortunate behavior. Only a few select handbooks of geomancy were henceforth to be consulted for determining a burial date. The officials above rank four were granted, on the classical model, three months, the officials below rank five one month to bury their dead.[71]

As in Koryŏ, funerals of high and meritorious officials were state affairs *(yejang)*.[72] Upon the announcement of the death of a high-ranking minister, the court adjourned for a few days *(ch'ŏlcho)*, and the king sent condolences *(choje)* and ceremonial gifts *(ch'ibu)* such as rice and beans. He also subsequently bestowed a posthumous name *(chŭngsi)* upon officials of the first rank. Inner and outer coffins were provided for official as well as private funerals by a government-run workshop, Kwihusŏ, located outside the city walls because of its unpropitious charge. Those too poor to afford the costs could draw support from the Department of Rites.[73]

The physical appearance of the graves also came under scrutiny. During Koryŏ, the construction of graves tended to display wealth and status, and large resources were lavished on them. A drastic curtailment was ordered early on, although the social position of the dead continued to be expressed by the height of the grave mound *(punmyo)*. But even high officials were no longer allowed to construct stone vaults *(sŏksil)* because these were not only unattested in the ritual literature, but also required enormous labor. They had to be replaced, following the *Chia-li*, with a layer of limestone.[74] Stone tables *(sŏksang, sŏgan)* and lanterns that customarily ornamented the tombs of high officials who had been honored with a state funeral were condemned as "useless things." For building the three stone steps leading up to the tomb, natural stone slabs were ordered to be used instead of the traditional polished ones. The number of corvée laborers who were recruited for such projects was therefore reduced.

Nevertheless, stone guardians *(sŏgin)*, stone grave markers *(p'yosŏk)*, and offering tables remained the hallmarks of *sadaebu* graves despite occasional criticism. Even some rich commoners at times marked their graves with stone posts in violation of the convention of their social standing.[75]

In the course of the fifteenth century, the siting of graves was increasingly based on geomancy *(p'ungsu)*. Although geomancy had been widely used during Koryŏ, its principles gained importance for locating propitious grave sites because of the grave's enhanced significance for both the dead and the living. The search for favorable locations *(kilchi)* was so intense that peasants were forced off their fields, and government orders were issued to prohibit burial in the neighborhood of rural villages. Soon the best sites facing south and promising great benefit *(namhyang taeri)* around the capital were all taken; and the government, concerned about future shortage, prohibited in 1431 further occupation of such grounds for private purposes within the capital province. Moreover, the Department of Rites proposed to import from China a number of geomancy manuals in order to disseminate solid knowledge and to stop the wild theories of "ignorant scholars." Toward the end of the century, the use of geomancy had become common property of the Confucian community, not because it had Confucian sanction—the *Chia-li* was vague in this respect—but because historical evidence from China was taken as testimony to its efficacy.[76]

Mourning behavior was rooted in "human feeling": this was the premise of the Confucian legislators' efforts to reform Korea's mourning customs. "Feeling," however, had been perverted during Koryŏ by Buddhist and shamanist notions and practices and therefore had to be newly cultivated by "right learning" *(chŏnghak)*. Ritual was part of such learning and, through its direct application to human action, was a valuable component of the reformatory process. The Confucian mourning ritual as laid down in the *Chia-li*, however, was not only a long, drawn-out sequence of separate actions, it also presupposed a particular social framework—a patrilineally structured society—within which such actions could gain meaning. In fifteenth-century Korea, the proper social milieu was not yet achieved, and it was difficult to sustain all parts of the mortuary ritual with the same emotional and practical commitment. The assessment of the situation at the end of the century was therefore mixed. Some enthusiastic officials reported in 1492 a "vast difference to Koryŏ customs": most *sadaebu* were complying with the *Chia-li,* and only a few were still adhering to Buddhist practices. Other observers were more pessimistic and discerned a lamentable decline of correct behavior.[77] Worse was to come, however. During the reign of the Yŏnsan'gun (r. 1494–1506), the mourning period for parents of *sadaebu* and commoners alike was shortened according to the old method of converting months to days, and the circle of mourning relatives was drastically curtailed.[78] After these turbulent years, the observance of the four rites again improved under King Chungjong, who was urged by his zealous Confucian advisers to pursue a ritually pure course. But even during the sixteenth century, reports abounded which drew attention to the survival of deviant customs. Clearly, nonconformity became an even more critical topic in a society that had after all reached a certain level of Confucian sophistication.[79]

Even in the high officialdom, which was frequently exhorted to display exemplary behavior, there were renegades who did not bury their dead within the prescribed time. Despite occasional warnings, funerals remained occasions for showing off wealth and status. Much of the basic funeral lore continued to be in the grip of Buddhist and shamanistic practitioners. For divining propitious gravesites *(pok t'aekcho, pogyŏng),* geomantic theories were in vogue on all social levels and contributed to the practice of moving a tomb to a new site *(ch'ŏnjang, kaejang)* if the original spot did not prove auspicious. Such beliefs even tempted King Myŏngjong to move his father's tomb against the protest of his advisers.[80]

From the beginning of the dynasty, the influence of the Confucian legislators was greatest in the capital city, and the thrust of their reformatory program only gradually pushed beyond the city walls. Seeing how the old customs persisted in the streets and alleys of the capital, concerned officials worried about the situation in the countryside. Such worries were not unwarranted, as reports from the provinces confirmed. The rich in the rural villages tried to outdo each other: during the night before the funeral of a parent, sumptuous feasts were given to which many guests were invited. The coffin was moved to a temporary tent, and loud music was played "to amuse the corpse" *(osi)*. Men and women danced all night. Extravagant food, especially the "oil and honey cakes" *(yumilkwa)*, filled dishes and platters, and wine was consumed in large quantities. In the southern provinces, Buddhist monks assisted at the festivities, which were popularly known as "the night of the soul's removal" *(yŏngch'ŏrya)*. If a fortune was not spent, and wine and music were missing, the neighbors disparaged the affair as a "shabby funeral" *(pakchang)*. In order to save up the necessary funds, poor people tended to postpone burials for years. Reports from the north made clear that funerary customs in the provinces of Hamgil and P'yŏngan were even more uncivilized. Coffins were unknown, even among the local elite. Instead, the corpses were exposed to the elements in open fields or on rocky cliffs, covered only lightly with a few stones. Occasionally good news was received in the capital that even commoners were using the *Chia-li* for conducting funerals and ancestor worship, but it was shockingly clear that what Chŏng Tojŏn had castigated as corrupt mores at the beginning of the dynasty was still prevalent at the outset of the sixteenth century. Neither admonitions and the distribution of the *Samgang haengsilto* (Illustrated Guide to the Three Relationships) nor stern warnings and legal sanctions seem to have broken the tenacious hold of some local traditions.[81]

FIVE

Inheritance

The institution of the rank-land system *(kwajŏnpŏp)* at the beginning of Chosŏn was the reformers' answer to the economic ills of the previous dynasty. It reasserted, even if only for a short period of time, the state's authority over the country's landed resources and reintroduced a certain degree of regularity and uniformity into its land management.[1] Its principal goal was to assure the livelihood of the new officialdom and to procure sufficient supplies for the military. The allocation of rank land was a prebendal system that entitled the recipients to collect, instead of the state or a local state agency, the tax *(cho)* from land presumably already owned by someone else. Such allocations were more restrictive than in Koryŏ. This may have been due partly to the limited land resources in Kyŏnggi from which the grants at first were made. In addition, a narrower definition of the recipients' qualifications may have restrained state largess.

Prebends of rank land in principle had to be returned to the state upon the recipient's death. This mechanism was designed, as the reformers repeatedly insisted, to forestall the alienation of such land from state control. From the start, however, there were certain special provisions that allowed the family members of a dead official to retain tax authority over the whole or portions of the rank land for their continued upkeep. Widows were granted "land to preserve faithfulness" *(susinjŏn)*, and orphans "land to safeguard upbringing" *(hyuryangjŏn)*. Both kinds of prebends were supposed, after serving their purpose, to revert back to the state; but in fact this often seems not to have been the case. To what extent such prebends were subject to manipulation is illustrated by the case of Kim Ha (?–1426). From childhood Ha had resided with his wife's family, but used his dead father's rank land to maintain himself. When he turned eighteen, he received a minor post and an appropriate portion of rank land whereupon he was to give up his *hyuryangjŏn*. Invoking the rule according to which orphans were allowed to enjoy such grants until the age of twenty, Ha asked that his prebend be transferred to his father-in-law, who lived on only five *kyŏl* of rank land.[2] Such illegal transfers of *susinjŏn* and *hyuryangjŏn* were relatively easy, and the pressure on rank land must have been equally great, especially if sons held lower ranks than their fathers and thus were tempted to secure unlawful adjustments of their income.[3]

THE STATE AND PRIVATE PROPERTY. While the state tried to retain control over rank land, other grants made by the state, most notably land granted to merit subjects *(kongsinjŏn)* and land awarded for special services *(pyŏlsajŏn)*, was intended from the outset to be handed down to the next generation. Consequently, large tracts of arable land that the state lavished on its faithful supporters were permanently lost to state control and either increased already existing private holdings or formed the nucleus of growing estates.[4] On the other hand, for many new officials without an adequate economic base of their own, the rank land grant was a major source of income, and its return to the state caused severe hardships—a situation that often forced the state to involuntary benevolence. These various factors which jeopardized state supervision over land became even more serious during T'aejong's reign when the land shortage in the capital province compelled the government to shift land allocations to the southern provinces, away from administrative surveillance. The adverse effects of this measure could not be countered by the replacement of the rank-land system by the more restrictive office-land system *(chikchŏn)* in 1466, which allotted land only to incumbent officials. With the gradual breakdown of the prebendal system toward the end of the fifteenth century, expansion of existing land holdings and reclamation of waste land were pushed even more aggressively; and the growing landed estates were, as disillusioned observers noted, scarcely different from their forerunners of late Koryŏ.[5]

The land reform efforts at the beginning of the Chosŏn dynasty were based on the premise that all land belonged to and was administered by the state. Although the state was probably in better control of the land in the early years of the dynasty than ever before, the existence of land in the hands of individuals had always been an established fact.[6] It was perhaps this inescapable reality that moved the government, in contradiction of its avowed ideal, to devise rules and regulations for gaining authority over one of the most crucial aspects of private property, namely inheritance.

The decision of the early Chosŏn legislators to extend state authority over an area of private life that hitherto had been outside its legal competence must have rested upon a number of considerations. Among the most disturbing features of the economic scene of late Koryŏ was not only the government's rapid loss of control over land, but the adverse influence the equally rapid privatization had on human behavior and relationships. The growth in the number and size of private holdings of land rendered individuals less dependent on state stipends so that they no longer felt compelled to seek government employment. This caused greater pressure on privately held land, and the customary practices which in Koryŏ had regulated the transmission of private property from one generation to the next broke down, giving rise to disputes among family members over land, slaves, and domestic property. Inheritance had become an important source of land, a fact the legislators could no longer afford to overlook.

The state's involvement with the inheritance of private property, which consisted largely of land and slaves, seems to have had a moral dimension. Those who received "ancestral land" *(choŏp)* from their parents, some memorialits stated, tended to forget their obligations toward the state. Moreover, discord over family wealth caused human relations to deteriorate. A disgruntled son who did not obtain the share he expected would treat his father like a stranger and even stop mourning for him prematurely. Such human estrangement could become still more acute among quarreling brothers.[7] Worse yet, the people's confidence in government was soured by such intrafamilial disputes when corruptible officials reached improper decisions.[8] This disturbing deterioration of the country's moral qualities called for urgent redress.

Inheritance also involved complex sociopolitical considerations that during the formative decades of the new dynasty received close attention. The most critical social innovation, the agnatic concept *(chongppŏp)*, had far-reaching implications for the distribution of property among the heirs. In particular, the ritual heir's pivotal role in descent group affairs demanded for him a greater share of the patrimony than for his siblings. This differential treatment eventually led to the disappearance of equal inheritance among siblings, male and female. Emphasis on the lineal principle also narrowed access to the ranks of the elite, and introduced sharper criteria for defining social status. This resulted in discriminatory treatment of an official's commoner *(yang)* and lowborn *(ch'ŏn)* children. In this new societal model, then, inheritance assumed unprecedented importance; and the government took steps to control it. However, whether it put forward economic, moral, or ritual arguments for justifying its involvement in inheritance matters, as long as the social scene remained unreformed and landed resources were still plentiful, the government's reform measures had only limited chance of success.

The land and slaves that constituted most private property were linked in close economic interdependence: the cultivation of land demanded a labor force of slaves; the slaves sustained themselves by land. The slaves not only worked the fields, they were also indispensable domestic servants. In short, slaves were the "hands and feet" of the elite, and their numbers indicated the degree of their master's prosperity. Unlike land, slaves were movable and thus were conveniently used as bribes and gifts; they were objects of sale and of ownership disputes; and, most importantly, they constituted,

besides land, the most valuable part of the inheritable patrimony
(choŏp in'gu). Illegal transactions involving slaves, even at the expense of the rightful heirs, contributed greatly to the unsettled socioeconomic atmosphere of late Koryŏ and early Chosŏn, and the
newly established government recognized that the slave problem
awaited a solution just as urgently as the land problem.

While T'aejo and his collaborators were confident that the institution of the *kwajŏnpŏp* in 1391 would reform the abuses of the land
system, they were at first apparently undecided about the best method
of how to come to grips with the slave issue. Only in 1395 did they
revive an older Koryŏ agency that had dealt with slaves under the
new name Nobi pyŏnjŏng togam (Office for the Management of
Slaves). The repeated reorganization of this office during the first
two decades of the new dynasty—it was finally abolished in 1414—
shows the government's dilemma: the situation called for an active
policy, yet opponents questioned the wisdom of the state's permanent involvement with issues that "did not bring it [the state] the
slightest profit." Nevertheless, T'aejong did make "the fights among
descendants over slaves" his concern, and during his and Sejong's
reigns the most fundamental legislation regulating the inheritance
of private property was formulated. Significantly, such legislation
was conceived in terms of slaves, and the *Kyŏngguk taejŏn* later also
adopted this format. Human labor was scarcer than land. Successive
developments, however, demonstrated the necessity to make both
land and slaves the foundation of the state's socioeconomic policies.[9]

THE AGNATIC PRINCIPLE AND INHERITANCE. The passing of property
to the next generation did not pose problems as long as there were
rightful heirs to receive their shares of the patrimony. In Koryŏ,
both sons and daughters customarily obtained equal portions of the
parental wealth. It was undoubtedly preferable to have natural children as heirs; but, failing them, collaterals were acceptable as substitute recipients. Since lineal continuation was not yet a social
priority, property could thus be transmitted horizontally. During
the chaotic last years of Koryŏ, ancestral property reportedly at times
even completely bypassed the prospective heirs and ended up in the

treasury of Buddhist temples or in the hands of influential personalities. Hereditary channels had grown fragile, and property was
alienated for purely personal gain.[10]

The early Chosŏn legislators viewed the problem of inheritance
within the newly established framework of linearity. The emphasis
on agnatic succession necessitated a fresh definition of the group
within which the patrimonial property was to be divided. By determining the amount of the inheritable share on the basis of the so-
cioritual position of the potential recipients, the legislators introduced a differential scheme with which they not only narrowed the
outer boundaries of this group, but also established within it a definite hierarchical ranking order.

Equal inheritance among sons and daughters, customary in Koryŏ,
was at first taken over in early Chosŏn. This custom was deeply
rooted, and therefore discrimination, not between the sexes but between the offspring of a man's various wives, was made the problem
of the day. According to the emerging concept of patriliny, only
the children of the primary wife were genuine members of the
descent group and thus bona fide heirs of their father's social status
as well as of his wealth. In contrast, the children of secondary wives
occupied only marginal positions within the descent group, and
therefore their shares of the inheritance were variable, depending on
social and ritual considerations.

The most immediate considerations were whether or not the primary wife had offspring and the social origin of the secondary wives.
Combined, they determined the proportion of the individual shares.
According to the first rules, issued in 1397, the children of secondary wives were allowed to partake in the inheritance only if there
were no primary offspring. Under such a condition, the children of
the commoner secondary wife were assigned all the slaves. In the
absence of commoner offspring, the children of slave mothers inherited certain fractions of the patrimony; the rest had to revert to
the state.[11] In other words, commoner and base offspring each had
a chance to inherit only if there were no heirs on the next higher
level of the social ranking order. The harshness of this concept—

perhaps the outcome of too restrictive thinking—was tempered by the more elaborate rules of 1405.

These rules significantly distributed the privilege of inheritance to all of a man's immediate descendants, even though their mother's social origin still determined individual shares. Accordingly, if a primary son existed, the commoner secondary son received one in seven shares, the lowborn secondary son one in ten. The latter's share increased in absence of a commoner half brother to one-seventh. Even if he was the sole male offspring, however, a lowborn secondary son could never become a full-fledged heir, as could a commoner son. In such a case, his father's nearest collaterals, usually the siblings, were assigned as coinheritors. The rules of 1405 clearly upgraded the secondary sons' standing as heirs, but equally reaffirmed the Koryŏ tradition of horizontal inheritance. The inclusion of the collaterals at the expense of the state inevitably put the lineal principle under pressure. This is illustrated by a request of the Office for the Establishment of Ceremonies in 1430 asking that, failing a primary son, the secondary commoner son be given only ten slaves, the remaining slaves being distributed among the collaterals. This proposal was rejected by Sejong who argued that the share of an heir with ritual responsibilities could not be reduced arbitrarily, an argument that revealed the king's commitment to safeguard the lineal principle against collateral attacks.[12]

The inheritance law of the Chosŏn dynasty was fully developed in the *Kyŏngguk taejŏn* of 1485.[13] Although based on the earlier formulations discussed above, this final version stands out by its expedient compromise between tradition and innovation. Tradition was reasserted in the confirmation of equal inheritance of sons and daughters. What was innovative was the clear revocation of horizontal inheritance by collaterals and the consequent firm implantation of the lineal principle. This meant that even lowborn secondary children no longer had to compete with greedy collaterals and could become their father's full-fledged heirs, under the condition that there were no higher ranking half siblings at all. For the rest, the *Kyŏngguk taejŏn* confirmed the differential shares of secondary sons laid down in 1405. Also new was the clear preferential treatment of the ritual heir *(sŭngjungja)*. Ancestor worship, only rudimentarily developed in 1405, assumed greater significance later in the fifteenth century, and consequently its economic basis had to be anchored in law. Regardless of his social standing, a ritual heir received in principle at least one share more than his siblings.[14]

What the sons and daughters of a primary marriage inherited in equal shares—this also applied to a deceased offspring—was the parental property that consisted of their father's and their mother's combined wealth. Although the portion the mother contributed to the common fund was usually managed by her husband, he did not receive title to it.[15] Therefore, when she died without issue of her own, her property was again separated, and the children of her husband's secondary wives, not being her direct heirs, received only fractions of it: one-seventh, if of commoner background; one-tenth, if of base background. These allotments were augmented by three or two shares, respectively, if the recipient was also the ritual heir. The rest of the female property had to be returned to her natal family *(ponjok)*.[16]

Spouses were granted the right, even without written confirmation, of usufruct in each other's property before it was given back to its original source. In order to prevent the dispersal of such property to unauthorized persons, the survivor was not allowed to pass it on to anybody outside the dead spouse's natal group, and even the shares distributed to those who legally were entitled to them were not to exceed the amounts fixed by law. As soon as the remaining spouse—the *Kyŏngguk taejŏn* mentioned only the widow— remarried, she lost her usufructuary rights. Clearly, the law was intended to hold together the patrimonial property and to forestall its alienation. This implied that selling it was prohibited. This implication, however, seems to have been often ignored by "uninformed" officials, and the discovery of various abuses stirred a major debate on the issue in 1490. Although the arguments differed as to the meaning of legal vocabulary—did the term "to manage" *(kuch'ŏ)* in the *Kyŏngguk taejŏn* connote "to sell" *(pangmae)?*—they converged toward the opinion that a poor, starving widow should be allowed for her sustenance to sell some of her husband's property. Granted that it was difficult to establish standards for judging poverty, a poor widow's actions were anyway restricted by the close watch of her husband's grudging relatives. The authorities, it was demanded, should be on guard against such irregularities as currying favor by gifts disguised as sales. A royal edict concluded that even though selling and buying was not expressly prohibited, any misuse of the patrimony should be checked for the sake of protecting the descent line *(chong)*. This rather loose statement was later corrected by the *Sok taejŏn,* which clearly prohibited the sale of ancestral property.[17]

The patrimony came to be recognized as the mainstay of the descent group, and therefore it was imperative to define and delineate the range of relatives within which it could be handed on, if the principal line remained without heir. The rules of 1405 mentioned kin of the fourth degree *(sach'on)* as the outer limit; and this criterion, frequently repeated in subsequent laws, was finally incorporated in the *Kyŏngguk taejŏn.* Not all members of a descent group *(ponjok),* then, were entitled to receive a share of such ownerless property. Only a segment of the nearest collaterals—siblings and relatives of the third *(samch'on)* and fourth degree, collectively known as *sason* or *ponson*[18]—were designated as the rightful recipients. The exact meaning of these terms as well as their temporal sequence, however, were unclear in this definition. If, according to the *Kyŏngguk taejŏn,* the relatives of the third degree were the beneficiaries after the siblings, did this exclude the children of a dead sibling from the inheritance? Or, did *samch'on* in fact include them?

These and similar uncertainties made the observance of this law problematic; and only two years after its promulgation, in 1487, a lengthy discussion among the highest officialdom tried to arrive at a clear-cut conclusion. The points of view, however, were divergent. The arguments in essence hinged upon the questions of whether or not the living *and* the dead siblings and their descendants were recognized as heirs, and whether or not the *samch'on* in the meaning of "paternal uncles" were placed immediately after the siblings. These possibilities derived from the incompatible traditions of horizontal and vertical inheritance. The officials who advocated the recognition of both the living and the dead siblings, in analogy to the distribution of the paternal inheritance, insisted on a division *per stirpes*, that is to say, they interpreted *samch'on* and *sach'on* lineally as nephews and grandnephews and consequently included them among the potential inheritors. The opponents, in contrast, demanded that if no living siblings existed, the privilege should be handed on to the father's siblings, that is, the paternal uncles, bypassing the siblings' descendants. This controversy was at last resolved in the *Taejŏn songnok* of 1493 in favor of the first argument, and the *Taejŏn chuhae* of 1555 clarified this decision still further: "Because the personal property of a person without offspring returns to the parents, the siblings' children and grandchildren form the descent group *(ponjok);* thus, the *samch'on* uncles and *sach'on* cousins are not given anything. If, however, there are no *sach'on* grandchildren [children of the deceased's nephew], the property reverts to the [generation of the] grandparents, and then the *samch'on* uncles and the *sach'on* cousins form the descent group . . ." This definition, which revealed clear lineal thinking, was clarified in a diagram (see Diagram 10). Called *sasondo,* this diagram depicted the right sequence of inheritors within the descent group and helped to implant in the minds of the officials in the early sixteenth century the essential of the principle of linearity.[19]

Collaterals, however judiciously selected, were at best residual heirs and therefore rarely the preferred recipients of property. During the troubled years of dynastic change, it was more profitable for a man without issue to "invest" his wealth in a son of an influential family from which he could expect some favors during his own lifetime. Such "economic adoptions," however, not only provoked conflicts with collateral kin, but also failed to correspond to the proper rules governing the artifical continuation of an heirless descent line.

It was therefore a major concern of the early Chosŏn legislators to hammer out regulations that would satisfy both social and economic considerations. Relying on Chinese legal models, already known in Koryŏ, they clearly distinguished two categories of adop-

Diagram 10. *Sasondo*

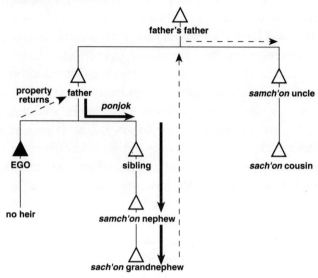

Diagram 11. The Case of Kang Hŭi-maeng

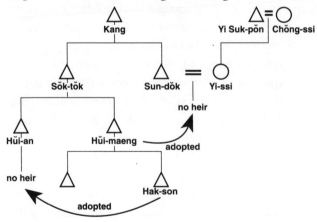

tion. The first category demanded the selection of a child under age three who came from either the husband's or the wife's stock or had been abandoned (and thus was of unknown origin). Although such a child was in most cases not agnatically related, its young age made it, like a natural child, totally dependent on its adoptive parents *(yangbumo)* whose surname *(sŏng)* it assumed—a condition even acknowledged by the Chinese who otherwise prohibited non-agnatic adoption.[20] Called "adopted son" *(suyangja)*, such an adoptee was considered a real son (or daughter) and was entitled to receive his adoptive parents' property *in toto.* To the second category belonged the foster son *(siyangja)*[21]—for him, no counterpart seems to have existed in China. He was acquired at a mature age and, in the absence of a clearly worded document, had to share his foster parents' property with the one who was in charge of ancestral services. This distinction between *suyangja* and *siyangja* was laid down in the early legal texts, but in popular usage it was apparently often blurred so that the concomitant economic benefits continued to be meted out according to sentiment rather than according to law. Moreover, adoption in any form was a disaster for the collaterals *(sason)* who had a legitimate claim to a sonless couple's fortune. It must have been due to their successful lobbying that the inheritance amounts of foster sons were repeatedly cut.[22]

This early form of adoption followed to an extent lineal considerations, but initially it provided a childless couple with an acceptable heir to their property rather than to their line. During the 1430s, official thinking gradually came to link this kind of adoption to the problem of lineal succession *(iphu)*. What indeed was the relationship between an "adopted son" *(suyangja)* and an "established heir" *(kyehuja)?* With the fixing of the line of succession in 1437, the *suyangja* seemed to possess the correct characteristics— those of a real son—to be recognized as a genuine heir to the descent line as well as to property rights. An examination of this issue by the state councillors in 1442, however, revealed some serious social reservations. A *suyangja,* even if taken in before age three, most often was a non-agnate and thus was not qualified to perform ancestral services for his adoptive parents. Moreover, his mourning obligations toward his own kin were not lightened. The ministers concluded that a child could not, by virtue of being taken in as a *suyangja,* automatically become a bona fide heir. Such social disqualification had an adverse effect on a *suyangja*'s economic expectations. Increasingly, his share of the inheritance was disputed; and when there were children by a secondary wife, his chances were still further reduced. These developments were reflected in the *Kyŏngguk taejŏn,* which granted adopted children smaller portions of the inheritance than had been common at the beginning of the dynasty: one share of seven when the adoptive parents did not have children of their own, one share of ten when primary offspring existed. The stipulation that a child adopted before his third year was to be given all of the property of his heirless adoptive parents remained in the lawbook, but such a child had little chance of becoming a fullfledged heir, particularly among the ritually conscious upper class. On the contrary, owing to the growing sophistication of agnatic thinking, social criteria came to prevail over purely economic concerns; and consequently the *suyangja* found himself in most cases supplanted by the *kyehuja,* in whom the social as well as the economic functions of adoption coexisted.[23]

WILLS AND REGULATIONS AFFECTING INHERITANCE. Following Koryŏ custom, the written document, usually signed by one or both parents, remained an important instrument for regulating inheritance matters in Chosŏn Korea. The importance of the will may have derived from the fact that Koryŏ Koreans thought of property as being under individual rather than corporate control. Moreover, inheritance may have been contingent on certain conditions, for example filial behavior of the inheritor. Although regarded as a family's "private affair," the validity of such a document was apparently confirmed by the law codes of early Chosŏn; and the officials who were called upon to arbitrate between disputants usually upheld the intention of the writ. Such a record could, of course, be tampered with. A dying father at times was pressured into changing his mind at the last moment; or falsifiers, knowing the officials' predilection for the written word, twisted its original intent after its author's death. On the other hand, parents were often partial toward certain offspring and thus were tempted to put their feelings in writing. Children, for example, who died before their parents were charged with lack of filial piety and were therefore often omitted in a will, with the result that their own children were disinherited.[24]

Parental arbitrariness gave rise to jealousy and discord among brothers and sisters, a problem grave enough to stimulate frequent debates among the highest officials. They were faced with the intricate question of whether or not they should cast custom *(sesok)* in legal terms *(pŏp)*. Customary practice since Koryŏ times had been more or less equal division of the parental estate among all siblings, a tradition still reflected in the few extant inheritance documents of the early Chosŏn period. To correct irregularities by law would, however, both infringe upon the father's authority to dispose of his property at will and relieve the younger generation of its obligation to maintain filial behavior in order to deserve a share of the heritage. As early as 1430, Chŏng Ch'o pleaded with King Sejong to put a stipulation into the lawbooks according to which the families of officials would be bound to observe equal division. Opposition against such a measure was obviously strong, and only the *Kyŏngguk taejŏn* of 1485 finally legislated the provision of equal shares *(p'yŏngbun)* for all children—male and female—of a primary wife.[25] This was a paradoxical act of legislation in several respects. Customary equal division became legalized at a time when the concept of patrilineal descent gained increased relevance even in economic matters. Clearly, however, the enforcement of the agnatic principle was still a matter of degree. To a certain extent, legal assurance of a daughter's inheritance share may have been offset by the legislators' efforts to incorporate a married woman's property into that of her affinal family. But whenever a daughter who married out inherited, a sizable piece of property did get lost to her natal family, and landholdings became widely scattered.[26] Moreover, the legal fixing of equal division deprived a parent's will of its original discretionary powers, and such documents tended to become mere inventories of land and slaves distributed to each inheritor.

There were two major times when a patrimony was passed on to the descendants: one was during the parents' (or grandparents') lifetime when they felt death approaching, and the other was after the mourning periods for them had ended. When the parents (often the father or the widowed mother alone) decided to distribute a portion of their property among their children—they usually retained some part of it for their own livelihood—an official document, known as "division writ" *(pun'gŭp mun'gi),*[27] was drawn up and authenticated by the signatures of the original owner, of the scribe, of a witness, and of the inheritors or their representatives present.[28] Despite the official nature of such a document, it could later be reversed, as the parental freedom to give or take away property was generally acknowledged. On an occasion such as an examination success, a birth, a wedding, or some other auspicious happening, some property could be given to an individual; and this was recorded in a "special gift writ" *(pyŏlgŭp mun'gi).* Although the writ was not an inheritance document in the strict sense, the property given away was generally part of the heritable estate.[29]

After the death of the father or of both parents, the surviving children—daughters at times represented by their husbands, dead sons by their children—gathered to draw up a document in which the patrimony, in full or what had been left after an earlier division, was apportioned among them.[30] Known as "writ on the mutual consent of the siblings" *(tongsaeng* [or *tongbok*] *hwahoe mun'gi),* it was often based on the testament *(yusŏ* or *yuŏn)* of the dead father or of a remoter ancestor *(chosang yusŏ);* and copies of the document were distributed to each inheritor. These documents seem in essence to have merely confirmed the general inheritance practice of the early Chosŏn dynasty, because almost all of those preserved from the fifteenth and sixteenth centuries give evidence of equal distribution of the inheritance among sons and daughters. Indeed, such equality was taken so literally—after 1485 often marked with "as based on the law" *(ŭibŏp)*—that even small and remote pieces of land were split up essentially equally among all the heirs, and each member of a slave family might be responsible to a different master (although the family was not actually separated).[31] Such fragmentation undoubtedly was often inconvenient; but underlying the custom was a belief that it would imbue a strong sense of thankfulness as well as obligation toward the ancestors; and each heir was to partake in this common emotional bond. Even if the arrangement resulted in a geographically unsatisfactory distribution of the ancestral property, the consciousness of common, albeit not necessarily agnatic, descent was nurtured and cooperation among close kin expedited.[32]

Concern about keeping the patrimony from being dispersed to outsiders often found passionate expression in the preface or postface of an inheritance document. "It is my wish," a father would write to his heirs, "that the ancestral fields, slaves, and household properties which I bequeath to you are forever, without fail, transmitted to my descendants." If poverty necessitated the selling of part of these belongings, this should be done among relatives lest "strangers enter your house, plough your fields, and use your possessions." Such a document was also intended to serve as evidence vis-à-vis the authorities in case an unfilial descendant sold his share to an unauthorized person, or somebody without offspring adopted an affinal relative and made him his heir, or a lowborn son turned against his father.[33] By "descendants" both sons and daughters were meant; and this is clear evidence of the still weakly developed sense of patriliny in the fifteenth century, for if daughters shared in the inheritance, land did pass out of the (patrilineal) descent group.

The stipulation in a testamentary document which prohibited the transmission of ancestral property beyond the lineal descendants (*mulgŭp sonoe* or *muryŏt'a*) was, however, often problematic because it disregarded the possibility that a ritual heir or an adoptee might come from outside this narrow circle of agnatic kin. Could the sanctity of a testament be called in question by a social action which, however unforeseen, was necessary for the continuation of the line? Or was an outside heir, even if taken in before age three, disinherited in principle by such a testament? This problem was repeatedly pondered, and the fear of losing ancestral property to unauthorized persons at first made strict adherence to the letter of the testament advisable. With the growing awareness, in the course of the 1430s, of the social importance of an established heir *(kyehuja)* or a ritual stepson *(pongsa ŭija)* this exclusionist view was revised; and in 1442 a share of the ancestral property was ruled to go to such an important adoptee, regardless of the testament's directives. This rule was later confirmed in the *Kyŏngguk taejŏn.*[34]

Various social issues could be tied together in a single testament. This was illustrated by the controversy over Kang Hŭi-maeng's (1424–1483) position as heir (see Diagram 11). According to the testament Yi Suk-pŏn (d. 1440) and his wife, Chŏng-ssi, drew up in 1415, the husband of their eldest daughter, Kang Sun-dŏk, was given a part of the inheritance. Because Sun-dŏk did not have children, he, with the consent of his wife, Yi-ssi, made Kang Hŭi-maeng, the second son of an elder brother, his jural heir *(iphuja).*[35] After both Suk-pŏn and Yi-ssi died, Chŏng-ssi, who in the meantime had become destitute, wanted to change the testament. She was unhappy about the fact that Sun-dŏk had adopted a nephew and had distributed Suk-pŏn's slaves among all his nephews, ignoring the potential inheritors on his wife's side. When Sun-dŏk did not comply with Chŏng-ssi's demand to return the testament, Chŏng-ssi appealed to the authorities and thereby evoked a heated high-level debate. Although it was not permissible, the officials argued, to let Chŏng-ssi change the entire testament—her intent to do so revealed her insubordinate attitude as a wife—she should nevertheless be allowed to have the say about her own property. Because there was no word in the testament that the bequest was not to be given beyond the range of grandchildren, Hŭi-maeng, who had been made heir with Yi-ssi's consent and thus had become Chŏng-ssi's direct, albeit non-agnatic, grandson *(oeson)*, was the rightful heir. Even though the establishment of an heir should not be motivated by economic gain, Hŭi-maeng's share was beyond dispute. In the end, the state councillors reached the verdict that Chŏng-ssi was entitled to control her own property and that Sun-dŏk was to be punished for insubordination because he failed in his filial obligation to come to Chŏng-ssi's rescue.[36]

The legal and therefore inviolable character of a testament remained at issue because the requirement of an official signature on such a document would have been a clear infringement upon the testator's free disposition. Without official authorization, however, a testament could easily become the focus of dispute among close kin or the means of letting slaves, a measure of the prestige of the rich, be removed from the proper inheritance channels. It was obviously not easy to find a solution for this dilemma, and the *Kyŏngguk taejŏn* of 1485 still exempted the documents written by and applicable to a narrow circle of kin (parents, paternal and maternal grandparents, wife's parents, husband's various wives, and siblings) from the compulsion of official sanction,[37] but the last wills *(yusŏ)* of grandparents and parents had to be handwritten to be valid.[38]

Of equal importance was the question of whether or not a testament could be changed later on, a problem that was a central point of discussion in Kang Hŭi-maeng's case. The early version of the *Kyŏngguk taejŏn* apparently permitted such an act as long as it was reported to the authorities; but after the recipient of the bequest died, change was no longer possible. In 1484, it was suggested that this wording be added to the sentence: "The parents' testament does not fall within this limitation." Official opinion unanimously approved such an addition because the restriction on changing a testament was only intended to protect the inheritance of an adoptee *(suyangja)*. The parents' authority over their own children, whether alive or dead, it was again argued, could not be touched by the state. Only King Sŏngjong opposed the amendment out of concern that the children of a dead son or daughter might by unfair means be deprived of their livelihood. The king, however, allowed himself to be persuaded otherwise; and the *Kyŏngguk taejŏn* of 1485 contained the additional sentence that parents and grandparents on both sides were permitted to change their testament vis-à-vis their children and grandchildren, a husband vis-à-vis his wives, primary and secondary.[39]

INHERITANCE AND WOMEN. The gradual implementation of Confucian-style legislation made noticeable inroads on women's traditional economic independence. In particular, the introduction of agnatic succession necessitated the ranking of wives, legislated in

1413, and made women generally more dependent on their husbands' family. This was underscored by the demand for virilocal residence, which often made the actual allocation of a woman's share of inheritance difficult—ancestral land could not be moved[40]—and also tended to subject a woman's assets more directly to her spouse's authority. This integrative tendency was particularly manifest in the fate of the property of a wife who died without offspring. A sizable percentage of her slaves and land came to be retained by her husband's family and given to the one who was appointed to conduct ancestral services for her before the rest was returned to her natal kin.

This growing involvement in her husband's descent group brought a woman certain acknowledged privileges when she became a widow. She could reclaim whatever she had brought in at the time of marriage or later and even retrieve her part of a bequest her husband had earlier made with her agreement.[41] Moreover, she enjoyed usufructuary rights over her late husband's estate. Equally important was her prerogative, if she was sonless, to select an heir to her husband's line. The legal stipulations that eventually came to restrict this power suggest that many a widow was guided in her choice by economic motives which undercut agnatic inheritance. For example, she might adopt a child from among her own kinsmen, who, if under age three, would legally inherit his adoptive father's complete personal holdings. Such manipulation alienated the patrimony from its proper recipients and compelled the legislators to outlaw it in the *Taejŏn chuhae*.[42]

The more a woman became part of her affinal family, the more intense grew the struggle over inheritable property among the different wives a man may have had. The customarily tenuous relationship between the dead first primary wife (*chŏnmo*) and her successor (*kyemo*) was also evident in economic matters. A second wife might begrudge the children of her dead predecessor their share of the paternal estate, and sell it or give it away, or hoard it up for her own progeny. But sometimes a father was partial toward his children by a second wife. Therefore, in 1554, a surviving second spouse who, vaguely supported by the *Kyŏngguk taejŏn,* took control of the

estate of a dead husband who had children by the previous marriage
was expressly denied the authority to dispose of it at will. This royal
order put an end to a second wife's possibly autocratic rule. It was
reaffirmed in the *Sok taejŏn*.[43]

From the outset, the competition for a childless wife's property
was severe. In 1435, half of a *kyemo*'s slaves were ordered to be given
to her ritual stepson *(pongsa ŭija)*. This high percentage was even
increased and made applicable to both the first and the second wife
by the *Kyŏngguk taejŏn:* it granted four out of five shares of a childless
wife's property to the ritual heir *(sŭngjungja);* his siblings divided
the remaining share. This division underlined the ritual heir's elevated position in the descent group and at the same time prevented
a large part of a stepmother's property from reverting back to her
natal family. This trend eventually went far beyond purely ritual
considerations, as is evident from an argument put forward in 1490.
At issue then was the fate of a first wife's property. If her son inherited his mother's wealth, then died without issue, it was postulated
that his younger half brother should be allowed to obtain it. Such a
demand was tantamount to making half brothers substitute heirs
for each other. Although a royal instruction found this request to
be in opposition to the *Kyŏngguk taejŏn,* the *Sok taejŏn* finally approved what had undoubtedly become general practice. It even expressly forbade the transfer of a first wife's slaves back to her own
kin. Clearly, then, the patriliny succeeded in incorporating into its
holdings, beyond the ritual recompense, the complete property of a
primary wife who, after her death, was given a surrogate son.[44]

Women were thought to be forever jealous beings, and this negative character trait was held responsible for the often reported friction between primary and secondary or minor wives. The elevation
of one woman as the primary wife marginalized all the other women
in the same household, and consequently their children's position
as heirs was greatly impaired. Secondary wives were known for
"scheming" to better their lot, persuading their master to leave
property to them and then disposing of it at will.[45] Whatever their
success, women were clearly differentiated in terms of property rights;

and lower economic status remained the hallmark of secondary wives throughout the dynasty.

Despite the fact that the law confirmed a daughter's right to inherit a share of the patrimony equal to that of her brother, during the first half of the dynasty the nature of a daughter's inheritance changed significantly. To be sure, even in the early sixteenth century, when there were no sons, daughters at times were designated as principal recipients of parental wealth with the express wish that their ancestral services be continued by non-agnatic descendants.[46] Such occasional (in Confucian eyes undoubtedly misguided) appropriations cannot, however, obscure the clear trend that daughters were gradually losing their qualification to inherit property in their own right. Although a woman's inheritance originally was quite independent of her marital arrangements and, in case she did not have children of her own, even reverted back to her natal family, the legal stipulations of the *Kyŏngguk taejŏn* significantly enlarged the stake her husband and his family had in her property and limited that of her natal family. In other words, a woman's inheritance, initially only loosely attached to her affines, was eventually turned into a weighty contribution to an inalienable conjugal fund. Whether it came in in the form of a dowry at the time of marriage or of an inheritance received later in life (upon the parents' death), the contribution to such a fund was an additional factor in establishing a bride as a primary wife and became an indivisible part of the husband's property. This transformation is documented by inheritance papers of the late sixteenth and early seventeenth centuries which list sons-in-law instead of daughters as the recipients of an inheritance share.[47] Property given to a son-in-law surely meant that the daughter, his wife, lost control over it, and that it became permanently detached from its original source. This development lowered a woman's economic power and made her increasingly dependent on her husband's estate.

FROM RITUAL TO ECONOMIC PRIMOGENITURE. During the first century of the new dynasty, then, the inheritance system emerged as a crucial part of the Confucian legislators' social reform program. By transposing the new social values into legal norms, it authoritatively imposed itself upon the daily life of the elite. The new laws stressed the lineal principle and thus clearly rerouted inheritance from horizontal to vertical channels. This shift might have loosened family cohesion—siblings who are no longer each other's heirs tend to disperse—had it not been for the strong ritual obligations that embedded fraternal relationships within a new frame of reference. Ritual principles elevated the eldest son and subordinated to him his younger brothers, and this hierarchical structure henceforth determined the distribution of wealth. Moreover, traditional status consciousness was narrowed by favoring primary over secondary issue. The only traditional feature that thwarted the complete enactment of this Confucian scheme was the distribution of property to daughters, a tradition that continued far into the seventeenth century, as a great number of surviving inheritance documents attest.[48]

Inheritance practices, however, changed little until the time when land began to be scarce and became an ever more precious determinant of higher social status within the elite group. This change was accompanied by important demographic developments, improvement of agricultural techniques, and heightened ritual awareness. The combination of all these factors—disparate, but reinforcing each other—brought about the conditions that made a revision of inheritance customs imperative and thus expedited the establishment of the ideal of economic primogeniture.[49]

At the beginning of the Chosŏn dynasty land was plentiful, but manpower scarce. This ratio began to change slowly in the course of time. The fifteenth century witnessed crucial agricultural innovations: irrigation facilities were expanded, and wetfield cultivation of rice became more widespread. The major crops, however, were still millet and soybeans; but the use of improved fertilizer allowed yearly cropping, and production consequently increased.[50] Such advances from extensive to intensive agriculture resulted in a sharp increase of population. The population growth seems to have reached a first peak around the middle of the sixteenth century, declined during the Japanese Wars of 1592–1598 and accelerated again in the second half of the seventeenth century.[51] Even though new land was put under cultivation, pressure on land intensified. The seventeenth century was also the time when the fragmentation of the patrimony caused by equal inheritance progressed to a critical stage and made the investments which advanced agriculture demanded increasingly unprofitable. These difficulties were reinforced by the decline of slave holdings as many slaves deserted their masters. Runaway slaves had to be replaced by tenants, a development that eventually subordinated the slave to the land as the most valuable economic asset. Serious repercussions on land cultivation patterns were the result.[52]

These economic factors prepared the ground upon which new ritual insights and forms could take root. Ritual innovations gained urgency when adverse economic developments called for stringent countermeasures. A most effective countermeasure, it was recognized, was the drastic curtailment of land fragmentation by revising existing inheritance practices. Strategies for doing so were presented in the ritual handbooks which advocated the recognition of the eldest son as the main inheritor of the patrimony and the setting aside of significant parts of the patrimony for serving the ancestors. During the seventeenth century, the confluence of economic demands and ritual concerns brought about profound change in the nature of the patrimony: instead of being a kind of economic insurance handed down by the ancestors to all of their descendants, the patrimony demanded correct ritual behavior of the agnatic descendants toward their ancestors. Focused on lineal continuity, this altered point of view hurt women's standing as heirs in their own right. As they were integrated into their husbands' family, the property they formerly had brought with them as inheritance or dowry became permanently detached from their natal families; and because they in turn could no longer function ritually in their brothers' ancestral shrines, the rationality of endowing them with property vanished. Ritual insignificance caused them loss of economic independence. Property, and thus also the mechanism of inheritance, became firmly implanted in the male domain.

The eldest son's gradual assumption of the ritual and economic prerogatives of the descent group, as postulated by Chu Hsi, elevated him in regard to both the living and the dead family members. His pivotal role was likened to that of a state ruler who was concerned that his descendants would preserve the patrimony from generation to generation so that "not a single inch of land and not a single slave might pass into somebody else's possession."[53] This concern eventually led to the discontinuation of rotating ancestor worship which, although disapproved by ritual experts, was customary during the early part of the Chosŏn dynasty.[54] Instead of sharing the economic burden of ancestral services, from the middle of the sixteenth century a special ritual allowance *(pongsajo)* became a distinct category that preceded all other stipulations in an inheritance document. Earlier, a ritual heir had rarely been given the extra share of inheritance guaranteed to him by law. The creation of ritual allowances was, for example, urged by Yi Hwang who castigated as lacking in respect the "large families that do not reserve slaves for their ritual heir and instead nonchalantly distribute them among [all] the sons."[55] Eventually the portions of land and slaves set aside for ancestral rites in fact began to surpass the legal one-fifth of the inheritance, and such ceremonial enthusiasm was increasingly justified as "being in conformity with the ritual manuals *(yejŏn)*."[56]

Ritual recognition of the eldest son, underlined by special economic provisions, gradually destroyed the customary equal division of the patrimony. Even though the reservation of an extra share for the ancestors initially did not necessarily lead to an unequal distribution of the remaining inheritance, the continuously increasing portion of the eldest son—well documented by inheritance papers from the second half of the seventeenth century—forced his younger siblings to be satisfied with much less, although it was rare that they would not inherit at all.[57] Justified in ritual terms, this development was closely linked to growing concern about the shortage and fragmentation of land and the inevitable consequence of downward mobility in many areas at that time. Although the *Sok taejŏn* reaffirmed equal inheritance, the prescriptions of the ritual manuals clearly came to eclipse the relevance of the lawbooks.[58]

The emergence of the eldest son as the undisputed ritual and economic head of the family had the most acute consequence for the female family members. Daughters, it was argued, married out and moved to distant places, and their offspring lost respect and devotion for their maternal grandparents. This line of reasoning was clearly expressed, for example, in the testament of Kwŏn Nae (n.d.), dated 1615:

> I have received the patrimony *(yuŏp)* of the previous generations. Land and slaves are more numerous than the family members, yet the daughters of the first and second wives are also very many. If each of them got an equal share, the extent [of the patrimony] would nevertheless not be sufficient, and I am very concerned that the lineal grandsons [lit. "the grandsons who continue the surname"] would not avoid poverty and thus would be unable to sustain the ancestral services. Moreover, since sons and daughters equally receive their physical appearance from their parents, human feelings are not lacking. Through the principle of inside and outside *(nae-oe chi ch'e)*, however, there is a great difference between them. Therefore, even if the lineal grandchildren were extremely poor, they would not bear to discontinue the burning of incense at the ancestral graves. [In contrast,] even if among the grandsons with a different surname were learned men, few would turn their sincerity toward their maternal ancestors. . . . If I come to think about all this, at the time of dividing up the property, I cannot but differentiate between sons and daughters. . . .[59]

This document pointed up in frank language the problems of the time: land had become so precious that even a large patrimony could no longer sustain the continued division among numerous sons and daughters. Loyalty to the descent group, moreover, was linked to agnatic membership, and therefore continued commitment to maternal ancestors was no longer expected. Such considerations necessitated differential division of the patrimony.

Similar sentiments were expressed in a testamentary statement *(chŏnhu munsŏ)* made by Kim Myŏng-yŏl (1613–?)[60] in 1669. Holding current ritual practices to be in violation of the prescriptions of the ritual manuals, its author deplored that the rules concerning the conduct of ancestral rites by the major line *(chongga)* had for long not been observed. He also regretted the established tradition of rotating ancestral services. The crux of the matter, he recognized, was the circumstance that when daughters married, they entered their husband's household, and that consequently their husbands and sons became unreliable performers of the rites for non-agnatic ancestors. Moreover, a married daughter's mourning obligations for her natal family were lowered. Recalling that rotating ancestor worship had long since been disapproved in his own family, the author stated emphatically, "There is no difference between sons and daughters as far as the human commitment between parent and child is concerned, but if there is no way [for daughters] to care for their parents as long as they [the parents] are alive and there is no ritual obligation [for daughters] to perform services for them after they die, how could they preferentially be given shares of land and slaves equal to those of sons? Considering both emotion and propriety, it is not at all impossible to give daughters [only] one-third portion of land and slaves. Would daughters and their sons dare harbor resentment?"[61] Resentment could not be ruled out, and thereafter the decision to cut the daughters' inheritance to one-third was repeatedly reaffirmed.[62] The one-third share undoubtedly was a calculation based on the fact that a married daughter's lowered mourning for her own parents amounted to only one-third of an eldest son's mourning of three years. Although the Puan Kim's solution may not have been a generally accepted rule, evidence is abundant enough to conclude that in the course of the seventeenth century daughters were gradually losing their traditional status as heirs of their ancestors' property.[63]

That daughters lost their ritual and economic claims on their natal families also resulted from changing residence patterns. Because husbands no longer took up permanent residence in their wives' house—brief initial periods notwithstanding—women moved in with their affinal relatives and became, for their own kin, outsiders. Geographic distance made the upkeep of female property increasingly cumbersome, and the inviolability of ancestral land was consequently no longer guaranteed. This is clearly manifested from the seventeenth century when exchange and sale of fields that had been acquired through wives began to be frequent. Such transactions usually were justified by citing the inconvenience of cultivating far-off and often small plots. At times land inherited by married sisters was sold to their eldest brother who administered the patrimony.[64] These measures must have contributed to the consolidation of fragmented landholdings.

With the eldest son's growing stature as his agnatic ancestors' main ritual heir and the consequent discontinuation of rotating ancestor worship, the land under his supervision became clearly more labelled. The most important such category was the land and slaves handed down from the ancestors *(sŭngjung minjŏn).*[65] This ancestral trust that also included the house of the descent group's main line *(chongga)* and the ancestral shrine *(sadang)* could no longer be divided among several sons, but had to be transmitted exclusively to the ritual heir *(chongja* or *chongson).* It in fact became the nucleus of newly developing corporate land because this property did not belong to the ritual heir as an individual, but to the entire descent group. The ritual heir merely administered it and was by law forbidden to sell it. A distinct part of the corporate estate was two kinds of ritual land: land and slaves for the services dedicated to the direct lineal antecedents *(chewijo)* and land and slaves for collateral members of the descent group who died without heirs *(panbujo).* This ritual land, at times called "ancestral service land" *(chejŏn),* also was under the ritual heir's control and could not be divided up among his siblings. With the exclusion of corporate and sacrificial land from the divisible inheritance, the only property that remained for distribution was the land and slaves acquired during a man's lifetime *(maedŭk minjŏn).* Although the eldest son usually received the largest share, fractions of such land continued to be occasionally given even to daughters.[66]

Moreover, the ruling elite of the early seventeenth century was further reminded by ritualists such as Hwang Chong-hae (1579–1642) that the ceremonies for an ancestor did not end when his tablet was removed from the domestic shrine, but had to be seasonally continued at his graveside. Ancestral service land thus turned into grave land *(myojŏn).* The dedication of such land to the ancestors was not only ritually appropriate but, as brothers and their descendants gradually dispersed, it also gave the master of the ancestral home the indispensable economic foundation for carrying on the family's ritual program. Except for the grave land of the apical ancestor, which also was under the ritual heir's control, the grave land of other ancestors was, often in rotation, taken care of by his younger brothers, based on the *Chia-li*. Because graves were frequently located on remote hillsides, far away from human habitations, they were tended by especially assigned slave grave keepers (*myojik, myono*).[67]

The recognition of the eldest son as exclusive ritual heir—a general phenomenon by the end of the seventeenth century—was the climax of a gradual process of deepened ritual awareness and knowledge that was accelerated by the need to counteract the adverse effects of land shortage and land fragmentation. The direction of change was toward reducing the property-sharing group, and the arguments were most often ritual. By the same token, the ritual group, too, narrowed. Ancestral property was no longer the concern of individuals, but was transformed into the inalienable asset of a corporate group. Inheritance documents thus gained renewed relevance. By setting forth the ritual imperatives of the time, they forced agnatic descendants who were not first sons to confront economic realities that increasingly turned against them. Women fared the worst. Although they were given some family heirlooms and at times even some slaves when they married, this could not hide the fact that sisters were in reality disinherited by their own brothers in the name of serving their ancestors.

SIX

Confucian Legislation: the Consequences for Women

Although Confucianism is a philosophy of agnation, it regards the union between man and woman as the root of all human relations. Furthermore, it holds this union to be the foundation of human morality and the mainspring of the socialization process that extends from the relationship between father and son to that between ruler and subject. In cosmological terms, heaven *(yang)* dominates earth *(yin);* and, correspondingly, male has precedence over female. The clear hierarchical order between the sexes is thus cosmologically sanctioned and is imperative for the proper functioning of the human order. This order can be preserved only when human passions are kept in check. To do this the Confucians drew a sharp distinction between the woman's "inner" or domestic sphere and the man's "outer" or public sphere. This asymmetry of the sexes *(namnyŏ chi pyŏl)* was necessary, they thought, to restrain sexual indulgence and selfishness, which would lead to social disorder, and to establish the different functions of husband and wife.

In the Confucian view, the law of nature thus accorded woman an inferior position. She had to obey her superiors: when unmarried, she had to follow her father's orders; when married, those of her husband; when widowed, those of her son. This was the subordination of the inner sphere to the outer sphere. In the domestic realm, however, the wife was supposed to assume leadership. The administration of the household was likened to that of a state. Domestic peace and prosperity depended on the way a wife exerted her authority. It was the wife's task to keep the customs pure. This was a heavy responsibility, for the purity of the customs as they were cultivated in the domestic sphere was directly correlated with the rise and fall of the dynasty.

The adoption and implementation of Confucian social tenets at the beginning of Chosŏn lastingly transformed the Korean social scene. At the core of this transformation was the domestic realm, represented by women. Women have rarely been innovators of social change, but social change often seems to have affected the lives of women more than those of men. Women therefore are a convenient focus for studying the acculturation of Confucian social thought.

THE INSTITUTIONALIZING OF PRIMARY AND SECONDARY WIVES. The early Neo-Confucian legislators were preoccupied with the "rectification of names" *(chŏngmyŏng)*, that is, with determining and identifying social status. For this, only a clear line of descent would provide the criteria on the basis of which descent group membership and thus social status could be verified. The singling out of one wife and her children as a man's rightful spouse and legitimate heirs was therefore of paramount importance. The legislative efforts had consequently to focus on the Koryŏ institution of plural marriage *(chunghon)*—a custom the Neo-Confucians regarded as principally responsible for social confusion at the beginning of the new dynasty. Censorial reports abundantly testified to the fact that high as well as low officials continued to have several wives,[1] a situation that prevented a clear delineation of status groups. The ranking of these women as primary *(ch'ŏ)* and secondary or minor *(ch'ŏp)* wives was thus a fundamental task for stabilizing society.

In 1402, urged by his Confucian conscience and encouraged by his Confucian advisers, King T'aejong ordered the Department of Rites and two prominent members of the Bureau of State Records (Ch'unch'ugwan), Ha Yun and Kwŏn Kŭn, to search through the history books to determine the number of royal consorts *(pi)* and concubines *(pin)* the feudal lords *(chehu)* of ancient China and the kings of Koryŏ used to keep. Perusing China's classical literature, the researchers found a very peculiar model of polygyny (multiple wives or female mates). As practiced by the nobility of feudal China, polygyny was regulated by two rules: a noble, when marrying, could take his wives only from one single family; he was strictly obligated to marry them all at the same time, and he could not marry again. These rules were intended to give the domestic sphere of a noble stability and peace because jealousy should not arise among women of the same status and family background. The rules also excluded rivalry between noble families by concentrating on a marriage alliance with one single family.[2]

It is not clear whether the Koreans fully understood the complexities of the feudal system, but they gained important numerical evidence: a feudal lord was entitled to take at one time nine women *(yŏ)*, a minister *(kyŏng)* or a great officer *(taebu)* one wife and two concubines, and a common officer *(sa)* one wife and one concubine.[3] This information furthermore allowed a significant conclusion: the ancient Chinese kings *(sŏnwang)* had classified women for the sake of clarifying human relationships and rectifying the domestic sphere.[4] This ancient system thus provided the Korean legislators with a rationale that could be used to determine unilineal descent by imposing upon the women's world a strictly hierarchical order.

These insights were first applied to the royal house. Because it had been rocked at short intervals by two succession struggles,[5] it became a convenient target for censorial criticism. The censors frequently angered King T'aejong with their blunt protests against instances when the proper distinction between women was violated in the royal house.[6] In analogy to the ancient Chinese system laid down in the *Li-chi* and the *Ch'un-ch'iu* (Spring and Autumn Annals), the Department of Rites suggested in 1411 that the inner quarters of the royal palace should house the queen *(wangbi)*, three royal concubines *(pin)*, and five ladies-in-waiting *(ing)*, all of whom should be descendants of merit subjects.[7] This suggestion borrowed the outer manifestation rather than the substance of feudal China's marriage institution, and it seems to have been too elaborate for King T'aejong. He limited the number of palace women to one concubine and two ladies-in-waiting.[8] The queen, who stood at the apex of the palace women, resided in the central palace. Her position was undisputed, and it was not deemed necessary to confer upon her a special title. She alone enjoyed the prestige and the privilege of being the royal primary wife.[9]

It was obviously not too complicated a task to straighten out the king's inner quarters by a game of numbers. The real test of strength lay in the legislators' attempt to introduce the new classification of women in the elite segment of society. As a first measure, to emphasize that the model of ancient China allowed the *sadaebu* only one legal wife *(ch'ŏ)*, the legislators granted honorary titles and land to the primary wife *(chŏngch'ŏ)*. It was up to the husband, however, to choose from among his wives the one he wanted to have recognized and honored by the state as his primary wife. The major criterion for his selection was what later Confucians disapprovingly called "the degree of mutual devotion and obligation" between the husband and one of his wives. Some lesser considerations for choosing a primary wife were the sequence of the marriages, the kind of wedding ceremonies, the length of time spent with a particular wife, and at times also the wife's moral qualities.

The delicacy of the choice may be inferred by the officials' reluctance to establish objective standards for the selection. The state's only conditions were that the woman to be selected had to have entered her husband's house as a virgin *(sillyŏ)* and that her family background had to be untarnished by lower-class ancestry.[10] It would seem that the state initially could not go further than this. In fact, the state was forced to lessen the ensuing social tension by issuing a legal ruling according to which a man's various wives would all be regarded as of equal standing regardless of their social origin *(chonbi sangdŭng)*. This clause conflicted, of course, with the strict interpretation of the ritual prescriptions that allowed a man to have only one main wife. It was undoubtedly a major concession to the social milieu of early Chosŏn, and it was later termed a temporary measure that would not be a permanent part of the dynastic founders' legal heritage.[11]

Zealously quoting from China's classical literature, the censors eventually tried to eliminate the inconsistency of the state's attitude toward women. They realized, however, that their efforts to "recapture the spirit of the Ch'un-ch'iu period" would be in vain without some legal sanctions. In a memorial presented to King T'aejong toward the end of 1412, they pleaded for the application of the Ming criminal code to force recalcitrant husbands to comply with the ritual prescriptions. In the spring of 1413, this request was granted, and a law was enacted that forbade a man who had a legal wife to take a second legal wife *(yuch'ŏ ch'wich'ŏ);* a man who broke this law was forced to separate himself *(ii)* from his illegally acquired second wife. This law, which was apparently promulgated in the *Sok yukchŏn* of 1413, was not made retroactive; in cases where men still had several wives *(ch'ŏ),* the only criterion for ranking them was thenceforth the sequence of marriage. Those who intentionally reversed or altered the ranking of their wives were to be punished according to the stipulations of the Ming code.[12]

The new social concept, expressed in the law of 1413, did not easily take root in Korean society. It went against tradition and its consequences for the various wives and their respective sons were grave. By ranking a man's wives, the state incited unusual competition in the domestic sphere. The state's criterion for singling out the primary wife did not in all cases coincide with the husband's personal preference; wives quarrelled about social standing and domestic finances; sons fought to prove their mothers' proper credentials in order to get for themselves the social recognition necessary to become legitimate heirs.

Throughout the first century of the Chosŏn dynasty, the censorial agencies were called upon to punish husbands who neglected or abandoned their primary wives to conclude second marriages, and to investigate claims of legitimacy brought forward by rival half brothers. The final rulings in such cases were particularly difficult when the mothers were of equal social background. For example, in 1437 Cho Yŏng-mu's (?–1414) two sons, who were half brothers, competed for official recognition as their father's legitimate heir. At the end of Koryŏ, the younger son's mother had been honored with an honorary title; but the elder son's mother was called *ch'ŏ,* legal wife. Trying to deprive her of this designation, the younger son called his older half brother *ch'ŏpcha,* the son of a secondary wife. He also desecrated his father's ancestral shrine by removing the memorial tablet the older brother had put there for his dead mother to prove his own legitimacy. The censors found the younger son guilty of violating human morality and recommended that he be punished with one hundred strokes of the heavy bamboo and three years of forced labor.[13] Clearly, women had become all the more key figures in transmitting the rights to descent group membership.

The distinction of 1413 between primary and secondary wives *(chŏkch'ŏp chi pun),* hailed as decisive means to clarify human relationships and social status, was a cornerstone of Confucian legislation and had far-reaching implications for the dynasty's social organization. The elevation of one spouse as a man's primary wife and his legitimate heirs' mother gave the lineal principle sharp contours and firmly bound that woman to her husband's descent group. By the same token, it introduced a built-in inequality into the women's world that was eventually correlated with social origin—primary wives were selected from the yangban elite, while secondary wives were of lower-class pedigree. In a wider perspective, then, the ranking of wives was intimately connected with dividing society into two broad categories: the superior and inferior *(chonbi)* or noble and base *(kwich'ŏn).* This "societal bulwark" *(taebang)* that separated the yangban as a practically endogamous status group from the rest of Korean society came eventually to be regarded as a genuinely Korean social institution that had originated from the wise precepts introduced by Korea's founding father, Kija. Illustrious scholars such as Yi Hwang defended it as the principle by which state and home were maintained.[14] This "social divide" depended largely on the proper social identification of women, and women therefore became the keepers as well as the victims of an unequal system.

MARRIAGE RULES AND STRATEGIES. Marriage with a primary wife was a transaction between two kin groups with strong legal, economic, and political connotations. For a society organized on the basis of structured patrilineal descent groups, the stated purpose of marriage, to bring forth male offspring, was the society's means of survival. The first sentence of the chapter on marriage in the *Li-chi* testifies to this: "The ceremony of marriage is intended to be a bond of love between two surnames, with a view, in its retrospective character, to securing the services in the ancestral temple, and in its prospective character, to securing the continuance of the family line."[15] Thus the purpose of marriage was to guarantee uninterrupted continuation of the descent group in two directions, taking the living as the starting point—toward the dead and toward the unborn.

To give Confucian ideology substance, the Neo-Confucian legislators of early Chosŏn demanded a rigorous reform of the pre-Confucian marriage institution of Koryŏ. As a first measure to rectify the "unnatural" family relationships that resulted from uxorilocal residence, in 1411 the Department of Rites demanded an extensive revision of the mourning-grade system. The lowering of mourning for matrilateral kin was an important attempt to create a new social milieu in which sentiment and allegiance would shift from matrilateral to patrilateral kin and the married couple would reside virilocally. The adaptation of the mourning system to Confucian usage, however, would be totally inadequate, a fervent reformer pointed out, if it were not placed into a much wider and more fundamental reform of the marriage institution itself.[16]

Foremost among the reform requests was the prohibition of intermarriage between close kin. Although marriages with patrilateral second cousins were no longer practiced at the beginning of Chosŏn, the *sadaebu* continued to marry matrilateral cousins. Because of uxorilocal residence, the matrilateral cousins lived under the same roof and were often attracted to each other; yet, since matrilateral first cousins had to wear mourning for each other, a ban on such marriages was imperative. In 1415, Yi Wŏn (1368–1429) was one of the first to demand that unions with matrilateral first cousins be prohibited.[17]

The adoption of the Confucian model not only went against sentimental values, but also raised some practical problems, most of which were economic. Daughters customarily inherited the same

share of land and other properties as their brothers. If the daughter now moved into her husband's house, she could not take land, but would have to be apportioned her share of the inheritance in the form of slaves, clothes, daily utensils, or perhaps some income from her family's land. If a bride's family was not able to provide her with her rightful inheritance, this could constitute an economic burden involving both sides of a marriage contract. A poor groom's family would find it difficult to accept a bride without property of her own.[18]

The principal reason, however, why the enforcement of marriage prohibitions with matrilateral kin was so difficult, it was recognized, was that descent groups had not been clearly differentiated during Koryŏ. The great familiarity with the mother's relatives especially blurred kinship limits. Moreover, marriages within the same descent group were often vaguely disguised as unions of the same surname but of different ancestral seats (pon'gwan). Nobody bothered to determine whether the origin had actually been the same[19]— research which, owing to traditionally vague descent group boundaries, would anyway have been difficult in most cases. As late as 1471, the Censorate still demanded the immediate drawing of a clear line between marriageable and unmarriageable matrilateral kin. This request was answered with an edict that prohibited marriage within the radius of second cousins.[20] Naturally, the same problem did not arise in regard to the wife's relatives because they were not regarded as consanguineous kin, and no legislation was enacted to delineate their marriageability. It became customary, however, to avoid, as a second marriage, a union with an affinal second cousin.[21]

By the end of the fifteenth century, descent-group exogamy was no longer disputed; but the question of what should be regarded as exogamous remained open. Confucian purists persisted in their demand for a ban on marriages between descent groups with either the same surname but different ancestral seats or the same ancestral seat but different surnames.[22] Finally, in 1669, the most outspoken and authoritative Confucian of his time, Song Si-yŏl (1607–1689), supported the long-standing request for more restrictive legislation and effected the enactment of a law that prohibited marriages between descent groups with the same surname but different ancestral seats.[23] This law intended to preclude the possibility that descent groups which had acquired different ancestral seats through segmentation would intermarry. Despite this struggle to deepen descent consciousness and to win general acceptance of restrictive legislation, pre-Confucian marriage customs, for example uxorilocal residence, remained a current that undercut the effectiveness of the Confucians' efforts.[24]

Social status was the principal determinant of political and economic advancement in Chosŏn society, and marriage was an important way of establishing affinal relationships with powerful descent groups. Thereby elite privileges were maintained and strengthened for the descent group in general and for the descendants in particular. The ruling elite was intent on keeping the prerogatives of political power and economic control within the confines of the group. This attitude especially forbade the introduction of marriage partners from outside the group. Although never explicitly stated in the law codes, the strong status consciousness of the *sadaebu* prohibited intermarriage with lower social groups so that group endogamy was a major factor in the marriage strategy.[25] Even within the ruling group, however, there were gradations of social standing and economic influence that affected the forming of conjugal ties. Political affiliation also played a weighty role,[26] so that from early in the dynasty Confucian idealists deplored the fact that political and economic considerations and not moral qualities often decided whether a union was a misalliance or a perfect match.[27]

Although the subject is largely unexplored, sketchy evidence for the second half of the Chosŏn period (observable until recently in rural areas) suggests that the marriage radius in geographical terms was more or less limited and may have been correlated with the social standing of the descent group. The more powerful a descent group, the wider its marriage radius. Although the bride's social credentials were considered of utmost importance, geographical distance was also a factor in the marriage calculation. Since a large proportion of the yangban population used to live in rural villages in which one descent group dominated *(tongjok purak)*, the search for a proper bride had to be conducted outside the village. The choice of a bride whose natal home was conveniently close was usually preferred.[28] The marriage radius of brides coming in and that of brides going out may not have been identical. Good marriage strategy ideally demanded the choice of a socially equal or higher spouse for daughters, whereas a daughter-in-law whose standing was slightly lower would eventually be raised to the husband's social level. The search for a proper partner for a daughter was therefore more difficult and covered a geographically wider range.[29]

It was not uncommon that a woman who had come into a descent group as a bride acted as matchmaker between unmarried members of her natal family and her husband's kin.[30] Affinal ties were thus spun, often repeatedly, with descent groups that lived scattered over several counties, but seldom beyond provincial boundaries. If national political prominence was achieved, the capital became the focal point for matchmaking, and daughters could even be sent as consorts to the royal palace. Marriage strategy was therefore an intricate game that could be played well only under certain conditions. A successfully concluded match could establish alliances that bore rich social dividends.[31]

Marriage was not an affair between individuals, but between families. It was the responsibility of a boy's or girl's most senior direct agnatic ascendants to take care of the marriage arrangements. Long before a marriage was actually concluded, preparations were made to defray the wedding costs. A piece of common property was set aside as "land for special obligations" *(ŭijang),* and the income from this property financed social duties such as weddings.[32] Another method was to establish an association of descent group members to finance the wedding *(hon'gye).* These economic dispositions underline the extent to which a wedding was the concern of the whole descent group.

The father or grandfather or even an elder of a boy's or girl's descent group was economically obligated to the younger generation, and he was also directly responsible for finding a suitable marriage partner within the proper time limits. Early in the Chosŏn dynasty, in 1427, the stipulations of Chu Hsi's *Chia-li* were adopted as law: a boy's marriageable age was fixed at between sixteen and thirty, that of a girl between fourteen and twenty. The *Kyŏngguk taejŏn* gave only base lines of fifteen for boys and fourteen for girls. It added that marriage could be proposed upon completion of the thirteenth year. Moreover, if one of the parents of either marriage party were chronically ill or over fifty, the limit could be lowered to twelve.[33]

The marriage ages in Chu Hsi's *Chia-li* were based on ancient Chinese tradition. The *Po-hu t'ung* gives the following explanation:

> Why does the man take a wife at thirty, while the woman marries at twenty? The number of *yang* is odd, the number of *yin* is even. Why [does] the man [marry at] an older age than the woman? The way of *yang* is slow, the way of *yin* is fast. At thirty a man's sinews and bones have become hard and strong, and he is ready to become the father of his children; at twenty a woman's flesh and muscles are fully developed, and she is ready to become the mother of her children. Combined together, they make [the age of] fifty, corresponding to the number of the Great Expansion, which begets the ten thousand things.[34]

Age regulations were aimed at suppressing the old custom, prevalent during Koryŏ, of marrying off children too early and not letting them mature to a proper age. The reason for early marriages, the officials of the Department of Rites complained, was the pursuit of wealth through affinal ties. Children who entered matrimony too young, they argued, were not aware of the principle that husband and wife are the mainstay of morality. They were unable, therefore, to fulfill their role of socializing their own children, and early marriage spelled sure disaster for descendants.[35]

Throughout the dynasty, voices were raised against the system of taking into the household a prospective son-in-law (*yesŏ*, Kor. *terilsawi*) or a prospective daughter-in-law (*yebu*, Kor. *minmyŏnŭri*). This system was a method of early marriage, usually contrived for economic reasons. Young children, often less than ten years old, were taken in by faking a wedding ceremony and put to work in the household or in the fields. Such sham marriages led to numerous

abuses and were practiced especially by the commoners, but yangban also were found guilty of violating the government-set age limits in this way.[36]

Statistical evidence is not available to document the youngest age
at which people married, but sporadic references suggest that
throughout the Chosŏn dynasty the limit was frequently lower than
that set by law. On the basis of data drawn from census registers
(hojŏk), the age difference between husband and wife, however, becomes clear. The common belief that the wife was generally older
than the husband is not valid for the whole dynasty. Data from the
late sixteenth and early seventeenth centuries reveal that especially
among the yangban, husbands tended to be up to ten years older
than their wives (in many cases, no doubt, because of second marriages). This trend was reversed in the nineteenth century when
wives seem to have been older than their husbands. In contrast,
among commoners and lowborn, husbands usually were older. It is
plausible that economic reasons prevented commoners from marrying their sons off at an early age. Among yangban, non-economic
considerations (for example the importance of affinal ties) must account for early marriage and especially for the brides' being older.[37]

As the dynasty moved into the late eighteenth and into the nineteenth century, yangban status came increasingly under pressure.
This circumstance suggests that the yangban may have found it
more important than ever to tie down proper affinal relationships to
maintain social status. The acquisition of affines became more crucial to the survival of a descent group than the immediate production of offspring. Because the act of marriage as such made a boy an
"adult," his age at the time of his wedding was of no great consequence. In contrast, a girl's marriageability depended on her physical maturity and therefore her age played a determining role. The
youth of the bridal couple and the groom's inability to start a household of his own may account for the often rather long time lapse
between the wedding and the actual induction of the bride into her
husband's house.

There were some conditions under which the conclusion of a marriage had to be postponed. The most important of these was the

death of a parent or close relative, such as a sibling for whom a year of mourning had to be observed. At the beginning of the dynasty it was deplored that *sadaebu* usually did not wait until after the mourning period to marry. Strict measures to eradicate such bad mores by enforcing the stipulations of the *Chia-li* were demanded. The Council of State therefore ruled in 1404 that during the three-year mourning period for parents and within one hundred days of the one-year mourning period marriages could not be concluded.[38] Offenders were accused of unfilial behavior and usually were punished with the confiscation of their patents of office.[39] The frequent demands of the censorial agencies to make proscriptive regulations stricter were realized only in the mid eighteenth century when it was ruled that if one parent on either side died, the wedding had to be postponed for three years even if the preliminary ceremonies had been held.[40] Other conditions under which marriage could not be concluded were, at the beginning of the dynasty, the times when girls were being selected as tribute for China and, during the whole dynasty, at times when the search for girls for the royal palace (*kan-t'aek*) was underway.

Marriage was the precondition for adulthood and to remain unmarried was socially inconceivable. It was of continuous concern to the Confucian legislators that economic reasons might prevent a family from marrying off its daughters at marriageable ages. Near the beginning of the dynasty, a law was passed that held a girl's closest paternal and maternal relatives responsible for getting her married at an appropriate time.[41] Negligence was to be severely punished. The *Kyŏngguk taejŏn* contained assurance of government help for needy girls and also carried a warning to family heads to keep within the prescribed time limits.[42] For a woman, the wedding signified a rite of passage from a childhood during which she received little attention to an adulthood during which she could become a full member of society.

THE CONFUCIAN-STYLE WEDDING CEREMONY. The Confucian wedding ceremony, which found its permanent form in Chu Hsi's *Chia-li,* was based principally on the *Li-chi* and the *I-li.* The six parts of the wedding procedure outlined in the *I-li* were collectively known as the six rites and became the blueprint for the Confucian-style wedding ceremony. They are 1) sending the present [from the groom's house to the bride's house] *(napch'ae)*, 2) asking the bride's name *(munmyŏng)*, 3) sending news of the favorable divination [to the bride's house] *(napkil)*, 4) the sending of the evidences [to the bride's house] *(napching)*, 5) asking the time of the ceremony *(ch'ŏnggi)*, and 6) the meeting in person *(ch'inyŏng)*.[43] In his *Chia-li*, Chu Hsi adopted this basic form, but tightened it and renamed its parts. His outline of procedure was as follows: 1) marriage proposal *(ŭihon)*, 2) betrothal *(napch'ae)*, 3) sending of wedding gifts *(napp'ye)* [to the bride's house], 4) bridegroom meeting the bride in person and inducting her into his home *(ch'inyŏng)*, 5) presentation of the bride to the parents-in-law *(pugyŏn kugo)*, and 6) presentation of the bride in the ancestral temple *(myogyŏn)*. Chu Hsi added a seventh step: the presentation of the bridegroom to the bride's parents *(sŏgyŏn puji pumo)*.

The climax of the wedding ceremony as prescribed by Chu Hsi was the rite during which the bridegroom personally inducted the bride into his own home *(ch'inyŏng)*; this was followed by the exchange of ceremonial bows between the bridal couple *(kyobae)*. The first three rites did not involve the wedding partners directly, but during the induction the bridegroom and the bride met for the first time. The rite symbolized the transfer of the bride from the natal home in which she grew up to the household in which she would spend her adult life.

No native ceremonial rite in Chosŏn Korea more persistently resisted Confucianization than the wedding rite. The fundamental conflict involved in introducing Chu Hsi's model was the Korean custom of uxorilocal marriage, which prevailed during Koryŏ and far into the new dynasty. As one of the chief architects of Chosŏn society, Chŏng To-jŏn, complained: "Since the groom moves into the bride's home, the wife unknowingly depends on her parents' love and cannot but hold her husband in light regard. Her arrogance thus grows with every day; and in the end there will be quarreling between husband and wife, whereby the right way of the family declines." The Confucians could not tolerate this custom by which *"yang* wrongly followed *yin,* thus abandoning completely the meaning of husband and wife."[44] The Confucian model demanded a reversal of Korean marriage customs so that the bride would be transferred to the bridegroom's house to become a member of his descent group.

In 1395, just after the inception of the new dynasty, royal orders went out to the famous Confucian Kwŏn Kŭn to settle the details of the four ceremonies: capping, wedding, funeral,and ancestor worship.[45] This was an expression of the dynasty's founder's desire to give Korean society the trappings of Confucian etiquette. In 1404, the highest ministers demanded that the *sadaebu* model their wedding ceremonies on Chu Hsi's *Chia-li.*[46] Ten years later, King T'aejong was still concerned that the Chinese would ridicule Korea's native marriage customs;[47] and he continued to demand that the Department of Rites study pure wedding forms as recorded in the Chinese classics and make recommendations to implement them in Korea.[48]

Confucian purists also demanded stringent austerity laws that would strip weddings of luxury items and put an end to the mindless display of wealth on such occasions. Already during the last years of Koryŏ the use of luxury items at weddings was prohibited.[49] Such prohibitions became even harsher at the beginning of Chosŏn. In 1394, gold could no longer be used, and only the highest civil and military officials were allowed to enjoy silk fabrics and jade ornaments.[50] Aiming at "straightening out the wedding ritual," the legislators pressed the king to ban all luxury goods and to restrict wedding expenditures.[51] As a result, strict laws against luxury were enacted in the *Kyŏngguk taejŏn.*[52]

Despite the fact that the reformers were aware of the inertia of tradition and realized the practical difficulties of ritual innovation, they pressed ahead to make Chu Hsi's *Chia-li* "the etiquette of the *sadaebu."* In 1434, the Department of Rites for the first time devised a ceremonial program for the wedding ceremony that was thought to be suitable for the ranked officialdom as well as for those without rank.[53] In all stages the proposed ceremony followed Chu Hsi's prescriptions punctiliously. Without changes, under the title

Chongch'in kŭp munmugwan ilp'um iha hollye (Wedding Rites for the Royal Relatives and the Civil and Military Officials of the First Rank and Below), it was attached to the Five Rites *(Orye)* and later incorporated into the *Kukcho oryeŭi.*[54] For easy reference, Chu Hsi's *Chia-li* was distributed among the *sadaebu*.

There was no visible effect resulting from either the royal example, which introduced the new-style wedding, or the legislative endeavors. No Confucian-style yangban wedding was reported in the fifteenth century, but under King Chungjong the issue drew new attention. He actively promoted the controversial rite of the groom's personal induction of the bride.[55] Rather than the king's performance of this rite in 1517, however, it was the great personal influence of Cho Kwang-jo (1482–1519) and his group that stimulated a young enthusiast, Kim Ch'i-un (n.d.), to become, in 1518, the first yangban to take his bride home in person.[56] Yet Kim's example did not set a new trend, and apparently few followed it.

After Chungjong's time the clamor for making the groom's personal induction of the bride the central part of the wedding ceremony was repeated occasionally,[57] but the issue never gained wide support. During the early part of the sixteenth century, a compromise formula known as "half *ch'inyŏng*" *(pan ch'inyŏng)* was devised. After the main ceremony in the bride's house was finished, the bride was presented to her parents-in-law on the following day.[58] How widely this was practiced is not clear. Even the ritualists in the seventeenth century had to acknowledge that the gap between native tradition and Confucian etiquette was unbridgeable,[59] and they did not, therefore, support their argument with much enthusiasm. They gave up their struggle to force the wedding ceremony into a Confucian framework and focused their discussions of the nuptial rite on inconsequential details and elaborate textual interpretations of relevant passages in the Chinese classics. They were unsuccessful in relating their learning to the social realities of their time as reflected in the wedding ceremony.

THE ROYAL WEDDING CEREMONY. The Confucian-style wedding ceremony was first performed in Korea not by the *sadaebu*, but by the royal house. The royal motive for assuming this pioneering role was the belief in the Confucian dictum that the exemplary behavior of the king would influence and eventually transform the conduct of his subjects. The first two occasions when Chu Hsi's *Chia-li* was used to some extent to program the wedding ceremonies at the royal court occurred during King T'aejong's reign.[60] It was King Sejong, however, who was the first Yi king confronted with the task of establishing the proper etiquette for the wedding of the crown prince who later became King Munjong (r. 1450–1452).

Assisted by an expert in ritual matters, Hŏ Cho, who served as minister of rites during his early years on the throne, King Sejong took special interest in adapting ancient Chinese rituals to use at the royal court. In the summer of 1426, the king ordered the Department of Rites to study the ritual handbooks and devise the details of the wedding ceremony. It is clear that Hŏ Cho and his assistants could not use the brief descriptions of the various stages of the wedding ritual as laid down in Chu Hsi's *Chia-li*. For fixing the fine points of the ceremony, they had to refer to such works as the *Ta-T'ang k'ai-yüan li* and the *T'ung-tien*.[61] A comparison of the sequence of ceremonies that Hŏ Cho drew up for the wedding of the crown prince with the precepts he found in the *T'ung-tien* illustrates the extent to which the Koreans were indebted to the Chinese ritual handbooks. Adapting official titles and some vocabulary to Korean usage, the officials of the Department of Rites adhered meticulously to the Chinese model. The crown prince's wedding to Kim O-mun's (n.d.) daughter[62] in the spring of 1427 was thus the first adaptation of Chinese imperial etiquette in Korea.[63]

The precedent set by the royal house was an impressive display of Sejong's intention to usher in a period of "revised etiquette," but its practical effect was small. Subsequent debate revealed that one part of the new ceremony, the bridegroom's personal induction of the bride *(ch'inyŏng)*, was the major obstacle to the successful adoption of the royal example by the *sadaebu*.[64] King Sejong understood the reasons for this seemingly open resistance to royal authority and was unwilling to force compliance by threatening punishment. However, supported by high officials who insisted on a fundamentalist interpretation and reenactment of the ancient Chinese wedding ceremony, he was unerring in his belief that the royal house had to continue to set a good example. In the spring of 1434, Sejong told the Department of Rites that if native marriage customs were abruptly changed, the result would be anger and frustration. He pledged, however, that thenceforth the royal house would strictly adhere to the ancient Chinese system; and he ordered the Department of Rites to devise ceremonial rules for the *sadaebu,* who were to follow the king's lead.[65]

The first wedding to follow the form decreed by King Sejong[66] was that between Yun P'yŏng (1420–1467) and the late King T'aejong's youngest daughter (by a secondary wife), Princess Suksun *(ongju),* in the spring of 1435.[67] A year later, in 1436, the Department of Rites devised a proper nuptial protocol for the crown prince on the basis of the ceremonial procedure of 1427.[68] This protocol became the blueprint for the wedding ceremony of the crown prince as laid down in the *Orye.*[69] The wedding ceremony of a king, which is described in the section of *Karye* (Festive Rites), was a simplified adaptation of the Chinese imperial ceremony as preserved in the *T'ung-tien.* It consisted of six parts: 1) betrothal *(napch'ae),* 2) sending of the wedding gifts *(napching),* 3) determination of the wedding date *(kogi);* 4) investiture of the queen *(ch'aekpi),* 5) induction of the queen *(pongyŏng wangbi),* 6) presentation of the queen at court *(wangbijo).*[70] It is significant that the ceremony upon which the Confucians laid the main emphasis, the personal induction of the bride by the bridegroom, was absent from the king's wedding ceremony. The ceremony that was established for the crown prince's wedding did not differ from that of the king in the first four stages, but concluded with three distinct acts: 1) the king's approaching the crown prince's sedan chair to give the last admonitions *(imhŏn ch'ogye),* 2) the bridegroom's personal induction of his bride *(ch'inyŏng),* and 3) the presentation of the royal daughter-in-law at court *(pinjogyŏn).*[71]

The establishment of the royal wedding etiquette thus was one facet of the ideological dialogue between the king and the Confucian officialdom. King Sejong was a monarch who was deeply interested in Confucian studies and in transforming Confucian ideology into normative guidelines of everyday life. In the case of the wedding ceremony, he had to deal with an especially sensitive issue because it was part of the much larger debate about the compatibility of native tradition and transmitted values. The debate split yangban officialdom into two camps: one that advocated heavy reliance on the Chinese example and one that defended Korean customs. The latter argued that Korea's customs differed from China's and that it would be fruitless to press for sudden changes. Although the scholar-officials were reluctant to model their own wedding ceremonies on the Confucian pattern, they demanded that the royal house strictly comply with Confucian etiquette. This contradictory attitude politicized and polarized the issue after Sejong's time: the yangban's demand for ideological purity in the royal wedding ceremony became a topic of intensive indoctrination which was binding for the king, but not for the yangban.[72]

After the years of the Yŏnsan'gun's disastrous reign (1494–1506), during which Confucian ideology was totally neglected, Neo-Confucianism was revived with new vigor. The scholar-officialdom intensified its indoctrination, and young King Chungjong proved a docile student. Under him Neo-Confucianism became firmly accepted as state ideology. This was also consequential for the royal wedding ceremony. King Chungjong deplored that King Sejong's efforts to Confucianize the wedding procedure had been largely ineffective and pledged to press for a nuptial ceremony that would include the bridegroom's personal induction of the bride as the central part. He also was confident that the right example given by the upper class would eventually have a reformative influence upon the lower classes.[73] The ideological correctness of the wedding ceremony, moreover, was thought to have sociopolitical implications. A royal edict issued in the winter of 1515 declared that only if the wedding rite were correct would the relationship between ruler and subject and between father and son be correct.[74]

King Chungjong himself soon had a chance to demonstrate the seriousness of his Confucian commitment. In the late summer of 1517, he climaxed the wedding with his third queen by personally

inducting her into the palace.[75] He was the first Yi king to perform
this ceremony, and his example was followed by later kings.[76] In
1702, this significant change in the royal wedding ceremony, which
symbolized the extent to which Confucian indoctrination was successful in the royal house, was incorporated in the *Oryeŭi*.[77]

At the time when the censoring bodies led by the group of men
around Cho Kwang-jo pressed for ideological purity, it is not surprising that King Chungjong's wedding had an ideological aftermath. Following the performance of the "proper rite," a controversy
was stirred up by the request of a member of the Office of Special
Counsellors (Hongmungwan), Yi Cha (1480–1533), that the king
conclude the wedding ceremony with the queen's presentation in
the ancestral temple. This rite, the memorialist argued, was the
most important part of the wedding ritual because it established the
bride as a married wife and secured her social position.[78] Since this
was a new rite that had not been performed before, King Chungjong ordered the Council of State and the Department of Rites to
study the proposal. While the censoring agencies insisted on an
exact interpretation of the ancient ritual literature and opined that
the already performed rite would be meaningless without the concluding ceremony, the state councillors and the officials of the Department of Rites argued that although the desire to perform this
rite was laudable, Korean usages differed from those of China.
Moreover, the bride had already been installed in the queen's quarters and her patent requested from China, acts that amply established her in her position as queen. The king sided with the state
councillors and rejected the censors' further presentations.[79] When,
however, the censors convinced the king of the simplicity of the
rite, the king reopened the debate.[80] It was unavoidable that the
continuing discussion threatened to become a futile exercise in hair-
splitting interpretations of ancient texts. The king repeatedly refused consent and finally ended the controversy with the somewhat
lukewarm argument that all the high officials of the government
had spoken against performing the rite.[81]

This last episode concluded a century of searching for the wedding rite befitting a Confucian king. Under King Sejong the royal

house had assumed the role of pioneering the development of a new ritual form; this act was thought to have an exemplary influence and to encourage the general compliance with Confucian precepts that was demanded of *sadaebu* society. But the issue was complicated by a variety of factors. There can be no doubt that the general commitment to Confucianizing Korean customs was genuine, but in no area of social mores was native tradition more resistant to change than in marriage rites. And in no other area of Korea's social life was the country's peculiarity more strongly defended against transmitted Chinese values. It was a formidable task to rationalize the acceptance of the Confucian system in some sectors and to insist on special precautions in others.

THE KOREAN WEDDING CEREMONY. A scholar-official of the sixteenth century, Cho Sik (1501–1572), pointed out that in Korea the Confucian precepts were followed only in general and not in detail,[82] an explanation as well as a justification for Korea's special wedding customs. Although the law prescribed compliance with the rules laid down in the *Chia-li*, the nuptial ceremony that was performed in yangban houses during the Chosŏn dynasty essentially continued native tradition.[83] Nevertheless, the native ritual incorporated certain features of the Confucian ceremony to highlight its principal parts. It was thus not a Confucianization of indigenous customs, but rather an indigenization of Confucian elements.

The Korean wedding ceremony came to consist of three distinct parts: the betrothal *(napp'ye)*, the presentation of a wild goose *(chŏnan)*, and the bride's entering the groom's house *(urye* or *ugwi).*[84] In the Confucian ceremony, the groom's presentation of a wild goose to the bride's parents was preliminary to the groom's personal induction of the bride, and it was performed just before the groom led the bride away to his house where the actual nuptial rite took place. In Korea, this act was made the centerpiece of the wedding ceremony. The goose, often a wooden replica, replaced other wild animals that had customarily been sent to the bridal home, usually three days in advance.[85] The gift was supposed to strengthen the marriage ties. This act set the stage for the climax of the ceremony, the ritual conjoining of the bridal couple. According to Korean custom, bridegroom and bride exchanged ceremonial bows and a nuptial cup in the house of the bride *(sŏbu kyobae)*, thus preserving Korean uxorilocal tradition. It was the merit of a prominent Neo-Confucian, Sŏ Kyŏng-dŏk (1489–1546), to combine *chŏnan* and *kyobae* and have them performed on the same day.[86] The *Chiali* was consulted only for some practical details of the ceremonial program.

The wedding ceremony,[87] the elaborateness of which depended on the wealth of the wedding partners, thus consisted of a series of acts that took place in different locations at different times. Because there were also distinct regional variations, it is impossible to describe a "typical" Chosŏn-dynasty yangban wedding. The description that follows is based on a variety of historical and ethnographic sources and gives a composite picture.

When a boy approached marriageable age, his parents started to look for a suitable bride for him. This was done informally by listening to reports about talented, pretty girls of acceptable social background. Personal interviews were impossible; but to verify hearsay, servants were sent out to take a look at the prospective bride. As soon as a desirable candidate was discovered, a middleman *(chungmae)*[88] was appointed to explore the social and economic background of the bride-to-be. If the result of this investigation was positive, the wedding masters *(honju)*,[89] usually the fathers of the future couple, got together in the men's quarters of the bridegroom's house to conclude the initial marriage negotiations *(myŏnyak)*.

Some time later—years could pass if the couple was very young— the groom's wedding master sent a formal letter to the bride's house asking that the wedding take place *(ch'ŏnghonsŏ)*.[90] This letter contained the groom's vital statistics: the four pairs of cyclical characters *(p'alcha)* that indicated the hour, the day, the month, and the year of his birth. Called the "four stars" *(sasŏng)* or the "four pillars" *(saju)*, these eight characters told the fortune of the person concerned. Signed by the wedding master and often also by the descent group elder *(munjang)*, the letter testified to the fact that the union was a matter that concerned the whole descent group. The receipt of a favorable reply *(hŏhonsŏ,* "letter granting the wedding") and of a letter that contained the dates for the betrothal and the wedding *(t'aegil* or *yŏn'gil)* set the stage for the first part of the wedding ceremony, the betrothal.

The betrothal established official relations with the bride's house by presenting the formal wedding contract *(honsŏ)* and a variety of gifts.[91] The groom's parents prepared gifts of colored silks or thread (typical colors were red and blue) and special items, most of them fertility symbols, such as millet ears, silkworm cocoons, and red pepper. The most important object placed in the lacquered wedding box was the wedding contract, which sealed the match as far as the two descent groups were concerned.[92]

Especially at the beginning of the dynasty, the question of when during the wedding procedure the union should be regarded as unbreakable was repeatedly raised. The censorial agencies had to deal with frequent complaints that betrothals were not honored, and brides and grooms were lightly abandoned. Consequently, a law was enacted, stipulating that the transmission of the marriage contract and the wedding gifts from the groom's house to the bride's would be irreversible evidence of affinal relations between two descent groups. This piece of legislation was confirmed in the *Kyŏngguk taejŏn.*[93]

This regulation eventually had grave consequences for the mutual mourning obligations. There came to be instances when the bride had to mourn for her future parents-in-law; but if the bride's parents died, the groom's family regarded this as a loss of influence and demanded the wedding gifts back. The legal stipulations of the *Kyŏngguk taejŏn* were not specific enough to forestall such cases; but in the middle of the seventeenth century, a royal edict ruled that if after the betrothal one parent of either partner died, the mourning period of three years had to be observed before the wedding ceremony could be concluded. This law was repeated in the *Sok taejŏn* of 1746.[94]

This law significantly regulated the mourning obligations between the two descent groups involved, but it left untouched the question whether the prospective bride should mourn for her dead fiancé or vice versa. Early in the dynasty this problem had arisen a few times. The cause célèbre was the controversy that was stirred up when Sejong's youngest son by a secondary wife, Prince Tamyang, died at the age of twelve in 1450. Shortly before the young prince's death, King Sejong had planned to marry him to Nam Kyŏng-u's (n.d.) daughter, but the wedding gifts had not yet been sent to Nam's house. King Munjong felt that the bride-to-be should mourn for the prince, whereas his highest ministers did not agree. The Department of Rites sided with the king and demanded that Nam's daughter mourn as if she had been fully married because the dates of the betrothal and induction had already been fixed. A dissenting voice was that of the minister of the Department of Rites, Chŏng In-ji. He was concerned that the handling of Prince Tamyang's case would set a precedent for the future and argued that on the basis of the Chinese classics and the *Chia-li* the wedding date was fixed only after the betrothal. If Nam's daughter were to mourn, she would have to be ennobled and later enshrined in Tamyang's ancestral shrine. This would be against the prescription of the classics which stipulated that as long as a bride was not presented to the ancestral shrine, she would not become a full-fledged member (*sŏngbu*) of the descent group. Therefore, Chŏng urged, Nam's daughter was under no mourning obligations. The other ministers eventually supported Chŏng's argument, and the king followed suit.[95] Although never put into the law books, this ruling in fact determined that the betrothal made the future bride a de facto wife, and that she therefore had to mourn for her dead fiancé for three years. Customarily a bride who had fulfilled her "wifely duties" was not supposed to marry again.[96]

Although not always performed in yangban houses, the capping (*kwallye*) of the bridegroom was a preliminary wedding rite. It had been demanded in the early sixteenth century, but without much effect except at the royal court.[97] Considered the "way into adulthood," it was performed on a propitious day shortly before the wedding day. In front of family and guests, the groom's freshly washed hair was put up in a topknot (*sangt'u*), and the headband (*manggŏn*) and the man's hat (*kat*) were added. Collectively, this ceremony was called *samga,* "the adding of the three things." If the groom was still very young, he wore a simple straw hat instead of the horsehair *kat;* and when he was about twenty years old, he changed to the *kat.* The groom was thus initiated into the men's world and went out to meet his bride as an adult.[98]

Usually within a year after sending the wedding gifts, the bridegroom prepared himself for the actual wedding ceremony which took place in the bride's house.[99] After announcing his impending wedding to his ancestors in the ancestral shrine *(komyo),* he rode on horseback to his bride's village *(ch'ohaeng).* He was accompanied by some closely related adults, his father, uncle, or grandfather—called *sanggaek*—and servants who carried the box containing the wedding presents, if it had not been sent a few days before, and a live or wooden goose. After the groom was welcomed into the bride's house by the bride's father, he first presented the goose to his parents-in-law and then proceeded to the ceremonial table which had been set up under a tent in the courtyard of the main hall of the house *(chungdang* or *taech'ŏng).* The bride, elaborately dressed and coiffed, was led by an elderly confidante to a position west of the ceremonial table *(ch'oryesang).* On this table, arranged in a specified order, were specially prepared foods—cooked rice, seaweed soup, honeycakes— and propitious items such as bamboo and pine branches, a live chicken, *taech'u* nuts, dried persimmons, cotton seeds, and various kinds of dried fish that were thought to help produce sons. The bride first bowed four times, then the groom, assisted by a master of ceremonies, bowed twice in reply.

The highlight of the ceremony was the exchange of the nuptial cup that was passed back and forth between the bridal couple by the two attendants *(kyogŭp* or *ch'orye).*[100] After this the bride was led back into an inner chamber, and the groom and his entourage ended the day with an elaborate banquet. These lavish ceremonies and feastings, witnessed by relatives and neighbors, publicly demonstrated the legality of the union and the legitimacy of its future offspring. Depending on regional wedding customs, during the first night the bridal chamber was surrounded by womenfolk who amused themselves by poking holes in the paper door and peeking into the room to make fun of the young couple. This was called "guarding the bridal chamber" *(susinbang)*. On the day after the wedding, the groom was roughed up and teased *(tongsangnye)*. [101]

On the following day, those who had accompanied the groom took an official look at the bride and left for home. The groom usually stayed three days in the bride's house and then returned home, only rarely taking his bride with him. Shortly thereafter, from three days to two months later, the groom went again to the bride's home *(chaehaeng)*, stayed there for a few days, and went back home. If the distance to the groom's house was very far, he stayed for one night in the house of some relative of the bride and proceeded from there to visit his bride for the second time. Three months after the actual wedding, the groom returned to the bridal house for the third time *(samhaeng)*. During his absence, there had been an intensive exchange between the two houses in the form of letters, presents, and visits. The bride's house sent expensive foodstuffs and presents to the groom's house, especially on holidays.

Years might pass before the last act of the wedding ceremony, the bride entering the groom's house *(sinhaeng* or *ugwi)*, took place. Depending on the economic situation of the newly related houses, and also on the ages of the wedding partners, the groom took his bride home shortly after his third visit or stayed on with his in-laws. In the latter case, the first child might be born before the couple returned to the husband's house. The bride's induction occurred on a carefully selected auspicious day. She took with her an array of gifts including cloth, wine, and special foods *(p'yebaek* or *chip'ye)*, which she presented to her parents-in-law after she had bowed to them and offered them wine *(hŏn'gurye)*. This scene was observed by the husband's relatives, to whom the new bride was introduced. [102] Thereafter, the bride had to pay her respects to her parents-in-law in the morning and in the evening, and three days later she was presented to her husband's ancestors *(komyo)*. [103]

Presentation to the ancestors was the final rite of the wedding ceremony, and it confirmed the bride as a full member of her husband's descent group. She then began her married life in the new environment, as daughter-in-law and as wife. If a bride died before she was presented to her parents-in-law and to her husband's ancestors, her spirit tablet was not enshrined in the ancestral shrine. This raised some ritual problems. Since the bride customarily entered her in-laws' house years after the actual wedding, and often after having borne her first child, it was thought ridiculous to make her status within the husband's descent group dependent on her visit to the ancestral temple. The more important criterion became, therefore, the existence of a son. [104]

TRAINING AND INDOCTRINATION OF WOMEN. The "virtuous conduct" prescribed by the Confucians for women had to be learned from the social precepts laid down in the Chinese classics. Because few women learned enough Chinese to read them, [105] vernacular versions propagated by the kings of the early Chosŏn dynasty for the instruction of women were their key to the classics. One of the earliest such works was the *Samgang haengsilto,* an illustrated collection of stories about the proper application of the three social principles: faithful minister, filial son, and chaste woman. [106] The traditional introductory text to Chinese wisdom was the *Ch'ŏnjamun* (One Thousand Character Classic) which listed one thousand basic Chinese characters arranged in groups of four for easy memorization.

The most important and influential textbook for women was compiled in 1475 by the mother of King Sŏngjong, Queen-Consort Sohye (her posthumous name). Entitled *Naehun* (Instructions for Women), this book consisted of quotations from educational works such as the *Sohak* (Chin. *Hsiao-hsüeh*), compiled as a primer for children by Chu Hsi. *Naehun* taught girls the four basics of womanly behavior: moral conduct—women need not have great talents, but must be quiet and serene, chaste and disciplined; proper speech—women need not have rhetorical talents, but must avoid bad and offensive language and speak with restraint; proper appearance—women need not be beautiful, but must be clean in dress and appearance; and womanly tasks—women need not be clever, but must pay attention to such duties as weaving and entertaining guests. *Naehun* also elaborated on the roles a married woman had to fill: she had to serve her parents-in-law, be an obedient and dutiful wife, and a wise and caring mother. [107]

Similar in content and didactic quality was the *Yŏsasŏ* (Four Books for Women), which was translated into the Korean vernacular by Yi Tŏk-su (1673–1744). The *Yŏsasŏ* combined four Chinese works written especially for the instruction of women. Another textbook was the *Tongmong sŏnsŭp* (First Training for the Young and Ignorant). This booklet, compiled by Pak Se-mu (1487–1554), elaborated on the five moral imperatives *(oryun)* by quoting passages from the Chinese classics and illustrating particular points with famous stories from Chinese history. These textbooks were often supplemented by biographies of virtuous women. [108]

Education for women was indoctrination. Its purpose was to instill in women, through the weight of China's classic literature, the ideals of a male-oriented society and to motivate them for the tasks of married life. Indeed, the pattern of behavior developed by the Confucians had the rigidity of a stereotype which did not allow for individual variations, so that Confucian society acclaimed particular women not for their individuality, but for the degree of prefection with which they were able to mimic the stereotype.

Before marriage, girls were not only instructed in Confucian ideology, but also experienced its practical consequences. After the age of seven, girls could no longer associate with boys or men. They were more and more confined to the inner quarters of the house where they received instruction in domestic duties from their mothers and grandmothers. They learned embroidery and the cultivation of silkworms, and were initiated into the intricacies of sacrificial food preparation.

Girls' cultural training was focused entirely on filling the role of married women. Training in ideology and in practical duties was based on the Confucian dictum that the moral human being was molded by the teachings of the sages. The successful application of these teachings was reflected in customs and manners. It was important to prepare girls for their future functions as moral guardians of the domestic sphere and providers for the physical needs of their families.

LIFE IN THE HUSBAND'S HOUSEHOLD. A woman became through marriage an adult member of society. When she left her natal home—

perhaps after several married years during which her husband had resided uxorilocally—and started her life in her husband's family, she found herself in an environment in which she was an outsider, and with her field of action hedged in by a set of Confucian social rules and values that stressed objective over subjective relationships. The descent group into which she married took precedence at all times over the family she had started or was about to start. Within the descent group, the members' roles were differentiated on the basis of age and sex. Ideologically, Confucianism postulated a clear delineation of the male and female spheres, with the public domain dominating the domestic. This social division was accentuated by the emphasis Confucianism laid on agnatic organization as the backbone of the patrilineal kinship system. As a result, the inter-generational relationship between father and son was given priority over the conjugal union.

The Confucian image of woman was thus a double one: she had to be modest and submissive, but also strong and responsible. On the level of Confucian idealism, the image was considered virtuous; on the level of daily life, it often meant bondage. Although the bride came to her husband's home fully indoctrinated with the values of sex-separation and agnation, she soon found herself subjected to the tension between an ideology that aimed at social harmony and a reality that was fraught with daily conflicts.

Easy interaction between the sexes had been natural during the Koryŏ period, but the Confucian moralists at the beginning of the Chosŏn dynasty were convinced that this unrestrained association jeopardized the integrity of the social structure. From the first years of the dynasty, the Censorate demanded legal provisions that would limit a yangban woman to having contact only with her closest kin.[109] Numerous reports of cases of adultery prompted the legislators to take severe measures to halt the "destruction of the human order." As a warning against future offenses, the wife of a high official who had committed adultery with a distant relative who had free access to the inner chambers was decapitated in 1423; her lover was banished. The king justified this harsh punishment by stating that a woman of such high social standing should have behaved with propriety.[110] Although King Sejong himself demanded the enactment of laws that would bar relatives outside the mourning grades from visiting each other, he was opposed to the request of the censors that capital punishment for notorious adulteresses be made mandatory. The heads of families were thenceforth held responsible for enforcing the separation of the sexes.[111]

The increasingly restrictive legislation also affected women's freedom of movement. From early in the dynasty, wives of high-ranking officials were no longer allowed to go around in open palanquins, as had been the custom during Koryŏ.[112] During King Sejong's reign the regulations concerning women's conveyances were further specified. Prototypes of a closed palanquin were built on royal command so that everybody could take them as models. In addition, palanquins had to be painted in different colors to identify the social ranks of the women who rode them. A later memorial handed in by watchful censors demanded that yangban women be banned from the streets during the daytime since they did not have to look after public affairs.[113]

Moreover, Neo-Confucian legislators, "to rectify the womanly way" and confine them to the domestic sphere, particularly censored women's frequent visits to Buddhist temples. In 1404, temples were declared off-limits to women except for memorial services for their parents.[114] Not only were they legally restricted from Buddhist temples and shrines, but shamans' houses were also found to have a corrupting influence and patronizing them was forbidden in 1431. Conniving officials and temple bonzes were threatened with harsh punishment; but laws and admonitions, the government complained, had little effect. The censors' efforts to bring temple-going women under control were rewarded in 1447 when the king approved their request that the heads of families and their closest agnates be charged with guilt by association for the trespasses of their womenfolk.[115] The Kyŏngguk taejŏn made women's temple visits and outings into the mountains a crime punishable by one hundred lashes.[116]

Not only were the Neo-Confucians of early Chosŏn concerned about checking the "corrupt" female mores inherited from the previous dynasty, but they also focused attention on reforming women's fashions. Dress style and color were convenient means for pointing up social differences. The Censorate complained that the indiscriminate use of style and fabrics had blurred the line between social status groups, and they demanded frugality.[117] By the middle of the fifteenth century, new dress and accessory styles still had not been found; but the Confucian legislators agreed that the female figure had to be clothed in such a way that no unauthorized eyes could catch a glimpse of it. They especially insisted that when primary wives went outside the house, they had to wear a veil or "screen-hat" (*yŏmmo*) that covered the face completely and was not to be lifted. Earlier, women had hidden their faces behind fans. In 1449, the use of silk gauze, patterned silks, and the color bright red became the exclusive privilege of yangban women and female entertainers. The *Kyŏngguk taejŏn* further restricted the choice of dress material and color to provide visual aid in differentiating social classes.[118]

In practical terms, the separation of "in" and "out" had a number of implications for the new bride who took up residence as primary wife[119] in the inner quarters of the house (*anch'ae*). Her freedom of movement was curtailed so that she virtually lost contact with the outside world. Only after being married for years would she venture forth on her first outing in a sedan chair accompanied by slave servants. The circle of men whom she could freely meet and talk with was usually limited to relatives up to and including the tenth degree, that is, fourth cousins, on the side of her own kin and the closest affines of her husband's family, that is, husbands of her husband's sisters and husbands of her husband's aunts.[120]

The bride who had just entered her husband's house had to try to find a place for herself in a female world in which authority and prestige were determined by the status of the men to whom the women were attached. The inequalities of the men's world were clearly reflected in the women's world. The most authoritative position was held by the husband's father, or possibly the husband's grandfather; and his counterpart was the husband's mother, the wife's mother-in-law.[121] The mother-in-law was the most important individual in the life of the young bride, since she stood at the apex of female social prestige and authority while the young bride was on the lowest level. The degree of tension created by the generational difference in position between the mother-in-law and the wife and by their competition for the attention and confidence of their common male worked with the need to avoid conflicts. This largely determined the daughter-in-law's behavior toward her superior. The filial daughter-in-law strove to follow the mother-in-law's orders punctiliously, and she avoided situations that might give rise to scoldings. She did not display insubordination by talking back. Smooth interaction with her mother-in-law was the young daughter-in-law's most important source of satisfaction and fulfillment, while friction and antagonism were the most important sources of frustration and unhappiness.

Domestic tranquility hinged upon more than the peaceful relationship between mother-in-law and daughter-in-law. The wife's position within the domestic group was also determined by the other daughters-in-law who happened to live under the same roof. The composition of the domestic group tended to be more complex the higher the social standing of the descent group. The large extended family was typical, however, for only a comparatively small, wealthy segment of yangban society. [122] In the extended family several married brothers lived together, their ranks fixed on the basis of the sequence of their births. This gave the oldest brother a definite position of prestige because he, as the ritual heir, would carry on the main line of descent. The latent rivalry between the brothers was ideologically smoothed over by the concept of brotherly love *(che)* that demanded the younger's deference to the older. The women who married into the descent group *(tongsŏ)* fitted into the brotherly hierarchy and carried into the inner chambers of the house the same conflicts and discord that might exist in the outer quarters. The wife of the eldest brother naturally held a position of eminence because she was to bear the son who would continue the primary descent line. She also had some ritual prerogatives in the domestic realm that the other wives did not have.

Human relationships within the female sphere of the house were further complicated by the presence of secondary wives and a large number of slave servants. The extent of a woman's influence and radius of action thus depended primarily on the position she received by marriage and only secondarily on the natural disposition and manipulating skills she acquired by birth and experience. Whatever the bride's qualifications, she knew that despite the inherent contradiction, her husband's family usually preferred the women who were born into it to those who married into it. Until the wife bore a son, her position in her husband's house was insecure. Only after the birth of a male heir had the wife fulfilled her duty and gained the privileges and authority of motherhood. With her husband, she eventually received filial piety, the expression of a new generation's respect and subordination.[123]

Women were rarely referred to by personal names. As girls, they were called by Korean-style names. Unlike the personal names given to sons that consisted of one or two Chinese characters, the girls' names were composed of single Korean elements and frequently ended with the diminutive *i*.[124] Lacking a respectable name and ultimately of little use to her natal family, a girl was rarely registered in the genealogical records of her descent group *(chokpo)*. After marriage, she was entered into her family's genealogy with her husband's name. In her husband's genealogy she was recorded as "spouse" *(pae)* and identified by the surname and ancestral seat of her natal descent group. Sometimes, the name and official title of her father and his immediate agnatic ascendants and of her maternal grandfather, collectively known as *sajo,* the four ancestors, were added to certify the impeccability of her ancestry. A married woman's natal family referred to her by her husband's surname and the title *sŏbang* to which the post-noun *taek* (house) was attached. In her husband's village, people called her by the name of her native place to which *taek* was added. A woman who had borne a child was simply designated as the mother of her son or daughter. Women who had married into the same descent group usually addressed each other by kin names.[125]

In official documents such as the census registers *(hojŏk),* the wife's social origin was clearly expressed in the terminology of the listing. The primary wife *(pae)* of a yangban householder was recorded by the surname and ancestral seat *(pon'gwan)* of her natal family. To the former the respectful term *ssi* was added; to the latter the term *chŏk* (register). This nomenclature contrasted with that used for commoner wives and, in the case of the ancestral seat, even with that of her husband: *ssi* was then replaced by *sosa* and *chŏk* by *pon*. In both cases, vital information about the four ancestors was added to the wives' names. [126]

As much as yangban women were isolated from the men's world, they were indirectly tied to the public sphere by the honorary titles they received on the basis of their husbands' official ranks. This privilege was reserved for women who were daughters of primary wives and who themselves were primary wives. [127] The granting of ranks to primary wives *(myŏngbu pongjak)* was instituted in the early years of the Chosŏn dynasty and codified in the *Kyŏngguk taejŏn*. Titles were conferred upon women only on their husbands' merits, but the seriousness with which the Confucian legislators put down the rules may have been an acknowledgment of the truth of the Confucian dictum that only a man whose wife worked for domestic peace and prosperity could rise in the official realm. [128]

THE MARRIED WOMAN'S LEGAL AND RITUAL FUNCTIONS. In Confucian terms, the family was a judicially self-sufficient unit within which domestic peace had to be preserved and disputes among its members smoothed over by ideological values that stressed the hierarchical structure of the family and the male-centered distribution of authority. Although women were responsible for the day-to-day operation of the family and thus largely determined the quality of the domestic atmosphere, highest authority over the family members and their behavior was lodged in the family or household head. [129] He had to judge right and wrong, arbitrate disputes, and take ultimate responsibility for keeping the family members in their places and for ensuring harmonious relations among them. The family head's authority was officially upheld by legal stipulations that ordered capital punishment for family members who defied their superiors. In judicial cases, the testimony of inferior family members—son, younger brother, wife, or slave—against their superiors was not accepted.[130] Within this power structure the woman's position was clearly subordinate. Although a woman as mother exerted lasting influence on her children's intellectual and emotional development, she had officially only limited authority over them.[131]

A woman could assume a leading role in the family only under one condition: her husband's death. If there was no adult son who could directly succeed to his father's position, the wife could become the head of the family or household.[132] Her tenure, however, was temporary. It ended as soon as the headship could be transferred to her son upon his maturity, that is, when he got married, or when it was entrusted to a legally established heir. In the latter case, the widow had one important prerogative: her will prevailed in the choice of such an heir.[133] With the passing of the household headship into the hands of the younger generation, the widowed mother became a member of the new household unit. She was not likely to establish a separate household.[134] A woman thus could not lead an independent existence. Her point of orientation for livelihood and domicile was at all times a male member of her family or household.

The woman was not only subject to male authority, her lot was intimately tied in with the fate of the household head. It was customary to punish the whole family when the head of the family was found guilty of a major crime. Only at the end of the eighteenth century did the law prohibit the capital punishment of the primary and secondary wives of the leader of an armed rebellion. Yangban women and children also could no longer be enslaved.[135] In criminal cases other than treason and rebellion, women of yangban status enjoyed certain privileges that women of the lower classes do not seem to have had. A yangban woman could be jailed only after a report was submitted to the judicial authorities. In case of conviction, she usually avoided punishment by paying a compensation.[136] After 1745, a woman could not be arraigned except in cases of rebellion and treason. She did not have to appear in court and could be represented by her son or son-in-law or even by a slave. A yangban woman had to submit to flogging only in rare cases.[137] Punishment of a pregnant woman was deferred until one hundred days after she had given birth.[138] From early in the dynasty on, men were responsible for preventing women from breaking laws and for keeping them in their place.[139]

The integration of women into their husbands' descent group as demanded by Confucian ideology is impressively illustrated by the daughters' gradual loss of inheritance rights. As has been discussed in Chapter Five above, by the middle of the dynasty daughters who upon marriage left their natal family were deprived of their stake in their families' ancestral property and entered their husbands' home without the land and slaves they had brought in earlier. All they may then have taken with them were some heirlooms and possibly some slaves. Women thus lost the economic independence they had enjoyed at the beginning of the dynasty. This development was closely connected with the gradual acceptance of the rule of primogeniture that concentrated a descent group's ancestral land and slaves in the hands of its primary agnatic heir. A concomitant factor was the change from uxorilocal to virilocal residence.

A married woman, upon her husband's death, could be called upon as widowed mother *(kwamo)* to oversee the distribution of her late husband's property. In case there was no male heir, she had the right to her husband's estate, but it was only a usufructuary right. As soon as an heir was established, she had to relinquish her claim to the property. Economically, then, a woman came to be completely dependent on wealth controlled by the male members of her affinal home.

Ritually, a married woman was assigned a marginal role. The only duty of the wife of the main officiant at the domestic ancestral rites was the presentation of the second libation *(chaehŏn* or *ahŏn)*.[140] On the mourning chart, a woman as mother was granted a three-year mourning period by her son *(chaech'oe);* but if her husband was still alive, this mourning was shortened to one year.[141] Although this reduction was not in tune with Chu Hsi's *Chia-li,* it was felt that the obligations of a three-year mourning period would make it difficult for a mourning son to serve his old father in a proper fashion.[142] For her own parents, a married woman mourned only for one year.[143]

A wife wore mourning for her husband for three years; but she, being replaceable as a wife, was mourned by her husband for only one year. For the death of an "inferior," the husband was originally not entitled to an official leave of absence. After a legally stipulated period of three years, a widower was urged to marry again as an act of filial piety toward his parents. This period could be reduced to one year if his parents wished it or if he was over forty and still sonless.[144]

The ultimate proof that a woman had been a primary wife, whether she had sons or not, came after her death. At the end of the mourning period, her spirit tablet was enshrined in her husband's ancestral shrine *(sadang)*; and, having become an ancestor, the dead wife was commemorated at regular memorial services.

SECONDARY WIVES AND THEIR SONS. The distinction between primary and secondary wives, legalized in 1413, ended the Koryŏ tradition of plural wives. It restricted a member of the officeholding elite to one primary wife. She was selected as spouse on the basis of a number of social criteria. She was inducted into the descent group by the proper rites and, most importantly, only she could assure her son a full share of the social recognition necessary for him to become the legitimate heir of his father's descent line and succeed in the world. Consequently, any other woman the husband may have taken into his house was, as far as his descent group was concerned, of secondary importance. The acquisition of a secondary or minor wife was a "private" arrangement. Such a wife lacked the primary wife's social prestige, and her attachment to a man's domestic group was precarious and, if she remained sonless, often only temporary.

The *Po-hu t'ung* explains the difference between a primary and secondary wife thus: "What do [the words] *ch'i* (Kor. *ch'ŏ*) and *ch'ieh* (Kor. *ch'ŏp*) mean? *Ch'i* means 'whole.' [The wife forms] one whole body with her husband. From the Son of Heaven down to the common man [the word *ch'i* is used with] the same meaning. *Ch'ieh* means 'to connect.' [The concubine] at regular times meets the man for connection."[145]

The clear differentiation of wives was also rationalized in cosmic terms. The loss of sequence between primary and secondary wives, it was warned, would result in cosmic disorder that would spell disaster for the human world.[146] The law consequently barred a secondary wife from ever advancing to the position of primary wife.[147] Strong ideological and legal considerations thus separated secondary wives from primary wives. The severity with which this discrimination was upheld had no counterpart in China and was uniquely Korean.

The social discredit that came to be attached to secondary-wife status eventually eliminated yangban daughters as potential secondary wives, except in cases of economic destitution, and limited the selection to the lower social classes.[148] The social origin of secondary wives was, therefore, varied. Often the daughters of secondary wives in turn became secondary wives of other yangban. Other candidates were girls of commoner status *(yangch'ŏp)*, professional entertainers *(kisaeng)*, and even slave girls *(ch'ŏnch'ŏp)*.[149] Widows who had no means of support occasionally also became secondary wives. Clearly, the taking of a secondary wife was not limited by rules of class endogamy.

The life of a secondary wife was subject to social rules that accentuated her inferior position within the descent group. At the beginning of Chosŏn, when a son by a secondary wife of commoner status could become his father's ritual heir, the reason for acquiring a secondary wife often was the primary wife's sonlessness. Later, as the system became increasingly inflexible owing to an ever more conscientious enactment of the agnatic principle that culminated in the institution of primogeniture, this criterion could no longer justify the existence of a secondary wife. Other reasons then may have been a particular woman's attractiveness as an entertainer and sexual partner and the social prestige the possession of several wives gave to a man of high political office and good economic standing.

Many aspects of a secondary wife's life came to be regulated by custom rather than by law—a circumstance that made her a rarely discussed person in official documents. Because secondary wives continued to be part of upper-class households well into the twentieth century, the following discussion also draws on information gathered in recent times.

There was no fixed ceremony when a man acquired a secondary wife.[150] It was customary, however, to conduct an abbreviated wedding ceremony if the bride was of commoner background. No ceremony was performed for a slave girl. For these secondary marriages, public recognition was of no great importance; they did not aim at tying affinal relations of any consequence, yet the husband was held responsible for the upkeep of his secondary wife. Some acknowledgment of a secondary wife's existence in a household was given by entering her name in the census register *(hojŏk)*; but even if she had a son, her name remained unrecorded in genealogical records. No numerical evidence therefore is available to allow an estimate of how widespread the keeping of secondary wives was. A secondary wife was commonly known by the name of her place of origin to which *taek* or *chip*[151] was added. Although the bond with her husband, or master *(kun)*, was not well defined, a secondary marriage could not be dissolved without good reason. For a woman, the arrangement was most often her only source of support.[152]

A secondary wife often lived in the same household as the primary wife. At times, one wife lived in the countryside, the other in the capital, and the place of residence may have been a device for ranking the wives at the beginning of the dynasty.[153] It was the primary wife's duty to maintain peace in the house, but accounts of domestic discord between the wives abound. A source of tension was the hierarchical order that was imposed upon the women's world. Also, the different social backgrounds of the wives gave rise to envy and dissatisfaction. Moreover, the marginal position of their mother within the descent group created for the children of a secondary wife personal frustration and resentment.

A secondary wife had no parental authority over her children. As long as her master was alive, such authority was vested in him. If after his death the primary wife became the temporary head of the household, parental authority was transferred to her *(ch'ŏngmo)*.[154]

In principle, a secondary wife could not become the head of a household; but after her master's death she might, with the consent of the new household head, form a separate domestic unit.[155] She also was not in line to receive a share of her husband's property, although he might have given her some. He, however, would get her property if she died without a son.[156] The concept of family was not fully applicable to the union with a secondary wife. If she was sonless, there was no need to adopt a son. A secondary wife's relationship with her master was intended to last only during his lifetime and was not supposed to form a social unit that had to be perpetuated.

The secondary wife's marginal position within a descent group was also evidenced by the lack of ritual obligations toward her master's ancestors. She was excluded from the regular services for his ancestors; and her spirit tablet, if there was one, was not placed in her husband's ancestral shrine. A secondary wife was, however, required to fulfill ritual duties toward her master, the master's primary wife, and the master's immediate lineal ascendants and descendants. The ritual concerns of her own descendants were accorded second place. Consequently, she had to mourn for her dead master for three years, whereas she herself was mourned for only three months, or not at all if she was sonless. She had to mourn for her master's eldest son by the primary wife for three years, whereas the mourning period for her own son lasted for only one year. She had to observe a one-year mourning period for the primary wife, although a primary wife had no mourning obligations toward a secondary wife. After her death, she was mourned by her own son for only one year and not, as was customary for mothers, for three years. If ancestral services were held, they had to be conducted in a purified room; and they were discontinued after her son's death.[157]

The social inequities that were created by the secondary-wife system were most acutely reflected in the discriminatory treatment of the sons of a secondary wife (*ch'ŏpcha* or *sŏja*).[158] The status of a secondary son in Chosŏn dynasty society became a vexing problem because it involved not only, in a narrow sense, a definition of who could be considered legitimate within a descent group, but also, in a wider sense, pertained to the delineation of social class boundaries. As suggested before, women played a decisive role in determining their offspring's legitimacy. Representing a certified and publicly recognized elite patriline by whose surname she continued to be known, a primary wife joined her social equal when she was ritually inducted into her husband's house. Their combined social credentials legitimized their progeny as full-fledged members of their father's family and patriline and, in addition, provided them with an enduring link to matrilateral kin. In contrast, a secondary wife, originating from the lower classes, lacked the social prestige of a well-established descent group and entered a yangban's house without public acclaim to take up the position of a subordinate. Although a secondary wife's son was recognized as having inherited his yangban father's "bones and flesh," he did not for this reason become a fully legitimate member of his father's descent group (although a secondary son by a base mother could, if his father held high office, become a commoner). It was not a question of paternity alone. What disqualified such a son was the fact that his mother had nothing to contribute to a socially determined "status fund" which would confirm his full legitimacy.

Legitimacy, that is, the affirmation of status, thus derived first of all from social rather than legal criteria. Already in Koryŏ, social status was primarily defined in terms of descent and heredity—a definition to which the matriline gave as much weight as the patriline. This tradition the Chosŏn Koreans upheld—against the dictates of Confucian agnation. For the elite, status ascription remained bilateral. This juxtaposition of genealogical and cultural values found expression in the uniquely Korean formula of the "four ancestors" (*sajo*) that included, besides a man's three lineal ascendants, his matrilateral grandfather. The latter's presumed non-existence in a secondary son's ancestral mix condemned such a son to a life as "half-yangban"—an admittedly unsatisfactory halfway station that, it was always feared, could give cause to insubordination and a consequent breakdown of the social hierarchy.

It was not only traditional status consciousness, however, that deprived a secondary son of legitimacy within his father's descent group. The Confucian patrilineal descent ideology equally pushed him to the sidelines. Early in the dynasty, a secondary son of commoner status was occasionally called upon to become the ritual heir of his father's descent line if there was no son by the primary wife; and this practice had legal backing. But with the gradual expansion of lineal thinking, which came to encompass the entire descent group, and the eventual implementation of ritual primogeniture, which even excluded second sons, a secondary son's heirship became unacceptable for his father's line as well as for the descent group as a whole. The strenuous efforts in mid sixteenth century to formulate comprehensive rules for regulating ritual heirship testify to the difficulty of reconciling the social status of the ritual performer with the dictates of the patrilineal principle. The ultimate solution was to remove secondary sons completely from heirship and succession, and this may also have been the time when their names started to drop out of genealogical records. When the continuation of a descent group was henceforth threatened by the lack of a lineal heir, adoption of an appropriate substitute, ideally an agnatic nephew, solved the problem. Adoption, increasingly practiced from the middle of the dynasty, thus destroyed one of the main reasons for concluding secondary marriages.

Moreover, a secondary son's precarious standing in the domestic realm prevented him from advancing in the political world. From the early days of the Chosŏn dynasty on, secondary sons were barred from holding regular government posts; and this discrimination was strengthened by the *Kyŏngguk taejŏn,* which explicitly excluded secondary sons and their descendants from taking the civil service examinations. [159] Secondary sons thus were unable to climb to political prominence. Even though from the middle of the sixteenth century occasional attempts were made to alleviate the secondary sons' predicament with the argument that the state was interested in selecting officials on the basis of ability, such initiatives largely proved ineffective. They clearly stood at cross-purposes with the yangban's insistence on keeping descent group legitimacy and, by extension, eligibility to political power within their own group. Legal and ritual discrimination against secondary sons remained one of the Chosŏn dynasty's most pernicious social issues.

THE DISSOLUTION OF THE CONJUGAL BOND. Ideologically, the dissolution of the conjugal bond was a social impossibility. Combining the husband's forbearance *(ŭn)* and the wife's sense of obligation *(ŭi)* was the ideological basis of marital harmony. If the wife failed in her role because of her "dark and ignorant nature" (she represented *yin* in the *yin-yang* duality), it was her husband's task to guide her to reform herself and to restore domestic peace. Would it not be cruelty to expel a wife without fully exhausting the possibilities of amending her conduct?[160] The sages of ancient China, however, granted the husband a number of criteria with which he could justify the expulsion of his wife: the seven instances of extreme disobedience *(ch'ilch'ul)*—disobedience toward the parents-in-law, failure to produce a son, adultery, theft, undue jealousy, grave illness, and extreme talkativeness. To prevent abuse in the application of the seven disobediences, the sages stipulated three instances when a wife could not be expelled *(sambulgŏ):* if the family fortune had improved greatly during the marriage, if the wife could not return to her own family, and if she had mourned for either or both parents-in-law.

In the Chosŏn dynasty, the Confucians recognized the two sets of criteria for and against the expulsion of a wife as a means of moral pressure rather than as of legal value. For a woman who received recognition and social standing in society only through marriage, the threat of being expelled from her husband's family and the social stigma attached to remarriage were effective means of keeping her obedient and submissive.[161] Since Confucian ideology attributed the ultimate responsibility for keeping peace in the domestic sphere to the morally superior husband rather than to the naturally inferior wife, the censors generally treated a husband harshly if he expelled his wife without weighty reason. They were backed by the provisions of the Ming criminal code, which prescribed eighty strokes of the heavy bamboo for a husband who expelled his wife without

having proof of one of the seven disobediences or who did not have
official permission to divorce her on the grounds of a criminal act.
For example, when a wife assaulted her husband the husband could
receive a judicial divorce *(ii)*. The judges usually dismissed undue
jealousy, grave illness, and extreme talkativeness as valid reasons for
a husband's separation from his wife because they were merely part
of a woman's natural disposition; in such cases, a reconciliation of
the spouses *(wanch'wi, pokhap)* was considered possible.

Of much greater moral and legal intricacy were the first four of
the seven disobediences because they were intimately connected with
descent group concerns and human morality. In the judgment of
such cases, the conflict between ideological considerations and the
application of legal stipulations was evident. The following example
makes this clear. A man's greatest offense was lack of filial piety,
and the most unfilial act of all was the failure to bring forth an heir.
This argument was presented in self-defense by a man who had
expelled his sonless wife and taken another wife. The censors originally refuted his plea with the counterargument that his first wife
had mourned for her father-in-law; they demanded a reconciliation.
Later they dropped this demand and had the husband punished with
ninety strokes of the heavy bamboo, the penalty for taking a primary wife when he already had one.[162]

The application of the criteria for and against the expulsion of a
wife depended to a large degree on the interpretations and the moral
attitudes of those who had to judge a case. Frequently the opinions
based on the two sets of criteria conflicted. This is illustrated by the
dispute King Sejong had with the censorial officials in the suit against
Yi Maeng-gyun (1371–1440) in 1440. Yi's seventy-year-old wife
had been jealous of her husband's secondary wife (who was a slave),
mistreated her, and eventually caused her death. Yi, who held high
office,[163] tried to cover up his wife's crime. The disclosure of the
facts stirred public sentiment, and the censors demanded the wife's
official expulsion *(ii)* on the grounds of jealousy; she also had no
son. The king declined to act on this recommendation because the
wife profited from two reasons for which she could not be expelled:
she had lived through her husband's climb to prominence, and she

had mourned for her parents-in-law. The king further argued that the wife's misdemeanor was closely connected with the husband's failure to keep peace in his house. He ordered Yi's dismissal from office and the invalidation of the wife's official patent. Pressed by the censors' demands for heavier punishment, the king finally agreed to Yi's banishment, but resisted further punishment of the wife.[164]

The dissolution of marriage, especially when it involved the first two of the seven disobediences, was an affair that went beyond the spouses' personal concerns. The parents' voice in their son's married life was licensed by the often quoted saying: "Dissatisfied parents make their son expel his wife even if he gets along with her; parents who like their daughter-in-law force their son to live with her, even though he does not like her." Expulsion of one's wife could therefore be a filial act. This is illustrated by the case of a higher official under King Sejong who justified the expulsion of his wife and his remarriage by claiming that he had done so upon his father's last request because he had no son. He had made his first wife leave after she had observed a three-year mourning period for her father-in-law. The censorial agencies were suspicious of the man's motives and demanded a reconciliation of the spouses because of the wife's filial act toward her father-in-law. The king, however, did not accept this recommendation, but insisted that a son was bound to obey his father's orders. To mourn for the parents-in-law was in Sejong's judgment not enough to make up for sonlessness.[165] King Sejong also ruled in favor of the father-in-law in the following instance: A father-in-law demanded a daughter-in-law's expulsion on the grounds that she had been disobedient. It turned out that the real reason for her father-in-law's displeasure with her was her maltreatment of the domestic slaves who had fled in great numbers. The censors pleaded for reconciliation, but the king upheld the patriarch's testimony and agreed to the expulsion.[166]

While the force of ideological arguments could control and at times even limit the applicability of the law, there were occasions when ideology was used in lieu of law. The seven disobediences were recognized as an important judicial weapon where the application of legal stipulations was problematic, most significantly in cases involving criminal women of yangban status.[167] On the other hand, when ideology did not complicate the judgment, the law was harshly applied. A husband who expelled his primary wife without sufficient reason and remarried had to expect heavy corporal punishment or, if he was a higher official, even dismissal from office and forced reconciliation. Numerous censorial reports illustrate the variety of unjustifiable motives for expelling a wife. One defendant wanted to use his second marriage as a vehicle for gaining official appointment. He did not receive the patent of office.[168] A bridegroom who was disappointed with his bride's physical appearance and her poor trousseau falsely accused her of adultery and expelled her. He was punished by sixty strokes of the heavy bamboo and one year of forced labor. He also had to take his bride back.[169]

Confucian society provided a married woman with neither ideological nor legal grounds that would have entitled her to seek a divorce from her husband. Once married into a descent group, a woman had no way of separating herself from this bond. In rare instances, when a woman wanted to leave her husband, she could do so only by using "male tactics." One such woman forced her spouse to give her written evidence of expulsion and then married another man. She and her second husband were severely punished.[170]

The dissolution of the conjugal bond thus was not an easy matter. Both ideology and law stressed the indissolubility of marriage and the security of the married woman. They held the husband responsible for maintaining order and harmony in his private life. The implications for the whole descent group as well as the moral ramifications therefore made the intentional termination of marriage an unwieldy instrument for settling marital and domestic discord.

WIDOWHOOD AND REMARRIAGE. Marriage was largely a descent group affair, and, as far as the wife was concerned, it lasted beyond her husband's death. After her spouse died, the wife's point of orientation shifted to the next generation: as mother, she became a senior member of her son's household. Confucian ideology stressed as the greatest of womanly virtues the wife's devotion to one husband,

and, in logical extension, to one descent group.[171] This emphasis on the exclusive nature of the marital relationship eliminated the rationale for taking a second husband. Adapted from Chinese sources, this ideal had influenced the Korean attitude toward marriage even before the Chosŏn dynasty.

During Koryŏ, remarriage of widows seems to have been rather common, and the anti-remarriage ideology was confined principally to the widows of high civil and military officials, who were ennobled if they did not remarry.[172] With the advent of Neo-Confucianism, remarriage became an important issue and the official attitude stiffened. In 1389, the highest government authority suggested that widows of aristocrats should not be allowed to marry for a second time, whereas widows of high officials could do so after the mourning period for their husbands. Remarriage was easier for women of lower social status, although those who chose not to marry again were, after they died, specially honored with commemorative tablets.[173]

At the beginning of Chosŏn, reports about women's serial marriages abounded. An amazing number of women, not always widows, concluded second and third marriages. Such behavior, it was argued, was injurious to the quality of the country's moral life. In 1406, the government revived the Koryŏ law that women who had married three times were to be recorded in the *Chanyŏan* (Register of Licentious Women). Now the law was made to apply specifically to primary wives of yangban status.[174] Compliance with this law seems to have been lax; but thirty years later, in 1436, stricter observance was demanded by the censors. The issue gained importance in 1468 with Kim Kae's (1405–1484) case when, despite the fact that his mother had been married three times, Kim was promoted to high official rank through special royal favor. The Censorate was outraged by King Sejo's seemingly insupportable gesture and argued that the son of a mother who had behaved so badly was not fit for office. The censors pointed to the strong correlation between an orderly domestic sphere and a healthy state.[175] Kim Kae was an isolated case, and the *Kyŏngguk taejŏn* repeated the stipulation that thrice-married women had to be registered.[176]

The Confucian legislators supported widows who "preserved their chastity" with special economic measures. The wife who was recognized as the primary wife was, after her husband's death, awarded a certain percentage of her husband's rank land *(kwajŏn):* two-thirds if she had sons, one-third if she was sonless. This land was called "land to preserve faithfulness" *(susinjŏn)* and was intended to guarantee the widow an independent existence, but it was a luxury the government found difficult to continue for long. With the conversion of the rank land into office land in 1466, the *susinjŏn* was abolished. There were frequent pleas later to restore it, but without results.[177]

More important than the economic incentives were the legal sanctions that the government took to correct "the ugly custom of remarriage." One of the first such measures was to deprive widows who remarried of their honorary titles.[178] Despite the many heroic stories about young widows who resisted their parents' pressure to remarry and fled to their parents-in-law's house—clear indication of uxorilocal residence—to serve as filial daughters-in-law or cut their hair and became nuns, it is evident that government policies did not deter even primary wives from entering a second marriage.

The subject continued to claim the legislators' attention throughout the first half of the fifteenth century. The Confucians expressed their disdain for serial marriages by putting them into the same category as secondary marriages and adultery: they all were aberrant forms of a woman's attachment to man. Because such marriages were common, they could not easily be outlawed; but severe restrictions were put on the offspring of such unions. The *Kyŏngguk taejŏn* of 1471, an edition which is not extant, apparently carried a provision that barred the sons and grandsons of thrice-married women from advancing into higher officialdom. A general debate on the problem of remarriage held in front of King Sŏngjong in 1477 revealed that the majority of officialdom favored restricting this prohibition to third marriages. It was argued that for young widows who had neither parents nor children the only way to escape destitution was remarriage and that, consequently, sonless widows should be allowed to remarry upon receiving permission from parents or descent group elders. Only a few officials demanded an amendment of the *Kyŏngguk taejŏn* that would contain a clear prohibition of second marriages. King Sŏngjong, who made the purification of yangban mores his special concern, sided with the minority opinion. To press his point didactically, he printed and distributed a vernacular treatise entitled *Samgang haengsil yŏllyŏdo* (Conduct of the Three Human Bonds with Illustrations of Virtuous Women).[179] Ideology, thus, was the principal reason the offspring of twice-married women were banned from official careers. The revised edition of the *Kyŏngguk taejŏn* of 1485 stipulated that the sons and grandsons of adulteresses and remarried women would not be eligible for civil or military office; and together with the descendants of secondary marriages, they were not allowed to compete in the lower and higher civil service examinations.[180] Remarriage as such was not outlawed, but the ideological and legal implications for the immediate descendants of a remarried woman made it well-nigh impossible for a widow to enter a second husband's house and function as a primary wife.

Remarriage, therefore, was, when it occurred, a lackluster affair concluded as a means of economic support; and since in most cases it was a secondary marriage, no particular rite marked the occasion. To remarry, a widow needed to get the consent of the head of her deceased husband's household or, sometimes, that of her own parents. If she had children, she lost her parental authority over them; and she could not claim a share of her late husband's estate.[181] Although chaste widowhood was regarded as a "beautiful custom," throughout the dynasty voices were raised in favor of abolishing the anti-remarriage laws. Nevertheless, despite its decidedly negative character, the custom of chaste widowhood became so well entrenched that a widow's remarriage bore a social stigma until recent times.[182]

Even for men, remarriage with a second primary wife was not unproblematic, for in ancient China second marriages were prohibited according to the principle that two primary wives could not coexist in one house.[183] While in ancient China these marriage rules had mainly functioned as political measures to minimize rivalry

among regional lords by prohibiting multiple marriage alliances, in
Korea they were given a purely social meaning. In China, when the
wife of a feudal lord died, she could be replaced by the wife next in
line who was her sister or cousin. [184] In Korea, because of the preferential status of the primary wife, no immediate substitute was
available. Remarriage after the primary wife's death, however, was
a social necessity: the female hierarchy in the inner chambers could
not be left without a leader, and some classical literature advised
against raising a secondary wife to the position of the primary wife. [185]

   The search for a viable solution to this ritual dilemma may have
been at least partly necessitated by the enactment of the law of 1413
which put special emphasis on the importance of the primary wife.
Close scrutiny of the Chinese model drew the Korean Confucians to
the conclusion that the Chinese remarriage prohibition had applied
primarily to the feudal lords and not to their retainers. The Koreans
thought they were on safe ritual ground with their assumption that
the royal house but not the *sadaebu* was subject to the remarriage
prohibition. Although a man like Pyŏn Kye-ryang regretted that
the ancient Chinese system was not applied more consistently in
Korea, King Sejong himself lent his voice to the argument that the
sadaebu were not bound by the same social rules as the royal house.
Nevertheless, he set an example (little heeded by later kings) by
refusing to remarry when he was urged to do so after the death of
his consort in 1446. [186]

THE CONFUCIANS' IMMUTABLE IMAGE OF WOMEN. The implementation
of Confucian ideology in Korea meant a rigorous regimentation of
women. By granting political and economic prestige to men, the
Confucian legislators allowed women to have status and authority
only within the domestic confines. The women's domain was the
"other world," a world the state did not wish to deal with directly.
It therefore inflicted its sanctions against women's misbehavior—
their deviations from assigned functions—rarely on the women
themselves, but on their male representatives—their husbands and
sons.

   Confucian ideology devised for women roles that called for specific behavior ("virtuous wife," "obedient daughter-in-law," "chaste widow"), and women were remembered either for their perfect enactment of these roles or for their rebellion against them. Biographies of women written by their kinsmen and appended to their collected works, therefore, only rarely yield information of a personal nature. Rather, such documents tended to depict women stereotypically as loyal personifiers of ideological dictates.

Whatever the lofty ideals were with which the women's incorporation into their husbands' descent group was rationalized, for women real life was neither tranquil nor serene. They naturally reacted to the functions and values ideology imposed upon the women's world. Within this system, women had to develop strategies to secure for themselves and for their offspring the best means of survival. When the curtain of ideology was lifted, realpolitik dominated the domestic scene. For the male onlookers, therefore, women were forever scheming and calculating, and conflict and tension were part of everyday life. To be sure, some women could make ideology work for them: a young widow, for example, who for whatever reason preserved her "chastity" by loyally serving her parents-in-law instead of giving in to her family's pressure to remarry was sure to be rewarded with public applause. Far more frequent, however, were the reports about wayward and jealous behavior. Women escaped ill-treatment from husband and parents-in-law by committing suicide. With the stakes in the well-being of their children so high, jealousy and discord between primary and secondary wives were endemic, and many a primary wife felt herself grievously betrayed by her husband's love affair with a low-status companion. Confronted with such "lack of propriety," the Neo-Confucians never relented in insisting on correct womanly behavior. After all, women were to give substance to the ideological standards and provide state and society with the "right men."

Conclusions: The Emergence of a Lineage Society

The developmental process Korean society underwent during the transition period from Koryŏ to Chosŏn can now be assessed and evaluated in a wider comparative perspective. A brief recapitulation of its most salient aspects and their juxtaposition against similar features in the social history of China will throw light upon the uniquely Korean dimensions of this process. It also will point out the consequences this transformation had for the constitution of the ruling elite of Chosŏn Korea and the role of ideology in the development of Korean society. It will be argued that this transformation resulted from a fundamental change of the structural conception of society initiated by the early Neo-Confucians.

To begin this discussion, it may be helpful briefly to restate the most conspicuous and decisive elements of the Koryŏ-Chosŏn transformation. Certainly the most striking aspect of change was the rigorous narrowing of the descent calculation. The all-inclusive Koryŏ descent group, in which descent was traced through female as well as male links, was forced into a strictly patrilineal scheme. This completely altered the basis of recruiting the descent group membership: the inclusive descent principle of Koryŏ was replaced by the exclusive principle of Chosŏn. This switch affected matrilateral kin most, for it was gradually deprived of the prominent place it had held in the kinship structure of Koryŏ. Women, generally, suffered a loss of status and economic independence as they were integrated into their husbands' groups through marriage. Residence consequently changed from uxorilocal to virilocal. Descent groups became uncompromisingly exogamous. Genealogical thinking that pursued non-agnatic lines as easily as agnatic ones gave way to strictly patrilineal reckoning on the basis of the unilineal principle of "line of descent" *(chong)*. In Koryŏ, descent from either a paternal or maternal ancestor, who perhaps had held high office several generations before, may have been haphazardly reconstructed by one descendant to receive for himself the protection privilege *(ŭm)*. In contrast, in Chosŏn a famous agnatic ancestor was remembered by his descendants to secure a starting point for the formation and continuation of their patrilineal descent group as a whole. Finally, this patrilineal contraction of the Koryŏ descent group culminated in the institution of primogeniture that ended fraternal succession and equal inheritance. After more than two centuries of legislation and indoctrination, the arduous and complicated shifting from horizontal to vertical thinking was thus concluded.

The undoubtedly most fundamental feature of the Confucianization of Korean society was the development of the patrilineal lineage system. Korean lineages came to be much more rigidly structured than those in China.[1] The crucial difference clearly lay in the extent to which primogeniture—the backbone of lineage organization in ancient China as described in the classics—was implemented in the two countries. In China, primogeniture had been defunct for many centuries, and only a "shadow" of preference for the eldest son survived in the extra share of inheritance that was usually given to him in recognition of his being the "primus" among his siblings.[2] Although inheritance practices varied, the basic rule was equal fraternal inheritance. In contrast, in Korea the singling out of the eldest son as the ideal and therefore preferred representative of his generation resulted from the greater emphasis on the continuation of the main line at the cost of collateral lines. Ritual primogeniture did not directly lead to a complete discontinuation of equal inheritance among brothers; but with the dynasty moving into its second half, the trend toward preferential, even if only rarely total, economic primogeniture is clearly discernible. However varied the practice may have been in specific cases, the idea of primogeniture became firmly implanted in the social consciousness and significantly narrowed the descent calculation—to the detriment of second as well as secondary sons.

The ideological ground from which this transformatory process took off was the ancestral cult. While patrifiliation was celebrated as the most fundamental human bond,[3] it had to be embedded into the larger genealogical context of descent to gain long-term structural significance. By defining each agnate's place in the descent group according to an unalterable scheme of generation and collaterality, ancestor worship translated agnation from an ideological postulate into lived reality. Ancestor worship clarified the lines of descent and marked kinship boundaries as well. It also fostered among the agnates gathered in front of the ancestral shrine consciousness of common descent and solidarity. Ancestral rites thus introduced a kind of ideological corporateness that, detached from political and economic conditions, functioned as a prime mover in the formation of patrilineal descent groups in Chosŏn Korea.

Ancestor worship defined first of all the socio-ritual criteria of a man's position in his descent group. Correlated to ritual status and function were the rights of inheritance and the obligations of mourning. Because Confucian ideology saw the political or public realm as a direct extension of the domestic sphere, the same restrictive criteria also applied to a man's chances in the public world. Only someone who enjoyed the recognition of full membership in his descent group could hope for advancement in the political sphere. The importance of ancestor worship as a social ordering device was nowhere better illustrated than in the case of secondary sons and women—persons who did not fit the ritual scheme.

Discrimination against secondary sons was in part a direct result of the restrictive manner with which ancestor worship was used in Korea. It had no counterpart in China. Although recognized as son of his father, a secondary son was marginalized by his descent group because he was, owing to his mother's inferior social status, genealogically and socially a weak link. At best he could therefore be entrusted with continuing his own father's line, but he was found unacceptable to bear the weight of the ancestral trust. This margin-alization became even more severe with the implementation of pri-mogeniture. Lacking full ritual membership in the domestic realm, secondary sons were also restricted in the public realm. They were barred from the examinations and thus could not hope for careers in government.[4]

Women did not fare much better for similar reasons: their stand-ing vis-à-vis the ancestors—their own and their husband's—was ambivalent. To be sure, in the early days of the dynasty when women were active members of their own descent groups, it seemed natural that they would share with their male siblings the ritual responsi-bilities toward their own ancestors. With their growing incorpora-tion into their husbands' descent groups, however, the symbolic and often also the geographic distance to their natal homes length-ened, and their own and their descendants' loyalty toward the (ma-ternal) ancestors was increasingly questioned. Separation from the ancestors resulted in the eventual loss of inheritance rights. As wives, women were strangers to their husbands' ancestors. They were therefore never accorded a function in the ancestral hall of their affines. At best they played a minor role in the domestic rites. As widows, women at first had a say in selecting an heir for their de-ceased husbands. But as soon as genealogical thinking began to encompass the whole descent group, they lost this decision-making power. Although their affines were obliged to ritually care for them, married women were excluded from the ritual life of their affinal families.

This analysis emphasizes the structural function of ancestral rites and leads to the conclusion that the lineage of late Chosŏn emerged first of all from a ritually motivated limiting of the Koryŏ descent group along patrilineal lines.

The Confucian transformation of Koryŏ society was a gradual process. It stretched over roughly the first 250 years of Chosŏn. The conceptualization of a Confucian society in the top ranks of govern-ment was much faster than its actual absorption among the rank and file. The fifteenth century was therefore still marked by a great deal of fluidity and uncertainty and, at times, even resistance—a situation that favored the survival of major Koryŏ traditions. But the ideological switches had been irreversibly thrown. As the dynasty moved into its second century, the internalization and application of lineage ideology developed momentum. Restrictive societal strategies not only were well-founded in the political realm, but gained added urgency by changing economic and demographic realities. It was then that the Korean aristocratic descent groups attained their full patrilineal structure, and the Confucian sociopolitical order reached maturity.

Despite this success, the Neo-Confucian theorists of the sixteenth and seventeenth centuries regretted the (in their eyes) all but perfect implementation of the ancient institutions. Korean ideosyncracies had created significant modifications of the original blueprints as found in the Chinese classics and in Neo-Confucian theory. Consequently, wide discrepancies emerged between the legal and ritual formulations concerning some central social features, for example secondary sons. The Neo-Confucians coined therefore the concept of *kuksok,* "national practice," which readily acknowledged the continued strength of Korean values—in particular, concern with descent and social status. In short, "national practice" encapsulated the distinctive nature of Korea's Confucian transformation: a unique blend of fundamentalistically interpreted models of China's pre-Confucian past and Korean readings of the Chinese Neo-Confucians' exegeses of the classical literature, with a strong ideosyncratic tradition of descent and status. This transformation owed its momentum to the Neo-Confucians' vision of a perfect society, but the society that eventually emerged represented its own version of Confucian rather than of Chinese society. The society of the Chosŏn period could claim to be as much "Confucian" as the society of contemporary China. Both differed critically—and the Koreans were well aware of this—from the prototypes of Chinese antiquity that the Neo-Confucians had taken as the point of departure of their social theories.

What, then, were some of the principal elements of Korea's social tradition that persisted despite the country's Confucianization and, indeed, contributed to what later Neo-Confucians apologetically called "national practice"? Most conspicuous was the continued strength of the maternal line of descent in determining and reproducing elite status. Women, as representatives of their respective patrilines, imparted the crucial hereditary essence that made their offspring full members or, if they lacked that essence, only half members of their husbands' descent group. For the elite, the reproduction of status remained bilateral. Assigning continued importance to a woman's ancestry in legitimizing her offspring, thus, was a significant remnant of the pre-Confucian past. Although contrasting with the Confucian stress on agnation, it worked in fact to heighten the exclusiveness of the Korean patrilineal descent group.

Alien to Confucian theory as well as to Chinese practice was consequently the wedding rite. It was the courtyard of the woman's natal home that provided the locus where the wedding ceremony publicly sealed the marital contract. The bride was then sent off, not endowed with a share of the patrimony, but with a share of her patriline's ancestral status that proved so vital for legitimizing her husband's children as full-fledged members of his descent group. This was an affirmation of status that, in contrast to the economic endowment of the Chinese bride, strengthened rather than loosened the Confucian underpinnings of the patrilineal group.

Status and its transmission, thus, were at the center of the secondary-son problem. Because the mother of a secondary son did not carry upper-class status, she could not impart this vital attribute to her offspring. Korean secondary sons were therefore genealogically as well as socially (and eventually also economically) outsiders who could not be entrusted with lineage heirship and the weight of the ancestral rites. In China, secondary sons seem generally to have been less marginalized, even though the pertinent literature speaks of great variability.[5] Because their mothers' lowly origin did not disenfranchise them of full lineage membership, they were readily made heirs to perpetuate their fathers' line and, at least in principle, had the same rights in their fathers' property as primary sons. The more loosely structured Chinese lineages could thus accommodate members who were excluded in Korea. Moreover, Chinese society after the T'ang was far less status conscious than Korean society and did not build social and political barriers against the secondary sons who in Korea were so feared as potential agents of social mobility.

Reminiscent of Koryŏ tradition was further the continued high esteem for the maternal grandparents as expressed by the custom of non-agnatic succession. Daughters' sons were occasionally assigned to conduct the ancestral services for their (sonless) maternal grandparents. Although it blatantly violated the dictates of Confucian agnation, this practice was sustained by strong sentimental values and thus survived until the middle of the dynasty. By that time, non-agnates disappeared from the genealogical records, and non-agnatic succession was forced into (never total) oblivion by agnatic adoption.

In late Chosŏn, the rigid structure of the descent groups led to a sharp distinction between a man's own patriline and that of his mother, expressed in the dichotomy of "inside" *(nae)* and "outside" *(oe)* kin.[6] Women became mere links between these two groups: in the genealogy of her natal family a married woman was recorded as someone's wife, in her husband's genealogy as someone's daughter. Ritually and economically far less protected than in Koryŏ, women in Chosŏn came to be more dependent on their affinal homes than their Chinese counterparts. Chinese women, especially from the Sung onwards, contributed with sizable dowries economically to a conjugal fund (always kept separate from common household property) that gave them as well as their husbands a certain degree of independence, and consequently they were less incorporated into their husbands' families than Korean women. Remarriage, therefore, was both more common and more feasible in China than in Korea.[7]

In sum, what the Neo-Confucians erected at the beginning of Chosŏn was a societal system that, by reflecting the Korean social milieu, represented a uniquely *Korean* interpretation and adaptation of the Confucian model. This interpretation incorporated values that significantly differed from the Chinese version of lineage system. Whereas in China (at least in the south) lineages were primarily built on property, in Korea's highly stratified society lineages were the quintessential expression of status and prestige. Rather than

eliminating status consciousness, the Korean Confucians drew strength
from it and modified the Confucian message in crucial areas to fit it
into their country's social tradition, thus creating an atmosphere
quite different from the Chinese social experience.

If it is valid to argue that the transformation of Koryŏ society
principally came about through a systematic application of Neo-
Confucian precepts by a small, Confucian-trained group of scholar-
officials, it is meaningful briefly to step back in time and consider
the transition period from T'ang to Sung and ask whether the Chinese
Neo-Confucians played a similar role of catalysts of change with
comparable results. Social historians of this period[8] emphasize that
the nature and social organization of the ruling class from T'ang to
Sung changed drastically. During T'ang, the upper stratum of society was constituted of "great families"—a group of high-status
clans whose definition was very broad. Although these clans traced
common patrilineal descent, no worshipping groups fixed on a common ancestor existed. The T'ang Chinese seem to have been almost
exclusively interested in kinship at the level of the mourning group
(wu-fu). In the ancestral temples a system of "major lineage" *(ta-
tsung)* and "minor lineages" *(hsiao-tsung)* was operable without ob-
serving primogeniture. A line of descent could never switch from
elder brother to younger brother. No property was corporately held,
and property was subject to fragmentation because of its equal division among the heirs. These "great families" were held together
by a strongly developed clan consciousness that manifested itself in
the compilation of genealogical records. Although the aristocratic
status of such families was upheld by birth, officeholding was an
eminently important condition for having high status certified by
the state. Therefore the upper echelons of government were virtually monopolized by aristocrats. Detailed lists inventoried those
clans that successfully combined aristocratic privileges with bureaucratic qualifications.

On the surface, the important clans of T'ang may possess certain
similarities to the Koryŏ descent groups. Both were loosely structured, but nevertheless placed great value on descent. In both so-

cieties primogeniture was unknown, and no common ritual or economic actions are discernible. High social prestige was dependent
on validation by the state, a circumstance that introduced a certain
ambiguity between ascriptive and achieved status. The most critical
difference between T'ang and Koryŏ, however, was the fact that
T'ang society was squarely patrilineal, while Koryŏ society was not.
This decisive difference, then, must surely have given rise to divergent responses to the Neo-Confucian challenge.

In early Sung, the old T'ang aristocracy fell from power, and a
new ruling class with a different social background emerged. Only
very few high officials traced their ancestry back to T'ang.[9] This
shift is generally attributed to the new civil service examination
system, a T'ang institution that was refined and elaborated under
the Sung. Even if vital, this was only one factor. Economic growth
through rapid commercial expansion, urbanization, and a burgeon-
ing printing industry were other signs marking the beginning of a
new epoch. But after less than 170 years, the Jurchen invaded North
China and established the Chin dynasty, forcing the Sung to retire
to the south. This traumatic event ushered in a second major shift
in the social circumstances of the elite, and it was during the Southern Sung that Chinese society acquired the traits that remained
characteristic until recent times.[10]

During the Sung, the values of social behavior and organization
came to center on the patrilineal descent group that recognized a
common ancestor and ordered that ancestor's agnatic descendants
on the basis of descent.[11] One of the new methods to foster agnatic
consciousness and bring agnatic kinsmen together apparently was
worship at ancestral graves.[12] Such early manifestations of descent-
group formation—another was the compilation of genealogies—seem
to have coincided in time with the Neo-Confucians' drive to reform
society by reviving the patrilineal descent line *(tsung)*. In the mid
eleventh century, scholars like Chang Tsai (1002–1078) and Ch'eng
I called for a recreation of the descent system of Chinese antiquity
that was described in great detail in the classics.[13] Shortly later,
Chu Hsi built upon the recommendations of his predecessors his
elaborate scheme of major and minor descent lines in which pri-

mogeniture was the main mechanism of lineal continuation. Although these precepts launched by the Neo-Confucians for renovating society were henceforth quoted in all ideological discussions on patrilineal organization, they were never followed to the letter because they did not tally well, and even stood in tension with, generally held notions of family structure and strategies. Nevertheless, regular ancestral services, corporate property, and the compilation of genealogical records eventually became institutionalized features typical of Chinese descent groups in the Ming and Ch'ing dynasties (even though the significance accorded to each of these features may have greatly varied according to time and geographic region).

How, then, does the Koryŏ-Chosŏn transition compare to the T'ang-Sung transition in the light of the Neo-Confucians' demand for a new social order? Most obvious is the fact that the Chinese Neo-Confucians were not involved in the fall of the T'ang. They developed their views of an ideal society in a sociopolitical environment that, after the collapse of the T'ang aristocracy, was conducive to a fundamental reorganization of kinship organization. A major shift toward more regulated relationships and activities among agnatic kinsmen seems to have been in the air. The Neo-Confucians may have merely underpinned this development with systematized schemes of descent-group formation which they unearthed from the classics and propagated as the guarantors of a stable social order. Their success, however, was greater at the ideological than at the practical front: they were respected teachers, but never gained much authority in government to legislate their ideas.

In contrast, in Korea there was no radical break between the ruling class of Koryŏ and that of early Chosŏn. The Confucian scholar-officials emerged from the old aristocratic matrix and carried over some distinct elements of this heritage, most notably an acute consciousness of status and descent. Their Neo-Confucian training equipped them with a professionalism that made them comparable to their contemporaries of late Yüan and early Ming rather than to the Sung Neo-Confucians. As the actual initiators of the dynastic change, they were directly involved in policy-making at all levels.

Their answer to the adverse social, economic, and political situation at the end of Koryŏ was an all-embracing program, the core of which was a fundamental social reconstruction—the implementation of the Neo-Confucian vision of a stable and organized society. In contrast to the Southern Sung where the Confucian-educated elite no longer coincided with the officeholders, and the officeholders came to supplant the hereditary aristocracy, in Chosŏn Korea the Neo-Confucians established themselves as the officeholders, the *sa-daebu,* and constituted the new dynasty's hereditary elite. They combined their insights in Confucian kinship organization with demands for an increasingly sophisticated and restrictive bureaucracy to delineate the boundaries between themselves and the rest of society. More than in Koryŏ, the definition of elite was made dependent on state legitimation.

This brief appraisal of a few aspects of the two transition periods, each of which had such a lasting impact on its own society, makes clear that the Korean experience was vastly different from the Chinese. Consequently, the development of kinship principles in the two countries can also be expected to have been quite divergent. In Korea, there seems to have been at once more continuity and more change than in China. How is this paradox to be explained? While in Sung China the aristocratic tradition was destroyed by the perfected examination system, in Korea the strong aristocratic element in society and politics survived the change of dynasties. More than ever before, however, ascriptive status criteria were counterbalanced by an element of achievement tested in state-controlled examinations. This unique blend of the aristocratic and bureaucratic, a hallmark of the new dynasty, prevented the growth of truly centralized power in Chosŏn Korea.[14]

But what role did Confucianism play in this? Is it sufficient to argue that the egalitarian and hierarchical strands, both present in Confucianism, tolerated this hybrid and therefore ensured its survival?[15] The crux of the problem indeed lies in Confucianism, but in the realm of social rather than political philosophy. Its egalitarian strand was clearly recognized by the Koreans, but as an ideal that was basically irreconcilable with the traditionally hierarchical order of their society. The difference between the Chinese and the Koreans lay most tellingly in the way they read the Neo-Confucian message in regard to social organization. The Chinese chose to ignore Chu Hsi's rigid system of major and minor descent lines perpetuated by primogeniture, perhaps because it was incompatible with egalitarian trends in Sung society. In contrast, the Koreans interpreted the Neo-Confucian societal blueprint more literally as a scheme suitable for narrowing the broad ascription of status by birth common in Koryŏ. The new "bureaucrats" of Chosŏn adopted the restrictive Confucian descent calculation to enhance their social position and political power in the long term and insure against any egalitarianism, whether in society or in the political realm. In sum, then, in Korea Confucianism not only helped preserve the aristocratic element, it also tightened its definition. At the same time, it supported a bureaucratic system that demanded increased loyalty toward the state through examinations, office-holding, and ideology.

Thus far, the practice of ancestor worship has been emphasized as a primary instrument in the formation of Chosŏn patrilineal descent groups, a process that was reflected in, as well as spurred on by, the compilation of genealogical records. Both these activities have corporate aspects, but were they sufficient as functional bases upon which the mature Korean lineage of late Chosŏn could grow? Most studies on Chinese lineage organization insist on landed estates as essential foci of lineage corporateness.[16] Historical studies that trace the development of corporate land in Korea are still lacking, and discussions of this topic usually are based on recent observations. The present investigation suggests that land in the form of ancestral trusts certainly came to play a crucial role as the corporate base of Korean lineages. Such corporately held land, however, developed slowly and basically in response to conscious and active application of Neo-Confucian precepts. Land may therefore have had only secondary significance in the formation of Korean lineages.

Ideology thus seems to have been the primary influence shaping the lineage of late Chosŏn. This is further suggested by the clear structural design of the Korean lineage, which distinguishes it from its more loosely organized Chinese counterpart. The Korean lineage focused on a central trunk, the most senior line of descent, from which junior lines branched off. Because of its ritual significance, the survival of the main line had to be guaranteed by all means, whereas junior lines at times disappeared. Such strong emphasis on seniority combined with primogeniture must have restrained, even if it could not prevent, segmentation; and if segmentation occurred, the new segment nevertheless remained ritually oriented toward the senior main line, whose genealogical superiority was undisputed. Organized around a new focal ancestor—an outstanding public or scholarly figure—and presumably sustained by its own corporate estate, the junior segment with its own primogeniture descendant then developed an independent existence and might economically and politically even have overtaken the senior line. But the consciousness that it was merely a "branch" did not fade. This was clearly expressed by the convention that such a branch *(p'a)* was always designated by the branch ancestor's office title or pen name *(ho)* and never by a place name denoting a new ancestral seat, thus avoiding a complete split from the original group. In general, Korean lineages were less segmented than Chinese lineages, whose corporate basis was primarily economic. As soon as enough land was available, the conditions for segmentation were given. In contrast, the Korean lineage, based on prestige and genealogy, clearly was under less pressure to segment for economic motives. Although the subject of segmentation in Korea is still largely unexplored, on the basis of the unique structural premises of Korean lineages it may be assumed that the "spinal cord" model, according to which the senior line persists while junior lines branch off at irregular intervals, describes this kind of segmentation better than the asymmetrical model typical for Chinese lineage segmentation.[17]

The primacy of Neo-Confucian ideology in the formation of Korean patrilineal descent groups has been variously demonstrated, but it remains to be shown how the gradual organization of such descent groups relates to the definition of the ruling elite at the beginning of Chosŏn. Most importantly, the introduction and adaptation of the patrilineal descent ideology through the medium of Neo-Confucian scholarship was an upper-class enterprise. Its rationale was dictated by the exigencies of the time: in a milieu that was overgrown by vested interests and destabilized by factional strife, social exclusiveness offered itself as the most effective means for a small group to assert political leadership. The *sadaebu* of early Chosŏn were, after all, not only scholars, but political activists who aimed at creating a sociopolitical order that would sustain their claim to power.

To gain the social and political upper hand, the *sadaebu* separated themselves from the rest of society by various means. They held the monopoly on Neo-Confucian learning, and they designed a ritual program that accentuated the special features of their unique style of life. Chu Hsi's *Chia-li* became in Korea a handbook for an elitist ritual life that was not intended to be shared (or at least only indirectly) by the lower social classes. Even within the upper layer, explicit legal rules supported ritual, and therefore social stratification. According to the *Kyŏngguk taejŏn,* only the incumbents of the highest offices were allowed to worship three generations of ancestors; all the others had to be satisfied with a reduced program. Rituals were status symbols and as such could not be shared.

For delineating themselves as a social group, it made sense for the *sadaebu* to adopt a societal scheme that would assign its members clear positions and, above all, keep the group small. The social models of ancient China, therefore, were not intended for everyone. They were manifestations of norms only the *sadaebu* were called upon to interpret and assimilate to their advantage. Even for them, it took generations until "lineage mentality" became second nature. But the initially small worshipping group gave structure to, and accentuated by its durability an old social value that retained its validity in Chosŏn Korea: heredity. Social status and its concomitant prestige, to be upheld, had to be transmitted to the next generation.

What provided the rationale for social exclusiveness in political terms? Surely it was the *sadaebu*'s claim to political power and leadership. This claim rested generally on the moral endowment the *sadaebu* believed they obtained through their Confucian education. This achieved qualification, however, they subordinated to the more fundamental notion of social qualification; and therefore access to political power, that is, to government office, had to be controlled by defining in social terms a candidate's eligibility to sit for the civil service examinations. In Korea, the examinations were never intended to introduce egalitarian standards for recruiting men to government service. On the contrary, the selection of talents was regarded as being intimately related to sharply delineated social boundaries, and therefore only someone who could prove his membership in a recognized descent group was deemed fit for advancing into the political realm. Before a candidate was admitted to sit for the examinations, his social background had to be verified. Intellectual abilities, however tested, would not be allowed to compromise social status. Because "the method of recruiting scholars *(sa)* was strict"—a statement made in the early years of the dynasty[18]—sons of primary wives alone were considered proper candidates, while secondary sons and sons of twice-married women were disqualified.[19]

In fact, at the beginning of Chosŏn, considerations of social origin and descent, already so prominent in Koryŏ, were inseparably welded to the exigencies of a more rationally built bureaucracy. This dual emphasis on inherited status and scholarly achievement created the typical aristocratic-bureaucratic hybrid, the scholar-official of the Chosŏn period.[20] With the preservation of the aristocratic element of heredity,[21] the traditional status hierarchy of Korean society was maintained and even reinforced, and consequently examination success and high office were preponderantly reserved to a relatively small number of productive lineages. During all of Chosŏn, 750 descent groups were represented among the passers of the higher civil service examinations, but the small total of 39 leading lineages produced 53 percent of all passers. The Chŏnju Yi, the descent group of which the royal house was the chief component, topped the list with 844 successful candidates.[22]

Political prominence conveyed entitlement to economic benefits, and the land and tax systems of Chosŏn Korea both favored the elite. The beneficiaries of the new land system implemented at the beginning of the dynasty (when a certain amount of land was confiscated from opponents to the new dynasty) were the merit subjects and the members of the new officialdom. Land received either as reward for supporting the founder of the new dynasty or as compensation for service in government, often added to already existing landed possessions, came to form the nucleus of landed estates. Their importance grew toward the end of the fifteenth century after all attempts by the state to control the apportionment of land had collapsed. Landed wealth, thus, was the basis upon which the Chosŏn elite depended for economic survival and ritual sustenance. Its preservation, however, eventually was threatened by increasing scarcity and successive division by inheritance. Plausible countermeasures then were land acquisition by legal and illegal methods and, above all, a rigid inheritance system that would reduce the number of potential recipients. The attempt to enforce primogeniture was the culmination of such defensive strategies. The primacy of land did not diminish even when at the end of the seventeenth century and especially during the eighteenth century commercial activities opened new avenues to economic enrichment. In the eyes of the Confucian officialdom, wealth acquired through mercantile enterprise never lost the odium of profit reaped by methods ill suited to high social status.

In sum, then, the *sadaebu* made good use of descent and heredity to monopolize the political life and the economic resources of Chosŏn Korea. But did the state not also profit from so stable a reservoir of servants? In Korea, lineage organization seems to have contributed to the longevity of the political system, apparently disproving the argument that lineage organization is incompatible with a centralized state.[23] This argument has only limited validity in Korea because the emergence of strong patrilineal descent groups did prevent complete centralization and the vestment of absolute power in the king. This is not to say that the aristocratic descent groups did not need the state. It was the state that conferred rank and office upon the successful examination candidates and thus validated their social status. The obligations to the state, however, especially in the economic realm, were often at odds with the interests of the descent groups. Political harmony and thus the state's survival depended therefore on the degree to which such conflicting interests could be balanced out.

A crucial variable was, of course, the relative strength or weakness of the royal house. After some despotic tendencies demonstrated during the fifteenth century by Sejo and Yŏnsan'gun were suppressed, the later Yi kings found their way back to the position from which their ancestor, T'aejo, had started out: that of first among equals. Since the Chŏnju Yi were of rather modest social background, it was the royal prerogative alone—a prerogative never really seriously challenged—that elevated them above other descent groups. This fact must have contributed to the generally weak and vulnerable status of the Yi king vis-à-vis the officeholding elite. Moreover, a king was surrounded by advantage-seeking in-laws rather than by supportive close kinsmen, for the descendants of a sovereign were for four generations barred from taking the examinations and entering office. Nevertheless, the Chŏnju Yi produced, as noted above, the highest number of successful examination passers and thus became closely enmeshed with the general bureaucracy.

It was, however, the aristocratic lineages who largely determined the political tenor of the dynasty. At the same time, they profited from the increasing bureaucratization because the holding of high office became one of the most important conditions for maintaining high social status. The state, thus, was an incomparably precious source of social legitimization, and it was within the king's power to reward meritorious servants with titles, land, and slaves—the accouterments of social prestige and dignity that benefitted the original recipient's entire descent group. However, with the numbers of eligible candidates for government positions proliferating toward the end of the dynasty's first century, competition among descent groups for rank and office sharpened; and deep, frequently unbridgeable, differences arose over often trivial issues and began to split the aristocracy into feuding political factions. The king could rarely keep himself aloof from such conflict and successfully play the role of arbiter.[24]

While social and political factors in the capital thus operated both to advance and threaten the interests of the ruling elite, the same was true for the countryside. Lineages were the informal channels through which law and order were maintained at the local level, where the central government was but weakly represented. On account of their strong attachment to land, localized lineages must have been interested in preserving order as well as in developing their respective localities by improving existing agricultural techniques and introducing new ones. Although such measures at least indirectly also benefitted the state through presumably higher tax revenue, lineages could grow into formidable bulwarks against state interference, especially where large tax-exempt tracts of land, perhaps attached to a local academy, were involved. Further research will have to illuminate in greater detail the ramifications of the dialectic of tension between kinship and power in Chosŏn Korea, but it may be suggested that while, on the one hand, the emergence of structured lineages introduced a sharper tone into the political discourse, on the other hand, by relating descent so closely to the political structure, lineages had to make the preservation of the state's viability the condition of their own survival.

One more important point remains to be considered. That is the elite's delineation vis-à-vis the other two social status groups, the commoners and the slaves.[25] As has been discussed above, the *sadaebu* constituted a "class"[26] that controlled extraordinary ritual, social, political, and economic privileges and was well aware of its identity. It also possessed a kind of "status honor" *(sap'ung)* that found frequent expression in the term "noble" *(kwi)* that was set in contrast to "base" *(ch'ŏn)*, a designation used for all the rest of society. Originating from the Great Appendix of the *I-ching* (Book of Changes),[27] these were subjective terms that denoted the dominant inequalities within Korean society, and were clearly not used as generic status labels.[28] Rather, they indicated the *sadaebu*'s purity versus all the others' impurity, and from the context in which they appeared in the original Chinese *loci classici*—most notably the *I-ching,* often quoted by the Korean Confucians[29]—it is evident that they point to the perfect social order within which everyone occupies the position to which his (inborn) capacities entitle him.[30]

Such division of society into two—albeit numerically uneven—halves was manifest in the fact that the *sadaebu* exclusively occupied all the ranked positions within the officialdom; that is to say, they did not share their functions with those below. More subtle and at the same time more incisive, however, was the *sadaebu*'s refusal to take primary wives from the lower classes. The *sadaebu* were therefore a practically endogamous group whose membership was basically determined by the fact of birth. As has been suggested before, it was not the men but the women who in fact preserved such exclusiveness. Consequently, only women whose agnatic kin belonged to the "noble" half of society could bring forth sons fully linked to their fathers' ancestral heritage. Conversely, sons of women originating from the lower ranks of society lacked the social purity to take over their fathers' ritual trust. A typical formula which evidenced a man's ancestral constellation at one glance was therefore "the four ancestors" *(sajo),* his three lineal ascendants and his maternal grandfather. This was a social passport that, only when "clean" on the maternal side, gave access to the official world.[31]

This interpretation helps explain the great insistence and frequency with which from the early days of the dynasty the differentiation of women as primary and secondary wives was correlated with the distinction between noble and base social status *(myŏng-bun).*[32] The early legislators were obviously well aware that the selection of women as spouses was a critical instrument for delineating social status groups and accentuating their hierarchical ranking. A woman's social rather than her material endowment ultimately determined her value as a wife. Intermarriage with low-class women (except as concubines) was therefore regarded as mésalliance that the consciousness of social status forbade the *sadaebu* to enter into.

This raises the question of the yangban lineages' social homogeneity. Although this question cannot be answered conclusively until more research is conducted, the above analysis seems to suggest that a Korean lineage normally accommodated only members who could prove the impeccability of their social background. Therefore, for reasons discussed before, most notably its genealogical orientation combined with acute status consciousness, a Korean lineage can be expected to be a socially homogeneous entity that did not cross social status boundaries.[33] Lineage organization in Korea was "by definition" an upper-class phenomenon that preserved its vitality for such a long time precisely because of its social, if not economic, uniformity. In this point it differed sharply from the Chinese lineage, which accommodated members of diverse social background but tended to split on economic grounds.[34] Korean lineages did tolerate considerable economic differences among their constituant parts, even though economic competition may have led to conflict among different segments. In the end, prolonged poverty and the consequent inability of certain segments to keep close ties with more influential kinsmen could cause downward mobility and a loss of yangban status (likely coupled with elimination from the genealogical records). What ultimately may have looked like a "commoner lineage" was in fact the result of downward mobility.

In conclusion, then, it seems appropriate to draw, as some contemporary observers did,[35] the major dividing line in Chosŏn society between the "noble" *(kwi)* and the "base" *(ch'ŏn)*. In other words, the society of Chosŏn Korea was first of all perceived as forming two major groups largely defined in terms of "purity," that is, the elite on the one hand and all the other social groupings on the other. This division was never used synonymously with the distinction between the commoners *(yang)*, that is, those who were not base, and the base people *(ch'ŏn)*, that is, slaves and those who pursued impure occupations as shamans, butchers, and leatherworkers—a distinction some modern Korean historians see as the most important dividing line.[36] The elite always stood above such categorization. In modern terms, Chosŏn society constituted a hierarchy of three distinct status groups that were based on hereditary and occupational criteria: the sociopolitical elite or the yangban; the commoners who did not belong to the ruling elite; and the slaves and other base people. Even though, at the beginning of the dynasty, a few commoners are known to have climbed through the examination system into government office, did they therefore ever gain recognition as yangban?[37] After all, the state could merely confirm, not confer, yangban status. As the dynasty moved into its second century, social discrimination intensified and made the dividing line between yangban and commoners increasingly inflexible. In such a society, then, downward mobility of yangban was far more likely than upward mobility of commoners.

Some of the points made in these conclusions have deliberately gone far beyond what is described in the preceding chapters and are intended merely to suggest ways in which the developments in the early part of the dynasty were relevant for bringing about the typical features of late Chosŏn society outlined in the introductory chapter. The validity of these suggestions will have to be tested in future research. What stands out with great clarity, however, is the fact that the patrilineal kinship organization of late Chosŏn is the product of a profound and lasting transformation set in motion at the beginning of the dynasty by the Neo-Confucian legislators. This transformation reached its climax in the course of the seventeenth century with the institution of primogeniture, an act the Korean Confucians, in contradistinction to their Chinese counterparts, had made the touchstone of their Confucianization of Korean society.

Notes
Select Bibliography
Glossary
Index

Notes

Traditional East Asian sources are cited by kwŏn and page number(s); b means the verso page. All *Sillok* citations refer to the *Chosŏn wangjo sillok* (The Veritable Records of the Chosŏn Dynasty), reprinted in 48 volumes by Kuksa p'yŏnch'an wiwŏnhoe, Seoul, 1955–1958. A Roman numeral indicates the volume number of a Western-bound work.

INTRODUCTION: SOCIETY AND IDEOLOGY

1. See Introduction by I. M. Lewis, ed., *History and Social Anthropology* (London: Tavistock Publications, 1968).
2. See, for example, James L. Watson's "Anthropological Overview: The Development of Chinese Descent Groups," in Patricia Buckley Ebrey and James L. Watson, eds., *Kinship Organization in Late Imperial China, 1000–1940* (Berkeley: University of California Press, 1986), pp. 274–292. See also James L. Watson, "Chinese Kinship Reconsidered: Anthropological Perspectives on Historical Research," *The China Quarterly* 92:589–622 (Dec. 1982).
3. The patrilineages were variously called *chok* (higher-order lineage), *p'a* (higher-order lineage or major segment of higher-order lineage), or *munjung* (sublineage). There is, however, no uniformity of nomenclature. The term *higher-order lineage* is borrowed from Maurice Freedman. It designates a number of local lineages grouped together on the basis that the ancestors of these lineages all are agnatic descendants from a common ancestor. See Maurice Freedman, *Chinese Lineage and Society: Fukien and Kwangtung* (London: The Athlone Press, 1966), pp. 20–21. My usage of such technical terms as *descent group, lineage,* etc., follows as far as possible the definitions given by Patricia B. Ebrey and James L. Watson in their introduction to *Kinship Organization*

in Late Imperial China, 1000–1940. For a recent study of Korean lineages, see Mutsuhiko Shima, "In Quest of Social Recognition: A Retrospective View on the Development of Korean Lineage Organization," *Harvard Journal of Asiatic Studies* 50.1:87–129 (June 1990).

4. The *Chŭngbo munhŏnbigo* (Revised Reference Compilation of Documents on Korea), an encyclopedic compilation first published at the end of the eighteenth century and last revised in 1908, lists 497 different surnames *(sŏng)*. Identical surnames were differentiated by adding the respective ancestral seats *(pon'gwan)*. Accordingly, for the surname Kim, for example, there were 499 different ancestral seats, for the Yi 451, and for the Ch'oe 326. Most surnames, however, did not have more than ten different ancestral seats. See *Chŭngbo munhŏnbigo,* kwŏn 47–53. For convenient tables of this material, see Zenshō Eisuke, *Chōsen no shūraku* (Keijō: Chōsen sōtokufu, 1933–1935), III, 60–121. Zenshō's voluminous work, which is based on fieldwork done in the early 1930s, is a remarkably comprehensive survey of Korean villages.

5. In this study, "secondary wives" and "secondary sons" are always used to indicate a man's minor wives and their offspring.

6. This is one of the most conspicuous differences between Korean and Chinese lineages. In China, a lineage could emerge whenever there was enough property to support its members.

7. The royal Yi of Chŏnju, for example, were subdivided into more than one hundred major segments *(p'a):* Zenshō Eisuke, III, 65–66. For a list of the localized major segments of the P'ungsan Yu in northwestern Kyŏngsang, see Kim Taek-kyu, *Ssijok purak ŭi kujo yŏn'gu* (Seoul: Ilchogak, 1979), p. 148.

8. For an extensive discussion of lineage formation and organization in Korea, see Roger L. Janelli and Dawnhee Yim Janelli, "Lineage Organization and Social Differentiation in Korea," *Man* (N.S.) 13:272–289 (1978). In this article, the Janellis investigate the applicability of Maurice Freedman's lineage models to Korea.

9. Zenshō Eisuke, III, 131–132.

10. For a discussion on the historical reliability of the *chokpo,* see Edward W. Wagner, "The Korean Chokpo as a Historical Source," in Spencer J. Palmer, ed., *Studies in Asian Genealogy* (Provo: Brigham Young University Press, 1972), pp. 141–152. See also Song Chun-ho, "Han'guge issŏsŏ ŭi kagye kirok ŭi yŏksa wa kŭ haesŏk," *Yŏksa hakpo* 87:99–143 (1980).

11. The older technical terms for the senior line, *taejong,* and the junior lines, *sojong,* seem to have been less in use by the early twentieth century. See *Chōsen saishi sōzoku hōron, josetsu* (Keijō: Chōsen sōtokufu, 1939), p. 489.

12. For descriptions of domestic and lineage rituals, see Roger L. Janelli and Dawnhee Yim Janelli, *Ancestor Worship and Korean Society* (Stanford: Stanford University Press, 1982). The classic discussion of Chinese ancestor worship

to which everyone concerned with ancestor worship in East Asia feels indebted is, of course, found in Maurice Freedman, *Lineage Organization in Southeastern China* (London: The Athlone Press, 1958).

13. For a comprehensive study of Korean villages during the Japanese colonial time, see Zenshō Eisuke, *Chōsen no shūraku,* 3 vols. Volume 3 is entirely devoted to single-lineage villages and contains invaluable descriptive and statistical materials.

14. Zenshō Eisuke, III, 217–218. For brief notes on the origin, development, and composition of famous one-lineage villages investigated in 1930, see III, 219–253, 349–351.

15. For a number of diagrams of famous compounds, see Zenshō Eisuke, III, 369–390.

16. For discussions of the economic aspects of Korean lineages, see Zenshō Eisuke, III, 413–452; *Chōsen saishi sōzoku hōron, josetsu,* pp. 520–529; Kim Taek-kyu, pp. 170–180; Yi Man-gap, *Han'guk nongch'on ūi sahoe kujo* (Seoul: The Korean Research Center, 1960), pp. 105–153.

17. For brief discussions of adoption, see Mark Peterson, "Adoption in Korean Genealogies," *Korea Journal* 14:28–35 (Jan. 1974); and Kim Taek-kyu, pp. 115–116. On adoption in late Chosŏn, consult Hattori Tamio, "Chosŏn sidae hugi ūi yangja suyang e kwanhan yŏn'gu," *Hankuk Hakpo* 11:111–154 (Summer 1978).

18. *Chŭngbo munhŏnbigo,* 229:25b–26. Quoted in Fujiya Kawashima, "Lineage Elite and Bureaucracy in Early Yi to Mid-Yi Dynasty Korea," *Occasional Papers on Korea* 5:9 (1977).

19. This point is made by Fujiya Kawashima, "Lineage Elite and Bureaucracy," pp. 14, 17. See also Wagner, "Korean Chokpo," pp. 150–151; and Edward W. Wagner, "The Ladder of Success in Yi Dynasty Korea," *Occasional Papers on Korea* 1:4–6 (1974).

20. Fujiya Kawashima has studied local elite culture in "A Study of the *Hyangan:* Kin Groups and Aristocratic Localism in the Seventeenth- and Eighteenth-Century Korean Countryside," *Journal of Korean Studies* 5:3–38 (1984).

21. For a list of *sŏwŏn,* see *Chŭngbo munhŏnbigo,* kwŏn 211–213; for a list of *sŏwŏn* that still existed in the 1930s, see Zenshō Eisuke, III, 644–645. The relationship between lineage and *sŏwŏn* is discussed, for example, in Kim Taek-kyu, pp. 40, 160. See also James B. Palais, *Politics and Policy in Traditional Korea* (Cambridge: Harvard University Press, 1975), pp. 113–115.

22. *Yangban* originally was not a status term, but designated the two ranks (*yangban*) of officials, the "east rank" (*tongban*), i.e., the civil officials, and the "west rank" (*sŏban*), i.e., the military officials. At the beginning of the Chosŏn dynasty, the term *yangban* was used, in continuation of Koryŏ tradition, in the specialized meaning of "those in office." At the same time, in a broader sense, *yangban* also denoted the officeholders and their immediate families,

i.e., the ruling elite. A similar term was "great and common officers" *(sadaebu)*.

23. Some of these problems are outlined in Song Chun-ho, "Han'guk ŭi ssijokche e issŏsŏ ŭi pon'gwan mit sijo ŭi munje," *Yŏksa hakpo* 109:91–136 (March 1986); and in Song Chun-ho, "Chosŏn ŭi yangbanje rŭl ŏttŏk'e ihae hal kŏsinga," in his *Chosŏn sahoesa yŏn'gu* (Seoul: Ilchogak, 1987), pp. 118–164. I am also grateful for long discussions on these issues with Prof. Song in the summer of 1986.

24. At the beginning of the dynasty, yangban were also liable for military service; but they could serve in elite units in the capital.

25. For a detailed discussion of this issue, see Yŏng-ho Ch'oe, "Commoners in Early Yi Dynasty Civil Examinations: An Aspect of Korean Social Structure, 1392–1600," *Journal of Asian Studies* 33.4:611–631 (Aug. 1974); and his book-length study entitled *The Civil Examinations and the Social Structure in Early Yi Dynasty Korea: 1392–1600* (Seoul: The Korean Research Center, 1987).

26. For examples, see Edward W. Wagner, "Social Stratification in Seventeenth-Century Korea: Some Observations from a 1663 Seoul Census Register," *Occasional Papers on Korea* 1:36–54 (1974). See also Susan S. Shin, "The Social Structure of Kŭmhwa County in the Late Seventeenth Century," *Occasional Papers on Korea* 1:9–35 (1974).

27. Lineages, however, could be formed by some social sub-groups. The passers of the technical examinations *(chapkwa),* called "middle people" *(chungin),* who ranked in the social hierarchy between yangban and commoners, are known to have had lineages. Moreover, the yangban offspring of secondary or minor wives *(sŏja)* were not bona fide members of their fathers' lineage, were often dropped from the genealogy, and therefore had to continue their own lines. For an example of such a "secondary line" *(sŏp'a)* still recognized in the 1960s, see Yi Man-gap, pp. 73–74.

28. For a brief overview of Confucian developments in United Silla, see Yi Ki-baek, "Yugyo suyong ŭi ch'ogi hyŏngt'ae," in his *Silla sidae ŭi kukka pulgyo wa yugyo* (Seoul: The Korean Research Center, 1978), pp. 122–139. Prof. Yi has also studied the *yuktup'um* in "Silla yuktup'um yŏn'gu," in *Silla chŏngch'i sahoesa yŏn'gu* (Seoul: Ilchogak, 1974), pp. 34–64.

29. See H. W. Kang, "Institutional Borrowing: The Case of the Chinese Civil Service Examination System in Early Koryŏ," *Journal of Asian Studies* 34.1:109–125 (Nov. 1974).

30. For two useful articles on private schools in late Koryŏ, see Yu Hong-nyŏl, "Raimatsu Sensho no shigaku," *Seikyū gakusō* 24:64–119 (May 1936); and Yi Pyŏng-hyu, "Yŏmal Sŏnch'o ŭi kwaŏp kyoyuk," *Yŏksa hakpo* 67:45–70 (Sept. 1975). Yun Sa-sun has surmised that Neo-Confucianism as developed in Northern Sung (960–1126) reached Korea as early as the first half of the

eleventh century. There is, however, no clear evidence for this assumption. See Yun Sa-sun, *Han'guk yuhak sasangnon* (Seoul: Yŏrŭmsa, 1986), pp. 11–12.

31. For a detailed discussion of the transmission of Neo-Confucianism and the careers of Chao Fu and Hsü Heng, see Wm. Theodore de Bary, *Neo-Confucian Orthodoxy and the Learning of the Mind-and-Heart* (New York: Columbia University Press, 1981), pp. 20ff. and 131–135.

32. *Koryŏsa chŏryo* 21:13. For a brief description of the Yuhak chegŏsa, see Ko Pyŏng-ik, *Tonga kyosŏpsa ŭi yŏn'gu* (Seoul: Sŏul taehakkyo ch'ulp'anbu, 1970), pp. 256–257.

33. *Hoehŏn silgi,* entry of 1290.

34. The *Hoehŏn silgi* contains a detailed chronology *(yŏnbo)* of An Hyang's life. An was later known as An Yu. His official biography is in *Koryŏsa* 105:28–31b. For a modern study of An's biography and thought, see Kim Pyŏng-gu, *Hoehŏn sasang yŏn'gu* (Seoul: Hangmunsa, 1983).

35. *Hoehŏn silgi,* entry of 1304.

36. All of these men have biographies in the *Koryŏsa.*

37. Paek I-jŏng is believed by some to have been the first transmitter of Neo-Confucianism to Korea. His biography insists on this fact. See *Koryŏsa* 106:2a–b; Paek Mun-bo, *Tamam ilchip* 2:18–19b. Also see Yun Yong-gyun, *Shushigaku no denrai to sono eikyō ni tsuite* (Keijō: Keijō Imperial University, (1933), pp. 20–31. In his brief note on the rise of Neo-Confucianism in China and its transmission to Korea, Hong Yŏ-ha (1621–1678) also clearly credited Paek I-jŏng with a major role in the transmission process: See Kil Chae, *Yaŭn sŏnsaeng sokchip, ha,* 23b–24b. It seems moot to speculate about which of the two, An Hyang or Paek I-jŏng, acquired a deeper understanding of Neo-Confucianism. The writings of neither are preserved.

38. *Koryŏsa* 34:20a–b; *Chŭngbo munhŏnbigo* 202:12b–13.

39. *Koryŏsa* 109:21a–b.

40. See his biography in *Koryŏsa* 107:15.

41. *Koryŏsa chŏryo* 24:3a–b.

42. *Koryŏsa chŏryo* 23:30b–1.

43. For a brief sketch on Yao Shu's activities, see de Bary, *Neo-Confucian Orthodoxy,* pp. 20–21.

44. For Yi Che-hyŏn's sojourn in Peking, see Kim Sang-gi, "Yi Ik-chae ŭi chae Wŏn saengae e taehayŏ," *Taedong munhwa yŏn'gu* 1:219–244 (Aug. 1963); Chŏng Ok-cha, "Yŏmal Chuja sŏngnihak ŭi toip e taehan si'go," *Chindan hakpo* 51:29–54 (April 1981). For references on the Chinese scholars, see Hok-lam Chan and Wm. Theodore de Bary, eds., *Yüan Thought: Chinese Thought and Religion under the Mongols* (New York: Columbia University Press, 1982).

45. Under the Mongol administration (Chŏngdong haengsŏng) "regional exam-

inations" *(hyangsi)* were instituted in Kaesŏng. After 1313, when the regular civil service examination system was revived in Peking, each administrative region of the Yüan empire was assigned a certain quota of passers of the regional examinations who had to be sent to Peking for the final examinations in the capital. The Korean quota was three candidates. The first three Koreans sent in 1315 failed the examinations: *Koryŏsa* 74:8. For a list of successful candidates, see *Chŭngbo munhŏnbigo* 185:23–25; see also Hŏ Hŭng-sik, *Koryŏ kwagŏ chedosa yŏn'gu* (Seoul: Ilchogak, 1981), pp. 250–251.

46. *Koryŏsa* 74:8; *Koryŏsa chŏryo* 24:9, 11.

47. *Koryŏsa* 74:8; *Koryŏsa chŏryo* 24:15; Chŏng Ok-cha, "Yŏmal Chuja sŏngnihak ŭi toip e taehan si'go," pp. 48–49.

48. Quoted from Wing-tsit Chan, "Chu Hsi and Yüan Neo-Confucianism," in Hok-lam Chan and de Bary, *Yüan Thought,* p. 210.

49. This work is extensively discussed by de Bary, *Neo-Confucian Orthodoxy,* p. 106ff.

50. The Five Classics are the *I-ching* (Book of Changes), the *Ch'un-ch'iu* (Spring and Autumn Annals), the *Shu-ching* (Book of Documents), the *Shih-ching* (Book of Poetry), and the *Li-chi* (Book of Rites). At times either the no longer extant *Yüeh-ching* (Book of Music) or the *Chou-li* (Rites of Chou) was included to make up the Six Classics.

51. For details, see de Bary, "The Rise of Neo-Confucian Orthodoxy in Yüan China," in his *Neo-Confucian Orthodoxy,* pp. 1–66.

52. Yi Che-hyŏn, *Yŏgong p'aesŏl, chŏnjip,* 1:12b–14.

53. *Koryŏsa* 110:34a–b.

54. *Koryŏsa* 115:6–7, 10b.

55. Such a thought had already been expressed by King Ch'ungsŏn in 1308 when he declared that it was not the scions of powerful families who should be used for government service, but talented and virtuous men living in seclusion: *Koryŏsa* 75:10b.

56. *Hoehŏn silgi,* entry of 1301.

57. See Liu Ts'un-yan and Judith Berling, "The 'Three Teachings' in the Mongol-Yüan Period," in Hok-lam Chan and de Bary, eds., *Yüan Thought,* pp. 479–503.

58. For details, see Fung Yu-lan, *A History of Chinese Philosophy,* Derk Bodde, tr. (Leiden: E.J. Brill, 1953), vol. 2, p. 469ff.

59. Paek Mun-bo, *Tamam ilchip* 2:1–2.

60. Pyŏn Kye-ryang, *Ch'unjŏng munjip* 12:4. For details, see Chapter Two.

61. *Works of Mencius,* bk. 3, pt. 1, sec. 12.

62. For the context of Chŏng To-jŏn's argument, see Chapter Four.

63. The ontological and psychological problems surrounding human nature became a major theme of the explorations of Korean philosophers of the sixteenth and seventeenth centuries.

64. In his book *The World of Thought in Ancient China* (Cambridge: Harvard University Press, 1985), Benjamin I. Schwartz discusses the various facets of *li* (proper behavior). See especially pp. 67–75.
65. For a discussion of restorationism in Neo-Confucianism, see Wm. Theodore de Bary, "Some Common Tendencies in Neo-Confucianism," in David S. Nivison and Arthur F. Wright, eds., *Confucianism in Action* (Stanford: Stanford University Press, 1959), pp. 34–36.
66. For an exhaustive discussion of Confucian professionals in the Yüan-Ming transition, see John W. Dardess, *Confucianism and Autocracy: Professional Elites in the Founding of the Ming Dynasty* (Berkeley: University of California Press, 1983), Chapter 1.
67. Here the term *ideology* is used in the sense outlined by Daniel Bell: "Ideology is the conversion of ideas into social levers . . . It is the commitment to the consequence of ideas . . . What gives ideology its force is its passion . . . For the ideologue, truth arises in action, and meaning is given to experience by the 'transforming moment.' " See Chaim I. Waxman, ed., *The End of the Ideology Debate* (New York: Simon and Schuster, 1968), p. 3.

1. THE PRE-CONFUCIAN PAST: A RECONSTRUCTION OF KORYŎ SOCIETY

1. *Koryŏsa* 2:15b.
2. *Koryŏsa* 73:1; 76:1; 78:2; 84:1a–b. For a discussion of the influence of T'ang law on legislation during Koryŏ, see Hanamura Yoshiki, "Kōrai ritsu," *Chōsen shakai hōseishi kenkyū* 9:6–13 (1937).
3. For a survey of Koryŏ's foreign relations during the Five Dynasties period, see Yi Ki-baek, "Koryŏ ch'ogi odae wa ŭi kwan'gye," in Yi Ki-baek, ed., *Koryŏ Kwangjong yŏn'gu* (Seoul: Ilchogak, 1981), pp. 135–152. For Koryŏ's relations with the Sung, see Michael C. Rogers, "Sung-Koryŏ Relations: Some Inhibiting Factors," *Oriens* 11:194–202 (1958).
4. *Koryŏsa* 93:16 (biography of Ch'oe Sŭng-no).
5. *Koryŏsa* 2:15b.
6. A similar case can be made for Japan, where the Chinese-style vocabulary also did not fit native usage. See Robert J. Smith, "Stability in Japanese Kinship Terminology: The Historical Evidence," in Robert J. Smith and Richard K. Beardsley, eds., *Japanese Culture: Its Development and Characteristics* (Chicago: Aldine, 1962), pp. 25–31.
7. For discussions of the compilation of the *Koryŏsa*, see Sin Sŏk-ho, *Han'guk saryo haesŏlchip* (Seoul: Han'guk sahakhoe, 1964), pp. 1–13; and Pyŏn T'ae-sŏp, "*Koryŏsa, Koryŏsa chŏryo* ŭi saron," *Sach'ong* 21/22:113–133 (Oct. 1977).
8. *T'aejong sillok* 3:3b.
9. For a discussion of the author and the contents of this work, see Werner

Sasse, *Das Glossar Koryŏ-pangŏn im Kyerim-yusa* (Wiesbaden: Otto Harrasso-witz, 1976), pp. 3–6.

10. *Kwijok* is a general and vague term denoting the upper layer of Koryŏ society. Other terms used in the documents are "great" *(taejok)*, "famous" *(myŏngjok)*, or "respected" *(mangjok)* descent groups.

11. Yi Kyu-bo, *Tongguk Yi Sanggukchip* (reprint; Seoul: Tongguk munhwasa, 1958), kwŏn 35, p. 20; Im Ch'un, *Sŏha-jip*, in *Koryŏ myŏnghyŏn-jip* (reprint; Seoul: Sŏnggyungwan taehakkyo, Taedong munhwa yŏn'guwŏn, 1973), II, Kwŏn 5, p. 3.

12. For discussions of the nature and development of the early Koryŏ aristocracy, see Yi Ki-baek, "Koryŏ chungang kwallyo ŭi kwijokchŏk sŏngkyŏk," *Tong-yanghak* 5:37–47 (1975); and Yi Ki-baek, "Koryŏ kwijok sahoe ŭi hyŏng-sŏng," *Han'guksa* (Seoul: Kuksa p'yŏnch'an wiwŏnhoe, 1974), IV, 152–212. Also Pyŏn T'ae-sŏp, "Koryŏjo ŭi munban kwa muban," in his *Koryŏ chŏngch'i chedosa yŏn'gu* (Seoul: Ilchogak, 1971), pp. 276–341; and Yi Sŏng-mu, *Chosŏn ch'ogi yangban yŏn'gu* (Seoul: Ilchogak, 1980), pp. 5–13. The most recent work discussing the formation of the Koryŏ aristocracy is by John B. Dun-can, "The Koryŏ Origins of the Chosŏn Dynasty: Kings, Aristocrats, and Confucianism," Ph.D. diss., University of Washington, 1988.

13. For a comprehensive survey of Koryŏ history, see Ki-baik Lee, *A New History of Korea*, Edward W. Wagner with Edward J. Shultz, trs. (Seoul: Ilchogak Publishers, 1984), pp. 110–124, 136–151.

14. *Koryŏsa* 33:21b–26.

15. For discussions of the late Koryŏ aristocracy, see Min Hyŏn-gu, "Koryŏ hugi ŭi kwŏnmun sejok," *Han'guksa* (Seoul: Kuksa p'yŏnch'an wiwŏnhoe, 1974), VIII, 13–59, esp. 28–30; Yi Sŏng-mu, *Chosŏn ch'ogi yangban yŏn'gu*, pp. 24–25; Duncan, "Koryŏ Origins of the Chosŏn Dynasty," pp. 78–81.

16. The glossary, *Koryŏ pangŏn*, is only one part of the *Kyerim-yusa*, which is presumed to have consisted of three parts. The two other parts are preserved only in fragments. For details about the contents of the glossary, see Werner Sasse, pp. 3–7.

17. The kinship terminology in the *Kyerim yusa* has been variously analyzed, but not put into proper historical perspective. The following articles were con-sulted, especially for the transcription of the terms: Yi Ki-mun, "Koryŏ sidae ŭi kugŏ ŭi t'ŭkching," *Tongyanghak* 6:299–305 (1976); Kwŏn Chae-sŏn, "Yŏdae ch'injok mit namnyŏ hoch'ingŏ e taehan koch'al," *Han'gugŏ munhak taegye*, (Seoul: Hyŏngsŏl ch'ulp'ansa, 1975), II, 135–173; Kang Sin-hang, "*Kyerim yusa* 'Koryŏ pangŏn' ŏsŏk," *Taedong munhwa yŏn'gu* 10:1–91 (Dec. 1975). Yi Kwang-gyu has discussed the vocabulary from an anthropological point of view in "Han'guk ŭi ch'inch'ŏk myŏngch'ing," *Yŏn'gu nonch'ong* 1:221–256 (1971). The identification of the terms can be found in Sasse, pp. 97–138.

18. The mourning system was introduced to Koryŏ in 985, but it was not used (or only very rarely) in the context of mourning. For a discussion of its ritual aspects, see the section on the mourning system in this chapter.

19. See David G. Johnson, *The Medieval Chinese Oligarchy* (Boulder, Colorado: Westview Press, 1977), p. 110.

20. Charts of the T'ang and Koryŏ mourning systems can be found in No Myŏng-ho, "Koryŏ ŭi obokch'in kwa ch'injok kwan'gye pŏpche," *Han'guksa yŏn'gu* 33:38, 40 (June 1981).

21. Based on T'ang and Sung precedents and reportedly instituted in Koryŏ in 1092, this law aimed at preventing conflict of interest in office by barring certain categories of kin from simultaneously holding important government posts: *Koryŏsa chŏryo* 6:16; *Koryŏsa* 84:4b–5. See also Kim Tong-su, "Koryŏ sidae ŭi sangp'ije," *Yŏksa Hakpo* 102:1–30 (June 1984); No Myŏng-ho, "Koryŏ ŭi obokch'in kwa ch'injok kwan'gye pŏpche," pp. 16–22 and the chart on p. 41. No thinks that the law of avoidance is based on reciprocity; that is, if the grandson is listed, the grandfather is automatically included, even if not listed. Therefore the law as it later appeared in the *Kyŏngguk taejŏn* of 1485 was not really an expansion of the Koryŏ version; its listings were simply more complete.

22. This is suggested by Yi Sung-nyŏng, "Chungse kugŏ ŭi kajok hoch'ing e taehayŏ," *Tongyang munhwa* 6/7:230 (1968).

23. The members of a *chok* were variously designated as *chogin, choksok, choktang,* and *chongnyu.*

24. For possible interpretations of the term *samjok,* see Karl Bünger, *Quellen zur Rechtsgeschichte der T'ang-Zeit* (Peiping: The Catholic University, 1946), pp. 115–117 (fn. 112). Affinal kin was also called *honjok* or *chogin. Koryŏsa* 64:22b–25 *(obok);* 84:4b–5 *(sangp'i).*

25. *Koryŏsa chŏryo* 13:34b; the respective entry in *Koryŏsa* 21:12 simply writes *chok* in place of *samjok.* A further example of *chok* including several surnames can be found in *Koryŏsa chŏryo* 11:9b. Surnames will be discussed in greater detail in the last section of this chapter.

26. For an example, see *Koryŏsa chŏryo* 11:16b. This presumably included cousins.

27. *Koryŏsa* 127:11b–24 (Yi Cha-gyŏm's biography). For further sources, see No Myŏng-ho, "Yi Cha-gyŏm ilp'a wa Han An-in ilp'a ŭi choktang seryŏk— Koryŏ chunggi ch'insoktŭl ŭi chŏngch'i seryŏkhwa yangt'ae," *Han'guk saron* 17:170–177 (Aug. 1987). For examples of the term *ch'inch'ŏk,* see *Koryŏsa* 78:2b, 14b. In both these cases it is combined with "sons and grandsons" to *chason ch'inch'ŏk.* See also *Koryŏsa* 79:1b; 104:30b; *Koryŏsa chŏryo* 24:35.

28. Another example is Ch'oe Ch'ung-hŏn's "action group" that included relatives with different surnames: *Koryŏsa chŏryo* 13:41. For an identification of the men, see Edward J. Shultz, "Institutional Developments in Korea under

the Ch'oe House: 1196–1258" (Ph.D. diss., University of Hawaii, 1976), p. 186. See also his "Twelfth-Century Koryŏ Politics: The Rise of Han Anin and His Partisans," *The Journal of Korean Studies* 6:14–17 (1988–1989).

29. *Koryŏsa* 73:3b–4; 95:2a–b.

30. Yi Nan-yŏng, comp., *Han'guk kŭmsŏngmun ch'ubo* (Seoul: Asea munhwasa, 1968), p. 133.

31. Koryŏ funerary inscriptions are collected, for example, in Hwang Su-yŏng, comp., *Chŭngbo Han'guk kŭmsŏk yumun* (Seoul: Ilchisa, 1976); and in Yi Nan-yŏng, comp., *Han'guk kŭmsŏngmun ch'ubo*. Funerary inscriptions point to the existence of family records that are variously called *kabo, kach'ŏp, sebo,* or *po* none of which, however, is extant.

32. *Sajo* is not listed in Morohashi Tetsuji, *Daikanwa jiten* (Tokyo: Daishūkan shoten, 1955). In China, the basic genealogical formula was "three ancestors" *(san-tai* or *san-tsu),* meaning father, grandfather, and great-grandfather.

33. *Koryŏsa* 74:2 (1273). The term *sajo* is rarely found in the *Koryŏsa;* this is perhaps its first appearance.

34. *P'alcho* literally means simply "eight ancestors," but obviously an individual had more than eight antecedents in the six ascending generations. The term, thus, cannot mean an enumeration of antecedents, but points to specific descent lines. For a description of this descent construct, see *T'aejong sillok* 30:39a–b; *Sejong sillok* 69:20a–b.

35. There was a differentiation between "inner homelands" *(naehyang)* meaning those on the father's side and "outer homelands" *(oehyang)* meaning those on the mother's side. See *Sejong sillok* 69:20a–b.

36. In this sense *hyang* originally coincided with "ancestral seat" *(pon'gwan).* Good examples for *hyang* meaning ancestral seat can be found in *Koryŏsa* 1:9; 56:6b; 80:28; 93:25b; 102:12b. *Hyang,* then, was often combined with *kwan* to *kwanhyang,* which seems to have been an older form of *pon'gwan.*

37. There are only eleven examples of such household registers extant, all dating from the fourteenth century. These sources are studied by Ch'oe Hong-gi, *Han'guk hojŏk chedosa yŏn'gu* (Seoul: Sŏul taehakkyo ch'ulp'anbu, 1975); Ch'oe Chae-sŏk, "Koryŏ hugi kajok ŭi yuhyŏng kwa kusŏng," *Hankuk Hakpo* 3:22–57 (Summer 1976); Hŏ Hŭng-sik, "Kukpo hojŏgŭro pon Koryŏmal ŭi sahoe kujo," *Han'guksa yŏn'gu* 16:51–147 (April 1977); Paek Sŭng-jong, "Koryŏ hugi ŭi p'alcho hogu," *Hankuk Hakpo* 34:191–213 (Spring 1984). The most comprehensive of these fragments, which contains at least three households recorded in the *p'alcho hogu* format, is the so-called "Household Register of Yi T'aejo" *(Yi T'aejo hojŏk wŏnbon),* which is designated as National Treasure No. 131. It is presumed to have been completed in 1391. All of the above mentioned authors have studied and analyzed this document.

38. Household registration was introduced from T'ang China at the beginning

of Koryŏ; the exact date is unknown. The T'ang household registers commonly included the names of the father and grandfather of the household head with their offices and titles. See Johnson, *Medieval Chinese Oligarchy*, p. 14. Extended households could comprise collateral kin (e.g., uncles and aunts), the spouses of brothers and sisters together with their children, or the close kin of the wife or the head of household. For a discussion of the T'ang household registers studied on the basis of the documents discovered at Tunhuang and Turfan, see Ikeda On, "T'ang Household Registers and Related Documents," in Arthur F. Wright and Denis Twitchett, eds., *Perspectives on the T'ang* (New Haven: Yale University Press, 1973), pp. 121–150.

39. For an analysis of the extant documents, see Paek Sŭng-jong, "Koryŏ hugi ŭi p'alcho hogu," pp. 197–201.

40. Officials of rank three to six had to record only six homelands, excluding the wife's two; officials of rank seven to nine, only four homelands, excluding in addition the paternal grandfather's and great-grandfather's maternal homelands; the brothers and sons of the elite without office, only two homelands, excluding in addition the father's and the mother's maternal homelands. See *Sejong sillok* 69:20a–b.

41. *T'aejong sillok* 30:39a–b; *Sejong sillok* 69:20a–b; Paek Sŭng-jong, "Koryŏ hugi ŭi p'alcho hogu," pp. 204–205.

42. *Koryŏsa* 79:3b.

43. Household size and structure have been studied by Hŏ Hŭng-sik, *Koryŏ sahoesa yŏn'gu* (Seoul: Asea munhwasa, 1981), pp. 59–79; Ch'oe Chae-sŏk, "Koryŏ hugi kajok ŭi yuhyŏng kwa kusŏng," pp. 22–57.

44. For such examples, see *Koryŏsa* 128:6; *Koryŏsa chŏryo* 12:23b.

45. For the T'ang succession rules, see Niida Noboru, *Tōryō shūi* (1933; reprint, Tokyo, 1964), pp. 304–314.

46. *Koryŏsa* 2:15b.

47. For Korean justification to China of fraternal succession, see, for example, *Koryŏsa* 21:2a–b.

48. For the history of the Royal Shrines of Koryŏ, see *Koryŏsa* 60:1ff; 61:34b–46. Yi Che-hyŏn was ordered in 1357 to settle anew the *chao-mu* sequence. See *Koryŏsa* 61:44b–46; 110:39; Yi Che-hyŏn, *Yŏgong p'aesŏl, chŏnjip*, pp. 19–25. The *chao-mu* system is discussed at some length by Claude Lévi-Strauss, *The Elementary Structures of Kinship* (London: Social Science Paperbacks, 1969), pp. 325–345; and by K. C. Chang, *Early Chinese Civilization: Anthropological Perspectives* (Cambridge: Harvard University Press, 1976), pp. 95–96.

49. The system of protection privilege has been studied by Pak Yong-un in "Koryŏ sidae ŭmsŏje ŭi silche wa kŭ kinŭng, sang," *Han'guksa yŏn'gu* 36:1–35 (March 1982); and "Koryŏ sidae ŭmsŏje ŭi silche wa kŭ kinŭng, ha," *Han'guksa yŏn'gu* 37:1–39 (June 1982); and "Koryŏ sidae ŭi ŭmsŏje e kwanhan myŏt

kaji munje," in Pyŏn T'ae-sŏp, ed., *Koryŏsa ŭi chemunje* (Seoul: Samyŏngsa, 1986), pp. 123–156; by Kim Yong-sŏn, *Koryŏ ŭmsŏ chedo ŭi yŏn'gu* (Ph.D. diss., Sŏgang University [Seoul], 1985); and by No Myŏng-ho, "Koryŏsi ŭi sŭngŭm hyŏlchok kwa kwijokch'ŭng ŭi ŭmsŏ kihoe," in *Kim Ch'ŏl-chun paksa hwagap kinyŏm sahak nonch'ong* (Seoul: Chisik sanŏpsa, 1983). Kim Yong-sŏn has compiled the most complete list to date of protection appointees; he gives 198 names.

50. It seems clear that even descendants of officials of the sixth rank and below occasionally enjoyed the privilege of protection appointments. Such cases, however, were rare. See Pak Yong-un, "Koryŏ sidae ŭmsŏje ŭi silche wa kŭ kinŭng, sang," p. 14. There is no evidence extant for a royal descendant receiving a protection appointment. See Kim Yong-sŏn, *Koryŏ ŭmsŏ chedo ŭi yŏn'gu*, p. 28.

51. Pak Yong-un provides interesting examples of multiple protection appointments in one kin group. See his "Koryŏ sidae ŭi ŭmsŏje e kwanhan myŏt kaji munje," pp. 139–144.

52. Praying for a male heir was not uncommon. For examples, see *Koryŏsa* 93:2, 99:22.

53. *Koryŏsa* 81:7b; 96:39b.

54. Niida Noboru, *Tōryō shūi*, pp. 305–314.

55. This translation follows the version of the *Koryŏsa chŏryo* 4:31b. For a comparison with the version in the *Koryŏsa*, see note 64.

56. The *Chŭngbo munhŏnbigo* gives an example for establishing a non-agnatic grandson *(oeson)* as heir *(sa):* 86:4. Where the firstborn son was specifically mentioned, terms such as *wŏnja* or *chŏkchang* were used. Later, the *Kyŏngguk taejŏn* designated the eldest son by the term *chŏkchangja.* For the T'ang usage, see Johnson, *Medieval Chinese Oligarchy*, p. 113.

57. For the legal stipulations, see *Koryŏsa* 84:40b, 41b; *Ku T'ang-lü shu-i* 12:8b–9. Ch'oe Chae-sŏk has thus far made the most thorough search for adoption cases in Koryŏ, but came up with only fourteen instances for the whole period. See his "Koryŏ sidae ŭi ch'injok chojik," *Yŏksa hakpo* 94/95:208–218 (Sept. 1982).

58. Although the literature on the Koryŏ land system is considerable, there is little or no consensus on some major issues such as land ownership, taxation, and modes of land cultivation. Owing to the lack of materials or the inadequacy of the extant sources, the subject will remain open to speculation and controversy, especially when the issues are treated in isolation and are not put into a larger context which includes, for example, social organization. For an overview of the Japanese and Korean scholarly literature since the 1930s, see Min Hyŏn-gu, "T'oji chedo," in *Han'guk saron*, vol. 2 (Koryŏ-p'yŏn) (Seoul: Kuksa p'yŏnch'an wiwŏnhoe, 1977), pp. 71–95. For a summary of the land system of Koryŏ, see Yi Sŏng-mu, "Kongjŏn-sajŏn-minjŏn

ŭi kaenyŏm—Koryŏ, Chosŏn ch'ogi rŭl chungsim ŭro," in *Han U-gŭn paksa chŏngnyŏn kinyŏm sahak nonch'ong* (Seoul: Chisik sanŏpsa, 1981), pp. 319–342. For a long, critical review article discussing old and new interpretations, see James B. Palais, "Land Tenure in Korea: Tenth to Twelfth Centuries," *Journal of Korean Studies* 4:73–205 (1982–1983).

59. *Koryŏsa* 78:6b. For a discussion of *chŏnsikwa*, see Kang Chin-ch'ŏl, *Koryŏ t'oji chedosa yŏn'gu* (Seoul: Koryŏ taehakkyo ch'ulp'anbu, 1980), pp. 30–61. The *chŏnsikwa* system was subsequently revised several times. See also Palais, "Land Tenure in Korea," p. 85ff.

60. The *Koryŏsa* states that the *chŏnsikwa* system was modelled on the T'ang equal-field system *(chün-t'ien)*. See *Koryŏsa* 78:2a–b. For a succinct description of the Chinese system, see Denis C. Twitchett, *Financial Administration under the T'ang Dynasty* (Cambridge: Cambridge University Press, 1963), pp. 1–23. Modern Korean and Japanese scholars have tried to disprove this general statement in an attempt to demonstrate the existence of private land ownership right from the beginning of Koryŏ. For a discussion of the revisionist view, which necessarily also involves a new understanding of the recipients of state land grants, see Palais, "Land Tenure in Korea," p. 73ff.

61. "Private land" is the literal meaning of *sajŏn;* but because it most likely was prebendal land, the term could perhaps best be rendered "land benefitting an individual." It should not, however, be confused with privately owned land belonging to the category of "people's land" *(minjŏn)*. *Minjŏn* supposedly was a sub-category of so-called "public land" *(kongjŏn)* from which the state collected taxes. For a discussion of *sajŏn*, see Kang Chinch'ŏl, *Koryŏ t'oji chedosa yŏn'gu*, pp. 62–172. For a summary of various attempts to interpret *sajŏn* and *kongjŏn*, see Palais, "Land Tenure in Korea," pp. 114–127, 144–150.

62. There is no consensus about the exact range of meaning of *chŏnjŏng*. Hatada Takashi takes it to mean land grants to soldiers and local functionaries *(hyangni):* "Kōrai jidai ni okeru tochi no chakuchōshi sōzoku to dohi no shijo kinbun sōzoku," in his *Chōsen chūsei shakaishi no kenkyū* (Tokyo: Hōsei daigaku shuppankyoku, 1972), p. 336. Takeda Yukio, in contrast, thinks that *chŏnjŏng* is a term used for all land grants, including those under the *chŏnsikwa* system: "Kōrai dentei no saikentō," *Chōsenshi kenkyūkai ronbunshū* 8:5–13 (March 1971). As Palais has pointed out, the definition of *chŏnjŏng* as prebend or land grant depends on whether such land had to be returned to the state or was permitted, as a matter of course, to be handed down to the next generation. See his "Land Tenure in Korea," pp. 86–94.

63. *Koryŏsa* 78:13b, 14a–b.

64. *Koryŏsa* 84:41b. The text of the law in the *Koryŏsa* differs slightly from that in the *Koryŏsa chŏryo*. Whereas the latter refers to the establishment of a sonless man's legal heir, the preamble of the former states as its purpose the

transfer of *chŏnjŏng (chŏnjŏng yŏllip)*. The difference between the T'ang model and its Korean adaptation lies in the fact that for the Koreans *sŏja* and *sŏson* did not mean the same as for the Chinese. In China, *sŏja* stood for a son of commoner status, that is to say, a son of a secondary marriage. For definitions of *sŏ* (Chin. *shu*), see Johnson, *Medieval Chinese Oligarchy*, p. 154, n. 1. In Koryŏ, however, the term *sŏja* had no such social meaning (as will be shown later, the institution of secondary marriages did not exist) and therefore was unusable. *Sŏson*, therefore, did not mean "son(s) of *sŏja*," as in China, but indicated any agnatic grandson besides the lineal grandson, i.e., the brothers of the latter as well as the son(s) of the *chŏkcha*'s younger brother(s). Typical for Koryŏ was the addition of non-agnatic grandsons *(yŏson)*. Hatada and Takeda are therefore not correct in their assumption that the Koreans copied the T'ang law wrongly. The Korean version is perfectly germane to the social situation of Koryŏ. See Hatada Takashi, "Chakuchōshi sōzoku," p. 327; Takeda Yukio, "Kōrai dentei," p. 14. Palais's translation of the law of 1046 is, therefore, also incorrect. See his "Land Tenure in Korea," p. 90. It was this law that made Hatada believe that at the beginning of the dynasty land was solely inherited by the eldest son, whereas slaves were equally divided among all the heirs.

65. *Koryŏsa* 78:14a–b. Takeda Yukio takes the law of 1069 as evidence for the prebendal rights being handed on to, besides son and grandson, "relatives" *(ch'injok* or *ch'inch'ŏk)*. He does not define "relatives" and seems to think that it was a wider circle of people than stipulated in the law of 1046. See his "Kōrai dentei," p. 15. *Ch'injok*, however, most probably was used as a summary term for the persons enumerated in the law of 1046: younger brother (by the same mother) and agnatic and non-agnatic descendants. It is therefore not an expansion of the law of 1046. For a discussion of the term *ch'inch'ŏk*, see pp. 38–39 above.

66. Yi Nan-yŏng, comp., *Han'guk kŭmsŏngmun ch'ubo*, No. 58, p. 157.

67. The evidence Takeda Yukio gives for these practices is relatively late, and therefore perhaps not representative for the early part of the dynasty. See his "Kōrai dentei," p. 18.

68. These terms were also used for reverting function and land back to the state. In much of the secondary literature on the Koryŏ land system, succession and inheritance are confused, giving rise to such hybrid terms as *sangsok yŏllip*. The term *sangsok*, "to inherit," does not appear in Koryŏ documents.

69. Takeda Yukio seems to agree with Yi U-sŏng that merit and protected land *(kongŭm chŏnsi)* was granted only to officials above rank five. Takeda Yukio, "Kōraichō ni okeru kōindensaihō no igi," in *Niida Noboru hakase tsuitō ronbunshū*, vol. 1 (Tokyo: Keisō Shobō, 1967), pp. 221–234. See also Hatada Takashi, "Chakuchōshi sōzoku," pp. 337–344.

70. Hatada Takashi interprets *chikcha* as *silcha*, "real son," in contrast to an adopted son. See his "Chakuchōshi sōzoku," p. 339.

71. *Koryŏsa* 78:15.

72. *Koryŏsa* 78:15b–16.

73. Sonless widows of civil and military officials and military personnel who would have been left without support were given residual portions of their husband's prebend *(kubunjŏn)*: *Koryŏsa* 78:13b, 14.

74. According to Hatada Takashi, *minjŏn* belonged to the third category of "public land" *(kongjŏn)*. The two other categories were land that provided for the royal house and land that paid the expenses of government agencies. *Minjŏn* was subject to a land tax amounting to one-fourth of its yield. For details, see Hatada Takashi, "Kōrai no kōden" and "Kōrai no minden ni tsuite," in his *Chōsen chūsei shakaishi no kenkyū* (Tokyo: Hōsei daigaku shuppankyoku, 1972), pp. 208–250 and 163–174 respectively. See also Kang Chin-ch'ŏl's discussion of *kongjŏn* in *Koryŏ t'oji chedosa yŏn'gu*, pp. 175–209.

75. On the question of private ownership, Palais has pointed out that its ultimate determinant is its defensibility against unwarranted attack. See his "Land Tenure in Korea," pp. 187–188. Ch'oe Chae-sŏk has collected evidence for buying and selling land and giving it away as a gift. See his "Koryŏjo e issŏsŏ ŭi t'oji ŭi chanyŏ kyunbun sangsok," *Han'guksa yŏn'gu* 35:37 (Dec. 1981). The examples Ch'oe gives for annexing others' land do not indicate, as he wants to see it, the private nature of land, but rather that its defensibility was weak.

76. For examples, see Ch'oe Chae-sŏk, "Koryŏ hugi kajok ŭi yuhyŏng kwa ku-sŏng," pp. 44–45; Hŏ Hŭng-sik, "Kukpo hojŏgŭro pon Koryŏmal ŭi sahoe kujo," p. 93.

77. *Koryŏsa* 84:40b. The Chinese model is in the T'ang code. See *Ku T'ang-lü shu-i*, 12:7b–8, 24:4b–5. The provision that demanded a guarantee for the older generation's livelihood the Koreans added from another T'ang law. See also Johnson, *Medieval Chinese Oligarchy*, p. 112.

78. See the illuminating article by Lutz K. Berkner, "Inheritance, land tenure and peasant family structure: a German regional comparison," in Jack Goody et al., eds., *Family and Inheritance* (Cambridge: Cambridge University Press, 1976), pp. 71–95.

79. *Koryŏsa chŏryo* 18:16b–17.

80. For examples, see the table in Hŏ Hŭng-sik, "Kukpo hojŏgŭro pon Ko-ryŏmal ŭi sahoe kujo," p. 90. The household also was a jural-administrative entity that was subject to regular registration for the purpose of levying taxes and assessing corvée labor. For this purpose, the households were legally divided into nine categories; but no numerical breakdown is available. The

tax burden was likely more tolerable for larger than for smaller households. See *Koryŏsa* 84:39b. Kang Chin-ch'ŏl has emphasized the collective nature of the tax burden. See his "Nongmin kwa ch'ollak," in *Han'guksa*, (Seoul: Kuksa p'yŏnch'an wiwŏnhoe, 1975), V, 277–290. For comparative T'ang data, see Ikeda On, pp. 121–150.

81. *Koryŏsa* 109:9; *Chōsen kinseki sōran* (reprint; Seoul: Kyŏngin munhwasa, 1974), I, 649–650. From Yun Sŏn-jwa's funerary inscription, it is clear that he had two sons and one daughter by his first wife, Yun-ssi, and two sons by his second wife, Pak-ssi. His firstborn son had died, and therefore it was actually his second, i.e., the eldest living son, who drafted the will. Similar admonitions are ascribed to Cho In-gyu (1237–1308). See *Koryŏsa* 105:40.

82. *Koryŏsa* 85:35b. The term *chŏkchang* should be noted here. It seems to refer specifically to the eldest son and not simply to any lineal descendant.

83. There are a few clear examples of the eldest son's important function of supervising the division of the patrimony. See *Koryŏsa* 95:16b, 109:9. For a discussion of the eldest son's role in property division in modern Taiwan, see Myron L. Cohen, *House United, House Divided: The Chinese Family in Taiwan* (New York: Columbia University Press, 1976), pp. 142–143.

84. *Koryŏsa* 102:17–18; *Koryŏsa chŏryo* 17:2b–3.

85. *Koryŏsa* 95:16b; *Koryŏsa chŏryo* 10:42a–b. The number of Yi Chi-jŏ's siblings is evident from his father's grave inscription. See Yi Nan-yŏng, comp., *Han-guk kŭmsŏngmun ch'ubo*, pp. 102–103.

86. Hong Sŭng-gi, *Koryŏ sidae nobi yŏn'gu* (Seoul: The Korean Research Center, 1981), pp. 90–109, 162–178. For property division in T'ang times, see Johnson, *Medieval Chinese Oligarchy*, p. 112.

87. *Koryŏsa* 85:4. The value of such hereditary items was expressed in amounts of cloth.

88. *Koryŏsa* 104:42a–b; *Chōsen kinseki sōran*, I, 637.

89. *Koryŏsa* 119:2b–3.

90. At the beginning of the dynasty, the slaves of an heirless man were apparently confiscated by the state. *Koryŏsa* 85:43. It is not clear when the term *sason* (collateral relatives) as the recipients of ownerless property began to be used. It is first mentioned in legal records of late Koryŏ. *Koryŏsa* 85:46b. Here it is not absolutely clear which categories of collateral kin are included in the term. Ch'oe Chae-sŏk and Hatada Takashi take *sason* as synonymous with *ponson, ch'inch'ŏk*, and *tongjong:* Ch'oe Chae-sŏk, "Koryŏ ŭi sangsokche wa ch'injok chojik," *Tongbang hakchi* 31:25–27 (June 1982); Hatada Takashi, "Chakuchōshi sōzoku," pp. 350–353. For a more detailed discussion on the fate of the property of childless heirs, see Chapter Five.

91. *Koryŏsa* 88:1a–b; *Koryŏsa chŏryo* 2:2.

92. *Koryŏsa* 91:19b–20b. For a list of these marriages, see Ha Hyŏn-gang, "Koryŏ wangjo ŭi sŏngnip kwa hojok yŏnhap chŏnggwŏn," *Han'guksa*, IV, 54.

93. *Koryŏsa chŏryo* 2:2.

94. For the marriage connections of the early Koryŏ kings, see chapter 88 of the *Koryŏsa*. For a list of further marriages with nieces and aunts within the royal house, see Ch'oe Chae-sŏk, "Koryŏ sidae ŭi ch'injok chojik," p. 226.

95. For detailed discussions of the first succession struggle, see Hugh Hi-Woong Kang, "Development of the Korean Ruling Class from Late Silla to Early Koryŏ" (Ph.D. diss., University of Washington, 1964), pp. 87–93; Ha Hyŏn-gang, "Hojok kwa wanggwŏn," *Han'guksa*, IV, 104ff. The two discussions differ in detail.

96. For details, see Yi Pyŏng-do, *Han'guksa, chungsep'yŏn* (Seoul: Ŭryu munhwasa, 1961), pp. 421–428; Yi Man-yŏl, "Koryŏ Kyŏngwŏn Yi-ssi kamun ŭi chŏn'gae kwajŏng," *Hankuk Hakpo* 21:2–29 (Winter 1980). A Kyŏngwŏn Yi *t'aehu* was recorded in King Ch'ungsŏn's list of 1308.

97. For details, see the biography of Ch'oe Ch'ung-hŏn in *Koryŏsa* 129:21b, 26b–27; Shultz, "Institutional Developments," pp. 119–123. For the marriage policies of Ch'oe Ch'ung-hŏn's son, U, see Shultz, "Institutional Developments," pp. 194–195.

98. For an example, see *Koryŏsa* 28:10b–11.

99. Ch'ungsŏn was only half Korean. His mother was Emperor Shih-tsu's daughter, and he spent his youth in Peking. He, thus, was presumably little committed to Koryŏ traditions and felt free to initiate reforms that went beyond the marriage institution. See Yi Pyŏng-do, *Han'guksa, chungsep'yŏn*, p. 635.

100. *Koryŏsa* 33:24a–b; *Chŭngbo munhŏnbigo* 89:3a–b.

101. This view is expressed by Min Hyŏn-gu, "Cho In-gyu wa kŭ ŭi kamun, sang," *Chindan hakpo* 42:27 (1976).

102. Evidence for the different ranges of consanguineous marriages is indirectly provided by the various laws, discussed below, which gradually prohibited them.

103. According to Lucy Mair, *Marriage* (Harmondsworth: Penguin Books, 1971), p. 29, one can speak of "endogamy" only if there are explicit rules. I therefore avoid this term here.

104. For an analysis of the marriage radius of the Andong Kim, see Hŏ Hŭngsik, *Koryŏ sahoesa yŏn'gu*, pp. 213–215. Further examples could be given. Yi Su-gŏn also suggests that the marriage radius of local families at the beginning of Koryŏ was narrow. See his "Koryŏ chŏn'gi t'osŏng yŏn'gu," *Taegu sahak* 14:70n64 (June 1978).

105. *Koryŏsa* 125:1b; Pak Yong-un, "Koryŏ sidae ŭi Haeju Ch'oe-ssi wa P'ap'yŏng Yun-ssi kamun punsŏk," *Paeksan hakpo* 23:131 (Dec. 1977).

106. *Koryŏsa* 99:17a–b. For Kim Po-dang's revolt, see Shultz, "Institutional Developments," p. 98.
107. See Hŏ Hŭng-sik, *Koryŏ sahoesa yŏn'gu,* pp. 213–219.
108. Im Wŏn-hu was Injong's father-in-law and the maternal grandfather of Ŭijong, Myŏngjong, and Sinjong. For details about the Chiksan Ch'oe and the Chŏngan Im, see Pak Yong-un, "Koryŏ chŏn'gi munban kwa muban ŭi sinbun munje," *Han'guksa yŏn'gu* 21/22:45–49 (Dec. 1978).
109. See the various articles on the Koryŏ aristocracy by Pak Yong-un. See also Yi Su-gŏn, "Koryŏ chŏn'gi t'osŏng yŏn'gu," p. 58. Min Hyŏn-gu has examined the marriage relations of Cho In-gyu and his descendants in "Cho In-gyu wa kŭ ŭi kamun (chung)," *Chindan hakpo* 43:14–32 (1977).
110. *Chŭngbo munhŏnbigo* 89:2b.
111. *Sung-shih* (Shanghai: Chung-hua shu-chü ch'u-pan, 1977), XL, 14047.
112. *Koryŏsa* 75:22b. Patrilateral cross-cousins were not touched by this measure. Kinship relationships were expressed by the five mourning grades introduced from China in 985.
113. *Koryŏsa* 95:28a–b; *Koryŏsa chŏryo* 5:40.
114. *Koryŏsa* 75:23.
115. *Koryŏsa* 75:23.
116. *Koryŏsa* 75:23b.
117. *Koryŏsa* 75:23b.
118. *Koryŏsa* 75:24.
119. *Koryŏsa* 75:24; 84:39 (headed "adultery"). Prohibited marriages across generations also were those with the daughter of a patrilateral first cousin (one generation below) and with the daughter of one's brother's son (two generations below). In *Chŭngbo munhŏnbigo* 89:2b, there is a similar version of the law of 1147; but it uses the term *tongsŏng,* "same surname," in the meaning of "father's surname group," within which intermarriage was prohibited.
120. In 1308 and 1367 demands for prohibiting marriages with matrilateral cross-cousins and with matrilateral second cousins, respectively, were voiced. *Koryŏsa* 84:39a–b.
121. Unions with relatives of a different surname, that is, matrilateral kin, were not prohibited as long as they did not violate the generational principle.
122. *Ku T'ang-lü shu-i* 14:1–4b; 16:18–19. Legal stipulations concerning adultery belonged to the category of "diverse laws" *(tsa-lü).*
123. *Koryŏsa* 84:39.
124. Hŏ Hŭng-sik, *Koryŏ sahoesa yŏn'gu,* p. 114; Yi Nan-yŏng, comp., *Han'guk kŭmsŏngmun ch'ubo,* pp. 232–233.
125. Hŏ Hŭng-sik, *Koryŏ sahoesa yŏn'gu,* pp. 114, 220. Hŏ maintains that especially among the local *hyangni* close kin marriages were common.
126. It is repeatedly asserted that in Koryŏ the (Confucian) rite of the groom's

personal induction of the bride *(ch'inyŏng)* was not performed. For an example, see *Sejong sillok* 48:25.

127. For tabulations of ages at marriage on the basis of funerary inscriptions and the "Household Register of Yi T'aejo," see Hŏ Hŭng-sik, *Koryŏ sahoesa yŏn'gu*, pp. 305–310; Ch'oe Chae-sŏk, "Koryŏ sidae ŭi honin chedo," *Koryŏ taehakkyo, inmun nonjip* 27:113–115 (1982). Both authors contend that ages at marriage, especially for women, were drastically lowered during the Mongol period when the Mongols demanded Korean women as tribute.

128. This information is based on the *Kyerim yusa* as quoted in *Kōrai izen no fūzoku kankei shiryō satsuyō* (Keijō: Chōsen sōtokufu, Chūsūin, 1941), p. 696; and Hsü Ching, *Kao-li t'u-ching*, p. 111. According to the latter source, commoners celebrated a wedding "only with wine and food."

129. *Koryŏsa* 85:20a–b, 22b–23; 108:6. Toward the end of the dynasty, several memorialists demanded measures that would have restricted the conspicuous consumption at weddings.

130. *Koryŏsa* 96:10; 109:15b–16; Yi Kyu-bo, *Tongguk Yi Sanggukchip* 37:14.

131. Ch'oe Chae-sŏk has tried to determine the duration of the husband's stay in his wife's house. He seems to make two assumptions: that all marriages were uxorilocal or at least started out as such, and that all uxorilocal marriages ended with the wife's "return" to her husband's house. For neither of these assumptions is there solid evidence. See his calculations in "Koryŏ sidae ŭi honin chedo," pp. 106–107.

132. Yi Kyu-bo, *Tongguk Yi Sanggukchip* 37:14.

133. Yi Kok asserts that the very rationale of uxorilocal marriage was the daughter's responsibility for taking care of her parents. This memorial, written in opposition to sending Korean girls to the Mongols, may have exaggerated the importance of a daughter's duties toward her parents. *Koryŏsa* 109:15b–16.

134. *Koryŏsa* 27:8; *Sejong sillok* 48:25.

135. For an example, see the biography of Cho Pyŏn (?–1288) whose father-in-law was Kim Pang-gyŏng (1212–1300): *Koryŏsa* 103:6b. If a new examination passer had no parents who could be honored, his parents-in-law could be substituted: *Koryŏsa* 74:3b.

136. For an example, see the biography of Ch'oe Sa-ch'u in *Koryŏsa* 96:1–3. His sons-in-law were Yi Cha-gyŏm, Mun Kong-in, and Yu In-jŏ (?–1113). All of them advanced to high office and were said to have contributed to the prosperity of Ch'oe's house.

137. *Koryŏsa* 94:28. For another example, see *Koryŏsa* 98:33a–b.

138. *Koryŏsa chŏryo* 17:13b.

139. *Koryŏsa chŏryo* 12:25.

140. A good example of a son-in-law receiving the protection privilege from his

father-in-law is the case of Yi Se-ch'ang (n.d.), Mun Kong-yu's (d. 1159) son-in-law. See the chart on p. 32 of Pak Yong-un, "Koryŏ sidae ŭmsŏje ŭi silche wa kŭ kinŭng, ha." Hwang-bo Yŏng (?–1047) made his non-agnatic grandson, the son of his son-in-law Kim Nok-sung (n.d.), his heir: *Koryŏsa* 7:4b.

141. *Koryŏsa* 64:24, 28. These mourning grades were exceptional in comparison to those commonly observed in T'ang China where the mourning period for the parents-in-law as well as for the son-in-law lasted only three months.

142. See, for example, *Koryŏsa* 96:10.

143. *Koryŏsa* 130:20b.

144. Hsü Ching, *Kao-li t'u-ching*, p. 111.

145. For example, see *Koryŏsa* 114:19; 123:19; 124:11b–12, 37. It may not be accidental that the compilers of the *Koryŏsa* made it a special point to mention such marriages in the biographies of personalities who were listed as "parasites" *(p'yehaeng)*. The fact that they were active during the Mongol period leads Hŏ Hŭng-sik to believe that it was under Mongol influence that plural marriage was introduced into Korea. See Hŏ Hŭng-sik, *Koryŏ sahoesa yŏn'gu*, p. 300. This, however, seems to be a mistaken notion; for clear evidence points to the existence of plural marriage long before Mongol domination.

146. Ch'oe Chae-sŏk has found fourteen tomb inscriptions which mention more than one marriage. See his "Koryŏ sidae ŭi honin chedo," p. 116.

147. For examples, see *T'aejong sillok* 19:2b; 23:9a–b; 25:13a–b; 27:46b–47; *Sejong sillok* 10:13. One term they used was *pyŏngch'uk*, "to keep [several wives] at the same time."

148. For a description of the "visiting husband" solution, although in a matrilineal society, see Robin Fox, *Kinship and Marriage* (Harmondsworth: Penguin Books, 1967), p. 101.

149. Neither Ch'oe Chae-sŏk nor Hŏ Hŭng-sik tries to interpret this remarkable phenomenon. Ch'oe Chae-sŏk, "Koryŏ hugi kajok ŭi yuhyŏng kwa kusŏng," pp. 22–57; and Hŏ Hŭng-sik, *Koryŏ sahoesa yŏn'gu*.

150. For an example, see Yun T'aek's (1289–1370) funerary inscription. Yun had four wives; two came from military, the others apparently from civil backgrounds. *Chōsen kinseki sōran*, I, 676–678.

151. Hsü Ching, *Kao-li t'u-ching*, pp. 103–104.

152. A good example is the case of Yun Sŏn-jwa, discussed in the section on inheritance.

153. Instead, such noncommital expressions as *sa*, "to have an affair," or *t'ong*, "to have intercourse," are used. The biography of Kwak Yŏ (1058–1130), for example, reports that Kwak never married *(ch'wich'ŏ)*, but had an affair with a singing girl *(ki)* and moreover kept a slave girl *(pich'ŏp)*:

Koryŏsa 97:9b–10. Hsü Ching writes that there were ladies-in-waiting *(ing)* in palace offices and servants *(ch'ŏp)* in government offices. It is hard to interpret these terms as "secondary wives." A synonym of *ch'ŏp* is *kwanbi*. See Hsü Ching, *Kao-li t'u-ching*, pp. 104, 106. For further examples of the usage of *ch'ŏp*, see Ch'oe Chae-sŏk, "Koryŏ sidae ŭi honin chedo," p. 121. When *ch'ŏp* is used in the monographic chapters *(chi)* of the *Koryŏsa*, it most often appears in quotations from the T'ang code or some Chinese-type legislation. The term *ch'ŏp* does not appear on funerary inscriptions.

154. Yi Saek, *Mogŭn mun'go* 16:7b (grave inscription of Yi Che-hyŏn); Chŏng Mong-ju, *P'oŭn-jip, songnok*, 1:5b (grave inscription of Haeyang-gun tae-buin Kim-ssi).

155. The interpretation of this passage hinges on the meaning of this term. In a contemporary piece, it is explained as "women of 'good' houses" *(yang-ganyŏ)*, that is, commoner women. In the same document "to marry" *(ch'wi)* is replaced by the derogatory "to keep" *(ch'uk)*. See biography of Kim Hon (1239–1311) in *Koryŏsa* 103:29b.

156. Hŏ Hŭng-sik, for example, insists that in Koryŏ "one husband–one wife" *(ilbu ilch'ŏ)* was the only form of married life and therefore interprets Pak's proposal as introducing a new polygamous system *(ilbu tach'ŏ)*, a system, Hŏ believes, that came about through contact with the Mongols. See his *Koryŏ sahoesa yŏn'gu*, pp. 302–303 and especially footnote 34 on p. 303 and footnote 50 on p. 70.

157. *Koryŏsa* 106:40–41. In the *Koryŏsa chŏryo* 19:28b, Pak's memorial is dated the second month of 1275. A similar concern with the decrease of the size of the households is voiced in Kim Hon's biography in which the king was about to order "officials and commoners" *(samin)* to keep commoner wives *(sŏch'ŏ): Koryŏsa* 103:29b. The fear that the population would decrease because of the Mongol demands was earlier also voiced in a document King Kojong (r. 1213–59) sent to the Mongols in 1232: *Koryŏsa* 23:12–13b. The demographic impact of the Mongol demands for Korean women remains to be studied.

158. Hsü Ching, *Kao-li t'u-ching*, p. 111; *Kyerim yusa* as quoted in *Kōrai izen no fūzoku kankei shiryō satsuyō* (Keijō: Chōsen sōtokufu, Chūsūin, 1941), p. 969.

159. *Koryŏsa* 88:26b–27.

160. *Koryŏsa* 102:19; *Koryŏsa chŏryo* 15:41b.

161. Arthur P. Wolf and Chieh-shan Huang, *Marriage and Adoption in China, 1845–1945* (Stanford: Stanford University Press, 1980), p. 182.

162. Hsü Ching, *Kao-li t'u-ching*, p. 111.

163. For example, *Koryŏsa* 99:1; 129:44b.

164. *Koryŏsa* 84:41. This provision is undated.

165. *Koryŏsa* 84:41b. Offspring of such unions were, according to a law of 1152, barred from office: *Koryŏsa* 75:24.
166. Hsü Ching, *Kao-li t'u-ching*, p. 117; *Kyerimyusa*, p. 696. The severity of legal provisions may have been a negative reflection of the generally easy contact between the sexes. Extramarital relations were heavily punished although the law, in imitation of T'ang precedent, specifically singled out only a small group of close relatives with whom illegal intercourse *(kanbi)* was punishable with strangulation: grandfather's concubine *(ch'ŏp)*, the wives of the paternal uncles, father's sister, sisters, the wives of son and grandson, and the brothers' daughters. See *Koryŏsa* 84:39. The typical housing arrangement with several married brothers and perhaps a uxorilocally residing brother-in-law living in the same household naturally provided opportunities for adulterous relationships. See *Koryŏsa* 95:30b for a case of adultery with the elder brother's daughter; or *Koryŏsa* 114:7b–8 for a case of adultery with the wife's younger sister; or *Koryŏsa* 26:14 for a case of adultery with the wife of a paternal uncle.
167. *Koryŏsa* 75:34; *Chōsen kinseki sōran*, I, 363; Yi Nan-yŏng, comp., *Han'guk kŭmsŏngmun ch'ubo*, pp. 185, 186.
168. Sŏngjong's first queen, Mundŏk wanghu, had lost her first husband before becoming queen: *Koryŏsa* 88:11b. Ch'ungnyŏl's third queen had also been a widow: *Koryŏsa* 89:12a–b. There are more such examples.
169. Yi Nan-yŏng, comp., *Han'guk kŭmsŏngmun ch'ubo*, p. 163; *Koryŏsa* 110:18, 124:12.
170. *Koryŏsa* 114:9b.
171. *Chōsen kinseki sōran*, I, 387, 418; *Koryŏsa* 11:25b, 129:45b.
172. *Koryŏsa* 64:25.
173. Kim Pu-sik, *Samguk sagi*, Kim Chong-gwŏn, tr. (Seoul: Kwangjin munhwasa, 1963), p. 62.
174. This was also the case in Japan. When in the early eighth century the Chinese-style mourning system was introduced, repeated revisions had to be made to bring it closer to Japanese mourning practices: G. B. Sansom, *Japan: A Short Cultural History* (London: The Cresset Press, 1952), pp. 161–162.
175. This diagram gives only a select number of mourning grades. For a complete chart, see No Myŏng-ho, "Koryŏ ŭi obokch'in kwa ch'injok kwan'gye pŏpche," p. 38.
176. *Koryŏsa* 64:27a–b.
177. *Koryŏsa* 64:28.
178. *Koryŏsa* 64:26b, 27; 85:8.
179. For descriptions of the Koryŏ *obok* system, see Yi P'il sang, "Koryŏ sidae pokche ŭi yŏn'gu," M.A. thesis of Seoul National University, 1974; No Myŏng-ho, "Koryŏ ŭi obokch'in kwa ch'injok kwan'gye pŏpche," pp. 1–

42. No incorrectly thinks that the absence of reference to a wife's ritual responsibilities toward her husband's family is an omission: see p. 5.

180. Biographies of filial sons are found in *Koryŏsa* 99:28b–30; 110:6b–8; 112:30b–31b, 31b–32b. For examples on grave inscriptions, see Yi P'il-sang, "Koryŏ sidae pokche ŭi yŏn'gu," p. 46.

181. *Koryŏsa* 112:32.

182. *Koryŏsa* 63:18; 64:25a–b; 84:5–7b.

183. *Koryŏsa* 64:25a–b; 94:37.

184. *Koryŏsa* 74:6b–7. As a rule, however, somebody in mourning could not take the exams. For examples, see Yi P'il-sang, "Koryŏ sidae pokche ŭi yŏn'gu," p. 52.

185. *Koryŏsa* 81:13b, 16b.

186. The method of converting the number of months to days was also used at the royal court because the king could not neglect his duties for the full length of the prescribed mourning periods. For details, see Yi P'il-sang, "Koryŏ sidae pokche ŭi yŏn'gu," pp. 52–54.

187. In the early Chosŏn period, the mourning period of one hundred days was considered typical for Koryŏ. See *Chŏngjong sillok* 1:3; *Sejong sillok* 58:19b.

188. *Koryŏsa* 64:20–22b. This section, entitled "Funerals of All Officials" (*che-sinsang*), gives examples from most periods of the dynasty.

189. *Koryŏsa* 85:6b.

190. *Koryŏsa* 85:13.

191. *T'aejong sillok* 12:13.

192. Yi Nan-yŏng, comp., *Han'guk kŭmsŏngmun ch'ubo*, pp. 111, 219; *Chōsen kinseki sōran*, I, 391.

193. *Sejong sillok* 26:29b.

194. Yi Nan-yŏng, comp., *Han'guk kŭmsŏngmun ch'ubo*, pp. 117, 229, 280; *Koryŏsa* 104:24. Although the burial sites are usually identified on grave inscriptions, it is difficult to locate them. A successful attempt to do so—undoubtedly extremely time consuming—would throw light on the historical formation of the capital elite.

195. See Yi Nan-yŏng, comp., *Han'guk kŭmsŏngmun ch'ubo*, pp. 218, 221, for two examples.

196. *Koryŏsa* 85:18; 111:4b; *T'aejong sillok* 33:57.

197. *Koryŏsa* 85:21b.

198. *Koryŏsa chŏryo* 10:8b.

199. *Koryŏsa* 64:26.

200. The *Koryŏsa* does not give information on the actual conduct of funerals. The grave inscriptions yield more detail. Here not always specifically acknowledged, three major collections of grave inscriptions were consulted: *Chōsen kinseki sōran;* Yi Nan-yŏng, comp., *Han'guk kŭmsŏngmun ch'ubo;* and Hwang Su-yŏng, comp., *Chŭngbo Han'guk kŭmsŏk yumun*.

201. *T'aejo sillok* 15:13a–b; *Sejong sillok* 44:2a–b.
202. *Koryŏsa chŏryo* 10:8b; *Koryŏsa* 84:19; *Sung-shih*, p. 14054; *Shuo-fu* as quoted in *Kōrai izen no fūzoku kankei shiryō satsuyō*, p. 696.
203. Such interpretations range from the view, held by Suematsu Yasukazu, that Silla society was originally matrilineal to the opinion, put forward by Yi Ki-dong, that Silla society was from its beginning patrilineal. Between these two poles there are many variations. A refutation of the matrilineal theory can be found in Kim Ŭi-gyu, "Silla mogyeje sahoesŏl e taehan kŏmt'o. Silla ch'injok yŏn'gu, kiil," *Han'guksa yŏn'gu* 23:41–64 (March 1979). For a review of various theories, see P'i Yŏng-hŭi, "Double Descent iron chŏgyong ŭl t'onghaesŏ pon Silla wang ŭi sinbun kwannyŏm," *Han'guk saron* 5:65–73 (October 1979).
204. The Japanese as well as Korean literature on Silla society is large and complex and cannot be reviewed here. For recent summaries of marriage and royal succession, see Ch'oe Chae-sŏk, "Silla wangsil ŭi honinje," *Han'guksa yŏn'gu* 40:1–32 (1983); and his "Silla wangsil ŭi wangwi kyesŭng," *Yŏksa hakpo* 98:39–105 (1983). The problem of whether or not *kol* is equal to *chok* is left out of my considerations here.
205. See Kim Ch'ŏl-chun, "Silla sangdae sahoe ŭi Dual Organization, sang," *Yŏksa hakpo* 1:15–47 (July 1952); and "Silla sangdae sahoe ŭi Dual Organization, ha," *Yŏksa hakpo* 2:85–115 (Oct. 1952). Although this work proved to be stimulating, its terminological vagueness has led to numerous misunderstandings and speculations. For a newer review of double descent, see P'i Yŏng-hŭi, "Double Descent iron chŏgyong ŭl t'onghaesŏ pon Silla wang ŭi sinbun kwannyŏm."
206. For a refutation of double descent as an analytical tool, see Elman R. Service, *Primitive Social Organization,* 2nd ed. (New York: Random House, 1971), pp. 118–121. George P. Murdock states that bilateral descent can be derived directly from either matrilineal or patrilineal, but not from double descent. See his *Social Structure* (New York: The Free Press, 1949), p. 327. For Korea, this whole complex awaits a thorough review. Terminological vagueness and inconsistency in Western anthroloplogical literature have exerted a confusing influence on Korean historical writing.
207. For a reconstruction of the kinship vocabulary of the fifteenth century, see Yi Sung-nyŏng, "Chungse kugŏ ŭi kajok hoch'ing e taehayŏ."
208. The *Kagero nikki* has been translated by Edward Seidensticker as *The Gossamer Years* (Tokyo: C. E. Tuttle, 1975).
209. These data are based on the seminal article by William H. McCullough, "Japanese Marriage Institutions in the Late Heian Period," *Harvard Journal of Asiatic Studies* 27:103–167 (1967). Also see Wakita Haruko, "Marriage and Property in Premodern Japan from the Perspective of Women's History," *The Journal of Japanese Studies* 10.1:73–99 (1984).

210. This is not to deny that the contemporary Sung also exerted influence on Korean society, but it was certainly much less remarkable.
211. The levirate, to be sure, was not unknown in Korea. It seems to have been an often practiced custom in Koguryŏ. For details, see Li Ogg, *Recherche sur l'Antiquité Coréenne* (Paris: Collège de France, Centre d'Etudes Coréennes, 1980), pp. 228–229.
212. For an illuminating article on social practices of the early Mongol and Yüan society, see Jennifer Holmgren, "Observations on Marriage and Inheritance Practices in Early Mongol and Yüan Society, with Particular Reference to the Levirate," *Journal of Asian History* 20.2:127–192 (1986).
213. See, for example, Hŏ Hŭng-sik, *Koryŏ sahoesa yŏn'gu*, pp. 300–301. Hŏ argues that in the household registers only the formula "one husband–one wife" appears, and that only a few officials closely associated with the Mongols kept several wives.
214. Holmgren, "Observations on Marriage and Inheritance Practices," pp. 147, 154–155. Holmgren sees Mongol polygamy as a prerequisite for the widespread custom of levirate.
215. For a detailed discussion of the adoption of surnames in Silla, see Yi Sungŭn, "Silla sidae sŏngssi ch'widŭk kwa kŭ ŭimi," *Han'guk saron* 6:3–65 (Dec. 1980).
216. The story is told in the *Yi-ssi karok* (Family Chronicle of the Yi). See Yi Man-yŏl, "Koryŏ Kyŏngwŏn Yi-ssi kamun ŭi chŏn'gae kwajŏng," p. 5, especially footnotes 4 and 5. Yi Man-yŏl has not ventured an explanation of the meaning of the double surname Yi-Hŏ. Because Ki is said to have descended from Karak, his immediate descendants undoubtedly wanted to remember this descent by also using Hŏ. Hŏ was the surname of King Suro's second son who took his mother's surname. The surname of the royal main line of Karak was Kim. See Yi Sun-gŭn, "Silla sidae sŏngssi ch'widŭk kwa kŭ ŭimi," p. 51. Yi quotes the *Han'guk sŏngssi tae'gwan* (Seoul: Ch'angjosa, 1973), p. 252, for the above legend.
217. For more such cases, see Yi Sun-gŭn, "Silla sidae sŏngssi ch'widŭk kwa kŭ ŭimi," p. 47. For a discussion of the difficulties surrounding the fixation of Wang Kŏn's ancestry, see Michael C. Rogers, "*P'yŏnnyŏn T'ongnok:* The Foundation Legend of the Koryŏ State," *Journal of Korean Studies* 4:3–17 (1982–1983).
218. See Johnson, *Medieval Chinese Oligarchy*, p. 91.
219. For a seminal treatment of the origin of the Korean *pon'gwan* system, see Song Chun-ho, "Han'guk ŭi ssijokche e issŏsŏ ŭi pon'gwan mit sijo ŭi munje." In its original sense, *pon'gwan* was identical with *ponjŏk*, "place of registration." Later, however, *pon'gwan* lost this primary meaning and was rarely ever identical with a man's place of birth or residence.
220. Song Chun-ho, "Han'guk ŭi ssijokche e issŏsŏ ŭi pon'gwan mit sijo ŭi

munje," p. 134. For a treatise on the formation of the Koryŏ aristocracy, see also Yi Ki-baek, "Koryŏ kwijok sahoe ŭi hyŏngsŏng."

221. Perhaps among other lists, the "Treatise on Clans" *(Shih-tsu chih)* of 632 with which Kao Shih-lien's name was connected was known in Kaesŏng: *Koryŏsa* 10:25. In T'ang, such national genealogies were apparently compiled in an attempt to make status dependent on officeholding: Johnson, *Medieval Chinese Oligarchy,* p. 48ff.

222. *Koryŏsa* 33:24a–b. For a discussion of the aristocratic descent groups of 1308, see Hwang Ul-long, *Koryŏ pŏlchok e kwanhan yŏn'gu* (Taegu: Ch'inhaksa, 1978), pp. 110–116.

223. See Johnson, *Medieval Chinese Oligarchy,* p. 92.

224. For examples, see *Koryŏsa* 104:55; 109:17. In the list of aristocratic families of 1308, the term "one descent line" *(ilchong)* was used to denote the direct descent line of a specific individual within a *chok*.

2. NEO-CONFUCIANISM: THE IDEOLOGICAL FOUNDATION OF SOCIAL LEGISLATION IN EARLY CHOSŎN

1. For a study of Sin Ton's political career, see Min Hyŏn-gu, "Sin Ton ŭi chipkwŏn kwa kŭ chŏngch'ijŏk sŏngkyŏk," *Yŏksa hakpo* 38:46–88 (Aug. 1968) and 40:53–119 (Dec. 1968).

2. Two important studies exploring the political and economic background of the transition period from late Koryŏ to early Chosŏn are Han U-gŭn, "Yŏmal Sŏnch'o ŭi pulgyo chŏngch'aek," *Sŏuldae nonmunjip, inmun sahoe kwahak* 6:1–80 (1957); and Yi Sang-baek, "Yubul yanggyo kyodae ŭi kiyŏn e taehan il yŏn'gu," in *Chosŏn munhwasa yŏn'gu non'go* (Seoul: Ŭryu munhwasa, 1948), pp. 1–170. The economic issues are also spelled out in Sudō Yoshiyuki, "Raimatsu Sensho ni okeru nōsō ni tsuite," *Seikyū gakusō* 17:1–80 (Aug. 1934). John B. Duncan discussed the politics of late Koryŏ in his "Koryŏ Origins of the Chosŏn Dynasty"; see esp. chap. 7.

3. *Koryŏsa* 115:1–9.

4. *Koryŏsa* 118:1–34 (Cho Chun's biography); 78:20–38 (memorials by Cho Chun, Yi Haeng, Hwang Sun-sang, Hŏ Ŭng, and Cho In-ok); Chŏng To-jŏn, *Chosŏn kyŏnggukchŏn, Sambong-jip,* pp. 214–215. For a good and detailed discussion of the land reform debates during the last years of Koryŏ, see Yi Sang-baek, *Yijo kŏn'guk ŭi yŏn'gu* (Seoul: Ŭryu munhwasa, 1959), pp. 117–120.

5. Besides these major lists, there were several minor lists, and the actual number of merit status recipients at the beginning of the Chosŏn dynasty is generally estimated at well over one thousand.

6. This overview is based on Chŏng Tu-hŭi, "T'aejo-T'aejongdae samgongsin ŭi chŏngch'ijŏk sŏngkyŏk," in *Chosŏn ch'ogi chŏngch'i chibae seryŏk yŏn'gu* (Seoul:

Ilchogak, 1983), pp. 7–56. An earlier version of this work, which appeared in *Yŏksa hakpo* 75/76:121–176 (Dec. 1976), contains complete lists of all three groups of merit subjects. See also Han Yŏng-u, "Chosŏn kaeguk kongsin ŭi ch'ulsin e taehan yŏn'gu," in *Chosŏn chŏn'gi sahoe kyŏngje yŏn'gu* (Seoul: Ŭryu munhwasa, 1983), pp. 117–180. This work contains biographical sketches for all merit subjects of 1392. See also Donald N. Clark, "Chosŏn's Founding Fathers: A Study of Merit Subjects in the Early Yi Dynasty," *Korean Studies* 6:17–40 (1982); and Yi Sang-baek, "Yi Sŏng-gye wa Koryŏ malgi ŭi chŏngch'aek," *Yijo kŏn'guk ŭi yŏn'gu,* pp. 3–116.

7. For a list of the rewards conferred upon T'aejo's merit subjects of 1392, see Clark, p. 19.

8. For a brief discussion of the marital ties between the merit subjects and the new royal house, see Clark, pp. 28–31.

9. Han Yŏng-u, "Chŏng To-jŏn ŭi in'gan kwa sahoe sasang," *Chindan hakpo* 50:123–135 (1980). Han seems to make too much of Chŏng To-jŏn's "illegitimate" ancestry. Although his maternal grandmother had apparently been a "secondary wife," in late Koryŏ this concept did not yet carry a social stigma. Instead, it is likely that Chosŏn critics who later attacked Chŏng's fateful misjudgment of 1398 used their own era's newly established legal standards, which depreciated a secondary wife's status, as a way of tarnishing Chŏng's image even more. It is anachronistic, therefore, to make this issue one of Chŏng's major motives for joining Yi Sŏng-gye's forces. See also Clark, pp. 24–25.

10. Cho Chun was a great-grandson of Cho In-gyu (1237–1308), who as interpreter for the Mongols built himself a powerful position in late Koryŏ society. See Min Hyŏn-gu, "Cho In-gyu wa kŭ kamun," parts "sang" and "chung." His obituary is in *T'aejong sillok* 9:24–27. Cho Chun's younger brother, Kyŏn (1351–1425), was made a second class merit subject in 1392.

11. Ha Yun's obituary is in *T'aejong sillok* 32:25b–27. See also Chŏng Tu-hŭi, *Chosŏn ch'ogi chŏngch'i chibae seryŏk yŏn'gu,* p. 34.

12. Kwŏn Kŭn was retroactively made a *wŏnjong kongsin,* a lesser category of merit subjects created by T'aejo in late 1392. In addition, in 1401, he became a T'aejong *chwamyŏng kongsin,* fourth class. Although his merit-subject status was thus not very impressive, Kwŏn Kŭn came to have close family ties to the royal house when his third son married T'aejong's third daughter.

13. Kwŏn Kŭn's obituary is in *T'aejong sillok* 17:8b–11. The most extensive biography is in Pak Ch'ŏn-gyu, "Yangch'on Kwŏn Kŭn yŏn'gu," *Sach'ong* 9:1–50 (Dec. 1964). Also see Chŏng Tu-hŭi, *Chosŏn ch'ogi chŏngch'i chibae seryŏk yŏn'gu,* pp. 34–35.

14. During roughly the first three decades of the new dynasty, for example, seventeen out of twenty high state councillors (senior first rank) were merit subjects. See Edward W. Wagner, *The Literati Purges: Political Conflict in*

Early Yi Korea (Cambridge, East Asian Research Center, Harvard University, 1974), p. 13.

15. It is interesting to note that the great descent groups from which during the first two centuries of the dynasty the highest number of *munkwa* passers emerged, for example the Andong Kim (ca. 65) or the Kwangsan Kim (78), produced only a few successful candidates during the reigns of the first three kings, the Andong Kim six, the Kwangsan Kim seven. A few members of both groups held high office in the first years of the dynasty, but no Andong Kim nor Kwangsan Kim was on the merit subject rosters promulgated during the reigns of T'aejo, Chŏngjong, and T'aejong. See the table in Clark, p. 39, n. 30, which is based on statistics compiled by Edward W. Wagner. These statistics have been slightly revised in the meantime.

16. Biographical data on these four men can be found in their respective obituaries in the *Sillok* and biographical sketches in their personal works. Also see *Han'guk inmyŏng taesajŏn* (Seoul: Sin'gu munhwasa, 1967). None of the descent groups of these four men can be found on the list of "leading clans" of late Koryŏ and early Chosŏn compiled by John B. Duncan. See his "The Social Background to the Founding of the Chosŏn Dynasty: Change or Continuity?" *Journal of Korean Studies* 6:52–53 (1988–1989).

17. This is based on Duncan's "Social Background to the Founding of the Chosŏn Dynasty." Duncan analyzed the available data for two periods: pre-Kongmin to 1392 and 1392 to 1400. He also shows the close marital ties which bound the highest officialdom together. This study seems to cast doubt on the view held by some Korean historians that a new *social* class of scholar-officials *(sinhŭng sadaebu)* came to power with the founding of Chosŏn. For such a view, see, for example, Han Yŏng-u, "Chosŏn wangjo ŭi chŏngch'i, kyŏngje kiban," *Han'guksa* IX, 25–29. Han Yŏng-u has in various publications expressed the opinion that the leadership in the transition period was provided by scholar-officials representing the small and medium-sized landlord class. For a critique of this point of view, see James B. Palais, "Han Yŏng-u's Studies of Early Chosŏn Intellectual History," *Journal of Korean Studies* 2:199–224 (1980).

18. For a discussion of the reestablishment of the Confucian Academy, see Hŏ Hŭng-sik, *Koryŏ kwagŏ chedosa yŏn'gu*, pp. 48–52.

19. Yi Saek's biography is in *Koryŏsa* 115:1–28 and his obituary in *T'aejo sillok* 9:6b–8. For a detailed biographical study, see Hans-Jürgen Zaborowski, *Der Gelehrte und Staatsmann Mogŭn Yi Saek (1328–1396)* (Wiesbaden: Otto Harrassowitz, 1976).

20. Chŏng Mong-ju's biography is in *Koryŏsa* 117:1–20. There is another short biography, written by Ham Pu-rim (1360–1410) and dated 1410, in Chŏng's collected works, *P'oŭn-jip* 4:30b–39. Some personal reminiscences of his con-

temporaries are found in Chŏng To-jŏn, "P'oŭn pongsago sŏ" of 1386 in his *Sambong-jip*, pp. 89–91. Pak Chong-hong tries to reconstruct the contours of Chŏng Mong-ju's thought on the basis of Hu Ping-wen's *Ssu-shu t'ung*. See Pak Chong-hong, "Tongbang ihak ŭi chorosŏ ŭi Chŏng P'oŭn," in his *Hanguk sasangsa non'go* (Seoul: Sŏmundang, 1977), pp. 24–29.

21. *Koryŏsa* 115:10b–11; Chŏng To-jŏn, *Sambong-jip*, p. 370.

22. Kwŏn Kŭn, commentary to Chŏng To-jŏn's *Simgirip'yŏn* in Chŏng To-jŏn, *Sambong-jip*, p. 286.

23. *Works of Mencius*, bk. 1, pt. 2, chap. 9, sec. 13.

24. Kwŏn Kŭn, "Preface" to Chŏng To-jŏn's *Pulssi chappyŏn* (dated 1398) in *Sambong-jip*, pp. 277–278. For a full study of Chŏng To-jŏn's thought, see Han Yŏng-u, *Chŏng To-jŏn sasang ŭi yŏn'gu*, rev. ed. (Seoul: Sŏul taehakkyo ch'ulp'anbu, 1983). See also Chai-sik Chung, "Chŏng Tojŏn: 'Architect' of Yi Dynasty Government and Ideology," in Wm. Theodore de Bary and JaHyun Kim Haboush, eds., *The Rise of Neo-Confucianism in Korea* (q.v.), pp. 59–88.

25. Kwŏn Kŭn, "Yŏnghŭngbu hakkyogi," in *Yangch'on munjip* 14:8–9b.

26. The *Iphak tosŏl* is available in a modern translation by Kwŏn Tŏk-chu as vol. 131 of Ŭryu mun'go (Seoul: Ŭryu munhwasa, 1974). For a discussion of this work, see Michael C. Kalton, "Early Yi Dynasty Neo-Confucianism: An Integrated Vision," in Laurel Kendall and Griffin Dix, eds., *Religion and Ritual in Korean Society* (Berkeley: Institute of East Asian Studies, University of California, 1987), pp. 9–25. By the same author, see also "The Writings of Kwŏn Kŭn: The Context and Shape of Early Yi Dynasty Neo-Confucianism," in Wm. Theodore de Bary and JaHyun Kim Haboush, eds., *The Rise of Neo-Confucianism in Korea* (q.v.), pp. 89–123.

27. For a discussion of "succession of the Way" *(tot'ong)* in Korea, see Martina Deuchler, "Self-cultivation for the Governance of Men: The Beginnings of Neo-Confucian Orthodoxy in Yi Korea," *Asiatische Studien* 34.2:9–39 (1980).

28. Han U-gŭn defines "concrete learning" *(sirhak)* of the early Chosŏn period in "Yijo sirhak ŭi kaenyŏm e taehayŏ," *Yijo hugi ŭi sahoe wa sasang* (Seoul: Ŭryu munhwasa, 1961), pp. 363–370.

29. *Sejong sillok* 120:14b.

30. *Koryŏsa* 93:19.

31. Yi Che-hyŏn, *Ikchae sŏnsaeng nan'go* 5:5b.

32. Han U-gŭn, "Yŏmal Sŏnch'o ŭi pulgyo chŏngch'aek," p. 9; Yi Ŭn-sun, "Yi Saek yŏn'gu," *Idae sawŏn* 4:64–65 (1962).

33. *Koryŏsa* 117:10b–11.

34. For the full text of this treatise, see Chŏng To-jŏn, *Sambong-jip*, pp. 254–279. For an evaluation of Chŏng To-jŏn's thought, see Yun Sa-sun, "Chŏng To-jŏn sŏngnihak ŭi t'ŭksŏng kwa kŭ p'yŏngkka munje," *Chindan hakpo* 50:151–160 (1980).

35. *Chŏngjong sillok* 3:2a–b.
36. *T'aejo sillok* 2:3b; *T'aejong sillok* 24:18a–b; *Sejong sillok* 23:27–29; 55:19a–b; 85:7b–8; Ch'oe Hang, *T'aehŏjŏng munjip*, vol. 2, kwŏn 1:30.
37. *Sejong sillok* 23:30–32.
38. *T'aejong sillok* 24:18a–b; *Sejong sillok* 23:27–9; Chŏng To-jŏn, *Sambong-jip*, pp. 270–279.
39. *Sejong sillok* 23:29.
40. *Sejong sillok* 50:32a–b; 64:8b; 77:24b; Sŏng Hyŏn, *Hŏbaektang-jip* 10:12a–b.
41. *Hung-fan* is a part of the *Shu-ching* (Book of History).
42. "Chosŏn" became the name of the new dynasty in 1393, when the Ming chose it from the two alternatives submitted by the Koreans. The other was "Hwaryŏng," which was another name for Yŏnghŭng (South Hamgyŏng), Yi T'aejo's birthplace. King T'aejo continued to use "Koryŏ" until 1393: *T'aejo sillok* 2:15b–16; 3:3b–4; Yi Sang-baek, *Han'guksa, kŭnse chŏn'gi-p'yŏn* (Seoul: Ŭryu munhwasa, 1962), pp. 63–65.
43. Chŏng To-jŏn, *Chosŏn kyŏnggukchŏn*, in his *Sambong-jip*, p. 205. The historicism of early Chosŏn was also expressed in the sacrifices to the mythical progenitor of the Korean people, Tan'gun, and to the respective founders of the previous dynasties of Silla, Koguryŏ, Paekche, and Koryŏ. The veneration of the dynastic founders was not only an expression of national independence, as Han Yŏng-u interprets it, but more importantly it was an effort to reconfirm a presumed historical link with Chinese antiquity and to put the founding of the new dynasty into a wider historical context. For a discussion of the various cults to Tan'gun, Kija, and the dynastic founders, see Han Yŏng-u, *Chosŏn chŏn'gi ŭi sahoe sasang* (Seoul: Han'guk Ilbosa, 1976), pp. 53–61. His "Kija Worship in the Koryŏ and Early Yi Dynasties: A Cultural Symbol in the Relationship between Korea and China" is in Wm. Theodore de Bary and JaHyun Kim Haboush, eds., *The Rise of Neo-Confucianism in Korea* (q.v.), pp. 349–374.
44. *T'aejong sillok* 3:3b; 25:14a–b; *Sejong sillok* 28:15; 41:16b–17, 19; 120:14b; Chŏng To-jŏn, *Chosŏn kyŏnggukchŏn*, in his *Sambong-jip*, p. 242.
45. *Kanggi* is the abbreviated form of *samgang yukki*, a phrase that combines the traditional "three major relationships" and "six social principles." The *samgang* are the relationships between ruler and subject, father and son, husband and wife. According to the *yukki*, fathers have paternal love *(sŏn)*, fathers-in-law righteousness *(ŭi)*, family members contact *(sŏ)*, brothers closeness *(ch'in)*, superiors the respect *(chon)* of their subordinates, friends longstanding friendship *(ku)*.
46. Cho Chun, *Songdang munjip*, vol. 2, kwŏn 4:23b. The analogy between the body's circulatory system and the state's executive channels was an often repeated theme. Kim Chang-saeng, for example, called the *kanggi* the state's

life lines *(myŏngmaek)*. The state's well-being was discernible by the upkeep of its life lines. *Sagye sŏnsaeng chŏnsŏ* 2:19.

47. Pyŏn Kye-ryang, *Ch'unjŏng munjip*, kwŏn 7, without pagination.

48. Chŏng To-jŏn, "Kyŏngje mun'gam, pyŏlchip," *Sambong-jip*, pp. 295–358.

49. *Yu* is often used synonymously with *sa*, official.

50. Sŏng Hyŏn, *Hŏbaektang-jip* 10:4a–b; Chŏng To-jŏn, *Sambong-jip*, kwŏn 3, pp. 83, 87; Han Yŏng-u, *Chŏng To-jŏn sasang ŭi yŏn'gu*, pp. 97–99.

51. Yi I, "Sŏnghak chibyo," part 7, in *Yulgok chŏnsŏ* 25:29b.

52. "To renovate the people" *(sinmin)* is a key concept mentioned in the first sentence of the *Ta-hsüeh*. Like Chu Hsi, Chŏng To-jŏn read it in this meaning and not in the original wording of "to love people" *(ch'inmin)*. See his *Pulssi chappyŏn* in *Sambong-jip*, p. 269. For an explanation of the different wordings of this passage, see Daniel K. Gardner, *Chu Hsi and the* Ta-hsüeh: *Neo-Confucian Reflection on the Confucian Canon* (Cambridge: Council on East Asian Studies, Harvard University, 1986), pp. 89–90.

53. *T'aejong sillok* 19:33b; Yang Sŏng-ji, *Nulchae-jip* 1:24b; 4:26a–b, 46; Yi Ŏn-jŏk, *Hoejae chŏnsŏ* 7:7.

54. Chŏng To-jŏn, *Chŏson kyŏnggukchŏn, Sambong-jip*, p. 232; Ch'oe Hang, *T'ae-hŏjŏng munjip* vol. 2, kwŏn 1:36; Sŏng Hyŏn, *Hŏbaektang-jip* 10:12b; Kang Hŭi-maeng, *Sasukchae-jip* 7:1b.

55. *Sejong sillok* 86:33; *Sŏngjong sillok* 35:1; Pyŏn Kye-ryang, *Ch'unjŏng munjip*, kwŏn 7, without pagination; Chang Hyŏn-gwang, *Yŏhŏn sŏngnisŏl* 7:59b; Yi Ik, *Sŏngho saesŏl*, I, 326.

56. *Sejong sillok* 52:27b; 89:32b; Chŏng To-jŏn, *Choson kyŏnggukchŏn*, in his *Sambong-jip*, p. 239; Yi Ik, *Sŏngho saesŏl*, I, 421; Yi I, *Yulgok chŏnsŏ* 25:24; Sŏng Hyŏn, *Hŏbaektang-jip* 10:8b–9. For a discussion of legal thought in early Chosŏn, see William Shaw, "The Neo-Confucian Revolution of Values in Early Yi Korea: Its Implications for Korean Legal Thought," in Brian E. McKnight, ed., *Law and the State in Traditional East Asia: Six Studies on the Sources of East Asian Law* (Honolulu: University of Hawaii Press, 1987), pp. 149–171.

57. For brief notes on the textual history of these works, see Charles S. Gardner, *Chinese Traditional Historiography* (Cambridge: Harvard University Press, 1961), pp. 56–57. The translations used here are: James Legge, *Li Chi, Book of Rites* 2 vols. (New York: University Books, reprint, 1967); John Steele, *The I-li or Book of Etiquette and Ceremonial*, 2 vols. (London: Probsthain, 1917); Edouard Biot, *Le Tcheou-li ou Rites des Tcheou*, 2 vols. (Paris: Imprimerie Nationale, 1851).

58. In 1045, for example, K'ung Ying-ta's *Li-chi cheng-i* (Correct Interpretations of the *Li-chi*) were presented to the king: *Koryŏsa* 6:34b. The three books on rites also were part of the materials studied for the civil service examinations during Koryŏ. See *Koryŏsa* 73:4a–b.

59. Kwŏn Kŭn, *Yegi ch'ŏn'gyŏllok* 1:1–4b; *Tanjong sillok* 10:42b. Kwŏn's work on the *Li-chi* is the only part which has survived of his *Ogyŏng ch'ŏn'gyŏllok* (Annotations of the Five Classics). For a brief note on this work, see Pak Ch'ŏn-gyu, pp. 7–8. Another edition of the *Li-chi* used during the early Chosŏn was Hu Kuang's (1370–1418) *Li-chi chi-shuo ta-ch'üan* (Great Compendium of Collected Annotations of the Book of Rites). The Karam Collection preserved in the Kyujanggak Library, Seoul National University, holds a woodblock edition printed during Sejong's reign. It was reprinted thereafter many times.

60. For a description of this work, see Robert C. Provine, *Essays on Sino-Korean Musicology* (Seoul: Il Ji Sa, 1988), pp. 90–92.

61. *T'aejong sillok* 5:27.

62. *Sejong sillok* 88:27.

63. *T'aejong sillok* 24:19; *Sejong sillok* 23:28a–b, 31b; 55:20b; 88:27.

64. For an overview of the various editions of the *Chia-li*, see *Chōsen tosho kaidai* (Keijō: Chōsen sōtokufu, 1919), pp. 22–4. A more detailed discussion of this work is found in Chapter Three. The most recent edition of the *Sarye pyŏllam* was edited by the antiquarian and medical expert, Hwang P'il-su, in 1900.

65. The *Ta-T'ang k'ai-yüan li* was compiled on imperial orders by Hsiao Sung (n.d.) and others and presented to the throne in 732. An expanded version is contained in the *T'ung-tien*, chaps. 106–140, and was probably known to the Koreans in this form. See Provine, pp. 71–72. The *T'ung-tien*, presented to the throne by Tu Yu (735–812) in 801, is a vast study of Chinese institutions from the time of the legendary Huang Ti down to the end of the *t'ien-pao* period (755). For brief bibliographical sketches of this work, see Robert Des Rotours, *Le Traité des Examens* (Paris: Librairie Ernest Leroux, 1932), pp. 84–85, and Ssu-yü Teng and Knight Biggerstaff, *An Annotated Bibliography of Selected Chinese Reference Works*, 2nd ed. (Cambridge: Harvard University Press, 1950), pp. 148–149.

66. The *Wen-hsien t'ung-k'ao* was compiled by Ma Tuan-lin who lived at the end of the Sung and at the beginning of the Yüan period. For details, see Teng and Biggerstaff, pp. 150–151; and Provine, pp. 95–96. See also *T'aejong sillok* 6:19; 16:4b; *Sejong sillok* 42:15b.

67. In the *Ta-Ming hui-tien*, Yi Sŏng-gye was mentioned as the son of Yi In-im, given in the Chinese text as Yi In-in. Together they were charged with murdering four kings of the Wang family between 1373 and 1395: *Ta-Ming hui-tien* 105:2. Yi In-im was the strong man who had King Kongmin of Koryŏ assassinated in 1374 and put King U on the throne. He himself was removed from power in 1388 by Yi Sŏng-gye. The problem showed up as early as the first years of T'aejong's reign, but then the Koreans were unable to acknowledge and change the error. For an account on the controversy over

the revision of the *Ta-Ming hui-tien* from a Chinese point of view, see L. Carrington Goodrich, "Korean Interference with Chinese Historical Records," *Journal of the North China Branch of the Royal Asiatic Society* 68:27–29 (1937). Goodrich says that the Korean envoy, Yi Kye-maeng (1458–1523), brought the *Ta-Ming hui-tien* to Korea. According to the *Sillok* the envoy was Yi Chi-bang (n.d.): *Chungjong sillok* 32:46, 64b; 33:5–6. Several petitions for revision of the misinformation about Yi Sŏng-gye were sent to China, but only the 1587 edition contained a supplement in which Yi Sŏng-gye's genealogy was corrected, and a short summary of Yi's coming to power was provided. The original misinformation, however, remained in the text: *Ta-Ming hui-tien* 105:2–4; *Chungjong sillok* 34:74b. The revised edition was brought to Seoul in the early summer of 1588: *Sŏnjo sillok* 22:11b–13.

68. *Chungjong sillok* 38:47; 64:2b; 81:57, 59; *Myŏngjong sillok* 11:51, 55b, 57; 13:12.

69. *T'aejo sillok* 8:5; *Sejong sillok* 77:26; 120:7b; *Sejo sillok* 1:12b, 21b. Rotours, p. 104.

70. *T'aejong sillok* 1:23; *Sejong sillok* 77:26. The *T'ung-chien kang-mu* is a condensation of Ssu-Ma Kuang's *Tzu-chih t'ung-chien* (Comprehensive Mirror for Aid in Government). See Charles S. Gardner, p. 14.

71. Kim Su-on, *Sigu-jip*, in *Yijo myŏnghyŏn-jip*, II, 661–663.

72. *T'aejo sillok* 15:11b–12b. A vernacular translation of the Four Books was made by the famous classicist, Kim Ku (?–1462), in Sejong's reign: *Sejong sillok* 119:19b.

73. *T'aejo sillok* 1:21; 2:13a–b; *T'aejong sillok* 22:47; 24:17b. Under King Sejong there was apparently a second printing with newly cast type: Pyŏn Kye-ryang, "Taehak yŏnŭi chuja pal," *Ch'unjŏng munjip* 12:28b–29.

74. The *Hsing-li ta-ch'üan* was compiled by imperial decree of 1414 under the editorship of Hu Kuang. It was completed in 1415.

75. *Sejong sillok* 30:4; 34:10b; 37:4b; 56:26a–b; 70:4b; Pyŏn Kye-ryang, "Sasŏ ogyŏng sŏngni taejŏn pal," *Ch'unjŏng munjip* 12:29b–30. According to the *Chŭngbo munhŏnbigo* 242:14, these works were first brought back from China by a Korean envoy in 1426. On the basis of *Sillok* information, however, this cannot have been their first transmission. Thereafter they were given to Korea by Ming China several times, and they were repeatedly reprinted.

76. Kim Chŏng-guk's version was prefaced by Chu Se-bung (1495–1554) presumably in 1541. Chu Se-bung, *Murŭng chapko* 7:28b–30. For the work's difficulty, see *Chungjong sillok* 96:62.

77. *Sejong sillok* 68:2b; *Chungjong sillok* 25:43b; 26:28, 34b–35, 36b; 32:18b. Chu Hsi wrote this work in 1175 in collaboration with Lü Tsu-ch'ien (1137–1181).

78. *T'aejong sillok* 13:14b; *Sejong sillok* 20:21; 43:26b; 84:32b–33; 94:6; *Munjong sillok* 5:13b; *Chungjong sillok* 28:21b–22; 34:3; *Myŏngjong sillok* 1:16; 12:29a–

b. The *Hsiao-hsüeh* seems to have been the work of Chu Hsi's disciple, Liu Ch'ing-chih. Chu Hsi added a preface dated 1187. Chu Hsi's *Chu Tzu yü-lei* (Classified Conversations of Chu Hsi) was brought from Peking by Korean envoys in 1476 and 1482 and presented to King Sŏngjong. Being a vast and rather amorphous collection, it does not seem to have been used much during the initial period of social legislation, and was not printed in Korea until 1570: *Sŏngjong sillok* 67:6b; 139:6; *Sŏnjo sillok* 5:7.

79. *T'aejong sillok* 20:14.

80. *Koryŏsa* 77:26. It was established in 1113, but its functions are largely unknown. It may have fallen into disuse because in 1352 a new, apparently similar office was set up with the title Yeŭich'ujŏng togam (Office for the Correction of Ceremonies): *Koryŏsa* 77:28b.

81. *Sejong sillok* 17:7.

82. There are two important studies on the various aspects of the Chiphyŏnjŏn: Ch'oe Sŭng-hŭi, "Chiphyŏnjŏn yŏn'gu," *Yŏksa hakpo* 32:1–58 (Dec. 1966) and 33:39–80 (March 1967); Chŏng Tu-hŭi, "Chiphyŏnjŏn haksa ŭi sahoejŏk paegyŏng kwa chŏngch'ijŏk sŏngjang," in his *Chosŏn ch'ogi chŏngch'i chibae seryŏk yŏn'gu,* pp. 125–194. While Ch'oe Sŭng-hŭi mainly analyzes the institutional aspects of the Chiphyŏnjŏn, Chŏng Tu-hŭi studies the social and political roles of the Chiphyŏnjŏn scholars. The Chiphyŏnjŏn's function as a reference library is described by Yi Chae-ch'ŏl, *Chiphyŏnjŏn ko* (Seoul: Hanguk tosŏ'gwan hyŏphoe, 1978).

83. For an extensive description of the Censorate's position and functions during the early Chosŏn dynasty, see Sohn Pow-key, "Social History of the Early Yi Dynasty, 1392–1592" (Ph.D. diss., University of California, Berkeley, 1963). A study of the censorial agencies during Sejong's period is given by Chŏng Tu-hŭi, "Sejongdae taegan ŭi chŏngch'ijŏk chiwi," in his *Chosŏn ch'ogi chŏngch'i chibae seryŏk yŏn'gu,* pp. 57–124.

84. *T'aejong sillok* 15:29; 32:1b–2; Yi Sang-baek, "Yubul yanggyo kyodae ŭi kiyŏn e taehan il yŏn'gu," pp. 122–125.

85. *T'aejong sillok* 29:11b; *Sejong sillok* 128:1. The work submitted to the king was entitled *Chesaŭi* (Ceremonies for Several Sacrificial Rites). Its attribution to Hŏ Cho becomes clear from the entry in the *Sejong sillok.*

86. Sejong's Five Rites are in the *Sillok,* referred to as *Oryeŭi chu* (Notes to the Five Rites and Ceremonials).

87. *Sejong sillok,* kwŏn 128–135; *Tanjong sillok* 3:8b–9. The *Kukcho oryeŭi* contains the descriptions and illustrations of all state rituals, which are divided into five categories: 1) the auspicious and sacrificial rites *(killye);* 2) the festive rites (for example, royal weddings; *karye*); 3) the rites for the reception of the state guests *(pillye);* 4) the military rites *(kullye);* 5) the mourning rites (royal funerals; *hyungnye*). Also consult Provine, pp. 34–38.

88. *Sŏngjong sillok* 161:7; *Chungjong sillok* 38:55; *Kukcho oryeŭi,* "Preface."

89. The term *sadaebu* was rarely used in Koryŏ. It originates from the Chinese classics, especially the *I-li*. *Taebu* designated the officials of rank four and above, *sa* those of rank five and below. Together they denoted the ranked officialdom. *Sadaebu* is often synonymous with *yangban*. Both these terms are used in this study interchangeably.

90. For a treatment of the *sadaebu*'s function in the bureaucracy and in the military, and their relation to land, see Yi Sŏng-mu, "Yangban," in *Han'guksa* (Seoul: Kuksa p'yŏnch'an wiwŏnhoe, 1974), X, 549–595; and his *Chosŏn cho'gi yangban yŏn'gu*.

91. *T'aejo sillok* 1:43b.

92. *T'aejo sillok* 8:8b.

93. *Sejong sillok* 11:21b.

94. For early *kahun*, see Kim An-guk, *Mojae sŏnsaeng-jip* 15:11b–12b; Sin Suk-chu, *Pohanjae-jip* 13:1–4b; Yu Hŭi-ch'un, *Miam sŏnsaeng-jip* 4:1–30. Chang Hyŏn-gwang, *Yŏhŏn sŏnsaeng munjip* 10:3 (biography of Kim Koeng-p'il); Ki Tae-sŭng, *Kobong sŏnsaeng-jip* 3:58a–b (biography of Kim Koeng-p'il). Kim Koeng-p'il (1454–1504) seems to have been one of the first to adopt *kahun*.

95. Chŏng To-jŏn, *Chosŏn kyŏnggukchŏn*, in his *Sambong-jip*, pp. 231, 242.

96. *Sejong sillok* 62:22b.

97. For a discussion of the *Kyŏngje yukchŏn*, see Hanamura Yoshiki, *Keizai roku-ten ni tsuite* (Keijō: Keijō Imperial University Studies in Law, no. 5, 1932).

98. *T'aejo sillok* 1:44b; *T'aejong sillok* 8:26a–b; 22:43b; 29:25b–26. The translation of 1395 was based on the Ming code edition of 1389. The Korean version, which differed only slightly from the Ming original, remained the authoritative criminal code until the end of the Chosŏn dynasty. For a summary of the adoption of Ming law in Korea, see *Richō hōten kō* (Keijō: Chōsen sōtokufu, Chūsū-in, 1936), pp. 76–128.

99. *Sejong sillok* 41:17b; 86:28; 120:15b, 17; 121:25b.

100. For a discussion of the compilation of the *Kyŏngguk taejŏn*, see Naito Kichi-nosuke, *"Keikoku taiten no nansan,"* *Chōsen shakai hōseishi kenkyū* 9:129–256 (1937); and Pak Pyŏng-ho, *Han'guk pŏpchesa-go* (Seoul: Pŏmmunsa, 1974), pp. 397–421. The *Kyŏngguk taejŏn* preserved today is the final version of 1485. It was amended a few times during the Chosŏn period: *Sok taejŏn* (Amended Great Code) of 1746; *Taejŏn t'ongp'yŏn* (Comprehensive Great Code) of 1785; *Taejŏn hoet'ong* (Updated Great Code) of 1865.

101. Just below the *sadaebu* were usually listed the "persons without rank" *(sŏin)*, presumably denoting those who were of aristocratic background but not part of the new bureaucracy. The social fate of these people was precarious as long as they did not secure rank and office. This is suggested by the gradual change of meaning of the term. By the middle of the sixteenth century it clearly denoted someone who no longer belonged to the elite.

Sŏin therefore became synonymous with "commoner" *(sŏmin, yangmin,* or *p'yŏngmin).* For examples, see *Sŏngjong sillok* 81:11b (where *sŏin* is taken to mean someone at the lower fringe of the elite) and *Myŏngjong sillok* 20:14, 15 (where *sŏ* is applied to non-yangban). In China, the term seems always to have denoted commoners. For the differentiation between "official" *(shih)* and "commoner" *(shu)* in T'ang China, see Johnson, *Medieval Chinese Oligarchy,* pp. 154–155.

102. Chŏng To-jŏn, *Chosŏn kyŏnggukchŏn,* in his *Sambong-jip,* p. 242.
103. Ibid., p. 222.
104. *Sejong sillok* 41:16b–17, 19; Sohn, pp. 27–31.
105. *Sejong sillok* 86:3; Ch'oe Hang, *T'aehŏjŏng munjip,* vol. 2, kwŏn 1:36b.
106. Yang Sŏng-ji, *Nulchae-jip* 1:26b–27, 30b–31.
107. *Sŏngjong sillok* 91:19, 20.
108. *Myŏngjong sillok* 15:37–39b; 17:44.
109. Ibid.
110. *Ki,* on the other hand, formed the five elements.
111. Cho Ik, *P'ojŏ sŏnsaeng-jip* 26:26b–27; Ki Tae-sŭng, *Kobong sŏnsaeng-jip* 1:9b. For a graph of the outlined concepts, see for example Cho Sik, *Nammyŏng-jip* 3:12.
112. Cho Ik, *P'ojŏ sŏnsaeng-jip* 26:27–28.
113. See James B. Palais, "Confucianism and the Aristocratic/Bureaucratic Balance in Korea," *Harvard Journal of Asiatic Studies* 44.2:427–468 (1984). Palais sees the combination of aristocratic and bureaucratic elements as the most outstanding characteristic of the scholar-officials of early Chosŏn.
114. For a discussion of professional elites in the founding of the Ming dynasty, see Dardess, *Confucianism and Autocracy.* For comparison, see also Edward L. Dreyer, *Early Ming China: A Political History, 1355–1435* (Stanford: Stanford University Press, 1982).

3. AGNATION AND ANCESTOR WORSHIP

1. The interdependence of Confucian-style ancestor worship and lineage organization has been discussed in various contexts. For examples, see Freedman, pp. 81–91, and C. K. Yang, *Religion in Chinese Society* (Berkeley: University of California Press, 1967), p. 253ff.
2. *Hsing-li ta-ch'üan* 67:1–2.
3. *Reflections on Things at Hand,* Wing-Tsit Chan, tr. (New York: Columbia University Press, 1967), pp. 227–228, 231–232.
4. *Li-chi,* "Sang-fu hsiao-chi," 6:36b; *Li Chi, Book of Rites,* James Legge, tr. (New York: University Books, 1967) II, 43. The father of the "major ritual heir" was called "separate son" *(pieh-tzu)* because as the younger son of a noble man he had to found a new line of his own.

5. *Li-chi,* "Sang-fu hsiao-chi," 6:36b–38; *Li-chi,* "Ta-chuan," 6:56–57; *Po-hu t'ung,* Tjan Tjoe Som, tr. (Leiden: E. J. Brill, 1949), II, 574–575; Ch'ü T'ung-tsu, *Law and Society in Traditional China* (The Hague: Mouton and Co., 1965), pp. 31–33.

6. *Po-hu t'ung,* II, 574.

7. Chu Hsi, *Chu Tzu yü-lei* (Reprint, 1978), 3:6, 10, 18b, 20.

8. For a description of the Shang and Chou lineage system, see K. C. Chang, pp. 72–92.

9. *Reflections on Things at Hand,* p. 229.

10. *Koryŏsa* 117:19b; *Chŭngbo munhŏnbigo* 86:1a–b.

11. *Koryŏsa* 118:23–24; Cho Chun, *Songdang munjip,* vol. 2, kwŏn 4:18a–b.

12. *Koryŏsa* 63:18–20; *Chŭngbo munhŏnbigo* 86:1a–b; Chŏng Mong-ju, *P'oŭn-jip, songnok,* 1:6–8.

13. *Koryŏsa* 121:21–22; *Chŭngbo munhŏnbigo* 86:1b–2.

14. *Koryŏsa* 78:19b, 23b, 30b.

15. *T'aejo sillok* 5:1; 8:15, 17b; 9:3b; 11:12a–b.

16. *T'aejong sillok* 2:22.

17. *T'aejong sillok* 11:29b.

18. *T'aejong sillok* 25:25a–b; *Sejong sillok* 35:14b.

19. *Sejong sillok* 54:24b, 33.

20. *Sejong sillok* 55:10.

21. *Li-chi,* "Tseng Tzu wen," 4:18a–b, 19b–20; *Li Chi, Book of Rites,* Legge, tr., II, 335–336; *Sejong sillok* 36:28; 41:16a–b. While Legge interprets *sŏja* as son by the secondary wife, the Koreans took it here as equivalent of "son next in order" *(ch'aja).*

22. *Sejong sillok* 43:23b–24b; 44:7a–b.

23. *Sejong sillok* 45:5b.

24. *Sejong sillok* 77:19b–21; *Hsing-li ta-ch'üan* 66:8.

25. *Kyŏngguk taejŏn,* p. 276.

26. Pyŏn Kye-ryang may have wrongly cited the *I-li.* The *Li-chi* discusses the differential cutoff line. See *Li-chi,* "Wang-chih," 3:13; *Li Chi, Book of Rites,* Legge, tr., I, 223.

27. *Sejong sillok* 41:17–18; *Ming hui-yao,* I, 223.

28. *Sejong sillok* 43:23b.

29. *Sejong sillok* 50:13b–14; *Kyŏngguk taejŏn,* p. 276.

30. For the case of T'aejo's brother, Yi Hwa, see *Sejong sillok* 67:23b.

31. *Sejong sillok* 64:11b.

32. *Sejong sillok* 68:27. This law reportedly was disputed.

33. *Sejong sillok* 77:33a–b. This rule was not applicable to the establishment of heirs for merit subjects, high officials, and members of the royal house. In those cases special arrangements had to be made.

34. In the *Koryŏsa* the technical terms "jural heirship" *(iphu)* and "ritual heir-

ship" *(pongsa)* cannot be found. That the *Chŭngbo munhŏnbigo* mentions Koryŏ succession rules under the heading "jural heirship" must have been for lack of a more appropriate category: see 86:4. In his reconstruction of the *Kyŏngje yukchŏn*, Hanamura Yoshiki does not have an entry headed *iphu* in his *Keizai rokuten no tsuite.*

35. *Sejo sillok* 13:38b–40b. The fact that Cho Kŭn became Mal-saeng's ritual successor is mentioned in neither the *Yangju Cho-ssi chokpo* of 1743 nor in the *Mansŏng taedongbo*. See also the case of Kang Hŭi-maeng discussed in Chapter Five.

36. For an example, see *Sejong sillok* 90:23.

37. Although the *Kyŏngguk taejŏn* of 1471 is no longer extant, much of its contents is known through its later versions and through references to it in the *Sillok.*

38. *Chungja* is thus synonymous with *ch'aja.*

39. For the relationship between *iphu* and *suyangja* (adopted child), see Chapter Five.

40. *Kyŏngguk taejŏn*, pp. 276, 277.

41. *Sŏngjong sillok* 32:1a–b; *Tae Myŏngnyul chikhae*, p. 170.

42. In official documents, a woman was referred to by her father's surname to which the post-noun *-ssi*, "lineage" or "family," was added.

43. *Sŏngjong sillok* 52:4a–b; 233:14–16b.

44. *Tanjong sillok* 3:12; *Sŏngjong sillok* 6:17a–b; 107:7–8, 12b–14; 150:3b–4.

45. *Chungjong sillok* 41:14b.

46. *Chungjong sillok* 41:15a–b.

47. *Taejŏn husongnok* (Contained in the *Taejŏn songnok kŭp chuhae*, Keijō: Chōsen sōtokufu, Chūsū-in, 1935), p. 161.

48. *Myŏngjong sillok* 13:54b–55.

49. *Myŏngjong sillok* 15:20b–21.

50. *Myŏngjong sillok* 15:52a–b.

51. *Taejŏn chuhae* (Contained in the *Taejŏn songnok kŭp chuhae*, Keijō: Chōsen sōtokufu, Chūsū-in, 1935), p. 270.

52. *Sok taejŏn*, pp. 234–236. The establishment of an heir was binding only if it was reported to the Department of Rites: *Kyŏngguk taejŏn*, p. 277. Later scholars repeatedly pointed out that this could not be an arbitrary, private act, but needed the sanction of the authorities. For example, see Ch'oe Sin, *Hagam-jip*, 2:5b.

53. *Myŏngjong sillok* 14:47; *Sŏnjo sillok* 14:17b–18; 15:5a–b; *Hyŏnjong sillok* 6:3b–4, 5a–b; *Sugyo chimnok*, p. 164; *Kaksa sugyo*, pp. 26–27.

54. *Sok taejŏn*, pp. 234–235; Yi I, "Iphu ŭi," *Yulgok chŏnsŏ* 8:25b–27b.

55. *Chungjong sillok* 27:2; 36:37a–b, 45b–46b. Another interesting discussion is found in *Sŏngjong sillok* 35:1b–2.

56. *Po-hu t'ung*, II, 257.

57. *Sejong sillok* 97:7b–8; 114:15a–b. For a general discussion of the secondary-son problem in Chosŏn Korea, see Martina Deuchler, " 'Heaven Does Not Discriminate': A Study of Secondary Sons in Chosŏn Korea," *Journal of Korean Studies* 6:121–163 (1988–1989).
58. *Sejong sillok* 64:10b–11b.
59. *Sejong sillok* 67:23a–b. An additional handicap for the secondary sons was that they could not enter the elite corps, Ch'ungŭiwi, to which only sons by primary wives were admitted. Those secondary sons of merit subjects, however, who did perform the ancestral services—this must have been very rare—were admitted to the Ch'ungŭiwi and to some other institutions otherwise open only to primary sons: *Kyŏngguk taejŏn*, p. 399. See also Deuchler, " 'Heaven Does Not Discriminate,' " p. 136.
60. *Kyŏngguk taejŏn*, pp. 276, 277. An additional clause stipulated that if a direct lineal heir had only a secondary son and wanted to establish a son of his younger brother as the ritual heir (of the main line), he could do so upon reporting it to the authorities. In such a case, he could set himself up with his secondary son as a separate branch line *(ilchi)*.
61. *Sŏngjong sillok* 35:1–3; 146:8b–9b.
62. *Myŏngjong sillok* 13:55; 15:19–20b; 20:13b–15; *Sugyo chimnok*, p. 164.
63. *Chōsenshi* 4.3:357; *Mansŏng taedongbo*, I, 123; *Yŏju Yi-ssi chokpo*, sang, pp. 4–5.
64. See, for example, Nam Hae's case in *Myŏngjong sillok* 15:19–21b. For a discussion of this case, see Deuchler, " 'Heaven Does Not Discriminate,' " pp. 131–133.
65. *Taejŏn husongnok*, p. 161.
66. *Myŏngjong sillok* 15:52a–b; *Sugyo chimnok*, p. 164.
67. *Myŏngjong sillok* 20:13b–15; *Taejŏn chuhae*, p. 269. The opinion that a secondary son—although low in status nevertheless his ancestor's descendant—could perform ancestral services if his half brothers by the primary wife were all dead was repeatedly voiced by ritually conscious Confucians. See Chŏng Kyŏng-se, *Ubok-chip* 13:28a–b; Song Chun-gil, *Tongch'undang-jip* 8:20b.
68. Yi Chae's *Sarye pyŏllam* does not mention secondary sons. The *Karye chŭnghae*, compiled by Yi Ŭi-jo and first published in 1792, contains the stipulations of *Kyŏngguk taejŏn* concerning the secondary sons' ritual role and adds a question-and-answer taken from Kim Chang-saeng's *Ŭirye munhae*. In his answer, Kim Chang-saeng confirmed that even a secondary son of lowborn origin, turned commoner, could perform ancestral rites *(pongsa)*. See *Ŭirye munhae* 1:13.
69. *Tŏksu Yi-ssi sebo* 2:27b.
70. The *Sok taejŏn*, however, contained a stipulation according to which the sons and grandsons of elite members *(sajok)* and court officials who did not have issue by their primary wives and thus were forced to make their sons

born of public slave women (i.e., slaves attached to governmental offices) their ritual heirs were allowed, upon verification, to substitute other slaves for such heirs who then were permitted to become commoners. See *Sok taejŏn,* p. 429.

71. *Sejong sillok* 41:19.
72. *Sejong sillok* 41:16b–17, 19; 44:7b; 120:15b–17b; *Kyŏngguk taejŏn,* p. 276. The law in the *Kyŏngguk taejŏn* reads: "As to the *sadaebu,* two wives (*ch'ŏ*) and more are enshrined together." The "two wives and more" was later thought to need some clarification. The *Taejŏn chuhae* of 1555 determined, on the basis of an analysis of some alternatives presented by Chu Hsi, that the passage meant that each primary wife (*chŏngsil*), whether the third or the fourth, would have to be enshrined in the ancestral shrine: *Taejŏn chuhae,* pp. 267–269.
73. Steele, tr., *I-Li,* II, 13.
74. *Sejong sillok* 50:3b–4; 64:8a–b, 31a–b; 65:5b, 6, 9b; 77:24–26b; 82:11b; *Kyŏngguk taejŏn,* p. 257.
75. *Kyŏngguk taejŏn,* pp. 491–492.
76. This provision was enacted in the *Taejŏn husongnok* of 1543: *Taejŏn husongnok,* p. 161.
77. The possible implications of partisan politics that pitted the censorial agencies against the state councillors must be further explored.
78. *Li-chi* 6:51a–b; *Li Chi,* Legge, tr., II, 59. In Legge's translation, the passage reads as follows: "When an eldest son and his wife could not take the place hereafter of his parents, then (in the event of her death) her mother-in-law wore for her (only) the five months' mourning." Legge's "eldest son and his wife" is obviously a misinterpretation of the term *chŏkpu,* "lineal wife," which must be considered synonymous with *ch'ongbu.* The Koreans did indeed take it in this meaning.
79. The relevant passages in the *Sillok* consulted for this study of the *ch'ongbu* are: *Chungjong sillok* 26:45–46; 38:32b; 41:15a–b, 15b–16; *Myŏngjong sillok* 6:17b–18; 10:93b; 11:44–45b, 66b; 12:1a–b, 3b–6b; 13:26a–b, 54b–55; 15:19a–b; 17:44b–45, 51b–52; 21:11b–12b; *Sugyo chimnok,* p. 164; *Taejŏn husongnok,* p. 161; *Taejŏn chuhae,* p. 270; *Sok taejŏn,* p. 234.
80. Sin Kŭn, *Ŭirye yusŏl* 8:38b.
81. *Sejong sillok* 30:3b.
82. *Sejong sillok* 97:24a–b, 28a–b. A *kyŏl* was the basic unit of area for arable land throughout the Chosŏn dynasty. It was used both in terms of productivity and as a unit of linear measure. Although variable in actual size, one *kyŏl* of grade one land measured approximately two acres. See Suan S. Shin, "Land Tenure and the Agrarian Economy in Yi Dynasty Korea: 1600–1800" (Ph.D. dissertation, Harvard University, 1973), Appendix I.
83. Yi Yu-ch'ŏl, *Yeŭi yujip* 24:33b–34.

84. For examples, see Sin Kŭn, *Ŭirye yusŏl* 8:38a–b; Pak Se-ch'ae, *Namgye yesŏl* 1:31b–34b; Yun Chŭng, *Myŏngjae ŭirye mundap* 1:7a–b, 8.

85. *Myŏngjong sillok* 26:60a–b.

86. *Sŏnjo sillok* 21:7b; 166:14b.

87. *Miryang Pak-ssi Sungmin-kongp'a sebo,* p. 10; Pak Pyŏng-ho, *Han'guk pŏpchesago,* pp. 371–377. Professor Pak found fifteen cases of non-agnatic succession in the *Suyang-siyang tŭngnok,* which covers the period from 1684 to 1772, and seven cases in the *Pŏboe kyehu tŭngnok* for the period from 1644 to 1741. These cases came to the attention of the authorities because of disputes over property. Cases of non-agnatic ritual succession were still known in the 1960s. See Kim Taek-kyu, pp. 133, 168.

88. *Li-chi,* "Ta-chuan," 6:57a–b (translated according to the paraphrase found in the introductory materials of genealogies).

89. For an example, see the outline genealogy *(segyedo)* of the Kwangsan Kim in *Kwangsan Kim-ssi Och'ŏn komunsŏ* (Sŏngnam-si: Han'guk chŏngsin munhwa yŏn'guwŏn, 1982), p. 9. See also Wagner, "Korean Chokpo" p. 146.

90. Preface by Sŏ Kŏ-jŏng to the *Andong Kwŏn-ssi taedongbo* of 1476, trans. by Martina Deuchler, in Peter H. Lee, ed., *Sources of Korean Tradition* (forthcoming).

91. Song Chun-ho, "Han'guge issŏsŏ ŭi kagye kirok ŭi yŏksa wa kŭ haesŏk," pp. 117, 141.

92. The earliest genealogy was reportedly published by the Munhwa Yu in 1423. The preface was written by Yu Yŏng (?–1430), an official under King Sejong. For a summary, see Kawashima, "Lineage Elite," p. 12. The edition of 1423, however, is not extant. The earliest surviving edition is that of 1565.

93. See Song Chun-ho, "Han'guge issŏsŏ ŭi kagye kirok ŭi yŏksa wa kŭ haesŏk," p. 118. For a careful comparative analysis of the Munhwa Yu and the Andong Kwŏn genealogies, see also Edward W. Wagner, "Two Early Genealogies and Women's Status in Early Yi Dynasty Korea," in Laurel Kendall and Mark Peterson, *Korean Women: View from the Inner Room* (New Haven, Conn.: East Rock Press, 1983), pp. 23–32.

94. Professor Edward W. Wagner has provided some information about this document in unpublished notes entitled "Some 15th Century Family Records: The 1476 Andong Kwŏn Genealogy." I am grateful to Dr. Mark Peterson who provided me with a photocopy of the Andong Kwŏn genealogy.

95. Preface written by Sŏng Hyŏn in 1493 to the first edition of *Ch'angnyŏng Sŏng-ssi Sasuk-kong p'abo.* (1836).

96. Preface of 1546 to *Sunhŭng An-ssi chokpo* (1864).

97. Preface by Kim Yuk, dated 1637, in *Ch'ŏngp'ung Kim-ssi sebo* (1750).

98. See *Pannam Pak-ssi sebo* with Pak Se-dang's preface dated 1683. Many further examples could be cited.

99. When, however, a secondary son was appointed ritual heir—in the latter half of the dynasty rare, but nevertheless occasionally practiced—the entry of his name preceded that of primary daughters *(chŏngnyŏ)* to mark his special position.

100. For example, see the editorial rules of *Paekch'ŏn Cho-ssi sebo* (1880). Here a primary wife is indicated by "mate" *(pae)*, a secondary wife by "[side] room" *({ch'ŭk}sil)*. It gives "died" *(chol)* for a member of a primary line and "ended" *(chong)* for a secondary son.

101. For a description of the usual information contained in a typical *chokpo* of the heyday of *chokpo* compilation, that is, from the latter part of the eighteenth century, see Song Chun-ho, "Han'guge issŏsŏ ŭi kagye kirok ŭi yŏksa wa kŭ haesŏk," p. 117.

102. *Sejong sillok* 35:14b; 65:27; 82:22; *Sejo sillok* 13:38b–40b; *Sŏngjong sillok* 32:1a–b; 35:1; 107:15; *Myŏngjong sillok* 19:61b; Ch'oe Chae-sŏk, "Chosŏn sidae ŭi sangsokche e kwanhan yŏn'gu," *Yŏksa hakpo* 53/54:129–136 (June 1972). Professor Ch'oe does not speculate about the significance of rotating ancestor worship.

103. *Kyŏngguk taejŏn*, p. 190; *Taejŏn chuhae*, pp. 264–265; *Sŏngjong sillok* 276:25; 277:15b.

104. *Kyŏngguk taejŏn*, pp. 491–492, 493, 495; *Sejong sillok* 97:7b–8; 102:29b; Yi Hwang, *T'oegye sangjerye tammun*, vol. 1, p. 37; Hwang Chong-hae, *Huch'ŏn-jip* 5:9; Ch'oe Chae-sŏk, "Chosŏn sidae ŭi sangsokche," pp. 132–136.

105. *Sasong yuch'wi* (Seoul: Pŏpchech'ŏ, 1964), pp. 504–505; *Sok taejŏn*, pp. 234–235. For a good example of an inheritance document that is concerned with the creation of corporate property, see Sŏng Hon, "Pongsa chŏnt'aek nobi sejŏn chongga yusŏ," in *Ugye-jip* 6:50b–51. For a more extensive discussion of such documents, see Chapter Five.

106. *T'aejo sillok* 2:6; *T'aejong sillok* 2:22; *Sejong sillok* 55:2b, 10.

107. *T'aejong sillok* 11:29b; *Sejong sillok* 54:24b; 55:6b–7; 56:35b–36; *Chu Tzu chia-li,* ch'üan 1.

108. *T'aejong sillok* 2:22; *Sŏngjong sillok* 107:7b; 166:11a–b; *Chungjong sillok* 29:13.

109. *Kyŏngguk taejŏn*, p. 276. The heirs of merit subjects were first ordered in 1456 to establish a special shrine, often called "extra shrine" *(pyŏlmyo)*, for their illustrious forefathers: *Sejo sillok* 7:15a–b; *Chŭngbo munhŏnbigo* 86:2b.

110. *Sejong sillok* 50:12b; 54:41b; 77:43b; *Sŏngjong sillok* 19:8; *Chungjong sillok* 29:13; *Myŏngjong sillok* 19:31b–32; *Kyŏngguk taejŏn*, pp. 275, 276–277. A ritual program for the observance of the seasonal rites was given in *Kukcho oryeŭi* 2:109–112.

111. Cho Ho-ik, *Chisan munjip* 2:18b–19b; Yi Hwang, "T'oegye sŏnsaeng ŏn-

haengnok," *Chŭngbo T'oegye chŏnsŏ,* vol. 4, kwŏn 2:19; Sŏng Hyŏn, *Yongjae ch'onghwa,* kwŏn 2, for a description of seasonal festivities. For an explanation of the *sokchŏl,* see Yi Ik, *Sŏngho saesŏl,* I, 338.

112. *Sejong sillok* 120:15a–b. Yi Hwang also approved the primary wife's participation at the ancestral rites. Yi Hwang, *T'oegye sangjerye tammun,* vol. 2, p. 133b.

113. *Chungjong sillok* 26:45b; 29:13; Kim Sŏng-il, "Pongsŏn chegyu," *Hakpong munjip* 7:1–3; Yi I, "Kyŏngmong yogyŏl," *Yulgok chŏnsŏ* 27:14b; Yi Hwang, *T'oegye sangjerye tammun,* vol. 2, pp. 40a–b, 134b–135. Ch'oe Chae-sŏk gives interesting examples of rotating ancestor worship. See his "Chosŏn sidae ŭi sangsokche," pp. 129–131. At times, even slaves conducted ancestral services for their masters who died without offspring and who had stipulated such an arrangement in their testaments. For an interesting example, see *Sŏngjong sillok* 81:11a–b, 11b–12.

114. Here *sŏin* does not refer to commoners, but to elite members without rank and office. For a definition of *sŏin,* see Chapter Two, note 101.

115. *Sejong sillok* 36:28; 41:17–18; *Kyŏngguk taejŏn,* p. 276; Pak Se-ch'ae, *Namgye-jip,* 45:33. According to ritual prescription, the spirit tablet of a descent group's founder was not to be buried after three generations, but the rites continued for "one hundred generations" *(paekse pulch'ŏn).* It was apparently rare that a special shrine *(sijomyo)* was built for the continued veneration of the first ancestor.

116. *Chungjong sillok* 35:30; Yi Hwang, *T'oegye sangjerye tammun,* vol. 2, pp. 125a–b, 147b; Kim Sŏng-il, *Hakpong munjip* 3:2a–b (letter to Yi Hwang) and 7:3b ("Pongsŏn chegyu"); Kim Chang-saeng, *Karye chimnam* 1:40a–b, 41; Pak Se-ch'ae, *Namgye-jip* 45:34a–b; Song Chun-gil, *Tongch'undang-jip* 8:20b–21b; Yi Ik, *Sŏngho saesŏl,* I, 351–352, 355–356; Ch'oe Chae-sŏk, "Chosŏn sidae ŭi sangsokche," pp. 126–127.

117. In present-day Korea, the cutoff rule is not uniform. According to the Janellis, the four generation limit is most common; Osgood reports for Kanghwa Island a limit of three generations. See Janelli and Janelli, *Ancestor Worship,* pp. 114–116; Cornelius Osgood, *The Koreans and Their Culture* (New York: The Ronald Press Company, 1951), p. 191.

118. Yi Ik discusses some of the difficulties in the *Chia-li* in *Sŏngho saesŏl,* II, 283–284.

119. Cho Chun, *Songdang munjip,* vol. 2, kwŏn 4:18; Yi I, "Kyŏngmong yogyŏl," *Yulgok chŏnsŏ* 27:15, 22–34.

120. For a brief discussion of the *Kukcho oryeŭi,* see Chapter Two. It was twice supplemented during the Yŏngjo period: *Kukcho sok oryeŭi* of 1744 and *Kukcho sok oryeŭibu* of 1751.

121. Chang Hyŏn-gwang, *Yŏhŏn sŏnsaeng munjip* 8:1; Yi Sik, *T'aektang-jip* 9:33a–b; *Myŏngjong sillok* 19:28b, 31b–32.

122. For a discussion of major trends in "ritual learning," see Yun Sa-sun,

"Sŏngnihak sidae ŭi yesasang," in *Han'guk sasang taegye* (Seoul: Sŏnggyun-gwan taehakkyo ch'ulp'anbu, 1984), IV, 599–624.

123. *Chungjong sillok* 34:73a–b. The colophon in the *Karye ŭijŏl (Chia-li i-chieh)* is dated 1626.

124. Kim Chang-saeng's preface is dated 1599, but the work was apparently not printed until the middle of the seventeenth century.

125. There are numerous similar works which cannot all be mentioned here. For a catalogue of this literature, see *Chōsen tosho kaidai*, pp. 14–27.

126. Kim Chang-saeng's son, Kim Chip (1574–1656), for example, made an extensive comparison of "ancient" and "present" rituals in "Ko'gŭm sang-nye idong ŭi." See the appendix to his *Ŭirye munhaesok*.

127. Kim Chang-saeng's *Ŭirye munhae* was amended by Kim Chip as *Ŭirye mun-haesok*.

128. For example, see Pak Kŏn-jung (n.d.), *Sangnye piyobo* (1645).

129. *Li-chi*, "Ch'ü-li, shang," 1:23b; *Li Chi, Book of Rites*, Legge, tr., I, 90.

130. Cho Chun, *Songdang munjip*, vol. 2, kwŏn 4:18; *T'aejo sillok* 2:6; 8:17b; 11:12a–b; *T'aejong sillok* 2:21b–22; 25:14a–b; *Sejong sillok* 53:3b–4; 65:20b; 76:15b–16; Han U-gŭn, "Chosŏn wangjo ch'ogi e issŏsŏ ŭi yugyo inyŏm ŭi silch'ŏn kwa sinang, chonggyo," *Han'guk saron* 3:151–152, 158–163 (1976).

131. *Li-chi*, "Chi-t'ung," 8:55.

132. *T'aejong sillok* 22:1b–22.

133. *Lun-yü* 1:3b–4; Arthur Waley, *The Analects of Confucius* (London: George Allen & Unwin, 1949), p. 85.

134. *T'aejong sillok* 11:29b; 25:25; *Sejong sillok* 40:22a–b; 45:4b–5; 54:41b; 55:10; *Sŏngjong sillok* 162:10a–b.

135. *Myŏngjong sillok* 15:20b–21b.

136. I borrow the terms "filiation" and "descent" from Meyer Fortes, *Kinship and the Social Order* (London: Routledge and Kegan Paul, 1969), p. 253ff.

137. For example, Kim Chip, *Ŭirye munhaesok*, p. 3.

138. The ritualists in general did not approve the exclusion of secondary sons from heirship; but because secondary-son status was in Korea closely related to lower social status, secondary sons came to be regarded as unacceptable heirs, especially for the main line.

139. This is, for example, extensively described in Pak Kŏn-jung's *Sangnye pi-yobo*. This exclusive status of the first son also necessitated a three-year mourning period for him. See Chapter Four.

4. MOURNING AND FUNERARY RITES

1. Quoted from the *Li-chi* of the elder Tai in Fung Yu-lan, *A History of Chinese Philosophy*, I, 354.

2. *Lun-yü* 1:3b–4; Waley, *Analects,* p. 85. For a more detailed discussion on classical interpretations of mortuary and sacrificial rites, see Yang, *Religion in Chinese Society* pp. 44–48.
3. The *fu* or *pok* is explained as meaning "to belong to," or "to submit oneself to." It has, thus, a passive connotation. For example, see Cho Ho-ik's *Karye kojŭng,* vol. 3, kwŏn 7.
4. The *Erh-ya* is a dictionary of glosses to ancient texts. See Charles S. Gardner, p. 61, fn. 80.
5. For a discussion of the mourning grades, see Freedman, *Lineage Organization,* pp. 41–45.
6. *Koryŏsa* 117:33–36.
7. *Koryŏsa* 120:34–41b.
8. Pak reportedly escaped this punishment through the personal intervention of Chŏng Mong-ju.
9. Yi Saek, *Mogŭn mun'go* 7:12b–13.
10. *Koryŏsa* 64:28b.
11. *Koryŏsa* 64:28b; 114:22; 115:41b–42; *Koryŏsa chŏryo* 26:27.
12. *Koryŏsa* 64:28b–29b.
13. *T'aejong sillok* 5:13.
14. Chŏng To-jŏn, *Chosŏn kyŏnggukchŏn, Sambong-jip,* p. 232.
15. *Lun-yü,* 1:8; Waley, *Analects,* p. 89.
16. *T'aejong sillok* 5:13b; 19:7, 35b–36; 22:54a–b; *Sejong sillok* 92:31b; *Kyŏngguk taejŏn,* pp. 244–265.
17. This diagram gives only select mourning grades to illustrate the transformation. For complete charts according to the *Kyŏngguk taejŏn,* see No Myŏng-ho, "Koryŏ ŭi obokch'in kwa ch'injok kwan'gye pŏpche," p. 39; or Kim Tu-hŏn's chart in his *Han'guk kajok chedo yŏn'gu* (Seoul: Sŏul taehakkyo ch'ulp'anbu, 1969), between pp. 570–571. A chart according to the Ch'ing Code can be found in Freedman, *Lineage Organization,* p. 45.
18. *T'aejo sillok* 7:14; *T'aejong sillok* 4:6; 5:12b.
19. *Lun-yü,* 9:5b–6b; Waley, *Analects,* p. 215.
20. Steele, *The I-li,* II, 15.
21. *Li Chi,* Legge, tr., II, 467.
22. In his *Chia-li,* Chu Hsi writes three years' hemmed sackcloth mourning *(chaech'oe samnyŏn),* whereas the Ming code has three years' unhemmed sackcloth *(ch'amch'oe samnyŏn).*
23. *Sejong sillok* 10:18.
24. *Sejong sillok* 38:4a–b; 52:4b–5; 54:17b–18b, 22, 28a–b; 56:2b, 9a–b; 76:32b; 77:5–6b; 111:27–28; 112:30a–b; *Sŏngjong sillok* 10:16a–b. There is, however, a difference between the stipulations of the *Kyŏngguk taejŏn* and the *Sarye pyŏllam:* the former does not give a fixed duration and simply lists the number of months after which various specific mourning sacrifices have to

be performed, suggesting that official mourning ends after fifteen months. The latter indicates one year of hemmed sackcloth mourning with staff *(chaech'oe changgi): Kyŏngguk taejŏn,* pp. 246–247; Yi Chae, *Sarye pyŏllam,* p. 113.

25. For the full argument on this point, see the section on ancestor worship and women in Chapter Three, where the full citations can be found. Interesting light is thrown on the legislative process by the controversy over fixing the mourning grade for the stepgrandmother *(kyejomo).* Because no mourning grade was assigned to her in the legal or ritual sources, the Department of Rites opined that she did not have to be mourned. Sejong opposed this view on the grounds of reciprocity and analogy and ordered the Department of Rites to reconsider the matter. The Department could not find a consensus and suggested in 1438 to submit this problem to the scrutiny of the Board of Rites (Li Pu) in Peking. In 1451, a Chinese reply was finally received in Seoul: because *kyemo* had to be treated like a real mother, the same treatment had to be accorded to *kyejomo.* On the basis of this evidence and on Sejong's earlier opinion, King Munjong (r. 1450–1452) finally gave his approval. This was reaffirmed in the *Kyŏngguk taejŏn.* See *Sejong sillok* 77:24–26b; 82:11b; 102:1b; *Munjong sillok* 6:32–33; *Kyŏngguk taejŏn,* p. 247. For a *kyemo* who was expelled by her husband, no mourning was observed: *Sejong sillok* 61:33.

26. Foster parents were defined as parents who took in a child before age three.

27. In Chosŏn Korea, the so-called "three fathers and eight mothers" *(sambu p'almo),* categorized by Chu Hsi and later mainly used in legal works, were taken up in the *Kyŏngguk taejŏn.* While all "three fathers" were stepfathers *(kyebu)* whose mourning grades differed according to whether or not the stepson was co-residing, the "eight mothers" were an exhaustive list of women's social functions toward the progeny as primary and secondary wives. The mourning grades assigned to them in the *Kyŏngguk taejŏn* followed Chu Hsi's model: *Kyŏngguk taejŏn,* pp. 256–259.

28. The *Sarye pyŏllam* prescribes only five months *(sogong)* for a *sŏmo* who either had a son or had raised the mourner when he was a child. Without such attributes, she was mourned for only three months. See *Kyŏngguk taejŏn,* pp. 158–159; Yi Chae, *Sarye pyŏllam,* p. 144.

29. This does not mean that a wife never mourned for her in-laws in Koryŏ. No documents, however, are available. It is possible that mourning for the husband's kin had already been mentioned in the *Kyŏngje yukchŏn.*

30. *T'aejong sillok* 16:31b; *Kyŏngguk taejŏn,* p. 244ff.

31. *T'aejong sillok* 29:2b.

32. *Sejong sillok* 48:25; *Kyŏngguk taejŏn,* p. 247. Undoubtedly as a concession, an additional fifteen days of leave from duty were given at the time of death of the maternal grandparents.

33. The maternal uncle's wife was assigned no mourning grade in the Ming code. Because she had been mourned in Koryŏ, the *Kyŏngguk taejŏn* prescribed three months. See *T'aejong sillok* 19:7; *Kyŏngguk taejŏn,* p. 250.
34. The Koryŏ mourning chart gives three months for matrilateral first cousins, female as well as male.
35. *T'aejong sillok* 22:54b; *Sejong sillok* 40:9a–b; *Kyŏngguk taejŏn,* p. 250.
36. *T'aejong sillok* 22:54b; 29:2b *Sejong sillok* 28:15b; 48:25, 30b; *Kyŏngguk taejŏn,* p. 246. The *Kyŏngguk taejŏn* gave an extra twenty-three days off-duty at the time of the wife's parents' death.
37. The third and fourth descending generations were uniformly mourned for three months—certainly rare events. A few further peculiarities must be mentioned. Non-agnatic grandsons naturally were not lineal heirs, but they were nevertheless mourned for three months. While the mourning grade for the direct lineal descendant as given in the *Kyŏngguk taejŏn* did not conform to the *I-li,* great pains were taken to determine the exact obligations of a jural heir *(iphuja)* toward his adoptive parents and their kin on the basis of the *I-li.* It was concluded that he had to be treated like a real son; consequently his mourning obligations toward his own parents were lowered: *Sejong sillok* 77:33a–b; 92:30b–31b. The *Kyŏngguk taejŏn,* however, did not yet contain stipulations for an established heir's *(kyehuja)* mourning toward his own parents. Such stipulations were first introduced in the *Sarye pyŏllam.*
38. *Kyŏngguk taejŏn,* p. 260.
39. The *Chia-li* noted that mourning for the eldest son was three years, but that under the "present system" (i.e., during the Sung period) only one year was observed.
40. There were four instances when three-year mourning was not worn: 1) for a first son who was incapacitated to serve in the ancestral hall; 2) for the lineal grandson who was called upon to function as ritual heir; 3) for a son other than the first son who was made ritual heir; and 4) for the lineal grandson who continued the ancestral charge. All of them lacked the proper qualifications *(chŏngch'e)* vis-à-vis the original heir's father and ancestors. For an explanation, see Pak Kŏn-jung, *Sangnye piyobo* (1645); also Chang Hyŏn-gwang, *Yŏhŏ sŏnsaeng munjip* 4:27b–28.
41. As a result of this change, for example, the meaning of the terms *ku* and *saeng* shifted. In Koryŏ, *ku* designated the wife's father, while *saeng* meant the son-in-law; at the same time, these terms stood for mother's brother and sister's son, respectively. This double meaning, also known in the *Erh-ya* and *I-li,* points to matrilateral cross-cousin marriages, prevalent in Koryŏ. In early Chosŏn, *ku* came to denote the husband's father, i.e., the wife's father-in-law, while *saeng* in the meaning of son-in-law seems to have disappeared. See *Koryŏsa* 64:22b–25; *Sejong sillok* 48:25; Han-yi Feng, *The Chinese Kinship System* (Cambridge: Harvard-Yenching Institute, 1948), pp. 44–45.

42. In his article "Koryŏ ŭi obokch'in kwa ch'injok kwan'gye pŏpche," No Myŏng-
ho reconstructs the mourning grades that were not specifically mentioned in
the *Koryŏsa*. His charts of the Koryŏ and early Chosŏn systems therefore look
almost identical and thus obscure the basic changes made in early Chosŏn.
43. The principle of *tanmun* is explained in the *Li-chi*. *Li Chi*, Legge, tr., II, 63.
Although not called *tanmun*, at times even matrilateral kin for whom no
mourning was required were given special consideration. They could, for
example, belong, like *tanmun* relatives, to the Battalion of Royal Kinsmen
(Chokch'inwi): see *Sŏngjong sillok* 104:16b; *Kyŏngguk taejŏn*, p. 399.
44. *T'aejong sillok* 10:7; 19:36; *Sejong sillok* 10:15; 27:14b.
45. *Lun-yü*, 1:8; Waley, *Analects*, p. 89; *Li-chi* 22:3; *Li Chi*, Legge, tr., II, 237–
238.
46. *Sejong sillok* 52:4b; *Sŏngjong sillok* 28:6b.
47. *Lun-yü*, 9:5b–6b; Waley, *Analects*, p. 215; *T'aejong sillok* 4:6; *Sejong sillok*
54:17b.
48. *T'aejo sillok* 15:11a–b; *T'aejong sillok* 1:17b; 4:6; 5:13b; 11:11b; 28:29b;
34:28b–29; *Sejong sillok* 27:18–19; 52:4b; 112:30–31; *Chungjong sillok* 5:13b;
34:32a–b; *Kyŏngguk taejŏn*, p. 483; *Tae Myŏngnyul chikhae*, pp. 285–286. A
mourner over seventy was allowed to eat meat and drink wine: *Sejong sillok*
125:9b–10.
49. According to a rule of 1404, weddings were prohibited during the three-
year mourning period for either father or mother and during one hundred
days when the mourning period lasted for one year: *T'aejong sillok* 8:5b.
50. *Kyŏngguk taejŏn*, p. 278.
51. This is only a selection of the most important sources: *Chŏngjong sillok* 1:3a–
b; *T'aejong sillok* 1:19b; 10:24b; *Sejong sillok* 22:8; 35:16; 38:4b; 40:8b; 43:26b;
Chungjong sillok 44:51b.
52. Mun Ik-chŏm was famous for introducing cotton to Korea.
53. *T'aejong sillok* 1:20b; *Sejong sillok* 22:21b; 54:13b–14b; 58:19b–20; 65:16b–
17; 88:3b–4.
54. *T'aejong sillok* 5:12b–14b; *Sejong sillok* 43:13b.
55. On the recommendation of the Council of State, the Department of Rites
issued a special certificate *(ŭich'ŏp)* to recall an official to duty. *Kyŏngguk
taejŏn*, pp. 284, 319–321.
56. *T'aejo sillok* 13:3a–b; 14:9b–10; *T'aejong sillok* 4:6a–b; 10:4b–5; *Sejong sillok*
10:4b–5; 11:4; 38:10; 43:5a–b, 19; 54:28a–b; 56:2b, 9b; 71:4b–5, 5b–
6, 11b–12, 12b; 76:32b; 77:12–13b; 80:32b–33; 92:15; 97:3a–b, 10a–b,
11b; 124:11–12; *Sejo sillok* 15:18, 21; 16:13b, 16b–17b; *Sŏngjong sillok* 10:16–
17b; 11:17b–18; *Chungjong sillok* 34:32a–b; *Kyŏngguk taejŏn*, pp. 245, 284.
57. *T'aejong sillok* 25:22a–b; *Sejong sillok* 11:8b; 16:12b; 51:26b–27; *Sŏngjong
sillok* 20:6; 150:10b; *Kyŏngguk taejŏn*, p. 246.
58. *Sejong sillok* 51:26b–27; 52:16b.

59. *Chungjong sillok* 15:25a–b; *Taejŏn songnok* (Contained in the *Taejŏn songnok kŭp chuhae*, Keijō: Chōsen sōtokufu, Chūsūin, 1935), p. 71.

60. It is interesting to note that the meaning of the term "those without rank and office" *(sŏin)*, used in the *Kyŏngguk taejŏn*, changed in the early sixteenth century to "commoners," i.e., those who no longer belonged to the elite. *Sŏin* was then used interchangeably with *sŏmin*, and the stipulation in the *Kyŏngguk taejŏn* was read accordingly.

61. *Chungjong sillok* 18:19b; 22:50; 23:5; 26:23a–b, 25b–26, 58, 59b–60, 60a–b, 62b; 31:49b; 44:51b.

62. *Sŏngjong sillok* 124:5b–6; 125:2b; 126:8; *Kyŏngguk taejŏn*, pp. 257–258.

63. *Li-chi* 2:35b; *Li Chi*, Legge, tr., I, 155–156. Legge translates *chang* with "hiding away."

64. *Koryŏsa* 85:21b–22b; *Sejong sillok* 10:14.

65. Yi Saek, *Mogŭn mun'go* 7:13.

66. *T'aejong sillok* 10:7a–b; *Sejong sillok* 10:14b; 27:14b; Chŏng To-jŏn, *Chosŏn kyŏnggukchŏn, Sambong-jip*, p. 232.

67. *T'aejong sillok* 25:5b.

68. *Sejong sillok* 10:14–15; 27:14b; 43:14. A ritual program for *sadaebu* and commoners, based on the *Chia-li*, was outlined in the *Kukcho oryeŭi* 8:72b–95.

69. *T'aejo sillok* 7:14; *T'aejong sillok* 19:35b.

70. *T'aejong sillok* 19:36.

71. *T'aejong sillok* 33:57–58; 34:38b; 36:8b; *Sejong sillok* 3:20a–b, 26b; Pak Ŭn, *Choŭn sŏnsaeng munjip* 1:40–42b; *Kyŏngguk taejŏn*, p. 279. In 1419, a group of officials presented a booklet entitled *Changil t'ongyo sujŏn* (Treatise on Common Principles of Burial Dates), compiled on royal order, that contained the proper knowledge about the selection of burial dates. Offenders who did not bury the dead according to the rites or delayed the funeral were punished according to the stipulations of the Ming code: *Tae Myŏngnyul chikhae*, pp. 287–288; *Sejong sillok* 4:28b; 20:24b.

72. *Yejang* stands in contrast to *kukchang*, royal funeral.

73. *T'aejong sillok* 10:30a–b; *Sejong sillok* 73:3b; 100:34b; 102:19; *Sŏngjong sillok* 152:14b; 163:16b–17; 164:12b–13; *Kyŏngguk taejŏn*, pp. 95, 278–279. Although the *Kyŏngguk taejŏn* provided as an extraordinary sign of esteem the attendance of "all officials" *(hoejang)* at the funeral of a high-standing person, this apparently never occurred during the Chosŏn dynasty because it was judged as inconvenient and too expensive.

74. *T'aejong sillok* 7:11b–12; 12:13; 35:56; *Kyŏngguk taejŏn*, p. 279.

75. *Sejong sillok* 26:29b; 28:32; *Sŏngjong sillok* 38:9a–b; *Chungjong sillok* 66:5.

76. *T'aejong sillok* 35:5; *Sejong sillok* 15:15; 51:5; 106:28b–29b; *Sŏngjong sillok* 3:3; 125:18b.

77. *Sŏngjong sillok* 234:14; 271:16a–b.

78. *Yŏnsan'gun sillok* 59:19a–b; 61:7b; 62:9.
79. Sin Hŭm (1566–1628), *Sangch'on-jip* as quoted in *Chōsen saishi sōzoku hōron, josetsu* (Keijō: Chōsen sōtokufu, 1939), p. 27.
80. *Chungjong sillok* 20:12a–b; 48:52b–53; 93:34a–b; *Myŏngjong sillok* 9:8b; 10:5b; 15:43a–b; 16:25b; 17:36b–37b; 25:32b–33b, 33b–34.
81. *Sejong sillok* 117:2b; 122:8a–b; *Sŏngjong sillok* 14:12–13; 15:16b–17b, 20b–22; 47:1; 99:7b–8; 228:3a–b; 251:4a–b; *Chungjong sillok* 5:13b; 8:47b; 22:30; 45:1; *Taejŏn songnok* pp. 68–69; Chŏng To-jŏn, *Chosŏn kyŏnggukchŏn, Sambong-jip,* pp. 231–232. It is interesting to compare the reports from the north with the description of mortuary customs in Koguryŏ; it is clear that in those remote areas Koguryŏ traditions survived into the Chosŏn dynasty. See Li Ogg, pp. 240–245.

5. INHERITANCE

1. For a detailed discussion of the rank land system and related problems, see Yi Sŏng-mu, *Chosŏn ch'ogi yangban yŏn'gu,* pp. 286–326.
2. *T'aejong sillok* 34:10a–b. King T'aejong was not happy about this request and ordered a general discussion, the outcome of which, however, is not reported.
3. *Koryŏsa* 78:40; *T'aejong sillok* 27:46b; 28:15; *Sejong sillok* 39:1; 53:10. It is clear that *susinjŏn* could be sizable tracts of land.
4. *Koryŏsa* 78:40b; *Kyŏngguk taejŏn,* p. 190.
5. For the details of these developments, see Yi Sang-baek, *Yijo kŏn'guk yŏn'gu,* pp. 196–219; Ch'ŏn Kwan-u, "Han'guk t'oji chedosa, ha," in *Han'guk munhwasa taegye* (Seoul: Koryŏ taehakkyo ch'ulp'anbu, 1965), II, 1387–1480; Sudō Yoshiyuki, "Raimatsu Sensho ni okeru nōsō ni tsuite," pp. 1–80.
6. For the development of private land, see Yi Sŏng-mu, *Chosŏn ch'ogi yangban yŏn'gu,* pp. 326–353.
7. *Koryŏsa* 78:23a–b, 32b–33.
8. *T'aejo sillok* 2:20b; *T'aejong sillok* 9:17a–b; 33:68.
9. *Koryŏsa* 85:45–46; *T'aejo sillok* 2:20b; 8:17; *T'aejong sillok* 9:17a–b; 27:22; 28:3a–b; 31:39b–40; 33:68. Under T'aejong, the Office for the Management of Slaves was renamed Nobi pyŏnjŏng (-chŏng) togam. The different *chŏng* character undoubtedly implied "rectification." For a detailed study of the establishment and development of this office, see Sudō Yoshiyuki, "Sensho ni okeru dohi no benshō to suisatsu to ni tsuite," *Seikyū gakusō* 22:5–37 (Nov. 1935). See also Ku Pyŏng-sak, *Han'guk sahoebŏpchesa t'ŭksu yŏn'gu* (Seoul: Tonga ch'ulp'ansa, 1968). Hatada Takashi explains the circumstance that the *Kyŏngguk taejŏn* expresses the inheritance shares in terms of slaves by suggesting that slaves were the most important part of the inheritance and that the privatization of land had not, at the beginning of Chosŏn, pro-

gressed significantly. See his "Kōrai jidai ni okeru tochi no chakuchōshi sōzoku to dohi no shijo kinbun sōzoku," in *Chōsen chūsei shakaishi no kenkyū,* p.
354.

10. *Koryŏsa* 85:45–46.

11. *T'aejo sillok* 12:1b–3b, 4a–b. The fractions were determined on the basis of
whether the mother was the father's own slave (one-half) or somebody else's
slave (one-seventh).

12. *T'aejong sillok* 10:9b–11b; *Sejong sillok* 48:2.

13. It is interesting to note that it is contained in the section on private slaves
(sach'ŏn) of the Code of Punishments *(Hyŏngjŏn).* This seems to indicate that,
although the interests of the state were not directly at issue, it intended to
lay down normative rules in order to forestall disputes among the members
of a descent group.

14. *Kyŏngguk taejŏn,* pp. 491–496.

15. In a property division document of 1429, for example, each share is clearly
marked according to its origin: "coming from father's side" *(pubyŏn chŏllae)*
and "coming from mother's side" *(mobyŏn chŏllae),* etc. See Ch'oe Sŭng-hŭi,
Han'guk komunsŏ yŏn'gu (Sŏngnam-si: Han'guk chŏngsin munhwa yŏn'guwŏn, 1981), pp. 291–293.

16. *Kyŏngguk taejŏn,* pp. 493–496.

17. *T'aejo sillok* 12:1b–3b; *T'aejong sillok* 10:11; 11:5b; *Sŏngjong sillok* 142:15b;
240:19a–b; 241:4b–6b, 6b–7, 9; *Kyŏngguk taejŏn,* p. 499; *Sugyo chimnok,* p.
239; *Sok taejŏn,* p. 440.

18. The term *sason* seems to be a typically Korean invention. It cannot be found
in any of the major Chinese and Japanese dictionaries, and its etymology
is obscure. It is often synonymously used with *ponson.* The first legal provision concerning the handing on of the slaves of an heirless owner seems to
date from the fourth month of 1405. It was then provided that such slaves
should be distributed "to limited *ch'on* of relatives *(chokch'in).*" *T'aejong
sillok* 9:14b. *Sason* may thus be a more definite term for a limited group of
chokch'in.

19. *T'aejong sillok* 10:11; 11:5b; 13:26b; *Sŏngjong sillok* 199:10b–12b; *Kyŏngguk
taejŏn,* pp. 493–494; *Taejŏn songnok,* p. 114; *Taejŏn chuhae,* pp. 281–282.
The diagram, *Sasondo,* was drawn up by Kim Paek-kan (?1510–?), the com-
piler of the *Sasong yuch'wi* of 1585 (Seoul: Pŏpchech'ŏ, 1964), p. 524. Kim's
diagram is here redrawn according to Western anthropological usage.

20. No explanation for the age limit of three years can be found. It may, however, be connected with the classical dictum that a child leaves his parents'
embrace only at the age of three and therefore reciprocates such care with a
corresponding mourning period of three years.

21. I use "foster son" in order to distinguish him from an "adopted son" *(suyangja).*

22. *Koryŏsa* 85:45b, 46a–b; *T'aejo sillok* 12:2; *T'aejong sillok* 7:1b–2; 10:10b; 13:26a–b; 25:25a–b; 26:32.

23. *Sejong sillok* 82:22; 97:7b–8; 102:29–30b; 120:3–4; 130:17a–b; *Chungjong sillok* 66:58; *Myŏngjong sillok* 20:60b–61; *Kyŏngguk taejŏn*, pp. 496–499; *Taejŏn chuhae*, p. 282; *Sok taejŏn*, p. 439. Non-agnatic adoption seems to have remained relatively important among the commoners. A *siyangja* who lacked all qualifications for becoming an heir was taken in for the purpose of gaining extra hands in house and fields and thus differed little from a slave. On both these issues, see Pak Pyŏng-ho, "Isŏng kyehu ŭi silchŭngjŏk yŏn'gu," in *Han'guk pŏpchesa-go*, pp. 361–371.

24. The *Kyŏngguk taejŏn*, p. 491, stipulated expressly that both the living and the dead children were to be given an appropriate share of the inheritance.

25. *T'aejong sillok* 13:26a–b; 26:22; *Sejong sillok* 31:7b; 49:34b–35; 59:12; 61:31b–32; 82:17a–b, 22; 102:29–30b; *Munjong sillok* 9:20a–b; *Tanjong sillok* 4:10b–15; *Sŏngjong sillok* 126:7a–b; 172:3b–4b; *Kyŏngguk taejŏn*, p. 491ff; Kim Yong-man, *Chosŏn sidae kyunbun sangsokche e kwanhan il yŏn'gu* (M.A. thesis, Academy of Korean Studies, 1982), pp. 13–14.

26. For a list of landed estates according to their provincial distribution, see Sudō Yoshiyuki, "Raimatsu Sensho ni okeru nōso ni tsuite," pp. 10–23.

27. There were still other terms used, often containing the character "collar" *(kŭm)*, in the meaning of portion. While the *pun'gŭp mun'gi* listed all the inheritors and thus were usually very extensive documents, there also were smaller documents known as "writ of transferal of one portion" *(kŭmbu mun'gi)* which recorded the share of one inheritor only.

28. For an example of such a document, see Ch'oe Sŭng-hŭi, *Han'guk komunsŏ yŏn'gu*, pp. 291–293. It concerns the property of Kim Mu (no dates) which was distributed among his four sons, two daughters, eight grandchildren, and two sons-in-law in 1429. A more complete version of this document is found in *Kwangsan Kim-ssi Och'ŏn komunsŏ*, pp. 150–156.

29. A similar document was the "promissory writ" *(hŏyŏ mun'gi)* which recorded any gift from a senior to a junior. Because its issuance could be quite arbitrary, it apparently gave rise to many disputes. It therefore had to be officially authorized. See Ch'oe Sŭng-hŭi, *Han'guk komunsŏ yŏn'gu*, pp. 305–314.

30. A document which clearly shows an earlier division can be found in *Kwangsan Kim-ssi Och'ŏn komunsŏ*, pp. 150–156. See also Ch'oe Sŭng-hŭi, *Han'guk komunsŏ yŏn'gu*, pp. 291–293.

31. A striking example for such fragmentation of the patrimony is given by Kim Yong-man, "Chosŏn sidae chaeji sajok ŭi chaesan soyu hyŏngt'ae I," *Taegu sahak* 27:124–125, fn. 60 (1985). On the basis of an inheritance paper of 1510, seven siblings—five sons and two daughters—received portions of land from plots in twenty-four different locations. The land in one location was

divided among six heirs; in two locations among five heirs; in another two among four heirs; in yet another two among three heirs; and in five locations among two heirs. Plots in twelve locations were not divided and were given in entirety to single heirs. None of them, thus, had a stake in all of the twenty-four plots. The eldest son, for example, inherited land in nine locations, the second son in only four, each daughter in eight.

32. Examples of such inheritance documents can be found in various sources, for example, Kim Yong-man, *Chosŏn sidae kyunbun sangsokche e kwanhan il yŏn'gu;* Ch'oe Sŭng-hŭi, *Han'guk komunsŏ yŏn'gu,* p. 281ff.; *Komunsŏ chipchin* (Seoul: Sŏul taehakkyo pusok tosŏgwan, 1972); *Chŏnju Yi-ssi Korim-gunp'a sŏnjo yumunjip* (Chŏnju, 1975).

33. Such a document is given in Yi Su-gŏn, comp., *Kyŏngbuk chibang komunsŏ chipsŏng* (Kyŏngsan: Yŏngnamdae ch'ulp'anbu, 1981), p. 128.

34. *Sejong sillok* 48:23b; 61:8b, 31b–32; 82:22; 97:7b–8; 102:29–30b; 120:3–4; *Kyŏngguk taejŏn,* p. 500. The *Taejŏn chuhae* of 1555 seems to have interpreted a stipulation in the *Kyŏngguk taejŏn,* according to which the ritual heir was like a real son and therefore not outside the circle of grandsons, as applicable to gifts and not to his lawful portion of inheritance. See *Taejŏn chuhae,* pp. 283–284.

35. This is not recorded in *Munhwa Yu-ssi sebo* (1565) 2:49b or *Andong Kwŏn-ssi sebo* (1476) 3:62.

36. *Tanjong sillok* 4:10b–15; 5:6b–7. Later, in 1476, Kang Hŭi-maeng's heirship was again discussed, but the testament no longer played a role. See *Sŏngjong sillok* 68:1a–b.

37. This law was preceded by an earlier one in the first version of the Code of Punishments *(Hyŏngjŏn)* of 1461. It is clear that the main concern of this law—itself based on a royal instruction of 1442—was the unrestrained giving and taking of slaves outside near kin: *Sejong sillok* 97:33b–34; *Sejo sillok* 25:3b–4b; *Kyŏngguk taejŏn,* p. 499.

38. *Kyŏngguk taejŏn,* pp. 499–500; *Taejŏn chuhae,* pp. 284–285. Those who were known to be unable to write, the sick, and women needed to have a relative who was a highstanding official as penman and witness.

39. *Sŏngjong sillok* 163:23b–24; 164:5; 165:10a–b; 172:3b–4b; *Kyŏngguk taejŏn,* p. 499; *Taejŏn chuhae,* p. 283; *Sok taejŏn,* p. 461.

40. *Sejong sillok* 50:33b.

41. See the case of Kang Hŭi-maeng in the above section.

42. *Kyŏngguk taejŏn,* pp. 496–497; *Taejŏn chuhae,* pp. 282–283; *Sasong yuch'wi,* pp. 516–517.

43. *T'aejong sillok* 13:26b; *Kyŏngguk taejŏn,* p. 499; *Sugyo chimnok,* p. 240; *Sasong yuch'wi,* p. 466; *Sok taejŏn,* p. 440.

44. *Sejong sillok* 68:13; *Sŏngjong sillok* 15:16; 39:12; *Kyŏngguk taejŏn,* p. 496; *Sugyo chimnok,* p. 240; *Sok taejŏn,* p. 439.

45. *T'aejong sillok* 26:21b–22; *Sejong sillok* 116:26a–b; *Sŏngjong sillok* 130:17a–b.

46. Two such documents, dated 1530 and 1528, respectively, can be found in *Komunsŏ chipchin*, p. 202; and Ch'oe Sŭng-hŭi, *Han'guk komunsŏ yŏn'gu*, pp. 315–316. In the latter document, the observance of the ancestral rites by a secondary son of lowborn origin *(ch'ŏnch'ŏpcha)* was considered inappropriate, and therefore the daughter was charged with ancestral duties.

47. Examples can be found in *Puan Kim-ssi Uban komunsŏ* (Sŏngnam-si: Han'guk chŏngsin munhwa yŏn'guwŏn, 1983), No. 5 (1581), pp. 201–202; No. 23 (1607), p. 207; No. 35 (1669), pp. 225–226.

48. Examples of inheritance documents which clearly show equal division of the patrimony between sons and daughters in the seventeenth century can be found in each of the document collections mentioned in note 32 above. Moreover, Yi Kwang-gyu has studied the inheritance papers preserved in the Kyujanggak Archives of Seoul National University. His findings are published in Chapter 8 of his *Han'guk kajok ŭi sajŏk yŏn'gu* (Seoul: Ilchisa, 1977), pp. 360–390.

49. The concept of economic primogeniture is here used in its anthropological rather than in its strictly legal sense. This means that the eldest son was not necessarily the sole heir at the expense of his younger brothers.

50. Yi T'ae-jin describes the development of agricultural techniques during the fifteenth century in "Nongŏp kisul ŭi paltal kwa sinhŭng sajok," in his *Han'guk sahoesa yŏn'gu* (Seoul: Chisik sanŏpsa, 1986), pp. 91–106. An earlier study is Yi Ch'un-nyŏng, *Yijo nongŏp kisulsa* (Seoul: Han'guk yŏn'guwŏn, 1964).

51. Any study of the demographic development of early Chosŏn is hampered by the sparse evidence available. Moreover, government statistics are unreliable because reporting was primarily concerned with able-bodied males for taxation and conscription. The manipulation of data was therefore common. Some general trends, however, are clear and succinctly explained by Tony Michell. See his "Fact and Hypothesis in Yi Dynasty Economic History: The Demographic Dimension," *Korean Studies Forum* 6:65–93 (1979/80). Michell's interpretations are largely supported by the more recent work by Hochol Lee, "Rice Culture and Demographic Development in Korea, c. 1429–1918," in Akira Hayami and Yoshihiro Tsubouchi, eds., *Economic and Demographic Development in Rice Producing Societies—Some Aspects of East Asian Economic History, 1500–1900* (1989), pp. 55–71. See also Song Ch'an-sŏp, "17•18 segi sinjŏn kaegan ŭi hwaktae wa kyŏngyŏng hyŏngt'ae," *Han'guk saron* 12:231–304 (Feb. 1985).

52. These developments are set forth on the basis of family documents of the Wŏlsŏng Son of Yangdong, the Chaeryŏng Yi, and the Andong Kwŏn by

Kim Yong-man, "Chosŏn sidae chaeji sajok ŭi chaesan soyu hyŏngt'ae I," pp. 89–159. Susan Shin describes changes in the agricultural labor force in "Some Aspects of Landlord-Tenant Relations in Yi Dynastý Korea," *Occasional Papers on Korea* 3:49–88 (1975).

53. *Myŏngjong sillok* 20:61.

54. Rotating ancestor worship continued to be mentioned in documents of the seventeenth century as a kind of safety measure in case the proper ritual heir was unable to fulfill the ritual charge all by himself. For examples, see Yi Kwang-gyu, *Han'guk kajok ŭi sajŏk yŏn'gu*, pp. 370–371.

55. Yi Hwang, *T'oegye chŏnsŏ* 27:16b.

56. Evidence of the gradual appearance of a special ritual allowance *(pongsajo)* can be found in the various document collections, for example *Kwangsan Kim-ssi Och'ŏn komunsŏ*, nos. 11, 12, 14 (all from the second part of the sixteenth century) on pp. 170–182; Yi Su-gŏn, comp., *Kyŏngbuk chibang komunsŏ chipsŏng*, pp. 178–180.

57. For examples, see Yi Kwang-gyu, *Han'guk kajok ŭi sajŏk yŏn'gu*, pp. 360–386.

58. *Sok taejŏn*, p. 234.

59. Yi Su-gŏn, comp., *Kyŏngbuk chibang komunsŏ chipsŏng*, p. 795.

60. Kim Myŏng-yŏl was a son of the Kim Hong-wŏn (1571–1645) who gained fame during the Japanese Wars. Hong-wŏn corresponded with many outstanding personalities of his time, and it is therefore not surprising that he and his descendants were well aware of the latest ritual developments.

61. *Puan Kim-ssi Uban komunsŏ*, no. 33, p. 224. The discovery of the papers kept by the Puan Kim of Uban was an especially fortunate event because they document social history from the early sixteenth century up to the colonial period. Inheritance documents are analysed by Mark Peterson in a paper entitled "The Puan Kims: A Case Study in Social Change in Mid Yi Korea," which he presented to a workshop in 1983.

62. For examples, see *Puan Kim-ssi Uban komunsŏ*, no. 26, p. 209; and no. 29, p. 213.

63. The *Kyŏngbuk chibang komunsŏ chipsŏng* contains several documents dating from the late seventeenth century with the same message: because daughters can no longer participate at ancestral rites, they do not deserve a share of the patrimony. For examples, see Yi Su-gŏn, comp., pp. 245, 401, 411. See also Yi Kwang-gyu, *Han'guk kajok ŭi sajŏk yŏn'gu*, pp. 384–385, for two documents of the first half of the eighteenth century in which daughters are no longer mentioned.

64. For examples, see Ch'oe Sŭng-hŭi, *Han'guk komunsŏ yŏn'gu*, pp. 322, 328–329; *Puan Kim-ssi Uban komunsŏ*, no. 28, pp. 211–213; Kim Yong-man, "Chosŏn sidae chaeji sajok ŭi chaesan soyu hyŏngt'ae I," p. 136. Kim Yong-

man analyzes the family documents of the Wŏlsŏng Son of Yangdong. He suggests that the increase in the sale and exchange of land was connected with the fact that from the late sixteenth century on, former non-resident landowners turned into resident landowners and became the founders of descent group villages *(tongjok purak)*. It would be interesting to substantiate this with more research on historic village formation.

65. The earlier division of the patrimony into the part which came from the father's side *(pubyŏn)* and that which came from the mother's side *(mobyŏn)* disappeared, of course, with the daughter's loss of inheritance.

66. The development of these different categories of property during the period from 1609 to 1799 can be perceived, for example, in the Puan Kim inheritance documents: see *Puan Kim-ssi Uban komunsŏ,* pp. 207–225.

67. Hwang Chong-hae, *Huch'ŏn-jip* as quoted in *Chōsen saishi sōzoku hōron, josetsu,* p. 554, fn. 8.

6. CONFUCIAN LEGISLATION: THE CONSEQUENCE FOR WOMEN

1. *T'aejong sillok* 19:2b, 11b; 23:9a–b.

2. For an exposition of the marriage customs of feudal China, see Marcel Granet, *La Polygynie sororale et le sororat dans la Chine féodale* (Paris: E. Leroux, 1920), esp. pp. 53–57.

3. *T'aejong sillok* 3:3b. The Department of Rites seems to have attributed this numerical evidence mistakenly to the chapter "Hun-i" of the *Li-chi.* It is a quotation from the *Ch'un-ch'iu Kung-yang chuan* (Spring and Autumn Annals, Tradition of Kung-yang), also contained in the *Po-hu t'ung,* I, 251.

4. *T'aejong sillok* 6:26b.

5. For a brief description, see Yi Sang-baek, *Han'guksa, kŭnse chŏn'gi-p'yŏn,* pp. 72–76. In the first incident, princes of T'aejo's two queens were involved.

6. *T'aejong sillok* 6:26b; 25:21b.

7. The term *hunhyŏn ch'ungŭi,* "meritorious and wise, loyal and faithful," I interpret as referring to the various merit subjects who had rendered special services to the throne under T'aejo, Chŏngjong, and T'aejong.

8. *T'aejong sillok* 22:25a–b. In 1414, a list of titles was put forward to regulate the hierarchical order of the various wives' offspring: *T'aejong sillok* 27:3a–b. These titles differ somewhat from those eventually codified in the *Kyŏngguk taejŏn,* pp. 35–38. The inner palace of the crown prince was similarly structured. See *Sejong sillok* 50:30b–31.

9. *Sejong sillok* 55:6b; 64:4. The wife of the crown prince was given the title *pin.* For a study of the royal women of early Chosŏn, see Kim Sŏn-gon, "Yijo ch'ogi pibin ko," *Yŏksa hakpo* 21:33–65 (Aug. 1963).

10. *T'aejo sillok* 9:8b. A woman who married again after her husband's death lost her honorary title. Although there is evidence that in the early part of the

dynasty the honorary titles were coupled with land grants, the *Kyŏngguk taejŏn* no longer carries such a stipulation.

11. *Sejong sillok* 120:14b–16b. The legal history of this clause granting equal status to the various wives regardless of social background cannot be easily established. It was apparently incorporated into the *Yukchŏn tŭngnok* (Records Attached to the *Kyŏngje yukchŏn*) and, being in conflict with later legislation, presumably was expurgated before the appearance of the revised *Sok yukchŏn* of 1426. None of these early legal codes are extant, and they can be partly reconstructed only on the basis of information given in the *Sillok*.

12. *T'aejong sillok* 25:13a–b; 27:46b–47; 33:16b–17; *Sejong sillok* 10:13; 117:21b; *Kyŏngguk taejŏn*, p. 518. The Ming criminal code provided three stipulations connected with the irregular acquisition and manipulation of wives: 1) making a primary wife into a secondary wife was to be punished with one hundred strokes of the heavy bamboo; 2) making a secondary wife into a primary wife while there existed a primary wife was to be punished with ninety strokes; 3) a man who took a second wife while he had a primary wife was to be punished with ninety strokes and judicial separation: *Tae Myŏngnyul chikhae*, p. 204.

13. *Sejong sillok* 76:30. For other examples, see *Sejong sillok* 23:30; 39:10b–11, 21a–b; 117:21b; *Munjong sillok* 12:42b; *Sejo sillok* 29:14; 35:8–9, 17b–18b; *Sŏngjong sillok* 68:1a–b; 74:1–2. The illegal keeping of two primary wives remained a theme even in King Chungjong's time. See, for example, *Chungjong sillok* 2:15a–b, 28b; 14:63; 18:30b; 60:4b.

14. *Myŏngjong sillok*, 15:38, 39.

15. *Li Chi*, Legge, tr., II, 428.

16. *Sejong sillok* 48:25.

17. *T'aejong sillok* 29:11b; *Sejong sillok* 40:9b.

18. *Sejong sillok* 50:33b.

19. *Sejong sillok* 50:32a–b; 83:23b. In 1443, members of the royal house were prohibited from marrying partners with the surname Yi, even if they did not belong to the royal line; but it seems clear that this prohibition was not well enforced: *Sejong sillok* 96:22.

20. *Sŏngjong sillok* 10:16b–17, 45. This prohibition of marriages with matrilateral second cousins seems to have also been binding for relatives of adoptive mothers *(yangmo)* and stepmothers *(kyemo)*. See Pak Pyŏng-ho, *Han'guk pŏpchesa-go*, pp. 347–351.

21. Pak Pyŏng-ho, *Han'guk pŏpchesa-go*, pp. 351–353.

22. There were many complaints about disregard of descent-group limits. Yi Sugwang (1563–1628) was concerned that yangban did not regard a marriage between descent groups of the same surname but different ancestral seats as shameful. His contemporary, Chŏng Kyŏng-se (1563–1633), complained

364 *Notes to pp. 239–240*

that a different ancestral seat was in many cases considered as a different surname. See Yi Nŭng-hwa, *Chosŏn yŏsok-ko* (reprint; Seoul, 1968), pp. 51–52.

23. *Hyŏnjong sillok* 16:3; 25:10b–11; Ch'oe Sin, *Hagam-jip* 2:27–28; *Sok taejŏn,* p. 236.

24. In 1556, it was found that on a remote island consanguineous marriages continued to be concluded: *Myŏngjong sillok* 20:30b–31.

25. For data which corroborate this statement, see Ch'oe Chae-sŏk, "Chosŏn hugi tosi kajok ŭi hyŏngt'ae wa kusŏng," *Koryŏ taehakkyo inmun nonjip* 19:144–146 (1974). Regulations that were established to determine the social identity of offspring of marriages between commoners and lowborn were an important sociopolitical instrument. See Yi Sang-baek, "Ch'ŏnja sumo-go," *Chindan hakpo* 25–27:155–183 (1964).

26. Yi Chung-hwan, *P'aryŏkchi* as quoted in Kim Tu-hŏn, p. 440. The relationship between marriage and political factions has not yet been sufficiently studied. Oda Shōgo touches on this problem in "Richō seiso ryakushi," in his *Chōsen shi kōza, bunrui shi* (Keijō: Chōsenshi gakkai, 1924), pp. 182–184.

27. In 1442, for example, the giving and receiving of slaves outside patrilateral, matrilateral, and affinal first cousins was prohibited. This regulation made it impossible to use slaves as gifts at times of weddings. *Sejong sillok* 97:33b–34; *Kyŏngguk taejŏn* ("Nobi kyŏlsong chŏnghan"), p. 521; Kim Chong-jik, *Ijollok,* second part, 4:18b.

28. There is no study yet which explores this subject on the basis of historical materials, for example genealogies or household registers. Kim Taek-kyu has given some indications on the basis of ethnographic fieldwork in Hahoe (North Kyŏngsang) in *Ssijok purak ŭi kujo yŏn'gu,* pp. 119–127. Yang Hoe-su corroborates Kim Taek-kyu's findings in *Han'guk nongch'on ŭi ch'ollak kujo* (Seoul: Koryŏ taehakkyo, 1967), p. 251. Ch'oe Chae-sŏk gives lists of the ancestral seats of the wives who married into two dominant descent groups, the Yŏgang Yi-ssi and Wŏlsŏng Son-ssi, but such lists do not explain marriage radius in geographical terms since ancestral seat and place of residence were most often not identical. See his *Han'guk nongch'on sahoe yŏn'gu* (Seoul: Ilchisa, 1975), pp. 500–503.

29. Kim Taek-kyu, pp. 123–127.

30. Kim Taek-kyu, pp. 134–135. Several examples are given: the husband's niece became the bride of the wife's nephew, or the wife's second cousin married the husband's father's first cousin.

31. This analysis, which is principally based on ethnographic data, must be strengthened and supplemented in the future with data drawn from historical sources.

32. Zenshō Eisuke, III, 414, 449.

33. *Sejong sillok* 37:24a–b; *Sejo sillok* 24:6b; *Kyŏngguk taejŏn*, p. 227.
34. *Po-hu t'ung*, I, 245.
35. *Sejong sillok* 88:26b–27. Marriageable age in the royal house was lower than that demanded for the yangban. Originally set at fourteen for boys and thirteen for girls, age limits were abolished in 1467. A year later, in 1468, an earlier ruling that forbade an age difference of more than six years between the prospective spouses was also abolished. See *Sejo sillok* 24:6b; 38:9b; 41:22.
36. *Sejong sillok* 85:46a–b; 88:21; Chŏng Tong-yu, *Chuyŏngp'yŏn* as quoted in Kim Tu-hŏn, p. 454.
37. For statistical data, see Ch'oe Chae-sŏk, "Chosŏn hugi panch'on kajok," in his *Han'guk kajok chedosa yŏn'gu* (Seoul: Ilchisa, 1983), pp. 419–422; see also his "Chosŏn hugi tosi kajok ŭi hyŏngt'ae wa kusŏng," pp. 147–148; and his "Chosŏn chŏn'gi ŭi kajok hyŏngt'ae," *Chindan hakpo* 37:155–156 (1974). Shikata Hiroshi seems to contradict Professor Ch'oe's findings; he shows a large percentage (50–60 percent) of husbands who were older than their wives. This result was obtained, as Professor Ch'oe points out, because Shikata Hiroshi did not differentiate between social groups. See Shikata Hiroshi, "Richō jinkō ni kansuru ichi kenkyū," *Chōsen shakai hōsei shi kenkyū* 9:289–298 (1937). A generally great age difference of ten years and more between husband and wife, common among yangban and commoners, was noticed already at the beginning of the dynasty: *Sejo sillok* 41:22. Kim Taek-kyu does not find it typical for Hahoe that wives were older than their husbands, although this was more common among yangban. (p. 129).
38. *T'aejong sillok* 8:4b. The latter rule was confirmed in 1429, although mourning clothes could be taken off after thirty days: *Sejong sillok* 43:13b.
39. For such cases, see, for example, *Sejong sillok* 35:16; *Sejo sillok* 35:6b–7; 36:7b–8; 37:32. The conclusion of marriages was also prohibited during official state mourning periods *(kuksang): Sejong sillok* 17:29b.
40. *Sok taejŏn*, p. 236. The ruling in the *Sok taejŏn* was preceded by repeated debates on the subject. Up to the first half of the sixteenth century, marriages were concluded during mourning periods. In 1545 an edict drew attention to the problem and empowered the authorities inside and outside the government to take appropriate measures: *Myŏngjong sillok* 3:93b–94; *Kaksa sugyo*, p. 22; *Sugyo chimnok*, p. 159. The law codes of the Chosŏn dynasty do not seem to have repeated a rule that had been in force during the Koryŏ period. That rule stipulated that to get married while either a parent or a grandparent was in prison was punishable with one hundred strokes: *Koryŏsa* 85:1.
41. This law apparently appeared in the *Sok yukchŏn* of 1413: *Sejong sillok* 10:12b.
42. *Sejong sillok* 23:24; 37:24a–b; 38:12b; 40:12b–13; 69:30b; *Kyŏngguk taejŏn*, p. 293. In 1472, the marriage allowance for needy yangban girls was fixed

at ten *sŏk* of rice and beans, that for commoner girls at five *sŏk*: *Sŏngjong sillok* 18:4; 249:5b; *Yŏnsan'gun sillok* 44:4b; *Sok taejŏn*, p. 236.

43. These translations are taken from Steele, *The I-li*, I, 18–27. The "sending of the evidences" is explained as follows: "The presents sent by the father of the young man to complete the preliminaries are a bundle of black and red silks and a pair of deerskins." Ibid., I, 21.
44. Chŏng To-jŏn, *Sambong-jip*, p. 231; Yu Hyŏng-wŏn, *Pan'gye surok* 25:19b.
45. *T'aejo sillok* 7:13b.
46. *T'aejong sillok* 8:5b.
47. *T'aejong sillok* 28:34.
48. *T'aejong sillok* 35:9.
49. *Koryŏsa* 85:20a–b, 22b–23; *Chŭngbo munhŏnbigo* 89:3b.
50. *T'aejo sillok* 6:5. Rankless persons were prohibited from using silver, silk clothes, and furs.
51. *T'aejong sillok* 35:9, 44; *Sejong sillok* 36:1; 43:13b.
52. *Kyŏngguk taejŏn*, p. 278. On the wedding night, officials above the second rank were allowed to use ten torches, those below the third rank only six. When the bride was presented to her parents-in-law, she could henceforth offer them one wine jug and five dishes of various foods. She could be accompanied by three female and ten male slaves.
53. *Sejong sillok* 67:18–20.
54. *Sejong sillok* 133:30–31b.
55. *Chungjong sillok* 12:61b–62; 22:57b–58; 23:66b; 24:13a–b.
56. *Chŭngbo munhŏnbigo* 89:6b. Kim Ch'i-un died in 1531 when he was a junior fifth counselor *(pugyori)* in the Office of Special Counsellors (Hongmungwan). He reportedly was an impetuous man and was much feared because of his association with men such as Hŏ Hang (?–1537), Kim Al-lo (1481–1537), and Ch'ae Mu-t'aek (?–1537).
57. For calls to perform *ch'inyŏng,* see, for example, *Myŏngjong sillok* 9:18b–19; *Sŏnjo sillok* 152:6b–7b, 11a–b; and *Yŏngjo sillok* 70:15b; 104:25.
58. *Chŭngbo munhŏnbigo* 89:6b.
59. For example, see Pak Se-ch'ae, *Namgye yesŏl* 3:31.
60. In 1407, King T'aejong's eldest son, Grand Prince Yangnyŏng, who was then the crown prince, married Kim Hal-lo's (1367–?) daughter and brought her personally to the royal palace: *T'aejong sillok* 14:5b–6. In 1414, T'aejong's fourth son, Grand Prince Sŏngnyŏng, married Sŏng Ŏk's (n.d.) daughter in the same way: *T'aejong sillok* 28:45b.
61. No royal wedding ceremony is described in the *Koryŏsa*. There is a brief protocol for the wedding of the crown prince entitled *Wangt'aeja nappiŭi: Koryŏsa* 66:27–32b.
62. Kim O-mun was Kim Ku-dŏk's (?–1428) son. Kim Ku-dŏk's one daughter had become a secondary wife of King T'aejong.

63. For the various stages of the wedding ritual, see *Sejong sillok* 35:13–14b, 17–18b, 23b; 36:2–4, 5a–b, 7–10. For the Chinese model of a crown prince's wedding, see *T'ung-tien*, kwŏn 127.
64. *Sejong sillok* 50:33b.
65. *Sejong sillok* 64:8b, 11b.
66. The rules were presented to the king by the Department of Rites at the end of 1434: *Sejong sillok* 67:16b–20.
67. *Sejong sillok* 67:21b. At the beginning of the year, the Department of Rites fixed the number of attendants who were allowed to accompany the members of the royal house when they performed *ch'inyŏng: Sejong sillok* 67:9b.
68. *Sejong sillok* 72:26b–34. The establishment of this protocol does not seem to be connected with the crown prince's (later King Munjong) acquisition of a third wife. His first wife, whom he married in 1427, was expelled from the palace in 1429 because of a palace scandal; and her name was erased in the royal genealogy: *Sejong sillok* 45:5, 7. His second wife was the daughter of Pong Yŏ (1375–1436) who became Sun-bin. In 1436, she was expelled from the palace because she had been unable to bear a son and was also accused of lesbian activities. She was demoted to commoner status and sent back to her own home. One of the crown prince's secondary wives, Kwŏn-ssi, then was selected as the new consort: *Sejong sillok* 46:3; 75:7b–9b, 26b–27b; 76:16–18, 19b–20.
69. *Sejong sillok,* kwŏn 128–135.
70. For the details, see *Sejong sillok* 133:1–10; *Chŭngbo munhŏnbigo,* 73:3–7; *T'ung-tien,* kwŏn 122.
71. For the details, see *Sejong sillok* 133:18–26b; *Chŭngbo munhŏnbigo* 73:7–14; *T'ung-tien,* kwŏn 127. In the following years, two of King Sejong's sons by a secondary wife married according to a similar, but simplified protocol: *Sejong sillok* 79:18; 87:31b. At the beginning of the Chosŏn dynasty, *karye* designated all weddings performed by members of the royal house. Toward the end of the dynasty the term *killye* was used for weddings performed by members of the royal house other than princes in order to emphasize the distinction between the royal main line and its branches. See Kim Yong-suk, *Yijo yŏryu munhak mit kungjung p'ungsok ŭi yŏn'gu* (Seoul: Sookmyung Women's University, 1970), p. 343.
72. For a discussion of the ideological struggle between the king and the officialdom, see Sohn Pow-key, "Social History."
73. *Chungjong sillok* 17:17b–18, 20b–21.
74. *Chungjong sillok* 23:27.
75. *Chungjong sillok* 28:36. For a discussion of the advisability for a king to perform *ch'inyŏng,* see *Chungjong sillok* 27:49b–50b. King Chungjong's first queen, Lady Sin, was expelled from the palace in 1506 because her father, Sin Su-gŭn (1450–1506), was Yŏnsan'gun's brother-in-law and was killed

in the deposition coup. For an analysis of the controversy surrounding Lady Sin's expulsion that arose in 1515, see Wagner, *Literati Purges*, p. 83ff. Chungjong's second queen had died while giving birth to the later King Injong in 1515.

76. King Sŏnjo performed the rite in 1601 and King Injo in 1638: *Sŏnjo sillok* 149:19; *Injo sillok* 37:34.

77. *Chŭngbo munhŏnbigo* 73:27b. The original ceremony, *pongyŏng wangbi*, during which specially appointed officials had brought the new queen to the royal palace, was changed into the king's personal induction of the queen.

78. *Chungjong sillok* 28:36a–b.

79. *Chungjong sillok* 28:36a–b, 38.

80. *Chungjong sillok* 28:42b.

81. *Chungjong sillok* 28:46a–b, 54a–b; 29:2b–3b, 4, 11–12, 19b–20.

82. Cho Sik, *Nammyŏng-jip* 5:10b.

83. *Sok taejŏn*, p. 236.

84. The term *ugwi* originates from the *Book of Odes*, Ode 6, where it is said, "this young lady is going to her future home."

85. In Korea, it seems to have always been the custom to send animals to the bride's house prior to the wedding. In Koguryŏ, for example, it was usually a pig. See Li Ogg, p. 225. In ancient China, it was customary to present a wild goose when visiting a superior. In the "Marriage of an Ordinary Officer" in the *I-li*, each stage of the wedding ceremony, except the *napching*, included the presentation of a wild goose. The *Li-chi* mentions the presentation of a wild goose only in connection with the groom's personal induction of the bride. For an interesting discussion of *chŏnan*, see Akiba Takashi, "A Study on Korean Folkways," *Folklore Studies* 16:62–73 (1957).

86. Cho Sik, *Nammyŏng-jip* 5:10b; *pyŏlchip* 1:5b; Nam Hang-myŏng, *Hoeŭn-jip* 5:1b; Yi Nŭng-hwa, *Chosŏn yŏsok-ko*, p. 70.

87. The Chinese expression for "wedding" most commonly used in Korea is the Chinese compound *honin*. Consisting of the elements "woman" and "dusk," *hon* indicates, according to the *Po-hu t'ung*, that the ceremony originally took place in the early evening. *In* means a woman who follows her husband: *Po-hu t'ung*, I, 244ff. A term that corresponds more closely to the Korean circumstances is *ip-changga* (mod. Korean: *changga kada*), meaning the husband's entering his bride's house. See Yu Hyŏng-wŏn, *Pan'gye surok* 25:19b. The Confucians, however, preferred the terms *honin*, *ch'wich'ŏ*, or *ch'wibu*, "to take a wife"; and *ka*, *chŏgin (chŏkpu)*, and *kwi*, "to take a husband." A modern Korean term used in the latter meaning is *sijip kada*, "to go to the house of the parents-in-law."

88. The role of a middleman could be played by a relative, usually a man, or a professional. When the marriage radius was more or less fixed, a woman who

had married into the descent group could effect a suitable match with a young member of her own family.

89. The *honju* were usually the fathers of the prospective couple. If a father had died, a relative (e.g., grandfather) could take his place. In rare cases, the mother could act as *honju*. See Chŏng Ku, *Han'gang munjip* 5:6b.

90. For examples of such letters, see Ch'oe Sŭng-hŭi, *Han'guk komunsŏ yŏn'gu*, pp. 410–414.

91. Akiba Takashi argues that *napp'ye* is not a bride price, but rather a present for establishing good relations: "A Study on Korean Folkways," pp. 41–42.

92. The terms *napch'ae* and *napp'ye* which designate two different stages in Chu Hsi's model were in Korea often used interchangeably. According to Pak Se-ch'ae, *napch'ae* designates the letter and *napp'ye* the gifts that were sent to formalize the match: *Namgye yesŏl* 3:22.

93. *T'aejong sillok* 24:16a–b; *Sejong sillok* 115:5b; 118:12a–b; *Sejo sillok* 4:29b; 38:39b–40; *Chungjong sillok* 73:52b; *Kyŏngguk taejŏn*, p. 484; Kim Chong-jik, *Ijollok,* second part, 4:18b.

94. *Chungjong sillok* 73:52b; *Sok taejŏn*, p. 236.

95. *Munjong sillok* 1:22–23b.

96. For such a case, see *Sejo sillok* 38:39b–40.

97. *Chungjong sillok* 26:66a–b; 31:45a–b; 34:20b.

98. Cho Ho-ik, *Chisan munjip* 3:5b–6; Nam Hang-myŏng, *Hoeŭn-jip* 5:1a–b.

99. The groom was dressed in the official gown of a civilian official *(tallyŏng),* a gauzed hat, square belt, and felt shoes *(samo kwandae).*

100. At times, the exchange of the nuptial cup was followed by a banquet attended only by groom and bride *(tongnoe).* The Korean usage of *ch'orye* really was a misnomer. *Ch'o* was the exhortation given by the fathers to bridegroom and bride before they left their respective homes on the wedding day. Although rarely possible, the exchange of the nuptial cup was performed again on the sixtieth wedding anniversary *(hoehollye* or *chungnoeyŏn).*

101. For a description and analysis of these customs, see Akiba Takashi, pp. 73–79; and Yi Nŭng-hwa, pp. 89–95.

102. At times the bride's presentation to her parents-in-law was followed by a ceremony that was the equivalent to the groom's capping. During the wedding ceremony the bride wore an elaborate hairdo of real and false hair. This hairdo was taken down, and the bride's hair was put up in a knot through which a hairpin was put. The "pinning up of the hair" *(kyerye)* marked the bride's coming of age.

103. If the bride was still very young, she usually returned home after being presented to her parents-in-law and entered her husband's house again upon reaching maturity. A special date was chosen for this second induction.

This sketch is based on the following sources: Yi Nŭng-hwa, pp. 76–89; Yu Hŭi-ch'un, *Miam-ilgi;* Nam Hang-myŏng, *Hoeŭn-jip* 5:1b; Kim Sŏng-il, *Hakpong munjip* 6:16–17; Yi Ik, *Sŏngho sŏnsaeng-jip,* kwŏn 48; *Kwangnye-ram* as appended to *Sarye pyŏllam* (reprint: Seoul, 1977), 3:10–19b; Hwang P'il-su, *Charae kwanhaeng hollye* as appended to *Sarye pyŏllam* (Seoul, 1967); Kim Taek-kyu, pp. 130–134; Chang Su-gŭn and Maeng In-jae, *Hahoe maŭl* (Seoul: Munhwajae kwalliguk, 1973), pp. 53–57; Chang Su-gŭn and Maeng In-jae, *Yangdong maŭl* (Seoul: Munhwajae kwalliguk, 1973), pp. 52–56; Chang Su-gŭn and Maeng In-jae, *Nagansŏng maŭl* (Seoul: Munhwajae kwalliguk, 1973), pp. 43–46; Akiba Takashi, pp. 64–65; Son Chin-t'ae, "Chosŏn honin ŭi chuyo hyŏngt'ae in solsŏ honsok ko," in his *Chosŏn minjok munhwa ŭi yŏn'gu* (Seoul: Ŭryu munhwasa, 1948), pp. 87–104.

104. Chang Hyŏn-gwang, *Yŏhŏn munjip* 4:46b–47; Han Wŏn-jin, *Namdang munjip* 16:20b–21; Chŏng Ku, *Han'gang munjip* 5:14b–15; Yi Ik, I, 249.

105. During a royal lecture, King Sejong stated that in contrast to Chinese women Korean women were unable to read, and therefore there was no danger of their meddling in politics: *Sejong sillok* 79:12.

106. *Sŏngjong sillok* 127:7; *Chungjong sillok* 98:39; *Kyŏngguk taejŏn,* p. 292.

107. For details, see Sohye wanghu Han-ssi, *Naehun.* There are several reprints of this work: see esp. *Naehun,* Kim Chi-yong, ed. (Seoul: Yŏnse taehakkyo, Inmun kwahak yŏn'guso, 1969); and *Naehun-Yŏsasŏ* (Seoul: Asea munhwasa, 1974).

108. About the educational experiences of some yangban women, see Sin Chŏng-suk, "Saengjon nobuin ŭi mun'gyŏn ch'aerok," *Kugŏ kungmunhak* 58–60:324–325 (Dec. 1972).

109. *T'aejo sillok* 2:3b–4. This rule dating from 1393 was laid down in the *Kyŏngje yukchŏn. Sejong sillok* 52:42b. Some time later, in 1416, the censors intensified their demands and sought a total confinement of women to the house (except for visits with their parents), but they did not receive royal approval: *T'aejong sillok* 32:12b–13.

110. *Sejong sillok* 22:3b.

111. *Sejong sillok* 44:27; 62:22b–23, 24a–b; 87:29.

112. *T'aejong sillok* 7:23.

113. *Sejong sillok* 19:19; 57:19; 58:8b; 123:4b–5. The censors' attention was mainly directed at conditions in the capital. Their efforts to include village women failed: *Sejong sillok* 62:22b.

114. *T'aejong sillok* 8:32b. Such a law must have been in the *Kyŏngje yukchŏn: Sejong sillok* 64:23.

115. *Sejong sillok* 52:42b; 53:4, 7; 57:15; 64:19b, 23–24; 108:9b–10; 116:10b. An edict of 1448 further clarified that the law not only prohibited visits to mountain temples, but also to temples in the capital: *Sejong sillok* 122:4b.

116. *Kyŏngguk taejŏn*, p. 481.
117. *T'aejong sillok* 17:15b; *Munjong sillok* 3:49b–50; *Tanjong sillok* 11:12b.
118. *T'aejong sillok* 24:24; 28:40b; *Sejong sillok* 21:1; 49:22; 94:11a–b; 114:25; 115:18; 123:6b–7; *Sŏngjong sillok* 10:24; *Kyŏngguk taejŏn*, p. 482.
119. There are various terms designating the primary wife: *ch'ŏ, myŏngbu, chŏk-ch'ŏ, chŏksil, yŏ'gun, chŏngbu.*
120. These limitations were customary until recent times: Sin Chŏng-suk, "Saengjon nobuin ŭi mun'gyŏn ch'aerok," pp. 329–330.
121. *Sejong sillok* 100:15b–16.
122. Census figures for the Taegu area for the period of 1675 to 1776, collected by Shikata Hiroshi, put the average number of people per household at 4.4 and 4.6. Unfortunately no ranges are given, but the four-person households accounted for 23 percent of all households studied. Ch'oe Chae-sŏk gives the following percentages for a yangban village (Yangjwadong, North Kyŏngsang province) for 1807: nuclear, 44.6 percent; stem, 41 percent; extended, 10.2 percent. In census registers for Sanŭm dating from the early seventeenth century, the percentage for three-generation households stood at only 3 percent. For statistical materials, see Shikata Hiroshi, "Richō jinkō ni kansuru ichi kenkyū," pp. 54–55; Ch'oe Chae-sŏk, "Chosŏn hugi panch'on e issŏsŏ ŭi kajok ŭi kusŏng," p. 296; and Ch'oe Chae-sŏk, "Chosŏn chŏn'gi ŭi kajok hyŏngt'ae," p. 147.
123. For a brief description of a yangban woman's daily life, see Martina Deuchler, "The Tradition: Women during the Yi Dynasty," in Sandra Mattielli, ed., *Virtues in Conflict: Tradition and the Korean Woman Today* (Seoul: Royal Asiatic Society, 1977), pp. 25–26.
124. Examples of girls' names are found in the *Sillok:* Sobi, Kammuri, Yŏriga, Kamdong, Chongbi. Some of these may have been commoner names: *Sejong sillok* 54:14b; 56:25b; 62:22b–23; 72:5b; *Sejo sillok* 5:8–10. For a study of women's names, see Ayugai Fusanoshin, *Zakkō* (reprint, 1973), pp. 119–132.
125. *Minji kanshū kaitō ishū* (Keijō: Chōsen sōtokufu, 1933), pp. 385–386. This is a collection of questions and answers compiled between 1909 and 1933 by legal institutions of the Japanese Government-General. It is a valuable sourcebook for social institutions.
126. Wagner, "Social Stratification in Seventeenth Century Korea," p. 41; John N. Somerville, "Success and Failure in Eighteenth Century Ulsan" (Ph.D. diss., Harvard University, 1974), pp. 168–169. *Sŏng* was an intermediate term between the commoner *sosa* and the aristocratic *ssi.* Wives of slaves were listed under their given name (*irŭm*); they did not have surnames. For an example of the use of the *hojŏk* for identifying the sequence of marriage, see *Sŏngjong sillok* 108:15b–16.
127. *T'aejo sillok* 9:8b.

372 *Notes to pp. 264–266*

128. *T'aejong sillok* 25:13a–b; 34:19b; *Sejong sillok* 48:4b; 55:6; 70:2b; 84:21b; *Kyŏngguk taejŏn*, pp. 30–32.
129. For an extensive discussion of the family head's powers within the traditional family, see Pak Pyŏng-ho, "Han'guk ŭi chŏnt'ong kajok kwa kajanggwŏn," *Hankuk Hakpo* 2.1:67–93 (Spring 1976).
130. *Sejong sillok* 47:24b, 25a–b; *Kyŏngguk taejŏn*, p. 479; *Sok taejŏn*, p. 402. An exception was made in the case of rebellion or treason.
131. The mother's consent, for example, was needed to finalize the marriage contracts of her children: *Minji kanshū kaitō ishū*, pp. 318–319.
132. For evidence of yangban widow householders, see Wagner, "Social Stratification in Seventeenth-Century Korea," p. 43. The line of succession to the household headship was: grandmother-in-law, mother-in-law, wife, daughter. In case a widow became the head of household, she also wielded parental authority over her children: *Minji kanshū kaitō ishū*, pp. 105–106; *Genkō Chōsen shinzoku sōzokuho ruishū* (Keijō: Toki to koseki kenkyūkai, 1939), pp. 365, 367.
133. *Myŏngjong sillok* 13:26b; *Minji kanshū kaitō ishū*, pp. 285–288. For details, see Chapter Three.
134. *Genkō Chōsen shinzoku sōzokuhō ruishū*, pp. 73–74.
135. *Sok taejŏn*, pp. 398–399; *Taejŏn t'ongp'yŏn* (Seoul: Pŏpchech'ŏ, 1963), pp. 590, 597.
136. *Chungjong sillok* 31:30b, 32, 37b; 90:46; *Myŏngjong sillok* 3:11a–b; 33:10.
137. In 1702, for example, a yangban woman killed a slave girl out of jealousy. After confessing the crime, she was flogged and banished. *Ch'ugwanji* (Keijō: Chōsen sōtokufu, 1937), p. 477.
138. *Sejong sillok* 50:31b; *Kyŏngguk taejŏn*, p. 470; *Sok taejŏn*, pp. 397, 404; *Ch'ugwanji*, pp. 597–598. The heaviest punishment the *Kyŏngguk taejŏn* prescribed for yangban women who committed crimes which normally drew the death sentence was the putting-on of the wooden neck collar (*mokk'al* or *kyŏngga*). A commoner woman, in contrast, who murdered her husband was decapitated: *Sejong sillok* 96:9.
139. This rule was not put into the *Kyŏngguk taejŏn*, but was considered to have the force of law: *Sŏngjong sillok* 10:19, 24; *Chungjong sillok* 82:58–59.
140. Yi Chae, *Sarye pŏllam*, pp. 287–288.
141. To differentiate the degree of mourning for the mother from that of the father, the son's mourning garments differed: for the father, he wore unhemmed sackcloth and carried a mourning staff made of bamboo, its roundness symbolizing heaven; for his mother, he wore hemmed sackcloth and carried a mourning staff made of elococca wood, the ends of which were squared off to symbolize earth. These prescriptions, which were based on passages in the *Li-chi* and *I-li,* are illustrated, for example, in Yi Chae, *Sarye pyŏllam*, pp. 150–156.

142. This reduction was initiated by King Sejong on the basis of personal experience. He had to mourn for his mother who had died in 1420 while his father, King T'aejong, was still alive: *Sejong sillok* 38:4a–b.

143. *Kyŏngguk taejŏn,* pp. 246, 260.

144. *Sejong sillok* 77:43b; 88:3b–4b; 112:22; *Kyŏngguk taejŏn,* pp. 259, 278. Only the *Taejŏn t'ongp'yŏn* of 1785 granted an official a two-day leave of absence on the occasion of the wife's death.

145. *Po-hu t'ung,* I, 261.

146. *Chungjong sillok* 80:33.

147. *Sejong sillok* 35:17b; *Sŏngjong sillok* 182:10. A man was called *pu* as the "husband" of a primary wife, and *kun* as the "master" of a secondary wife.

148. In 1482 King Sŏngjong prohibited royal sons-in-law and courtiers from taking yangban daughters as secondary wives: *Sŏngjong sillok* 141:1. On the other hand, to take the daughter of a secondary wife of lowborn status *(ch'ŏn)* as wife *(ch'ŏ)* was considered inappropriate for a civil official *(tongban): Sejong sillok* 92:12b.

149. For examples of social origin, see *T'aejong sillok* 12:37b; 26:4, and many subsequent entries.

150. There is no evidence that in Korea secondary wives were bought, or that there was a market for them. The term "to marry" *(ch'wi)* was often used in connection with acquiring a secondary wife. For a description of specialized markets for concubines in China, see Patricia Ebrey, "Concubines in Sung China," *Journal of Family History* 11.1:1–24, esp. p. 7ff (1986).

151. Whether a secondary wife was called *taek* or *chip* by the primary wife reportedly depended on her status in the household. Her husband's secondary wife (presumably of commoner background) she called *taek,* whereas her son's secondary wife she called *chip.*

152. According to the *Kyŏngguk taejŏn,* a lowborn girl (whether she was a private or a public slave) who became a secondary wife of an official of second rank and above and had children could buy commoner status upon providing a substitute slave: *Kyŏngguk taejŏn,* p. 486. *Minji kanshū kaitō ishū,* pp. 82–84; *Genkō Chōsen shinzoku sōzokuhō ruishū,* pp. 36, 88, 146–147, 173; Sin Chŏng-suk, "Saengjon nobuin ŭi mun'gyŏn ch'aerok," p. 328.

153. For examples, see *Sejong sillok* 30:20a–b; 116:26a–b; *Munjong sillok* 3:52.

154. *Minji kanshū kaitō ishū,* pp. 265–266.

155. *Genkō Chōsen shinzoku sōzokuhō ruishū,* pp. 60–61, 372, 376. The Seoul Census Register of 1663 lists six widowed commoner householders who had been secondary wives in yangban households. See Wagner, "Social Stratification in Seventeenth-Century Korea," p. 47.

156. The sequence of heirs of a secondary wife's property was: son, grandson, master, household head: *Genkō Chōsen shinzoku sōzokuhō ruishū,* pp. 400, 415; *Minji kanshū kaitō ishū,* pp. 125–126, 379–382.

374　　　*Notes to pp. 270–279*

157. *Sejong sillok* 67:15b; Kim Chang-saeng, *Ŭirye munhae* 1:18; Song Chun-gil, *Tongch'undang munjip* 8:42a–b; 9:28b–29; Yi Chae, *Sarye pyŏllam*, p. 150.
158. For a detailed discussion of secondary sons, see Deuchler, " 'Heaven Does Not Discriminate,' " pp. 121–163; and Chapter Three above.
159. *Kyŏngguk taejŏn*, p. 208. From the middle of the sixteenth century on, the barring of secondary sons' descendants from the examinations was gradually relaxed. For the details, see Deuchler, " 'Heaven Does Not Discriminate.' "
160. Cho Kwang-jo, *Chŏngam munjip*, purok 2:1a–b.
161. Yi Ik, *Sŏngho saesŏl*, I, 255–256.
162. *Sejong sillok* 30:14a–b.
163. Yi Maeng-gyun had become a left vice-councillor of the Council of State in 1430.
164. *Sejong sillok* 89:25b–26, 29b–30, 32–33b. This case is also an interesting example for the restraint with which a yangban woman was punished.
165. *Sejong sillok* 32:28b.
166. *Sejong sillok* 100:15b–16; *Sejo sillok* 30:22.
167. *Chungjong sillok* 82:59; *Ch'ugwanji*, p. 138. There was a terminological difference between a husband's expulsion of his wife: "to make go" *(kŏ)*, and the government's order to get rid of an illegally acquired wife, "to separate" *(ii)*.
168. *T'aejong sillok* 30:9b.
169. *Sejong sillok* 110:2b.
170. *Sejo sillok* 3:2b.
171. *Sŏngjong sillok* 82:10.
172. *Koryŏsa* 75:34. This applied to widows of civil and military officials above the third rank.
173. *Koryŏsa* 84:42b–43; *Chŭngbo munhŏnbigo* 89:3b.
174. *T'aejong sillok* 11:29; *Sejong sillok* 72:35.
175. *Sejo sillok* 43:23–24, 27–28. For a detailed discussion of this case, see Yi Sang-baek, "Chaega kŭmji sŭpsok ŭi yurae e taehan yŏn'gu," in *Chosŏn munhwasa yŏn'gu non'go* (Seoul: Ŭryu munhwasa, 1948), pp. 212–218.
176. *Kyŏngguk taejŏn*, pp. 483–484. This code clearly equates the term *kaengjŏk sambuja*, "thrice-married woman," with *sirhaengja*, "women who misbehave." The latter term refers to adultery.
177. *T'aejong sillok* 14:49; 27:46b; 28:15; *Sŏngjong sillok* 4:28b; 130:8b; 261:18b–19; *Chungjong sillok* 2:40; 21:58b, 60a–b.
178. *T'aejo sillok* 9:8.
179. *Sŏngjong sillok* 82:9b–16, 18b, 19b–20; 127:7. For a detailed analysis of the debate of 1477, see Yi Sang-baek, "Chaega kŭmji sŭpsok ŭi yurae e taehan yŏn'gu," pp. 218–229.
180. *Kyŏngguk taejŏn*, pp. 34, 208.

181. The mourning grade for a remarried mother was lowered to one year with mourning staff *(chaech'oe changgi): Kyŏngguk taejŏn*, p. 258; *Minji kanshū kaitō ishū*, pp. 236–237, 413–414.

182. For examples, see *Chungjong sillok* 64:11a–b, 12, 13b; *Myŏngjong sillok* 7:36b; *Sukchong sillok* 31:38; *Chŏngjo sillok* 1:55b–56. Officially the Kabo reforms of 1894 ended the widow's predicament by ruling that widows of any social class were henceforth free to remarry. Yi Sŏn-gŭn, *Han'guksa, hyŏndae-p'yŏn* (Seoul: Ŭryu munhwasa, 1963), p. 243.

183. *Po-hu t'ung*, I, 252, 254–255. The passage on the prohibition of remarriage reads, "Why must he [the son of heaven] marry only once? It is to avoid debauchery and to prevent him casting away virtue and indulging in passion. Therefore he only marries once; the Lord of men has no right to marry twice."

184. Granet, pp. 65–66.

185. *Po-hu t'ung*, I, 257–258; *Sejong sillok* 41:16b.

186. *T'aejong sillok* 32:13a–b; *Sejong sillok* 41:16b–17, 19; 122:6.

CONCLUSIONS: THE EMERGENCE OF A LINEAGE SOCIETY

1. If not further specified, references to China mean China after the Ming period. Because of the great variation of social practices across social groups and between regions, it is obviously risky to generalize for "China." But the risk is taken here for the sake of argument.

2. This point was formulated by Professor Maurice Freedman in a lecture given in an Oxford seminar in the spring of 1972.

3. For examples emphasizing the bond between father and son, see *Sejong sillok* 103:23b; Pak Su-ch'un, *Kuktam-jip* 2:29; Pak Se-ch'ae, *Namgye-jip* 21:12b.

4. For details, see Deuchler, " 'Heaven Does Not Discriminate.' "

5. See, for example, Hugh D. R. Baker, *Chinese Family and Kinship* (London: The MacMillan Press, 1979), p. 36; Ebrey, "Concubines in Sung China," pp. 14–15; S. van der Sprenkel, *Legal Institutions in Manchu China* (London: The Athlone Press, 1962), p. 15.

6. The kin terms for matrilateral kin were, and still are, therefore prefixed with "outside" *(oe)*.

7. These points on China are made by Jack Goody, *The Oriental, the Ancient and the Primitive* (Cambridge: Cambridge University Press, 1990), pp. 58, 81ff. They are elaborated by Patricia B. Ebrey, "Shifts in Marriage Finance from the Sixth to the Thirteenth Century," in Rubie S. Watson and Patricia B. Ebrey, eds., *Marriage and Inequality in Chinese Society* (Berkeley: University of California Press, 1991), pp. 102–123.

8. Two works are most relevant: David G. Johnson, *The Medieval Chinese Oligarchy;* and Patricia B. Ebrey, *The Aristocratic Families of Early Imperial China*

(Cambridge: Cambridge University Press, 1978). For the details on social organization, Johnson's work was used.

9. For details, see Johnson, *Medieval Chinese Oligarchy.*

10. This summary draws on the brief, but illuminating discussion of the background of the T'ang-Sung transition by Robert P. Hymes, *Statesmen and Gentlemen* (Cambridge: Cambridge University Press, 1986), pp. 2–6. See also Robert Hartwell, "Demographic, Political, and Social Transformations of China, 750–1550," *Harvard Journal of Asiatic Studies* 42:2:365–442 (Dec. 1982).

11. James L. Watson has characterized the shift from T'ang to Sung in anthropological terms as one from alliance to descent as a major organizing principle of society. See his "Chinese Kinship Reconsidered."

12. See Patricia B. Ebrey, "The Early Stages in the Development of Descent Group Organization," in Patricia B. Ebrey and James L. Watson, eds., *Kinship Organization in Late Imperial China, 1000–1940* (Berkeley: University of California Press, 1986), pp. 16–61. In the same work, see James Watson's "Anthropological Overview," pp. 279–282, for a discussion of Ebrey's findings and interpretations.

13. For a discussion of the Neo-Confucians' ideas on descent groups, see Chapter Three above. See also Ebrey, "Early Stages in the Development of Descent Group Organization," pp. 35–39; and Patricia B. Ebrey, "Conceptions of the Family in the Sung Dynasty," *Journal of Asian Studies* 43.2:221–222, 229–232 (Feb. 1984).

14. James B. Palais has devoted a provocative article to this phenomenon in his "Confucianism and the Aristocratic/Bureaucratic Balance in Korea." Palais ascribes the persistence of this phenomenon in Korea to the absence of major wars and the lack of economic change of any magnitude during the Chosŏn period. He also speaks of the egalitarian versus hierarchical influence of Confucianism, but in this discussion he generally seems to underestimate the impact of Neo-Confucianism on the restructuring of Korean society.

15. This is a crude rendition of Palais' argument in the much more reasoned article mentioned above.

16. For a recent formulation of this proposition, see Patricia B. Ebrey and James L. Watson, eds., *Kinship Organization in Late Imperial China,* p. 5.

17. For a theoretical description of the "spinal cord" method of segmentation, see Fox, *Kinship and Marriage,* pp. 124–125. Maurice Freedman was the first to suggest that in Korea primogeniture might have prevented lineages from segmenting internally. See his *Lineage Organization in Southeastern China,* pp. 135–136, 137. This view is refuted by Roger L. Janelli and Dawnhee Yim Janelli, who argue that the absence of internal segmentation among Korean local lineages is attributable not to primogeniture but to cultural values, i.e.,

status assertion. See their "Lineage Organization and Social Differentiation in Korea," pp. 279, 287. For a detailed description of the asymmetrical segmentation of Chinese lineages, see Jack M. Potter, "Land and Lineage in Traditional China," in Maurice Freedman, ed., *Family and Kinship in Chinese Society* (Stanford: Stanford University Press, 1970), pp. 121–138. The most recent work on Korean lineages is by Mutsuhiko Shima, "In Quest of Social Recognition."

18. *T'aejong sillok* 33:17; *Sejong sillok* 56:1b.
19. It is true that no legal stipulations barred commoners from taking the examinations, and at the beginning of the dynasty there were a few commoners who did successfully pass them and advance to government offices. Seen from the total number of examination passers, however, they were the exception. Ch'oe Yŏng-ho has explored the fate of these commoners in *The Civil Examinations and the Social Structure in Early Yi Dynasty Korea: 1392–1600*. For a discussion of the secondary sons' position in the public realm, see Deuchler, " 'Heaven Does Not Discriminate.' "
20. See also Palais, "Confucianism and the Aristocratic/Bureaucratic Balance in Korea."
21. The aristocratic element was reinforced through the continuation of the "protection privilege" *(ŭm)*, although this may have been less important than in Koryŏ. For a description of this institution in early Chosŏn, see Yi Sŏng-mu, *Chosŏn ch'ogi yangban yŏn'gu,* pp. 44–49.
22. Song June-ho, "The Government Examination Rosters of the Yi Dynasty," in Spencer J. Palmer, ed., *Studies in Asian Genealogy,* p. 154. For a table listing the 38 lineages with the number of their respective examination passers, see p. 166. In the course of the dynasty the *munkwa* examinations were given 745 times, producing some 14,600 successful candidates, an average of 28 per year. Subsequent refinement of the data by Edward W. Wagner has resulted in small changes in the totals of some lineages, but the overall picture remains the same.
23. This argument has been put forward by Meyer Fortes. See his "The Structure of Unilineal Descent Groups," *American Anthropologist* 55.1:17–41 (1953). The Janellis also make this point. See their "Lineage Organization and Social Differentiation in Korea," p. 274.
24. To date, only Fujiya Kawashima has studied the interaction between a powerful lineage and the state. See his "Lineage Elite."
25. Of course, there was still another status group, the *chungin,* most importantly consisting of the technical specialists employed by the central government (translators, interpreters, medical practitioners, astronomers, court painters, calligraphers, etc.) and local functionaries who served under the magistrates at county level. Although they shared the educational accomplishments and Confucian ideological orientation of the elite, they could not intermarry with

it. Similarly, although they could achieve high rank, they were never entrusted with major responsibilities in the central government. Capital-bound *chungin* formed their own lineages and kept the same kind of genealogical records. (Personal communication from Professor E. W. Wagner).

26. This term is here used loosely in the meaning of a group sharing some important characteristics, for example the primacy of birth. It does not imply legal definition. See Georges Balandier, *Political Anthropology* (London: Allen Lane, The Penguin Press, 1970), p. 89.

27. In the opening sentence of the Great Appendix, it is said, "Heaven is lofty and honourable; earth is low." See James Legge, tr., *I Ching: Book of Changes,* ed. with Introduction and Study Guide by Ch'u Chai with Winberg Chai (New York: University Books, 1964), p. 348.

28. For a similar usage of these terms in T'ang China, see Johnson, *Medieval Chinese Oligarchy,* pp. 5–6.

29. See, for example, *T'aejong sillok* 5:32b; 29:23b; *Sejong sillok* 47:9.

30. This is, for example, clearly expressed in *Hsün-tzu,* chap. 4 *(yung-ju)* where it is said that the kings of antiquity established specific rules for differentiating the various social status groups. Here *kwi* and *ch'ŏn* are used in parallel with "old" and "young." The same combinations are also found in the *Chou-li.*

31. This was a uniquely Korean formula. The Chinese scrutinized only the three patrilineal ascendants. For the Koreans, there had to be at least one "generally known high official" *(hyŏn'gwan)* among the four ancestors. Those who could not produce such evidence (perhaps because of insufficient genealogical records) needed three guarantors who could vouch for the social background of the candidate. See *Taejŏn husongnok,* pp. 165–166. See also the discussion on this issue by Yŏng-ho Ch'oe, *The Civil Examinations,* pp. 129–131. Ch'oe uses this material to show that commoners were not barred from the civil service examinations.

32. Some of the early references are *T'aejong sillok* 25:21b; *Sejong sillok* 47:9; 56:1b; *Sŏngjong sillok* 35:1a–b; 146:9; 202:14a–b. See also Deuchler, " 'Heaven Does Not Discriminate.' " Synonyms of *kwi* and *ch'ŏn* were "honored" *(chon)* and "despised" *(pi).*

33. This view is at odds with the interpretation of the Janellis who maintain that "gentry" (yangban) status did not entail more than the exemption from a military tax, and that there was an enormous difference in status between a literate officeholder and his kinsmen who worked in the fields. This discrepancy of views may stem from the fact that the Janellis have studied localized lineages from the perspective of the twentieth century, whereas my emphasis is on elite lineages of the early part of the Chosŏn dynasty. See their "Lineage Organization and Social Differentiation in Korea."

34. For a differentiated analysis of this problem, see Rubie S. Watson, *Inequality among Brothers* (Cambridge: Cambridge University Press, 1985).

35. See for example Kwŏn To's (1387–1445) argument and definition of commoner status dated 1434 in *Sejong sillok* 64:10b–11, and the discussion on social status in 1487 in *Sŏngjong sillok* 202:13b–14b.

36. The problem of how to distinguish the status groups of early Chosŏn has led to a prolonged and heated controversy among Korean historians, a controversy too long and complicated to be discussed here in full. The point of departure seems to have been Yi Sŏng-mu's seminal work *Chosŏn ch'ogi yangban yŏn'gu* (1980), in which Yi contends that the society of early Chosŏn was broadly divided into two status groups, the "good people" *(yangin)* and the "base people" *(ch'ŏnin)*. The broad category of "good people" thus was taken to include the yangban, the civil and military officeholders of early Chosŏn. The relationship between this sociopolitical elite segment and the remaining "good people," however, did not become clear. Yi's work was criticized in a book review by Han Yŏng-u in *Sahoe kwahak p'yŏngnon* 1 (June 1982). Han reviewed earlier opinions and put forward his own views on the issue in "Chosŏn chŏn'gi yŏn'gu ŭi chemunje" in his *Chosŏn chŏn'gi sahoe kyŏngje yŏn'gu* (1983). Han insists that at the beginning of Chosŏn there was no privileged ruling class, and that the term yangban was solely used to designate the civil and military officials. He, too, interprets "good people" as including the officeholders and sees the more specialized meaning of yangban as ruling elite as a development of the sixteenth century. Han moreover equates "noble" *(kwi)* and "base" *(ch'ŏon)* with "good" *(yang)* and "base" *(ch'ŏn)*, contending that in early Chosŏn all people who were not slaves were thus "good." Yi Sŏng-mu's and Han Yŏng-u's viewpoints are discussed by Song Chun-ho in a substantial article entitled "Chosŏn yangban ko," *Han'guk sahak* 4:27–357 (1983). Song refutes the view of a two-tiered society in early Chosŏn and upholds the "traditional" division of society into three social status groups. The last word on this issue does not seem to have been written. It is, however, a fallacy to concentrate on the analysis of terms as such—their usage is never consistent—and not to see them in the various contexts of social institutions in which they were used.

37. Such seeming "upward mobility" of commoners and slaves is discussed by Yŏng-ho Ch'oe, *The Civil Examinations*.

Select Bibliography

Akiba Takashi. "A Study on Korean Folkways," *Folklore Studies* 16:1–106 (1957).

Andong Kwŏn-ssi sebo 安東權氏世譜 (Genealogy of the Andong Kwŏn). 1476.

Arii Tomonori 有井智徳. "Richō shoki no kosekihō ni tsuite" 李朝初期の戸籍法について (On the Household Registration System in Early Chosŏn), *Chōsen gakuhō* 朝鮮学報 39–40:42–93 (1966).

Ayugai Fusanoshin 鮎貝房之進. *Zakkō* 雑攷 (Miscellaneous Studies). Reprint, 1973.

Baker, Hugh D. R. *Chinese Family and Kinship*. London: The MacMillan Press, 1979.

Balandier, Georges. *Political Anthropology*. London: Allen Lane, The Penguin Press, 1970.

Beattie, Hilary J. *Land and Lineage in China: A Study of T'ung-ch'eng County Anhwei, in the Ming and Ch'ing Dynasties*. Cambridge: Cambridge University Press, 1979.

Bendix, Reinhard, and Seymour Martin Lipset, eds. *Class, Status, and Power: Social Stratification in Comparative Perspective*. 2nd ed. London: Routledge & Kegan Paul, 1967.

Berkner, Lutz K. "Inheritance, land tenure and peasant family structure: a German regional comparison," in Jack Goody et al., eds., *Family and Inheritance*. Cambridge: Cambridge University Press, 1976.

Biot, Edouard. *Le Tcheou-li ou Rites des Tcheou*. 2 vols. Paris: Imprimerie Nationale, 1851.

Bünger, Karl. *Quellen zur Rechtsgeschichte der T'ang-Zeit*. Peiping: The Catholic University, 1946.

Buxbaum, David C. *Chinese Family Law and Social Change in Historical and Comparative Perspective*. Seattle: University of Washington Press, 1978.

Chan, Hok-lam, and Wm. Theodore de Bary, eds. *Yüan Thought: Chinese Thought and Religion under the Mongols.* New York: Columbia University Press, 1982.

Chan, Wing-Tsit, tr. and comp. *A Source Book in Chinese Philosophy.* Princeton: Princeton University Press, 1963.

———. "Chu Hsi and Yüan Neo-Confucianism," in Hok-lam Chan and de Bary, eds., *Yüan Thought* (q.v.)

Chang Hyŏn-gwang 張顯光. *Yŏhŏn sŏnsaeng munjip* 旅軒先生文集 (Collected Works). 11 kwŏn. Date uncertain.

———. *Yŏhŏn sŏnsaeng sŏngnisŏl* 旅軒先生性理説 (Neo-Confucian Theories). 6 vols. Date uncertain.

Chang, K. C. *Early Chinese Civilization: Anthropological Perspectives.* Cambridge: Harvard University Press, 1976.

Chang Su-gŭn 張籌根 and Maeng In-jae 孟仁在. *Hahoe maŭl* 河回마을 (Hahoe Village). Seoul: Munhwajae kwalliguk 文化財管理局, 1973.

———. *Yangdong maŭl* 良洞마을 (Yangdong Village). Seoul: Munhwajae kwalliguk, 1973.

———. *Nagansŏng maŭl* 樂安城마을 (Nagansŏng Village). Seoul: Munhwajae kwalliguk, 1973.

Ch'angnyŏng Sŏng-ssi Sasuk-kong p'abo 昌寧成氏思肅公派譜 (Genealogy of the Ch'angnyŏng Sŏng, Sasuk-kong Branch), 1836.

Cho Chun 趙浚. *Songdang munjip* 松堂文集 (Collected Works). 2 vols. 1901.

Cho Ho-ik 曹好益. *Chisan munjip* 芝山文集 (Collected Works). 5 vols. No date.

———. *Karye kojŭng* 家禮考證 (Investigations of the *Chia-li*). 3 vols. 1646.

Cho Ik 趙翼. *P'ojŏ sŏnsaeng-jip* 浦渚先生集 (Collected Works). 18 vols. Date uncertain.

Cho Sik 曺植. *Nammyŏng-jip* 南冥集 (Collected Works). 8 vols. 1764.

Ch'oe Chae-sŏk 崔在錫. "Chosŏn hugi panch'on e issŏsŏ ŭi kajok ŭi kusŏng" 朝鮮後期班村에 있어서의 家族의 構成 (The Family Structure of a Yangban Village in the Late Yi Dynasty), in *Sŏk Chu-sŏn kyosu hoegap kinyŏm minsokhak nonch'ong* 石宙善教授回甲紀念民俗学論叢 (Festschrift for Professor Sŏk Chu-sŏn). Seoul: 1970.

———. "Chosŏn sidae ŭi sangsokche e kwanhan yŏn'gu" 朝鮮時代의 相續制에관한研究 (Study of Inheritance during the Chosŏn Period), *Yŏksa hakpo* 歷史学報 53–54:99–150 (June 1972).

———. "Chosŏn hugi tosi kajok ŭi hyŏngt'ae wa kusŏng" 朝鮮後期都市家族의形態와構成 (Morphological Structure of Urban Families in the Late Yi Dynasty), *Koryŏ taehakkyo, inmun nonjip* 高麗大学校人文論集 19:125–155 (1974).

———. "Chosŏn chŏn'gi ŭi kajok hyŏngt'ae" 朝鮮前期의家族形態 (Family Structure in the Early Yi Dynasty), *Chindan hakpo* 震檀学報 37:133–159 (1974).

———. *Han'guk nongch'on sahoe yŏn'gu* 韓國農村社會研究 (Study of Korean Rural Society). Seoul: Ilchisa 一志社, 1975.

———. "Koryŏ hugi kajok ŭi yuhyŏng kwa kusŏng" 高麗後期家族의類型과構成 (Family Structure in the Late Koryŏ Dynasty), *Hankuk Hakpo* 韓國学報 3:22–57 (Summer 1976).

———. "Koryŏjo e issŏsŏ ŭi t'oji ŭi chanyŏ kyunbun sangsok" 高麗朝에 있어서의土地의子女均分相續 (Equal Inheritance of Land by Sons and Daughters in Koryŏ), *Han'guksa yŏn'gu* 韓國史研究 35: 33–44 (Dec. 1981).

———. "Koryŏ sidae ŭi honin chedo" 高麗時代의婚姻制度 (The Marriage System of Koryŏ), *Koryŏ taehakkyo, inmun nonjip* 27:105–128 (1982).

———. "Koryŏ sidae ŭi ch'injok chojik" 高麗時代의親族組織 (Kinship Organization in Koryŏ), *Yŏksa hakpo* 94–95:208–218 (1982).

———. "Koryŏ ŭi sangsokche wa ch'injok chojik" 高麗의相續制와 親族組織 (Kinship Organization and Inheritance of Koryŏ), *Tongbang hakchi* 東方学志 31:5–39 (June 1982).

———. "Silla wangsil ŭi wangwi kyesŭng" 新羅王室의王位繼承 (Royal Succession in Silla), *Yŏksa hakpo* 98:39–105 (1983).

———. "Silla wangsil ŭi honinje" 新羅王室의婚姻制 (Royal Marriages in Silla), *Han'guksa yŏn'gu* 40:1–32 (1983).

———. *Han'guk kajok chedosa yŏn'gu* 韓國家族制度史研究 (Study of the Korean Family System). Seoul: Ilchisa, 1983.

———. "Koryŏ sidae pumojŏn ŭi chanyŏ kyunbun sangsok chaeron" 高麗時代父母田의子女均分相續再論 (Reexamination of Equal Inheritance by Sons and Daughters of Parental Property in Koryŏ), *Han'guksa yŏn'gu* 44:1–46 (March 1984).

Ch'oe Hang 崔恒. *T'aehŏjŏng munjip* 太虛亭文集 (Collected Works). 2 vols. 1625.

Ch'oe Hong-gi 崔弘基. *Han'guk hojŏk chedosa yŏn'gu* 韓國戶籍制度史研究 (Study on the Census Register System in Korea). Seoul: Sŏul taehakkyo ch'ulp'anbu 서울大学校出版部, 1975.

Ch'oe Sin 崔慎, *Hagam-jip* 鶴菴集 (Collected Works). 6 kwŏn. 1894.

Ch'oe Sŭng-hŭi 崔承熙. "Chiphyŏnjŏn yŏn'gu" 集賢殿研究 (Study on Chiphyŏnjŏn), *Yŏksa hakpo* 32:1–58 (Dec. 1966) and 33:39–80 (March 1967).

———. *Han'guk komunsŏ yŏn'gu* 韓國古文書研究 (Study of Old Documents of Korea). Sŏngnam-si: Han'guk chŏngsin munhwa yŏn'guwŏn 韓國精神文化研究院, 1981.

Ch'oe Yŏng-ho. "Commoners in Early Yi Dynasty Civil Examinations: An Aspect of Korean Social Structure, 1392–1600," *Journal of Asian Studies* 33.4:611–631 (Aug. 1974).

——. *The Civil Examinations and the Social Structure in Early Yi Dynasty Korea: 1392–1600.* Seoul: The Korean Research Center, 1987.

Ch'ŏn Kwan-u 千寬宇. "Han'guk t'oji chedosa, ha" 韓國土地制度史, 下 (The Land System of Korea, Part 2), in *Han'guk munhwasa taegye* 韓國文化史大系 (Handbook of Korean Culture), vol. 2. Seoul: Koryŏ taehakkyo ch'ulp'anbu 高麗大学校出版部, 1965.

Chŏng Ch'ŏl 鄭澈. *Songgang-jip* 松江集 (Collected Works). 7 vols. 1894.

Chŏng Ku 鄭逑. *Han'gang munjip* 寒岡文集 (Collected Works). 12 kwŏn. Date uncertain.

Chŏng Kyŏng-se 鄭經世. *Ubok-jip* 愚伏集 (Collected Works).

Chŏng Mong-ju 鄭夢周. *P'oŭn-jip* 圃隱集 (Collected Works), in *Yŏgye myŏnghyŏn-jip* (q.v.).

Chŏng Ok-cha 鄭玉子. "Yŏmal Chuja sŏngnihak ŭi toip e taehan si'go" 麗末朱子性理学의導入에對한試考 (On the Introduction of Chu Hsi's Neo-Confucianism in Late Koryŏ), *Chindan hakpo* 51:29–54 (April 1981).

Chŏng To-jŏn 鄭道傳. *Sambong-jip* 三峯集 (Collected Works). Seoul: Kuksa p'yŏnch'an wiwŏnhoe 國史編纂委員會, 1961.

Chŏng Tu-hŭi 鄭杜熙 *Chosŏn ch'ogi chŏngch'i chibae seryŏk yŏn'gu* 朝鮮初期政治支配勢力研究 (The Political Elite of the Early Chosŏn Dynasty: Its Formation and Political Roles). Seoul: Ilchogak 一潮閣, 1983.

Ch'ŏngp'ung Kim-ssi sebo 清風金氏世譜 (Genealogy of the Ch'ŏngp'ung Kim), 1750.

Chŏnju Yi-ssi Korim-gunp'a sŏnjo yumunjip 全州李氏高林君派先祖遺文集 (Documents Left by the Ancestors of the Korim-gun Branch of the Chŏnju Yi). Chŏnju, 1975.

Chōsen kinseki sōran 朝鮮金石總覧 (General Survey of Korean Epigraphy). 2 vols. Reprint. Seoul: Kyŏngin munhwasa 景仁文化社, 1974.

Chōsen saishi sōzoku hōron, josetsu 朝鮮祭祀相續法論序説 (An Introduction to the Inheritance Law of Korean Ancestor Worship). Keijō: Chōsen sōtokufu, Chūsū-in 朝鮮總督府, 中樞院, 1939.

Chōsen tosho kaidai 朝鮮圖書解題 (Annotated Bibliography of Korean Books). Keijō: Chōsen sōtokufu, 1919.

Chōsenshi 朝鮮史 (Chronological Abstracts of Historical Documents on Korea). Comp. by Chōsen sōtokufu. 37 vols. Keijō: Chōsen sōtokufu, 1932–1940.

Chosŏn wangjo sillok 朝鮮王朝實錄 (Veritable Records of the Chosŏn Dynasty). 48 vols. Reprint. Seoul: Kuksa p'yŏnch'an wiwŏnhoe, 1955–1958.

Chu Hsi 朱熹. *Wen-kung chia-li* 文公家禮 (The House Rules of Master Chu). Shanghai, 1918.

——. *Chu Tzu yü-lei* 朱子語類 (Classified Conversation of Chu Hsi). Reprint. Seoul, 1978.

Chu Se-bung 周世鵬. *Murŭng chapko* 武陵雜稿 (Various Writings). 9 vols. 1859.

Ch'ü, T'ung-tsu. *Law and Society in Traditional China.* The Hague: Mouton & Co., 1965.

Ch'ugwanji 秋官志 (Records on Punishment). Keijō: Chōsen sōtokufu, 1937.

Chung, Chai-sik. "Chŏng Tojŏn: 'Architect' of Yi Dynasty Government and Ideology," in de Bary and Haboush, eds., *The Rise of Neo-Confucianism in Korea* (q.v.).

Chŭngbo munhŏnbigo 增補文獻備考 (Revised Reference Compilation of Documents on Korea). Reprint. 3 vols. Seoul: Kojŏn kanhaenghoe 古典刊行會, 1957.

Clark, Donald N. "Chosŏn's Founding Fathers: A Study of Merit Subjects in the Early Yi Dynasty," *Korean Studies* 6:17–40 (1982).

Cohen, Myron L. *House United, House Divided: The Chinese Family in Taiwan.* New York: Columbia University Press, 1976.

Dardess, John W. *Confucianism and Autocracy: Professional Elites in the Founding of the Ming Dynasty.* Berkeley: University of California Press, 1983.

Davenport, William. "Nonunilinear Descent and Descent Groups," *American Anthropologist* 61.4:557–572 (1959).

de Bary, Wm. Theodore. "Some Common Tendencies in Neo-Confucianism," in Nivison and Wright, eds., *Confucianism in Action* (q.v.).

——. *Neo-Confucian Orthodoxy and the Learning of the Mind-and-Heart.* New York: Columbia University Press, 1981.

——, Wing-tsit Chan, and Burton Watson, eds. *Sources of Chinese Tradition.* New York: Columbia University Press, 1960.

—— and JaHyun Kim Haboush, eds. *The Rise of Neo-Confucianism in Korea.* New York: Columbia University Press, 1985.

Deuchler, Martina. "The Tradition: Women during the Yi Dynasty," in Sandra Mattielli, ed., *Virtues in Conflict: Tradition and the Korean Woman Today.* Seoul: Royal Asiatic Society, 1977.

——. "Self-cultivation for the Governance of Men: The Beginnings of Neo-Confucian Orthodoxy in Yi Korea," *Asiatische Studien* 34.2: 9–39 (1980).

——. "'Heaven Does Not Discriminate': A Study of Secondary Sons in Chosŏn Korea," *Journal of Korean Studies* 6:121–163 (1988–1989).

Dreyer, Edward L. *Early Ming China: A Political History, 1355–1435.*

Stanford: Stanford University Press, 1982.

Duncan, John B. "The Koryŏ Origins of the Chosŏn Dynasty: Kings, Aristocrats, and Confucianism." Ph.D. dissertation, University of Washington, 1988.

———. "The Social Background to the Founding of the Chosŏn Dynasty: Change or Continuity?," *Journal of Korean Studies* 6:39–79 (1988–1989).

Ebrey, Patricia Buckley. *The Aristocratic Families of Early Imperial China. A Case Study of the Po-ling Ts'ui Family.* Cambridge: Cambridge University Press, 1978.

———. "Conceptions of the Family in the Sung Dynasty," *Journal of Asian Studies* 43.2:219–243 (1986).

———. "Concubines in Sung China," *Journal of Family History* 11.1: 1–24 (1986).

———. "The Early Stages in the Development of Descent Group Organization," in Ebrey and Watson, eds., *Kinship Organization in Late Imperial China, 1000–1940* (q.v.).

——— and James L. Watson, eds. *Kinship Organization in Late Imperial China, 1000–1940.* Berkeley: University of California Press, 1986.

Feng, Han-yi. *The Chinese Kinship System.* Cambridge: Harvard-Yenching Institute, 1948.

Fortes, Meyer. "The Structure of Unilineal Descent Groups," *American Anthropologist* 55.1:17–41 (1953).

———. *Kinship and Social Order: The Legacy of Lewis Henry Morgan.* London: Routledge and Kegan Paul, 1969.

Fox, Robin. *Kinship and Marriage.* Harmondsworth: Penguin Books, 1967.

Feedman, Maurice. *Lineage Organization in Southeastern China.* London: The Athlone Press, 1958.

———. *Chinese Lineage and Society: Fukien and Kwangtung.* London: The Athlone Press, 1966.

———. ed., *Family and Kinship in Chinese Society.* Stanford: Stanford University Press, 1970.

Freeman, J. D. "On the Concept of the Kindred," as reprinted in Paul Bohannan and John Middleton, eds., *Kinship and Social Organization.* New York: The Natural History Press, 1968.

Fung Yu-lan. *A History of Chinese Philosophy.* Derk Bodde, tr. 2 vols. Leiden: E.J. Brill, 1953.

Gardner, Charles S. *Chinese Traditional Historiography*. Cambridge: Harvard University Press, 1961.

Gardner, Daniel K. *Chu Hsi and the* Ta-hsueh: *Neo-Confucian Reflection on the Confucian Canon*. Cambridge: Council on East Asian Studies, Harvard University, 1986.

Genkō Chōsen shinzoku sōzokuhō ruishū 現行朝鮮親族相續法類集 (Collection of Existing Laws on Kinship and Inheritance). Keijō: Toki to koseki kenkyūkai 登記と戶籍研究會, 1939.

Goodrich, L. Carrington. "Korean Interference with Chinese Historical Records," *Journal of the North China Branch of the Royal Asiatic Society of the Year 1937* 68:27–34 (1937).

Goody, Jack. "The Classification of Double Descent Systems," *Current Anthropology* 2:3–26 (1961).

———. "Inheritance, marriage and property in Africa and Eurasia," *Sociology* 3:55–76 (1969).

———. "Sideways and downwards," *Man* (N.S.) 5:627–638 (1970).

———. *Production and Reproduction: A Comparative Study of the Domestic Domain*. Cambridge: Cambridge University Press, 1976.

———. *The Oriental, the Ancient and the Primitive: Systems of Marriage and the Family in the Pre-Industrial Societies of Eurasia*. Cambridge: Cambridge University Press, 1990.

———. ed., *Succession to High Office*. Cambridge: Cambridge University Press, 1966.

Granet, Marcel. *La Polygynie sororale et le sororat dans la Chine féodale*. Paris: E. Leroux, 1920.

Ha Hyŏn-gang 河炫綱. "Koryŏ wangjo ŭi sŏngnip kwa hojok yŏnhap chŏnggwŏn" 高麗王朝의成立과豪族聯合政權 (The Establishment of Koryŏ and the Sharing of Power with the *hojok*), in *Han'guksa* 한국사 (History of Korea), vol. 4 (q.v.).

———. "Hojok kwa wanggwŏn" 豪族과王權 (The *hojok* and Royal Power), in *Han'guksa*, vol. 4 (q.v.).

Han U-gŭn 韓㳓劤. "Yŏmal Sŏnch'o ŭi pulgyo chŏngch'aek" 麗末鮮初의佛教政策 (Buddhist Policy at the End of Koryŏ and at the Beginning of Chosŏn), *Sŏuldae nonmunjip, inmun sahoe kwahak* 서울大学校論文集, 人文社會科学 6:1–80 (1957).

———. *Yijo hugi ŭi sahoe wa sasang* 李朝後期의社會와思想 (Society and Thought in Late Yi Dynasty Korea). Seoul: Ŭryu munhwasa 乙酉文化社, 1961.

———. "Sejong e issŏsŏ ŭi taebulgyo sich'aek" 世宗에있어서의對佛教施策 (Buddhist Policies under Sejong), *Chindan Hakpo* 25–27: 67–154 (Dec. 1964).

———. "Chosŏn wangjo ch'ogi e issŏsŏ ŭi yugyo inyŏm ŭi silch'ŏn kwa sinang, chonggyo" 朝鮮王朝初期에 있어서의儒教理念의實踐과信仰·宗教 (The Practice of Confucianism and Religion at the Beginning of the Chosŏn Dynasty), *Han'guk saron* 韓國史論 3:147–228 (1976).

Han Wŏn-jin 韓元震. *Namdang munjip* 南塘文集 (Collected Works). 22 vols. Date uncertain.

Han Yŏng-u 韓永愚. "Chosŏn wangjo ŭi chŏngch'i, kyŏngje kiban" 朝鮮王朝의政治·經濟基盤 (The Political and Economic Basis of the Chosŏn Dynasty), *Han'guksa*, vol. 9 (q.v.).

———. *Chosŏn chŏn'gi ŭi sahoe sasang* 朝鮮前期의社會思想 (Social Thought at the Beginning of the Chosŏn Dynasty). Seoul: Han'guk Ilbosa 한국日報社, 1976.

———. "Chŏng To-jŏn ŭi in'gan kwa sahoe sasang" 鄭道傳의人間과社會思想 (Chŏng To-jŏn's Social Thought), *Chindan hakpo* 50: 123–135 (1980).

———. Book review of Yi Sŏng-mu's *Chosŏn ch'ogi yangban yŏn'gu* 李成茂.朝鮮初期兩班研究, *Sahoe kwahak p'yŏngnon* 社會科學評論 1:81–109 (June 1982).

———. *Chosŏn chŏn'gi sahoe kyŏngje yŏn'gu* 朝鮮前期社會經濟研究 (Studies of the Economy and Society of Early Chosŏn). Seoul: Ŭryu munhwasa, 1983.

———. *Chŏng To-jŏn sasang ŭi yŏn'gu* 鄭道傳思想의研究 (A Study of the Thought of Chŏng To-jŏn). Rev. ed. Seoul: Sŏul taehakkyo ch'ulp'anbu, 1983.

———. *Chosŏn chŏn'gi sahoe sasang yŏn'gu* 朝鮮前期社會思想研究 (Studies on the Social Thought in the Early Chosŏn Period). Seoul: Chisik sanŏpsa 知識產業社, 1983.

———. "Kija Worship in the Koryŏ and Early Yi Dynasties: A Cultural Symbol in the Relationship between Korea and China," in de Bary and Haboush, eds., *The Rise of Neo-Confucianism in Korea* (q.v.).

———. "Chosŏn ch'ogi sahoe kyech'ŭng yŏn'gu e taehan chaeron" 조선초기사회계층연구에대한재론 (Reexamination of Studies on the Social Structure of Early Chosŏn), *Han'guk saron* 12:305–358 (Feb. 1985).

Hanamura Yoshiki 花村美樹. *Keizai rokuten ni tsuite—Richō kokusho no hōten ni kansuru ichi kōsatsu* 經濟六典について, 李朝國初の法典に関する一考察 (Study on the *Kyŏngje yukchŏn* of the Early Yi Dynasty). Keijō: Keijō Imperial University Studies in Law, no. 5, 1932.

———. "Kōrai ritsu" 高麗律 (Koryŏ Law), *Chōsen shakai hōseishi kenkyū* 朝鮮社會法制史研究 9:1–127 (1937).

Han'guk inmyŏn taesajŏn 韓國人名大事典 (Korean Biographical Dictionary). Seoul: Sin'gu munhwasa 新丘文化社, 1967.

Han'guk sasang taegye 韓國思想大系 (Collection of Essays on Korean Thought), vol. 2: "Sahoe-kyŏngje sasang-p'yŏn" 社會經濟思想編 (Social and Economic Thought). Seoul: Sŏnggyun'gwan taehakkyo 成均館大学校, 1976.

Han'guk sŏngssi tae'gwan 韓國姓氏大觀 (Compendium of Korean Surnames). Seoul: Ch'angjosa 創造社, 1973.

Han'guksa 韓國史 (History of Korea). 25 vols. Seoul: Kuksa p'yŏnch'an wiwŏnhoe, 1973–1979.

Hartwell, Robert. "Demographic, Political, and Social Transformation of China, 750–1550," *Harvard Journal of Asiatic Studies* 42.2:365–442 (Dec. 1982).

Hatada Takashi 旗田巍. *Chōsen chūsei shakaishi no kenkyū* 朝鮮中世社會史の研究 (A Study on the Medieval Society of Korea). Tokyo: Hōsei daigaku shuppankyoku 法政大学出版局, 1972.

Hattori Tamio 服部民夫. "Chosŏn sidae hugi ŭi yangja suyang e kwanhan yŏn'gu" 朝鮮時代後期의養子收養에關한研究 (On Adoption in the Late Chosŏn Period), *Hankuk Hakpo* 11:111–154 (Summer 1978).

Hŏ Hŭng-sik 許興植. "Kukpo hojŏguro pon Koryŏmal ŭi sahoe kujo" 國寶戶籍으로본高麗末의社會構造 (The Social Structure at the End of Koryŏ as Seen through Census Registers), *Han'guksa yŏn'gu* 16:51–147 (April 1977).

―――. *Koryŏ sahoesa yŏn'gu* 高麗社會史研究 (Studies of Koryŏ Society). Seoul: Asea munhwasa 亞細亞文化社, 1981.

―――. *Koryŏ kwagŏ chedosa yŏn'gu* 高麗科擧制度史研究 (Studies of the Examination System in Koryŏ). Seoul: Ilchogak, 1981.

―――. comp. *Han'guk chungse sahoesa charyojip* 韓國中世社會史資料集 (Collection of Documents Concerning the Social History of Koryŏ). Seoul: Asea munhwasa, 1976.

Hoehŏn silgi 晦軒實記 (Records on An Hyang). No date.

Holmgren, Jennifer. "Marriage, kinship and succession under the Ch'itan rulers of the Liao dynasty (907–1125)," *T'oung Pao* 72:44–91 (1986).

―――. "Observations on Marriage and Inheritance Practices in Early Mongol and Yüan Society, with Particular Reference to the Levirate," *Journal of Asian History* 20.2:127–192 (1986).

Hong Sŭng-gi 洪承基. *Koryŏ sidae nobi yŏn'gu* 高麗時代奴婢研究 (Study of Slaves in Koryŏ). Seoul: The Korean Research Center, 1981.

Hsing-li ta-ch'üan 性理大全 (Great Compendium on Human Nature and Principle). Reprint. Seoul. 1978.

Hsü Ching 徐兢. *Kao-li t'u-ching* 高麗圖經 (Report on Koryŏ). Seoul: Asea munhwasa, 1972.

Hucker, Charles O. *The Ming Dynasty: Its Origins and Evolving Institutions.* Ann Arbor: Center for Chinese Studies, The University of Michigan, 1978.

Hwang Chong-hae 黃宗海. *Huch'ŏn-jip* 朽淺集 (Collected Works). 4 vols. 1713.

Hwang Su-yŏng 黃壽永, comp. *Chŭngbo Han'guk kŭmsŏk yumun* 增補韓國金石遺文 (Supplemented Epigraphy of Korea). Seoul: Ilchisa, 1976.

Hwang Ul-long 黃雲龍. *Koryŏ pŏlchok e kwanhan yŏn'gu* 高麗閥族에關한研究 (Study of the Koryŏ Aristocracy). Taegu: Ch'inhaksa 親學社, 1978.

Hymes, Robert P. *Statesmen and Gentlement: The Elite of Fu-Chou, Chiang-Hsi, in Northern and Southern Sung.* Cambridge: Cambridge University Press, 1986.

Hyŏn Sang-yun 玄相允. *Chosŏn yuhaksa* 朝鮮儒学社 (History of Korean Confucianism). Seoul: Minjung sŏgwan 民衆書館, 1949.

Ikeda On, "T'ang Household Registers and Related Documents," in Arthur F. Wright and Denis Twitchett, eds., *Perspectives on the T'ang.* New Haven: Yale University Press, 1973.

Im Ch'un 林椿. *Sŏha-jip* 西河集 (Collected Works), in *Koryŏ myŏnghyŏn-jip* (Works of Famous Confucians of Koryŏ), vol. 2. Seoul: Sŏnggyun'gwan taehakkyo, Taedong munhwa yŏn'guwŏn, 1973.

Johnson, David G. *The Medieval Chinese Oligarchy.* Boulder, Colorado: Westview Press, 1977.

Janelli, Roger L., and Dawnhee Yim Janelli, "Lineage Organization and Social Differentiation in Korea," *Man* (N.S.) 13:272–289 (1978).

———. *Ancestor Worship and Korean Society.* Stanford: Stanford University Press, 1982.

Kaksa sugyo 各司受教 (Royal Edicts Received by Various Government Agencies). Contained in *Sugyo chipyo* (q.v.).

Kalton, Michael C. "The Writings of Kwŏn Kŭn: The Context and Shape of Early Yi Dynasty Neo-Confucianism," in de Bary and Haboush, eds., *The Rise of Neo-Confucianism in Korea* (q.v.).

———. "Early Yi Dynasty Neo-Confucianism: An Integrated Vision," in Laurel Kendall and Griffin Dix, eds., *Religion and Ritual in Korean Society.* Berkeley: Institute of East Asian Studies, University of California, 1987.

Kang Chin-ch'ŏl 姜晋哲. *Koryŏ t'oji chedosa yŏn'gu* 高麗土地制度史

研究 (Land System of Koryŏ). Seoul: Koryŏ taehakkyo ch'ulp'anbu, 1980.

Kang, Hugh Hi-Woong. "The Development of the Korean Ruling Class from Late Silla to Early Koryŏ." Ph.D. dissertation, University of Washington, 1964.

————. "Institutional Borrowing: The Case of the Chinese Civil Service Examination System in Early Koryŏ," *Journal of Asian Studies* 34.1:109–125 (Nov. 1974).

Kang Hŭi-maeng 姜希孟. *Sasukchae-jip* 私淑齋集 (Collected Works). 5 vols. 1942.

Kang Sin-hang 姜信沆, "*Kyerim yusa* 'Koryŏ pangŏn' ŏsŏk" 鷄林類事「高麗方言」語釋 (The *Koryŏ pangŏn* in the *Kyerim yusa*), *Taedong munhwa yŏn'gu* 大東文化研究 10:1–91 (Dec. 1975).

Kanshū chōsa hōkokusho 慣習調査報告書 (Report on Investigations into Korean Customs). Keijō: Chōsen sōtokufu, 1912.

Kawashima, Fujiya. "Lineage Elite and Bureaucracy in Early Yi to Mid-Yi Dynasty Korea," *Occasional Papers on Korea* 5:8–19 (1977).

————. "A Study of the *Hyangan*: Kin Groups and Aristocratic Localism in the Seventeenth- and Eighteenth-Century Korea Countryside," *Journal of Korean Studies* 5:3–38 (1984).

Kendall, Laurel, and Mark Peterson, eds. *Korean Women: View from the Inner Room.* New Haven, Conn.: East Rock Press, 1983.

———— and Griffin Dix, eds. *Religion and Ritual in Korean Society.* Berkeley: Institute of East Asian Studies, University of California, 1987.

Ki Tae-sŭng 奇大升. *Kobong sŏnsaeng munjip* 高峰先生文集 (Collected Works). 5 vols. 1630.

Kil Chae 吉再. *Yaŭn sŏnsaeng sokchip* 冶隱先生續集 (Collected Works), in *Yŏgye myŏnghyŏn-jip* (q.v.).

Kim An-guk 金安國. *Chŏngsok ŏnhae* 正俗諺解 (Vernacular Version of *Chŏngsok*). No date.

————. *Mojae sŏnsaeng-jip* 慕齋先生集 (Collected Works). 15 kwŏn. 1687.

Kim Chang-saeng 金長生. *Ŭirye munhae* 疑禮問解 (Questions and Answers on Doubtful Passages of the Rites). 4 kwŏn. 1646.

————. *Karye chimnam* 家禮輯覽 (Collected Commentaries to the *Chia-li*).

————. *Sagye sŏnsaeng chŏnsŏ* 沙溪先生全書 (Collected works of Kim Chang-saeng). 24 vols. Date uncertain.

Kim Chip 金集. *Ŭirye munhaesok* 疑禮問解續 (Supplement to Questions and Answers on Doubtful Passages of the Rites). Date uncertain.

Kim Ch'ŏl-chun 金哲埈. "Silla sangdae sahoe ŭi Dual Organization" 新羅上代社會의 Dual Organization (Dual Organization in the Society of Early Silla), *Yŏksa hakpo* 1:15–47 (July 1952) and 2:85–115 (Oct. 1952).

Kim Chŏng-guk 金正國. *Kyŏngminp'yŏn* 警民編 (For Advising the People). Date uncertain.

Kim Chong-jik 金宗直. *Ijollok* 彝尊錄 (Records on Morality). 1528.

Kim Pu-sik 金富軾. *Samguk sagi* 三國史記 (Historical Records of the Three Kingdoms). Kim Chong-gwŏn 金鍾權, tr. Seoul: Kwangjin munhwasa 光進文化社, 1963.

Kim Pyŏng-gu 金柄九. *Hoehŏn sasang yŏn'gu* 晦軒思想研究 (Study of An Hyang's Thought). Seoul: Hangmunsa 学文社, 1983.

Kim Sang-gi 金庠基. *Koryŏ sidaesa* 高麗時代史 (History of Koryŏ). Seoul: Tongguk munhwasa 東國文化社, 1961.

―――. "Yi Ik-chae ŭi chae Wŏn saengae e taehayŏ" 李益齋의在元生涯에對하여 (Yi Che-hyŏn's Life in Yüan). *Taedong munhwa yŏn'gu* 1:219–244 (Aug. 1963).

Kim Si-sŭp 金時習. *Maewŏltang-jip* 梅月堂集 (Collected Works). Reprint. Seoul: Asea munhwasa, 1973.

Kim Sŏn-gon 金善坤. "Yijo ch'ogi pibin ko" 李朝初期妃嬪考 (A Study on the Queen and the Royal Concubines in the Early Yi Dynasty), *Yŏksa hakpo* 21:33–65 (Aug. 1963).

Kim Sŏng-il 金誠一. *Hakpong munjip* 鶴峯文集 (Collected Works). 16 kwŏn. 1851.

Kim Su-on 金守溫. *Sigu-jip* 拭疣集 (Collected Works), in *Yijo myŏnghyŏn-jip*, vol. 2 (q.v.).

Kim Su-t'ae 金壽泰. "Koryŏ pon'gwan chedo ŭi sŏngnip" 高麗本貫制度의成立 (The Establishment of the *pon'gwan* System in Koryŏ), *Chindan hakpo* 52:41–64 (Oct. 1981).

Kim Taek-kyu 金宅圭. *Ssijok purak ŭi kujo yŏn'gu* 氏族部落의構造研究 (Study on the Structure of Single-Surname Villages). Seoul: Ilchogak, 1979.

Kim Tong-su 金東洙. "Koryŏ sidae ŭi sangp'ije" 高麗時代의相避制 (The Law of Avoidance during Koryŏ), *Yŏksa hakpo* 102:1–30 (June 1984).

Kim Tu-hŏn 金斗憲. *Han'guk kajok chedo yŏn'gu* 韓國家族制度研究 (Study of the Korean Family System). Seoul: Sŏul taehakkyo ch'ulp'anbu, 1969.

Kim Ŭi-gyu 金毅圭. "Silla mogyeje sahoesŏl e taehan kŏmt'o―Silla ch'injok yŏn'gu, kiil" 新羅母系制社會説에對한檢討. 新羅親族研究, 其一 (A Critical Study of Matrilinealism in Silla Dynasty―Kinship System of Silla, Part I), *Han'guksa yŏn'gu* 23:41–64 (March 1979).

Kim Yong-man 金容晚. *Chosŏn sidae kyunbun sangsokche e kwanhan il yŏn'gu* 朝鮮時代均分相續制에關한一研究 (A Study of the Equal Inheritance Law of Chosŏn Korea). Sŏngnam-si: M.A. thesis, Han'guk chŏngsin munhwa yŏn'guwŏn, 1982.

―――. "Chosŏn sidae chaeji sajok ŭi chaesan soyu hyŏngt'ae I" 朝鮮時代在地士族의財産所有形態 I (Property of the Landed Aristocracy of the Chosŏn Period), *Taegu sahak* 大丘史学 27:89–159 (1985).

Kim Yong-sŏn 金龍善. *Koryŏ ŭmsŏ chedo ŭi yŏn'gu* 高麗蔭敍制度의研究 (Study of the Protection Privilege in Koryŏ). Ph.D. dissertation, Sŏgang University (Seoul), 1985.

Kim Yong-suk 金用淑. *Yijo yŏryu munhak mit kungjung p'ungsok ŭi yŏn'gu* 李朝女流文学및宮中風俗의研究 (The Works of Women Writers and Court Ways during the Yi Dynasty). Seoul: Sookmyung Women's University, 1970.

Ko Pyŏng-ik 高柄翊. *Tonga kyosŏpsa ŭi yŏn'gu* 東亜交渉史의研究 (Study of East Asian Diplomatic History). Seoul: Sŏul taehakkyo ch'ulp'anbu, 1970.

Komunsŏ chipchin 古文書集真 (Collection of Old Documents Preserved in Seoul National University). Seoul: Sŏul taehakkyo pusok tosŏgwan 서울大学校附属圖書館, 1972.

Kōrai izen no fūzoku kankei shiryō satsuyō 高麗以前の風俗關係資料撮要 (Materials Concerning Customs of the Koryŏ Period). Keijō: Chōsen sōtokufu, Chūsū-in, 1941.

Koryŏ-Chosŏn ch'ogi ŭi hakcha kuin 高麗-朝鮮初期의学者9人 (Nine Scholars of Koryŏ and the Beginning of Chosŏn). Seoul: Sin'gu munhwasa, 1974.

Koryŏsa 高麗史 (History of Koryŏ). Reprint. Seoul: Yŏnhŭi taehakkyo, Tongbanghak yŏn'guso 延禧大学校, 東方学研究所, 1955.

Koryŏsa chŏryo 高麗史節要 (Condensed History of Koryŏ). Reprint. Seoul: Kojŏn kanhaenghoe, 1960.

Ku Pyŏng-sak 丘秉朔. *Han'guk sahoebŏpchesa t'ŭksu yŏn'gu* 韓國社會法制史特殊研究 (A Study on the History of Law in Korea). Seoul: Tonga ch'ulp'ansa 東亜出版社, 1968.

Ku T'ang-lü shu-i 舊唐律疏義 (Law Code of the T'ang Dynasty). Reprint. Taipei: no date.

Kukcho oryeŭi 國朝五禮儀 (Manual of the Five State Rites). Reprint. Seoul: Kyŏngmunsa 景文社, 1979.

Kwangsan Kim-ssi Och'ŏn komunsŏ 光山金氏烏川古文書 (Old Documents of the Yean Branch of the Kwangsan Kim). Sŏngnam-si: Han-guk chŏngsin munhwa yŏn'guwŏn, 1982.

Kwŏn Chae-sŏn 權在善. "Yŏdae ch'injok mit namnyŏ hoch'ingŏ e taehan koch'al" 麗代親族및男女呼稱語에對한考察 (Study of Terms of Address between Male and Female and between Relatives during Koryŏ), in *Han'gugŏ munhak taegye* 韓國語文学大系 (Handbook of

Korean Language and Literature), comp. by Han'gugŏ munhakhoe 韓國語文学會. Seoul: Hyŏngsŏl ch'ulp'ansa 螢雪出版社, 1975.

Kwŏn Kŭn 權近. *Yangch'on munjip* 陽村文集 (Collected Works). 2 vols. Reprint. Seoul: 1969.

———. *Iphak tosŏl* 入学圖説 (Illustrated Treatises for the Beginner), Kwŏn Tŏk-chu 權德周, tr. *Ŭryu mun'go*, vol. 131. Seoul: Ŭryu munhwasa, 1974.

———. *Yegi ch'ŏn'gyŏllok* 禮記淺見錄 (Annotations to the Book of Rites). Reprint. Seoul: no date.

Kyŏngguk taejŏn 經國大典 (Great Code of Administration). Keijō: Chōsen sōtokufu, Chūsū-in, 1934.

Lee, Hochol. "Rice Culture and Demographic Development in Korea, c. 1429–1918," in Akira Hayami and Yoshihiro Tsubouchi, eds. *Economic and Demographic Development in Rice Producing Societies—Some Aspects of East Asian Economic History, 1500–1900.* Papers presented to the Tokyo Workshop on "Economic and Demographic development in Rice Producing Societies," September 11–15, 1989.

Lee, Ki-baik. *A New History of Korea.* Edward W. Wagner tr., with Edward J. Shultz. Seoul: Ilchogak, 1984.

Legge, James, tr. *I Ching: Book of Changes*, ed. with an Introduction and Study Guide by Ch'u Chae with Winberg Chai. New York: University Books, 1964.

———. tr. *Li Chi: Book of Rites*. See *Li Chi*.

Lévi-Strauss, Claude. *The Elementary Structures of Kinship*. J. H. Bell, J. R. von Sturmer, and Rodney Needham, trs. London: Social Science Paperbacks, 1969.

Lewis, I. M., ed. *History and Social Anthropology*. London: Tavistock Publications, 1968.

Li-chi 禮記 (Book of Rites).

Li Chi: Book of Rites. An Encyclopedia of Ancient Ceremonial Usages, Religious Creeds, and Social Institutions. James Legge, tr. Ed. with Introduction and Study Guide by Ch'u Chae and Winberg Chai. 2 vols. New York: University Books, 1967.

Li Ogg. *Recherche sur l'Antiquité Coréenne: Ethnie et Société de Koguryŏ*. Paris: Collège de France, Centre d'Etudes Coréennes, 1980.

Liu, Ts'un-yan, and Judith Berling, "The 'Three Teachings' in the Mongol-Yüan Period," in Chan and de Bary, eds., *Yüan Thought* (q.v.)

Lun-yü 論語 (The Analects of Confucius). Szu-pu pei-yao, ed. Reprint. Shanghai: Commercial Press, no date.

Mair, Lucy. *Marriage*. Harmondsworth: Penguin Books, 1971.

Mansŏng taedongbo 萬姓大同譜 (Genealogical Recordings). Reprint. No date.

McCullough, William H. "Japanese Marriage Institutions in the Late Heian Period," *Harvard Journal of Asiatic Studies* 27:103–167 (1967).

McMullen, I. J. "Non-Agnatic Adoption: A Confucian Controversy in Seventeenth- and Eighteenth-Century Japan," *Harvard Journal of Asiatic Studies* 35:133–189 (1975).

Mencius, Works of.

Michell, Tony. "Fact and Hypothesis in Yi Dynasty Economic History: The Demographic Dimension," *Korean Studies Forum* 6:65–93 (1979–1980).

Min Hyŏn-gu 閔賢九. "Sin Ton ŭi chipkwŏn kwa kŭ chŏngch'ijŏk sŏng-kyŏk" 辛旽의 執權과 그 政治的 性格 (Sin Ton's Seizure of Power and His Political Significance), *Yŏksa hakpo* 38:46–88 (Aug. 1968) and 40: 53–119 (Dec. 1968).

———. "Koryŏ hugi ŭi kwŏnmun sejok" 高麗後期의 權門世族 (The Powerful Families of Late Koryŏ), in *Han'guksa*, vol. 8 (q.v.).

———. "Cho In-gyu wa kŭ ŭi kamun, sang" 趙仁規와 그의 家門, 上 (Cho In-gyu and His family, part 1), *Chindan hakpo* 42:17–28 (1976).

———. "Cho In-gyu wa kŭ ŭi kamun, chung" 趙仁規와 그의 家門, 中 (Cho In-gyu and His Family, Part 2), *Chindan hakpo* 43:5–32 (1977).

———. "T'oji chedo" 土地制度 (Land System), in *Han'guk saron* 韓國史論 (*Koryŏ-p'yŏn* 高麗編). Seoul: Kuksa p'yŏnch'an wiwŏnhoe, 1977.

Ming hui-yao 明會要 (Statutes of the Ming Dynasty). 2 vols. Peking, 1957.

Minji kanshū kaitō ishū 民事慣習回答彙集 (Collection of Customary Replies in Civil Litigations). Keijō: Chōsen sōtokufu, Chūsū-in, 1933.

Miryang Pak-ssi Sungmin-gongp'a sebo 密陽朴氏肅愍公派世譜 (Genealogy of the Miryang Pak, Branch of Mr. Sungmin [Pak Sŭng-jong 朴承宗]). Date uncertain.

Morohashi Tetsuji 諸橋轍次. *Daikanwa jiten* 大漢和辭典 (Great Chinese-Japanese Dictionary). Tokyo: Daishūkan shoten 大修館書店, 1955.

Morris, Ivan. *The World of the Shining Prince: Court Life in Ancient Japan*. London: Oxford University Press, 1964.

Munhwa Yu-ssi 文化柳氏世譜 (Genealogy of the Munhwa Yu), 1565.

Murdock, George P. *Social Structure*. New York: The Free Press, 1949.

———. "Cognatic Forms of Social Organization," as reprinted in Paul Bohannan and John Middleton, eds., *Kinship and Social Organization*. New York: The Natural History Press, 1968.

Naehun 內訓 (Instructions for Women). Kim Chi-yong 金智勇, ed. Seoul: Yŏnse taehakkyo, Inmun kwahak yŏn'guso, 1969.

Naehun-Yŏsasŏ 內訓, 女四書 (Instructions for Women). Reprint. Seoul: Asea munhwasa, 1974.

Naitō Kichinosuke 内藤吉之助. "*Keikoku taiten* no nansan" 經國大典の難産 (Difficult Origin of *Kyŏngguk taejŏn*), *Chōsen shakai hōseishi kenkyū* 9:129–256 (1937).

Nam Hang-myŏng 南鶴鳴. *Hoeŭn-jip* 晦隱集 (Collected Works). 5 kwŏn. Date uncertain.

Niida Noboru 仁井田陞. *Tōryō shūi* 唐令拾遺 (Remnants of T'ang Law). 1933. Reprint. Tokyo, 1964.

———. "Kōrai oyobi Rishi Chōsen no zaisan sōzokuhō to Chūgokuhō" 高麗および李氏朝鮮の財産相續法と中國法 (Property Inheritance Law of Koryŏ and Yi Dynasty and Chinese Law), *Chōsen gakuhō* 30:1–10 (1964.1).

Nivison, David S., and Arthur F. Wright, eds. *Confucianism in Action*. Stanford: Stanford University Press, 1959.

No Myŏng-ho 盧明鎬. "Koryŏ ŭi obokch'in kwa ch'injok kwan'gye pŏpche" 高麗의 五服親과 親族關係法制 (Relatives within the Five Mourning Grades and the Legislative System of Kinship in Koryŏ), *Han'guksa yŏn'gu* 33:1–42 (une 1981).

———. "Koryŏsi ŭi sŭngŭm hyŏlchok kwa kwijokch'ŭng ŭi ŭmsŏ kihoe" 高麗時의 承蔭血族과 貴族層의 蔭敍機會 (Protection Appointments of the Aristocracy in Koryŏ), in *Kim Ch'ŏl-chun paksa hwagap kinyŏm sahak nonch'ong* 金哲埈博士花甲紀念史学論叢 (Festschrift for Kim Ch'ŏl-chun). Seoul: Chisik sanŏpsa, 1983.

———. "Koryŏ ch'ogi wangsil ch'ulsin ŭi hyangni seryŏk—Yŏch'o ch'insoktŭl ŭi chŏngch'i seryŏkhwa yangt'ae" 高麗初期王室出身의 '鄕里' 勢力－麗初親屬들의 政治勢力化樣態 (Local Power of the Members of the Royal House in Early Koryŏ), in Pyŏn T'ae-sŏp, ed., *Koryŏsa ŭi chemunje* (Problems of Koryŏ History). Seoul: Samyŏngsa, 1986.

———. "Yi Cha-gyŏm ilp'a wa Han An-in ilp'a ŭi choktang seryŏk—Koryŏ chunggi ch'insoktŭl ŭi chŏngch'i seryŏkhwa yangt'ae" 李資謙一派와 韓安仁一派의 族黨勢力－高麗中期親屬들의 政治勢力化樣態 (Factional Power of Yi Cha-gyŏm's and Han An-in's Factions—The Political Strengthening of Kin Groups in Mid Koryŏ), *Han'guk saron* 17:167–225 (Aug. 1987).

Oda Shōgo 小田省吾. "Richō seisō ryakushi" 李朝政爭畧史 (An Outline History of Political Strife in the Yi Dynasty), in his *Chōsen shi kōza, bunrui shi* 朝鮮史講座, 分類史 (Lectures on Korean History). Keijō:

Chōsenshi gakkai 朝鮮史学會, 1924.

Osgood, Cornelius. *The Koreans and Their Culture.* New York: The Ronald Press Company, 1951.

Paek Mun-bo 白文寶. *Tamam ilchip* 淡庵逸集 (Collected Works), in *Koryŏ myŏnghyŏn-jip* 高麗名賢集 (Works of Famous Confucians of Koryŏ), vol. 5. Seoul: Sŏnggyun'gwan taehakkyo, Taedong munhwa yŏn'guwŏn, 1980.

Paek Sŭng-jong 白承鍾. "Koryŏ hugi ŭi p'alcho hogu" 高麗後期의 八祖戶口 (On the *p'alcho hogu* in Late Koryŏ), *Hankuk Hakpo* 34:191–213 (Spring 1984).

Paekch'ŏn Cho-ssi sebo 白川趙氏世譜 (Genealogy of the Paekch'ŏn Cho). 1880.

Pak Ch'ŏn-gyu 朴天圭. "Yangch'on Kwŏn Kŭn yŏn'gu" 陽村權近研究 (Study of Kwŏn Kŭn), *Sach'ong* 史叢 9:1–50 (Dec. 1964).

Pak Chong-hong 朴鍾鴻. *Han'guk sasangsa non'go* 韓國思想史論攷 (Studies of Korean Thought). Seoul: Sŏmundang 瑞文堂, 1977.

Pak Kŏn-jung 朴建中. *Sangnye piyobo* 喪禮備要補 (Supplement to *Sangnye piyo*). 1645.

Pak Pyŏng-ho 朴秉濠. *Han'guk pŏpchesa-go* 韓國法制史攷 (Studies of the Legal History of Korea). Seoul: Pŏmmunsa 法文社, 1974.

———. "Han'guk ŭi chŏnt'ong kajok kwa kajanggwŏn" 韓國의 傳統家族과家長權 (The Traditional Family and Right of Family Head in Korea), *Hankuk Hakpo* 2.1:67–93 (spring 1976).

Pak Se-ch'ae 朴世采. *Namgye yesŏl* 南溪禮説 (Namgye's Theories on Ritual). 1718.

———. *Namgye-jip* 南溪集 (Collected Works). 9 vols. Date uncertain.

Pak Se-mu 朴世茂. *Tongmong sŏnsŭp* 童蒙先習 (First Training for the Young and Ignorant). Original text with translation by Yi Sŏk-ho 李錫浩. Seoul: Ŭryu munhwasa, 1971.

Pak Su-ch'un 朴壽春. *Kuktam-jip* 菊潭集 (Collected Works). 2 vols. 1725.

Pak Ŭn 朴訔. *Choŭn sŏnsaeng munjip* 釣隱先生文集 (Collected Works of Pak Ŭn). Reprint. Seoul, 1979.

Pak Yong-un 朴龍雲. "Koryŏ sidae ŭi Haeju Ch'oe-ssi wa P'ap'yŏng Yun-ssi kamun punsŏk" 高麗時代의海州崔氏와坡平尹氏家門分析 (An Analysis of the Haeju Ch'oe-ssi and the P'ap'yŏng Yun-ssi), *Paeksan hakpo* 白山学報 23:121–153 (Dec. 1977).

———. "Koryŏ chŏn'gi munban kwa muban ŭi sinbun munje" 高麗前期文班과武班의身分問題 (Problems Concerning the Social Status of Civil and Military Officials in Early Koryŏ), *Han'guksa yŏn-gu* 21–22:33–66 (Dec. 1978).

———. "Koryŏ sidae ŭi Chŏngan Im-ssi, Ch'ŏrwŏn Ch'oe-ssi, Kongam Hŏ-ssi kamun punsŏk" 高麗時代의定安任氏, 鐵原崔氏, 孔巖許氏家門分析 (An Analysis of the Chŏngan Im-ssi, the Ch'ŏrwŏn Ch'oe-ssi, and the Kongam Hŏ-ssi), *Han'guksa nonch'ong* 韓國史論叢 3:43–81 (Dec. 1978).

———. "Koryŏ sidae ŭmsŏje ŭi silche wa kŭ kinŭng, sang" 高麗時代蔭敍制의實際와그機能, 上 (On the Protection Privilege in Koryŏ and Its Function, Part 1), *Han'guksa yŏn'gu* 36:1–35 (March 1982).

———. "Koryŏ sidae ŭmsŏje ŭi silche wa kŭ kinŭng, ha" 高麗時代蔭敍制의實際와그機能, 下 (On the Protection Privilege in Koryŏ and Its Function, Part 2), *Han'guksa yŏn'gu* 37:1–39 (une 1982).

———. *Koryŏ sidaesa, sang* 高麗時代史, 上 (History of Koryŏ, Part 1). Seoul: Ilchisa, 1985.

———. "Koryŏ sidae ŭi ŭmsŏje e kwanhan myŏt kaji munje" 高麗時代의蔭敍制에關한몇가지問題 (On Various Problems Concerning the Protection Privilege in Koryŏ), in Pyŏn T'ae-sŏp, ed., *Koryŏsa ŭi chemunje* (Problems of Koryŏ History). Seoul: Samyŏngsa, 1986.

Palais, James B. *Politics and Policy in Traditional Korea.* Cambridge: Harvard University Press, 1975.

———. "Han Yŏng-u's Studies of Early Chosŏn Intellectual History," review article in *Journal of Korean Studies* 2:199–224 (1980).

———. "Land Tenure in Korea: Tenth to Twelfth Centuries," *Journal of Korean Studies* 4:73–205 (1982–1983).

———. "Slavery and Slave Society in the Koryŏ Period," *Journal of Korean Studies* 5:173–190 (1984).

———. "Confucianism and the Aristocratic/Bureaucratic Balance in Korea," *Harvard Journal of Asiatic Studies* 44.2:427–468 (1984).

Pannam Pak-ssi sebo 潘南朴氏世譜 (Genealogy of the Pannam Pak). 20 vols. 1831.

Peterson, Mark. "Adoption in Korean Genealogies," *Korea Journal* 14:28–35 (Jan. 1974).

———. "The Puan Kims: A Case Study in Social Change in Mid Yi Korea." Unpublished paper. 1983.

———. "The Mid Yi Dynasty Transformation of the Korean Family and Lineage: An Examination of Adoption and Inheritance Practices." Ph.D. dissertation, Harvard University, 1987.

P'i Yŏng- hŭi 皮瑛姫. "Double Descent iron chŏgyong ŭl t'onghaesŏ pon Silla wang ŭi sinbun kwannyŏm" Double Descent 理論適用을通해서본新羅王의身分觀念 (Social Status of the Silla Royal House Seen through the Applicability of the Double-Descent Theory), *Han'guk saron* 5:65–105 (Oct. 1979).

Po-hu t'ung 白虎通 (The Comprehensive Discussions in the White Tiger

Hall). Tjan Tjoe Som, tr. 2 vols. Leiden: E. J. Brill, 1949.

Potter, Jack M. "Land and Lineage in Traditional China," in Maurice Freedman, ed., *Family and Kinship in Chinese Society* (q.v.).

Provine, Robert C. *Essays on Sino-Korean Musicology: Early Sources for Korean Ritual Music.* Seoul: Il Ji Sa, 1988.

Puan Kim-ssi Uban komunsŏ 扶安金氏愚磻古文書 (Old Documents of the Puan Kim). Sŏngnam-si: Han'guk chŏngsin munhwa yŏn'guwŏn, 1983.

Pyŏn Kye-ryang 卞季良. *Ch'unjŏng munjip* 春亭文集 (Collected Works). 12 kwŏn. 1824.

Pyŏn T'ae-sŏp 邊太燮. *Koryŏsa ŭi chemunje* 高麗史의諸問題 (Problems of Koryŏ History). Seoul: Samyŏngsa 三英社, 1986.

――――. "*Koryŏsa, Koryŏsa chŏryo* ŭi saron" 高麗史, 高麗史節要의史論 (Discussion on the *Koryŏsa* and the *Koryŏsa chŏryo*), *Sach'ong* 21–22:113–133 (Oct. 1977).

――――. *Koryŏ chŏngch'i chedosa yŏn'gu* 高麗政治制度史研究 (Studies of the Political System of Koryŏ). Seoul: Ilchogak, 1971.

――――. "Musillan e ŭihan sinbun chedo ŭi pyŏnjil" 武臣亂에依한身分制度의變質 (Changes of the Social Status System through the Military Upheavals), *Sahak yŏn'gu* 史学研究 13:144–153 (June 1962).

P'yŏngsan Sin-ssi kyebo. 平山申氏系譜. (Genealogy of the P'yŏngsan Sin). 1976.

Reflections on Things at Hand: The Neo-Confucian Anthology Compiled by Chu Hsi and Lü Tsu-ch'ien. Translated with Notes by Wing-tsit Chan. New York: Columbia University Press, 1967.

Richō hōten kō 李朝法典考 (Study of the Law Codes of the Yi Dynasty). Keijō: Chōsen sōtokufu, Chūsū-in, 1936.

Richō no zaisan sōzoku hō 李朝の財産相續法 (The Inheritance of Property in the Yi Dynasty). Keijō: Chōsen sōtokufu, Chūsū-in, 1936.

Rogers, Michael C. "Sung-Koryŏ Relations: Some Inhibiting Factors," *Oriens* 11:194–202 (1958).

――――. "*P'yŏnnyŏn T'ongnok*: The Foundation Legend of the Koryŏ State," *Journal of Korean Studies* 4:3–72 (1982–1983).

Rotours, Robert Des. *Le Traité des Examens.* Pairs: Librairie Ernest Leroux, 1932.

Sansom, G. B. *Japan: A Short Cultural History.* London: The Cresset Press, 1952.

Sasong yuch'wi 詞訟類聚 (Collection of Judicial Cases). Seoul: Pŏp-chech'ŏ 法制處, 1964.

Sasse, Werner. *Das Glossar Koryŏ-pangŏn im Kyerim-yusa.* Wiesbaden:

Otto Harrassowitz, 1976.

Schwartz, Benjamin I. *The World of Thought in Ancient China*. Cambridge: Harvard University Press, 1985.

Service, Elman R. *Primitive Social Organization*. 2nd ed. New York: Random House, 1971.

Seidensticker, Edward, tr. *The Gossamer Years: Kagero nikki, The Diary of a Nobleman of Heian Japan*. Tokyo: C.E. Tuttle, 1975.

Shaw, William. "The Neo-Confucian Revolution of Values in Early Yi Korea: Its Implications for Korean Legal Thought," in Brian E. McKnight, ed., *Law and the State in Traditional East Asia: Six Studies on the Sources of East Asian Law*. Honolulu: University of Hawaii Press, 1987.

Shikata Hiroshi 四方博. "Richō jinkō ni kansuru ichi kenkyū" 李朝人口に関する一研究 (Study of the Korean Population during the Yi Dynasty), *Chōsen shakai hōsei shi kenkyū* 9:257–368 (1937).

Shima, Mutsuhiko. "In Quest of Social Recognition: A Retrospective View on the Development of Korean Lineage Organization," *Harvard Journal of Asiatic Studies* 50.1:87–129 (June 1990).

Shin, Susan S. "Land Tenure and the Agrarian Economy in Yi Dynasty Korea: 1600–1800." Ph.D. dissertation, Harvard University, 1973.

————. "The Social Structure of Kŭmhwa County in the Late Seventeenth Century," *Occasional Papers on Korea* 1:9–35 (1974).

————. "Some Aspects of Landlord-Tenant Relations in Yi Dynasty Korea," *Occasional Papers on Korea* 3:49–88 (1975).

Shultz, Edward J. "Institutional Developments in Korea under the Ch'oe House: 1196–1258." Ph.D. dissertation, University of Hawaii, 1976.

————. "Twelfth-Century Koryŏ Politics: The Rise of Han Anin and His Partisans," *The Journal of Korean Studies* 6:3–38 (1988–1989).

Sin Chŏng-suk 申貞淑. "Saengjon nobuin ŭi mun'gyŏn ch'aerok" 生存老婦人의 聞見採錄 (Materials from Interviews of Old Ladies), *Kugŏ kungmunhak* 국어국문학 58– 60:321–340 (Dec. 1972).

————. "Han'guk chŏnt'ong sahoe punyŏ ŭi hoch'ingŏ wa chonbiŏ" 韓國傳統社會婦女의 呼稱語와 尊卑語 (Terminology and Speech Levels of Traditional Korean Women), *Kugŏ kungmunhak* 65–66:199–213 (Dec. 1974).

Sin Kŭn 申近. *Ŭirye yusŏl* 疑禮類説 (Various Theories on Doubtful Passages in the Rites). 1792.

Sin Sŏk-ho 申奭鎬. *Han'guk saryo haesŏlchip* 韓國史料解説集 (Collection of Commentaries on Historical Materials of Korea). Seoul: Han-guk sahakhoe 韓國史学會, 1964.

Sin Suk-chu 申叔舟. *Pohanjae-jip* 保閑齋集 (Collected Works). 4 vols. 1645.

Smith, Robert J. "Stability in Japanese Kinship Terminology: The Historical Evidence," in Robert J. Smith and Richard K. Beardsley, eds., *Japanese Culture: Its Development and Characteristics.* Chicago: Aldine Publishing Company, 1962.

Sohn Pow-key. "Social History of the Early Yi Dynasty, 1392–1592." Ph.D. dissertation, University of California, Berkeley, 1963.

Sohye wanghu Han-ssi 昭惠王后韓氏. *Naehun* 內訓 (Instructions for Women). 1475. Reprint. Seoul: Asea munhwasa, 1969.

Sok taejŏn 續大典 (Amended Great Code). 1746. Reprint. Keijō: Chōsen sōtokufu, Chūsū-in, 1938.

Somerville, John N. "Success and Failure in Eighteenth Century Ulsan." Ph.D. dissertation, Harvard University, 1974.

Son Chin-t'ae 孫晋泰. "Chosŏn honin ŭi chuyo hyŏngt'ae in solsŏ honsok ko" 朝鮮婚姻의主要形態인率婿婚俗考 (Study on Chosŏn's Principal Marriage Form: *solsŏ*), in *Chosŏn minjok munhwa ŭi yŏn'gu* 朝鮮民族文化의研究 (Studies on Korean Folk Culture). Seoul: Ŭryu munhwasa, 1948.

Song Ch'an-sŏp 宋讚燮. "17·18 segi sinjŏn kaegan ŭi hwaktae wa kyŏngyŏng hyŏngt'ae" 17·18世紀新田開墾의擴大와經營形態 (The Expansion of Land Reclamation and Its Management in the Seventeenth and Eighteenth Centuries), *Han'guk saron* 12:231–304 (Feb. 1985).

Song Chun- gil 宋浚吉. *Tongch'undang-jip* 同春堂集 (Collected Works). 18 vols. 1768.

Song Chun-ho (Song June-ho) 宋俊浩. "The Government Examination Rosters of the Yi Dynasty," in Spencer J. Palmer, ed., *Studies in Asian Genealogy.* Provo: Brigham Young University Press, 1972.

———. "Han'guge issŏsŏ ŭi kagye kirok ŭi yŏksa wa kŭ haesŏk" 韓國에있어서의家系記錄의歷史와그解釋 (An Interpretative History of Family Records in Traditional Korea), *Yŏksa hakpo* 87:99–143 (1980).

———. "Chosŏn yangban ko" 朝鮮兩班考 (A Study of Yangban in Chosŏn Korea), *Han'guk sahak* 4:27– 357 (1983).

———. "Han'guk ŭi ssijokche e issŏsŏ ŭi pon'gwan mit sijo ŭi munje" 韓國의氏族制에있어서의本貫및始祖의問題 (The Origin and Nature of *pon'gwan* and *sijo* in the Korean Clan System), *Yŏksa hakpo* 109:91–136 (March 1986).

———. *Chosŏn sahoesa yŏn'gu* 朝鮮社會史研究 (Studies on the Social History of Chosŏn). Seoul: Ilchogak, 1987.

Sŏng Hon 成渾. *Ugye-jip* 牛溪集 (Collected Works). Reprint. Seoul: Asea munhwasa, 1979.

Sŏng Hyŏn 成俔. *Hŏbaektang-jip* 虛白堂集 (Collected Works). 8 vols. Date uncertain.

———. *Yongjae ch'onghwa* 慵齋叢話 (Collected Tales of Sŏng Hyŏn). Reprint. Taipei: The Oriental Cultural Service, 1971.

Song, June-ho. *See* Song Chun-ho.

Sprenkel, S. van der. *Legal Institutions in Manchu China: A Sociological Analysis.* London: The Athlone Press, 1962.

Steele, John. *The I-li or Book of Etiquette and Ceremonial.* Translated from the Chinese with Introduction, Notes and Plans. London: Probsthain, 1917.

Sudō Yoshiyuki 周藤吉之. "Raimatsu Sensho ni okeru nōsō ni tsuite" 麗末鮮初における農莊について (On the Estates of the Late Koryŏ and Early Chosŏn Dynasties), *Seikyū gakusō* 青丘学叢 17:1–80 (Aug. 1934).

———. "Sensho ni okeru dohi no benshō to suisatsu to ni tsuite" 鮮初における奴婢の辨正と推刷とに就いて (On the Management of Slaves in the Early Yi Dynasty), *Seikyū gakusō* 22:1–61 (Nov. 1935).

Sugyo chimnok 受教輯錄 (Collection of Royal Edicts). Contained in the *Sugyo chipyo* (q.v.).

Sugyo chipyo 受教輯要 (Compendium of Royal Edicts). Keijō: Chōsen sōtokufu, Chūsū-in, 1943.

Sung-shih 宋史 (History of Sung). 40 vols. Shanghai: Chung-hua shu-chü ch'u-pan, 1977.

Sunhŭng An-ssi chokpo 順興安氏族譜 (Genealogy of the Sunhŭng An). 1864.

Tae Myŏngnyul chikhae 大明律直解 (Literal Explanation of the Ming Code). Reprint. Keijō: Chōsen sōtokufu, Chūsū-in, 1937.

Taejŏn songnok kŭp chuhae 大典續錄及註解 (Additions to *Kyŏngguk taejŏn* and Annotations). Keijō: Chōsen sōtokufu, Chūsū-in, 1935.

Taejŏn t'ongp'yŏn 大典通編 (Comprehensive Great Code). 1785. Seoul: Pŏpchech'ŏ 法制處 1963.

Takeda Yukio 武田幸男. "Kōraichō ni okeru kōindensaihō no igi" 高麗朝における功蔭田柴法の意義 (The meaning of *kongŭm* and *chŏnsikwa* in Koryŏ), in *Niida Noboru hakase tsuitō ronbunshū* 仁井田陞博士追悼論文集 (Collection of Articles in Memory of Niida Noboru), vol. 1. Tokyo: Keisō Shobō, 1967.

———. "Kōrai dentei no saikentō" 高麗田丁の再檢討 (Further Investigation of the *chŏnjŏng* in Koryŏ), *Chōsenshi kenkyūkai ronbunshū* 朝鮮史研究會論文集 8:1–37 (March 1971).

Ta-Ming hui-tien 大明會典 (Statutes of the Great Ming). Reprint of 1587 ed., 1963.

Teng, Ssu-yü, and Knight Biggerstaff. *An Annotated Bibliography of Selected Chinese Reference Works.* Rev. ed. Cambridge, Harvard University Press, 1950.

Tŏksu Yi- ssi sebo 德水李氏世譜 (Genealogy of the Tŏksu Yi).

T'ung-tien 通典 (Encyclopedia of Rites). Tu Yu 杜佑, comp. Reprint. Taipei, 1963.

Twitchett, Denis C. *Financial Administration under the T'ang Dynasty.* Cambridge: Cambridge University Press, 1963.

Wagner, Edward W. "The Korean Chokpo as a Historical Source," in Spencer J. Palmer, ed., *Studies in Asian Genealogy.* Provo: Brigham Young University Press, 1972.

———. *The Literati Purges: Political Conflict in Early Yi Korea.* Cambridge: East Asian Research Center, Harvard University, 1974.

———. "The Ladder of Success in Yi Dynasty Korea," *Occasional Papers on Korea* 1:1–8 (1974).

———. "Social Stratification in Seventeenth-Century Korea: Some Observations from a 1663 Seoul Census Register," *Occasional Papers on Korea* 1:36–54 (1974).

———. "Two Early Genealogies and Women's Status in Early Yi Dynasty Korea," in Kendall and Peterson, eds., *Korean Women* (q.v.).

Wakita, Haruko. "Marriage and Property in Premodern Japan from the Perspective of Women's History," *The Journal of Japanese Studies* 10.1:73–99 (1984).

Waley, Arthur. *The Analects of Confucius.* London: George Allen and Unwin, 1949.

Watson, James. L. "Anthropological Overview: The Development of Chinese Descent Groups," in Ebrey and Watson, eds., *Kinship Organization in Late Imperial China, 1000–1940* (q.v.).

———. "Chinese Kinship Reconsidered: Anthropolotical Perspectives on Historical Research," *The China Quarterly* 92:589–622 (Dec. 1982)

Watson, Rubie S. *Inequality among Brothers: Class and Kinship in South China.* Cambridge: Cambridge University Press, 1985.

——— and Patricia B. Ebrey, eds. *Marriage and Inequality in Chinese Society.* Berkeley: University of California Press, 1991.

Waxman, Chaim I., ed., *The End of the Ideology Debate.* New York: Simon and Schuster, 1968.

Wolf, Arthur P., and Chieh-shan Huang, *Marriage and Adoption in China, 1845–1945.* Stanford: Stanford University Press, 1980.

Yang, C. K. *Religion in Chinese Society.* Berkeley: University of California Press, 1967.

Yang Hoe-su 梁會水. *Han'guk nongch'on ŭi ch'ollak kujo* 韓國農

村의村落構造 (Study of the Structure of the Korean Farming Village). Seoul: Koryŏ taehakkyo, Asea munje yŏn'guso 亜細亜問題研究所, 1967.

Yang Sŏng-ji 梁誠之. *Nulchae-jip* 訥齋集 (Collected Works). Reprint. Seoul: Asea munhwasa, 1973.

Yangju Cho-ssi chokpo 楊州趙氏族譜 (Genealogy of the Yangju Cho). 1743.

Yi Chae 李縡. *Sarye pyŏllam* 四禮便覽 (Easy Manual of the Four Rites). Seoul: Sech'ang sŏ'gwan 世昌書館, 1967.

———. *Sarye pyŏllam* 四禮便覽 (Easy Manual of the Four Rites) with *Kwangnyeram* 廣禮覽 (Broad Survey of Rites). Reprint. Seoul, 1977.

Yi Chae-ch'ŏl 李載喆. *Chiphyŏnjŏn ko* 集賢殿考 (Study of the Chiphyŏnjŏn). Seoul: Han'guk tosŏ'gwan hyŏphoe 韓國圖書館協會, 1978.

Yi Che-hyŏn 李齊賢. *Ikchae sŏnsaeng man'go* 益齋先生亂藁 (Jottings by Yi Che-hyŏn), in *Yŏgye myŏnghyŏn-jip*, vol. 2 (q.v.).

———. *Yŏgong p'aesŏl* 櫟翁稗説 (Secret Memoranda), in *Yŏgye myŏnghyŏn-jip*, vol. 2 (q.v.).

Yi Ch'un-nyŏng 李春寧. *Yijo nongŏp kisulsa* 李朝農業技術 (History of Agricultural Techniques of the Yi Dynasty). Seoul: Han'guk yŏn-guwŏn, 1964.

Yi Hwang 李滉. *T'oegye sangjerye tammun* 退溪喪祭禮答問 (T'oegye's Questions and Answers on Funeral and Ancestral rites), 2 vols.

———. *Chŭngbo T'oegye chŏnsŏ* 增補退溪全書 (Supplemented Collected Works). 5 vols. Reprint. Seoul: Sŏnggyun'gwan taehakkyo, Taedong munhwa yŏn'guwŏn, 1971.

Yi I 李珥. *Yulgok chŏnsŏ* 栗谷全書 (Collected Works). 2 vols. Reprint. Seoul: Sŏnggyun'gwan taehakkyo, Taedong munhwa yŏn'guwŏn, 1971.

Yi Ik 李瀷. *Sŏngho saesŏl* 星湖僿説 (Collected Works). 2 vols. Reprint. Seoul: Kyŏngin munhwasa 景仁文化社, 1970.

———. *Sŏngho sŏnsaeng-jip* 星湖先生集 (Collected Works). 2 vols. Reprint. Seoul: Kyōngin munhwasa, 1974.

Yi Ki-baek 李基白. *Silla chŏngch'i sahoesa yŏn'gu* 新羅政治社會史研究 (Study of the Political and Social History of Silla). Seoul: Ilchogak, 1974.

———. "Koryŏ kwijok sahoe ŭi hyŏngsŏng" 高麗貴族社會의形成 (The Formation of the Koryŏ Aristocratic Society), *Han'guksa* (History of Korea), vol. 4 (q.v.).

———. "Koryŏ chungang kwallyo ŭi kwijokchŏk sŏngkyŏk" 高麗中央官僚의貴族的性格 (The Aristocratic Nature of the Central Officialdom in Koryŏ), *Tongyanghak* 東洋学 5:37–47 (1975).

———. *Han'guksa sillon* 韓國史新論 (New History of Korea). Rev. ed. Seoul: Ilchogak, 1976.

———. *Silla sidae ŭi kukka pulgyo wa yugyo* 新羅時代의國 家佛教와儒教 (Confucianism and State Buddhism in Silla). Seoul: The Korean Research Center, 1978.

———. ed., *Koryŏ Kwangjong yŏn'gu* 高麗光宗研究 (Studies of the Kwangjong's Reign in Koryŏ). Seoul: Ilchogak, 1981.

Yi Ki-mun 李基文. "Koryŏ sidae ŭi kugŏ ŭi t'ŭkching" 高麗時 代의國語의特徵 (Characteristics of the Language of the Koryŏ Period), *Tongyanghak* 6:299–305 (1976).

———. "Ajabi wa ajami" 아자비와아자미 (On *ajabi* and *ajami*), *Kugŏhak* 國語學 12:3–12 (1983).

Yi Kwang-gyu (Kwang Kyu Lee) 李光奎. "Han'guk ŭi ch'inch'ŏk myŏngch'ing" 韓國의親戚名稱 (Kin Terminology in Korea), *Yŏn'gu nonch'ong* 研究論叢 1:221–256 (1971).

———. *Han'guk kajok ŭi kujo punsŏk* 韓國家族의構造分析 (Structural Analysis of the Korean Family). Seoul: Ilchisa, 1975.

———. "Chosŏn wangjo sidae ŭi chaesan sangsok" 朝鮮王 朝時代의財産相續 (Property Inheritance in the Chosŏn Dynasty), *Hankuk Hakpo* 3:58–91 (summer 1976).

———. *Han'guk kajok ŭi sajŏk yŏn'gu* 韓國家族의史的研究 (Historical Studies of the Korean Family). Seoul: Ilchisa, 1977.

———. "Conflict and Harmony in Korean Rural Communities," *Journal of Korean Studies* 6:193–210 (1988–1989).

Yi Kyu-bo 李奎報. *Tongguk Yi Sanggukchip* 東國李相國集 (Collected Works). Reprint. Seoul: Tongguk munhwasa 東國文化社, 1958.

Yi Man-gap 李萬甲. *Han'guk nongch'on ŭi sahoe kujo* 韓國農 村의社會構造 (The Social Structure of the Korean Village). Seoul: The Korean Research Center, 1960.

Yi Man-yŏl 李萬烈. "Koryŏ Kyŏngwŏn Yi-ssi kamun ŭi chŏn'gae kwajŏng" 高麗慶源李氏家門의展開過程 (The Development of the Kyŏngwŏn Yi-ssi), *Hankuk Hakpo* 21:2–29 (winter 1980).

Yi Nan-yŏng 李蘭暎, comp. *Han'guk kŭmsŏngmun ch'ubo* 韓國金 石文追補 (Additions to Korean Epigraphy). Seoul: Asea munhwasa, 1968.

Yi Nŭng-hwa 李能和. *Chosŏn yŏsok-ko* 朝鮮女俗考 (Study of Customs of Korean Women). Reprint. Seoul: Hangmungak 學文閣, 1968.

Yi Ŏn-jŏk 李彥迪. *Hoejae chŏnsŏ* 晦齋全書 (Collected Works). Reprint. Sŏnggyun'gwan taehakkyo, Taedong munhwa yŏn'guwŏn, 1973.

Yi P'il-sang 李弼相. *Koryŏ sidae pokche ŭi yŏn'gu* 高麗時代服制의研究 (Study of the Mourning System of the Koryŏ Period). Seoul: Sŏul taehakkyo, taehagwŏn 大学院, 1974.

Yi Pyŏng-do 李丙燾. *Han'guksa, chungsep'yŏn* 韓國史, 中世編 (Korean History: The Medieval Period). Seoul: Ŭryu munhwasa, 1961.

Yi Pyŏng-hyu 李秉烋. "Yŏmal Sŏnch'o ŭi kwaŏp kyoyuk" 麗末鮮初의科業教育 (The Education Preparing for the Civil Service Examination in the Late-Koryŏ and Early-Chosŏn Dynasties), *Yŏksa hakpo* 67:45–70 (Sept. 1975).

Yi Saek 李穡. *Mogŭn mun'go* 牧隱文藁 (Collected Literary Works), in *Yŏgye myŏnghyŏn-jip* (q.v.).

Yi Sang-baek 李相伯. "Yubul yanggyo kyodae ŭi kiyŏn e taehan il yŏn'gu" 儒佛兩教交代의機緣에對한一研究 (Study on the Supplanting of Buddhism by Confucianism), in *Chosŏn munhwasa yŏn'gu non'go* 朝鮮文化史研究論攷 (Some Studies of the Origin of Korean Social Customs). Seoul: Ŭryu munhwasa, 1948.

———. "Chaega kŭmji sŭpsok ŭi yurae e taehan yŏn'gu" 再嫁禁止習俗의由來에對한研究 (Study on the Sources of Anti-Marriage Customs), in *Chosŏn munhwasa yŏn'gu non'go* (See previous entry).

———. *Yijo kŏn'guk ŭi yŏn'gu* 李朝建國의研究 (Study of the Founding of the Yi Dynasty). Seoul: Ŭryu munhwasa, 1959.

———. *Han'guksa, kŭnse chŏn'gi-p'yŏn* 韓國史, 近世前期編 (History of Korea, Early Modern Period). Seoul: Ŭryu munhwasa, 1962.

———. "Ch'ŏnja sumo-go" 賤者隨母考 (Study on the Determination of Low-born Status through the Mother), *Chindan hakpo* 25–27:155–183 (1964).

Yi Sik 李植. *T'aektang-jip* 澤堂集 (Collected Works). 17 vols. 1747.

Yi Sŏng-mu 李成茂. "Yangban" 兩班 (The Yangban), in *Han'guksa*, vol. 10 (q.v.).

———. "Chosŏn chŏn'gi ŭi sinbun chedo" 朝鮮前期의身分制度 (The Social Status System of the Early-Chosŏn Period), *Tonga munhwa* 13:173–191 (June 1976).

———. *Chosŏn ch'ogi yangban yŏn'gu* 朝鮮初期兩班研究 (Study of the Yangban in the Early-Chosŏn Period). Seoul: Ilchogak, 1980.

———. "Kongjŏn-sajŏn-minjŏn ŭi kaenyŏm—Koryŏ, Chosŏn ch'ogi rŭl chungsim ŭro" 公田·私田·民田의概念—高麗, 朝鮮初期를中心으로 (The Concepts of *kongjŏn*, *sajŏn*, and *minjŏn* in Koryŏ and Early Chosŏn), in *Han U-gŭn paksa chŏngnyŏn kinyŏm sahak nonch'ong* 韓祐劤博士停年紀念史学論叢 (Festschrift for Professor Han U-gŭn). Seoul: Chisik sanŏpsa, 1981.

———. "Chosŏn ch'ogi sinbunsa yŏn'gu ŭi chaegŏmt'o" 朝鮮初期身分史研究의再檢討 (Reexamination of Studies of Social Status in Early Chosŏn), *Yŏksa hakpo* 102:205–233 (June 1984).

Yi Su-gŏn 李樹健. "Koryŏ chŏn'gi t'osŏng yŏn'gu" 高麗前期土姓研究 (A Study of the *t'osŏng* in Early Koryŏ), *Taegu sahak* 14:29–70 (June 1978).

————. comp., *Kyŏngbuk chibang komunsŏ chipsŏng* 慶北地方古文書集成 (Collection of Old Documents of the Kyŏngbuk Area). Kyŏngsan: Yŏngnamdae ch'ulp'anbu, 1981.

————. *Han'guk chungse sahoesa yŏn'gu* 韓國中世社會史研究 (Study of the Social History of Medieval Korea). Seoul: Ilchogak, 1984.

Yi Sun-gŭn 李純根. "Silla sidae sŏngssi ch'widŭk kwa kŭ ŭimi" 新羅時代姓氏取得과그意味 (The Adoption of Surnames in the Silla Period and Its Meaning), *Han'guk saron* 6:3–65 (Dec. 1980).

Yi Sung-nyŏng 李崇寧. "Chungse kugŏ ŭi kajok hoch'ing e taehayŏ" 中世國語의家族呼稱에대하여 (On the Kinship Terminology of Middle Korean), *Tongyang munhwa* 6–7:229–246 (1968).

Yi T'ae-jin 李泰鎮. "Sipsa-o segi nongŏp kisul ŭi paltal kwa sinhŭng sajok" 14·5世紀農業技術의發達과新興士族 (Development of Agricultural Techniques in the Fourteenth and Fifteenth Centuries and the Newly Rising Elite), *Tongyanghak* 9:15–34 (Oct. 1979).

————. *Han'guk sahoesa yŏn'gu* 韓國社會史研究 (Study of Korea's Social History). Seoul: Chisik sanŏpsa, 1986.

————. *Chosŏn yugyo sahoe saron* 朝鮮儒教社會史論 (Studies of the Confucian Society of Chosŏn). Seoul: Chisik sanŏpsa, 1989.

Yi U-sŏng 李佑成. "Han'in-paekchŏng ŭi sinhaesŏk" 閑人·白丁의新鮮釋 (New Interpretation of *han'in* and *paekchŏng*), *Yŏksa hakpo* 19:53–89 (Dec. 1962).

Yi Ŭn-sun 李銀順. "Yi Saek yŏn'gu" 李穡研究 (Study on Yi Saek), *Idae sawŏn* 梨大史苑 4:37–69 (1962).

Yi Yu-ch'ŏl 李惟哲. *Yeŭi yujip* 禮疑類輯 (Collection of Doubtful Passages on the Rites). Date uncertain.

Yijo myŏnghyŏn-jip 李朝名賢集 (Works of Famous Confucians of the Yi Dynasty). Seoul: Sŏnggyun'gwan taehakkyo, Taedong munhwa yŏn'guwŏn, 1977.

Yŏgye myŏnghyŏn-jip 麗季名賢集 (Collection of Works of Famous Confucians of the Late Koryŏ Period). Seoul: Sŏnggyun'gwan taehakkyo, Taedong munhwa yŏn'guwŏn, 1959.

Yŏju Yi-ssi chokpo 驪州李氏族譜 (Genealogy of the Yŏju Yi).

Yŏkchu Koryŏsa 譯註高麗史 (Translated and Annotated *Koryŏsa*). Tonga taehakkyo kojŏn yŏn'gusil 東亜大学校古典研究室, 1971.

Yŏkchu Kyŏngguk taejŏn 譯註經國大典 (Translated and Annotated *Kyŏngguk taejŏn*). 2 vols. Sŏngnam-si: Han'guk chŏngsin munhwa yŏn'guwŏn, 1985–1986.

Yŏsasŏ 女四書 (Four Books for Women). Reprint. Seoul: Asea munhwasa, 1974.

Yu Hong-nyŏl 柳洪烈. "Raimatsu Sensho no shigaku" 麗末鮮初の私学 (Private Schools in Late-Koryŏ and Early-Yi Korea), *Seikyū gakusō* 24:64–119 (May 1936).

Yu Hŭi-ch'un 柳希春. *Miam sŏnsaeng-jip* 眉巖先生集 (Collected Works). 3 vols. Date uncertain.

———. *Miam-ilgi* 眉巖日記 (Diary of Yu Hŭi-ch'un).

Yu Hyŏng-wŏn 柳馨遠. *Pan'gye surok* 磻溪隨錄 (Collected Works). Reprint. Seoul: Tongguk munhwasa, 1958.

Yun Chŭng 尹拯. *Myŏngjae ŭirye mundap* 明齋疑禮問答 (Questions and Answers on Rites by Myŏngjae).

Yun Sa-sun 尹絲淳. "Chŏng To-jŏn sŏngnihak ŭi t'ŭksŏng kwa kŭ p'yŏngkka munje" 鄭道傳性理學의特性과그評價問題 (The Characteristics of Chŏng To-jŏn's Neo-Confucianism and Its Evaluation), *Chindan hakpo* 50:151–160 (1980).

———. "Sŏngnihak sidae ŭi yesasang" 性理學時代의禮思想 (Thought on Rites during the Period of Neo-Confucianism), in *Han'guk sasang taegye* 韓國思想大系 (Encyclopedia on Korean Thought), vol. 4. Seoul: Sŏnggyun'gwan taehakkyo ch'ulp'anbu, 1984.

———. *Han'guk yuhak sasangnon* 한국유학사상론 (Studies of Korean Confucianism). Seoul: Yŏrŭmsa, Yŏrŭm sasang ch'ongsŏ No. 3 여름사, 여름사상총서 Nr. 3, 1986.

Yun Yong-gyun 尹瑢均. *Shushigaku no denrai to sono eikyō ni tsuite* 朱子学の傳來とその影響に就いて (Transmission of Neo-Confucianism and Its Influence). Keijō: Keijō Imperial University, 1933.

Zaborowski, Hans-Jürgen. *Der Gelehrte und Staatsmann Mogŭn Yi Saek (1328–1396)*. Wiesbaden: Otto Harrassowitz, 1976.

Zenshō Eisuke 善生永助. *Chōsen no shūraku* 朝鮮の聚落 (Korean Villages). 3 vols. Keijō: Chōsen sōtokufu, 1933–1935.

Glossary

ahŏn　亜獻
an　安
An Chin　安震
An Hyang　安珦
anch'ae　안채
Andong Cho-ssi　安東曺氏
Andong Kim-ssi　安東金氏
Andong Kwŏn-ssi　安東權氏
Ansan Kim-ssi　安山金氏
An-ssi　安氏

chabi　慈悲
Ch'ae Mu-t'aek　蔡無擇
chaech'oe　齋衰
chaech'oe changgi　齋衰杖期
chaech'oe kinyŏn　齋衰朞年
chaech'oe samnyŏn　齋衰三年
chaehaeng　再行
chaehŏn　再獻
Chaejong　載宗
ch'aekpi　冊妃
chaemul　財物
Chaeryŏng Yi-ssi　載寧李氏
chaesang chi chong　宰相之宗
chagŭn chip　작은 집
ch'aja　次子
ch'amch'oe samnyŏn　斬衰三年
chang　葬 (to bury)
chang　藏 (to preserve)

chang　長 (eldest)
Ch'ang　昌王
Chang Tsai　張載
changga kada　장가 가다
changgi　杖期
Changil t'ongyo sujŏn
　葬日通要隨箋
changja　長子
changjach'ŏ　長子妻
Chanyŏan　恁女案
chao　昭
Chao Fu　趙復
chao-mu　昭穆
chapkwa　雜科
Charae kwanhaeng hollye
　自來慣行昏禮
chason ch'inch'ŏk　子孫親戚
Chaunsa　慈雲寺
che　悌
chehu　諸候
chejo　提調
chejŏn　祭田
chen-kuan　貞觀
Chen-kuan cheng-yao　貞觀政要
Chen Te-hsiu　真德秀
Ch'eng Hao　程顥
Ch'eng I　程頤
Ch'eng-Chu　程・朱
ch'erip　遞立

chesa 祭祀

Chesaŭi 諸祀儀

chesil 祭室

chesinsang 諸臣喪

chewijo 祭位條

chi 志

ch'i 氣 (mind-matter)

ch'i 治 (political order)

ch'i 妻 (primary wife)

Chi-lin lei-shih 鷄林類事

Chi Nog-yŏn 智祿延

chi-szu 祭祀

"Chi-t'ung" 祭統

chia 家

Chia-li 家禮

Chia-li i-chieh 家禮義節

ch'ibu 致賻

ch'ido 治道

ch'ieh 妾

chien 姦

chi'ga 支家

chih-cheng 至正

Chih-cheng t'iao-ke 至正條格

chih-tao 治道

chija 支子

Chijŭng 智證王

chikcha 直子

chikchŏn 職田

Chiksan Ch'oe-ssi 稷山崔氏

ch'ilch'ul 七出

ch'in 親

ch'inch'ŏk 親戚

ch'indang 親黨

ch'injok 親族

Chinju 晋州

ch'inmin 親民

Chin-ssu lu 近思錄

ch'inyŏng 親迎

chinyu 真儒

chip 집

chip'ae 紙牌

Chiphyŏnjŏn 集賢殿

chip'ye 贄幣

Ch'iu Chün 丘濬

cho 租 (tax)

cho 祖 (ancestor)

ch'o 醮

ch'ŏ 妻

Cho In-gyu 趙仁規

Cho In-ok 趙仁沃

Cho Kŭn 趙菫

Cho Kwang-jo 趙光祖

Cho Kyŏn 趙狷

Cho Mal-saeng 趙末生

Cho Pang-nim 趙邦霖

Cho Pok-hae 趙福海

Cho Pu-rim 趙傅霖

Cho Pyŏn 趙忭

Cho Yŏng 趙涘

Cho Yŏng-mu 趙英茂

Ch'oe Ch'i-wŏn 崔致遠

Ch'oe Ch'ung 崔冲

Ch'oe Ch'ung-hŏn 崔忠獻

Ch'oe Hae 崔瀣

Ch'oe Hong-jae 崔弘宰

Ch'oe Myŏng-gil 崔鳴吉

Ch'oe Sa-ch'u 崔思諏

Ch'oe Sŭng-no 崔承老

Ch'oe Tan 崔端

chŏgin 適人

chogin 族人

ch'ohaeng 初行

choje 吊祭

ch'ŏjok 妻族

chojong 祖宗

chok 族

chŏk 嫡 (direct lineal descendant; first-born son)

chŏk 籍 (register)

chŏkcha 嫡子

chŏkchang 嫡長

chŏkchangja 嫡長子

chokch'in 族親

Chokch'inwi 族親衛

chŏkch'ŏ 嫡妻
chŏkch'ŏp chi pun 嫡妾之分
chŏkp'a 適派
chokpo 族譜
chŏkpu 嫡(適)婦 (lineal wife)
chŏkpu 適夫 (to take a husband)
Ch'ŏkpulso 斥佛疏
chŏksil 嫡室
choksok 族屬
chŏkson 嫡孫
choktang 族黨
chol 卒
ch'ŏlcho 輟朝
Chŏlla 全羅
chon 尊
ch'on 寸
chŏnan 奠雁
chonbi 尊卑
chonbi sangdŭng 尊卑相等
ch'ŏnch'ŏp 賤妾
ch'ŏnch'ŏpcha 賤妾子
chong 終 ("ended")
chong 宗 (descent line)
chŏng 政
Chŏng Ch'o 鄭招
Chŏng Ch'ŏk 鄭陟
Chŏng In-ji 鄭麟趾
Chŏng-ssi 鄭氏
Chŏng Tong-yu 鄭東愈
chŏn'gaek 田客
Chŏngan Im-ssi 定安任氏
Chongbi 終非
chŏngbu 正婦
ch'ongbu 冢婦
chŏngch'e 正體
Chongch'in kŭp munmugwan
   ilp'um iha hollye 宗親及文武
   官一品以下婚禮
chŏngch'ŏ 正妻
Chŏngdong haengsŏng 征東行省
chongga 宗家
ch'ŏnggi 請期

chŏnghak 正学
chonghoe 宗會
ch'ŏnghonsŏ 請婚書
chongja 宗子
chongja chi pŏp 宗子之法
chongjang 宗長
Chŏngjong 定宗
Chŏngjong (r. 1034–1046) 靖宗
chŏngmo 嫡母
chŏngmun 旌門
chŏngmyŏng 正名
chŏngnye 正禮
chŏngnyŏ 正女
chongnyu 宗類
chongppŏp 宗法
chŏngsil 正室 (primary wife)
chŏngsil 淨室 (purified room)
chongson 宗孫
chongt'o 宗土
chŏnhu munsŏ 傳後文書
ch'ŏnin 賤人
Ch'ŏnjamun 千字文
ch'ŏnjang 遷葬
chŏnjŏng 田丁
chŏnjŏng yŏllip 田丁連立
Chŏnju Yi-ssi 全州李氏
ch'ŏnmin 賤民
chŏnmo 前母
chŏnsikwa 田柴科
choŏp 祖業
choŏp chi chŏn 祖業之田
choŏp in'gu 祖業人口
choŏpchŏn 祖業田
ch'ŏp 妾
ch'ŏpcha 妾子
ch'orye 醮禮
ch'oryesang 醮禮床
chosang yusŏ 祖上遺書
Chosŏn 朝鮮
Chosŏn kyŏnggukchŏn
   朝鮮經國典
Chou 周

Chou-li 周禮
Chu Hsi 朱熹
Chu Se-bung 周世鵬
Chu Tzu chia-li 朱子家禮
Chu Tzu yü-lei 朱子語類
"Ch'ü- li" 曲禮
chubu 主婦
ch'uch'ŏn 追薦
chujeja 主祭者
ch'uk 畜
ch'ŭksil 側室
ch'ulmo 出母
Ch'un-ch'iu 春秋
Ch'un-ch'iu Kung-yang chuan
春秋公羊傳
Ch'unch'ugwan 春秋館
Chung- yung 中庸
chungdang 中堂
chunghon 重婚
chungin 中人
chungja 衆子
chungjo 中祖
chŭngjojong 曾祖宗
Chungjong 中宗
chungmae 仲媒
Ch'ungmok 忠穆
chungmun 中門
ch'ungmun 祝文
chungnoeyŏn 重牢宴
Ch'ungnyŏl 忠烈
Ch'ungsŏn 忠宣
Ch'ungsuk 忠肅
chŭngsi 贈諡
Ch'ungŭiwi 忠義衛
chungwŏl 仲月
ch'uwŏn 追遠
Chuyŏngp'yŏn 晝永篇
chün-t'ien 均田
chün-tzu 君子
chwamyŏng kongsin 佐命功臣
ch'wi 娶
ch'wibu 娶婦
ch'wich'ŏ 娶妻

Erh-ya 爾雅

fu 服
fu-ku 復古

Ha Yun 河崙
Haeju Ch'oe-ssi 海州崔氏
Haeyang-gun taebuin Kim-ssi
海陽君大夫人金氏
Hahoe iltong 河回一洞
Ham Pu-rim 咸傅霖
Hamch'ang Kim-ssi 咸昌金氏
Hamgil 咸吉
Hamgyŏng 咸鏡
hapchang 合葬
ho 號
Hŏ Cho 許稠
Hŏ Hang 許沆
Hŏ Ŭng 許應
hoehollye 回婚禮
Hoehŏn 晦軒
hoejang 會葬
hogu 戶口
hŏhonsŏ 許婚書
hojok 豪族
hojŏk 戶籍
hoju 戶主
hon 魂
Hongmungwan 弘文館
hŏn'gurye 献舅禮
hon'gye 婚契
honin 婚姻
honin chi che 婚姻之制
honjok 婚族
honju 婚主
honsŏ 婚書
hŏyŏ mun'gi 許與文記
Hsia 夏
Hsiao-ching 孝經
Hsiao-hsüeh 小学
Hsiao Sung 蕭嵩
hsiao-tsung 小宗
hsiao-tsung-tzu 小宗子

Hsien-tsung 憲宗
hsing 姓
Hsü Heng 許衡
Hsüan-tsung 玄宗
Hsün-tzu 荀子
hu-hun 戶婚
Hu Kuang 胡廣
Hu-Paekche 後百濟
Hu Ping-wen 胡炳文
Huang Ti 黃帝
hubi 后妃
Hui-an 晦奄
Hŭijong 熙宗
hŭisa 喜捨
humo 後母
"Hun-i" 昏義
Hung-fan 洪範
hunhyŏn ch'ungŭi 勳賢忠義
hunyo 訓要
hwajang 火葬
Hwang-bo Yŏng 皇甫穎
Hwang Hŭi 黃熹
Hwang P'il-su 黃泌秀
Hwang Sun-sang 黃順常
Hwaryŏng 和寧
hyang 鄉
hyangdo 香徒
hyangni 鄉吏
hyangsi 鄉試
Hyejong 惠宗
hyŏn 賢
hyŏnjo 顯祖
Hyŏnjong 顯宗
hyŏngje ch'inch'ŏk 兄弟親戚
Hyŏngjŏn 刑典
hyŏn'gwan 顯官
hyung 凶
hyungnye 凶禮
hyuryangjŏn 恤養田

i 理
I-ching 易經
I-li 儀禮

I-li ching-chuan t'ung-chieh
　　儀禮經傳通解
Ich'adon 異次頓
idan 異端
idu 吏讀
igŭp 移給
ihak 理學
ii 離異
iil yŏgwŏl 以日易月
ijang 移葬
ijong 禰宗
ilbu ilch'ŏ 一夫一妻
ilbu tach'ŏ 一夫多妻
ilchi 一支
ilchong 一宗
illyun 人倫
Im Wŏn-hu 任元厚
Im Yŏn 林衍
imhŏn ch'ogye 臨軒醮戒
in 仁
ing 媵
Injo 仁祖
Injong 仁宗
ip-changga 入丈家
iphu 立後
"Iphu ŭi" 立後議
iphuja 立後者
ipsa 立嗣
irŭm 이름
isŏng 異姓

ju 儒

ka 家 (family; household)
ka 嫁 (to take a husband)
kabo 家譜
kach'ŏp 家牒
Kaegyŏng 開京
kaejang 改葬
kaengjŏk sambuja 更適三夫者
Kaesŏng 開城
kahun 家訓
kajang 假葬

Kamdong 甘同
Kammuri 甘勿伊
kamo 嫁母
kamyo 家廟
kamyo chi che 家廟之制
kanbi 奸非
Kang Sun-dŏk 姜順德
kanggi 綱紀
Kangjong 康宗
Kangnŭng Kim-ssi 江陵金氏
kant'aek 揀擇
Kao Shih-lien 高士廉
kao-tsu-tsung 高祖宗
kaŏp 家業
kapsa 甲士
Karak 駕洛
karye 嘉禮
Karye chŭnghae 家禮增解
Karye ŏnhae 家禮諺解
Karye ŭijŏl 家禮義節
kat 갓
ki 氣 (material substance)
ki 妓 (singing girl)
kibok 起服
kiilche 忌日祭
Kija 箕子
kije 忌祭
kil 吉
kilchi 吉地
killye 吉禮
Kim 金
Kim Al-lo 金安老
Kim Chi-suk 金之淑
Kim Ch'i-un 金致雲
Kim Ching 金澄
Kim Ch'o 金貂
Kim Ha 金何
Kim Hal-lo 金漢老
Kim Hon 金琿
Kim Hong-wŏn 金弘遠
Kim Hwi-nam 金輝南
Kim Ik-su 金益壽

Kim Kae 金漑
Kim Koeng-p'il 金宏弼
Kim Ku 金鉤
Kim Ku-dŏk 金九德
Kim Ku-yong 金九容
Kim Kŭng-nyul 金兢律
Kim Kyŏn-su 金堅壽
Kim Mu 金務
Kim Mun-jŏng 金文鼎
Kim Myŏng-yŏl 金命説
Kim Nok-sung 金祿崇
Kim O-mun 金五文
Kim Paek-kan 金伯幹
Kim Pang-gyŏng 金方慶
Kim Po-dang 金甫當
Kim Pu 金傅
Kim Tŏk-hŭng 金德興
Kim Tŏk-saeng 金德生
Kim Ŭn-bu 金殷傅
Kim Yŏn-ji 金連枝
Kim Yuk 金育
Kim Yun 金倫
kinyŏn 期年
kisaeng 妓生
kisŏn 其先
kŏ 去
kogi 告期
"Ko'gŭm sangnye idong ŭi"
    古今喪禮異同議
Koguryŏ 高句麗
koje 古制
kojojong 高祖宗
Kojong 高宗
komyo 告廟
kongjŏn 公田
Kongmin 恭愍
kongsin 功臣
kongsinjŏn 功臣田
kŏn'guk kongsin 建國功臣
kongŭm chŏnsi 功蔭田柴
Kongyang 恭讓
korye 古禮

Koryŏ 高麗

Koryŏ pangŏn 高麗方言

Koryŏguk yuhak chegŏsa
高麗國儒学提擧司

ku 舅 (wife's father)

ku 舊 (longstanding friendship)

Ku-su 龜壽

kubunjŏn 口分田

kuch'ŏ 區處

kukchang 國葬

Kukcho sok oryeŭi 國朝續五禮儀

Kukcho sok oryeŭibo
國朝續五禮儀補

kuksang 國喪

kuksok 國俗

kullye 軍禮

kŭm 衿

kŭmbu mun'gi 衿付文記

Kŭmsŏng 金城

kun 君

kŭn 勤

k'ŭn chip 큰집

K'ung Ying-ta 孔穎達

kun'gwan 軍官

kunja 君子

kunsa 軍士

kwajŏn 科田

kwajŏnpŏp 科田法

kwallye 冠禮

Kwak Yŏ 郭輿

kwamo 寡母

kwan 貫

kwanbi 官婢

kwanhyang 貫鄉

kwanjang 官葬

Kwangjong 光宗

Kwangnyeram 廣禮覽

Kwangsan Kim-ssi 光山金氏

kwi 歸

kwich'ŏn 貴賤

Kwihusŏ 歸厚署

kwijang 歸葬

kwijok 貴族

kwŏn 權

Kwŏn Nae 權來

Kwŏn Pu 權溥

Kwŏn-ssi 權氏

Kwŏn To 權蹈

kwŏnmun sega 權門世家

kye 系

kyebu 繼父

kyehuja 繼後者

kyeja 系者

kyejomo 繼祖母

kyemo 繼母

Kyerim yusa 鷄林類事

kyerye 筓禮

kyobae 交拜

kyogŭp 交卺

kyŏl 結

kyŏng 經 (classic; constant rule)

kyŏng 卿 (minister)

kyŏng 敬 (reverence)

kyŏngga 頸枷

"Kyŏngje mun'gam, pyŏlchip"
經濟文鑑別集

Kyŏngje yukchŏn 經濟六典

Kyŏngjong 景宗

Kyŏngju 慶州

Kyŏngju Kim-ssi 慶州金氏

"Kyŏngmong yogyŏl" 擊蒙要訣

Kyŏngwŏn [Inju] Yi-ssi
慶源〔仁州〕李氏

kyŏngyŏn'gwan 經筵官

kyŏre 겨레

Li-chi 禮記

Li-chi cheng-i 禮記正義

Li-chi chi-shuo ta-ch'üan
禮記集説大全

Li Pu 禮部

Liu Ch'ing-chih 劉清之

Lü Tsu-ch'ien 呂祖謙

Lun-yü 論語

Ma Tuan-lin　馬端臨
Maech'iwŏn　埋置院
maedŭk minjŏn　買得民田
Maeng Sa-sŏng　孟思誠
manggŏn　網巾
mangjok　望族
Man'gwŏndang　萬卷堂
Meng-tzu　孟子
Mi-su　眉壽
Min Sŏng-hwi　閔聖徽
Ming　明
Ming T'ai-tsu　明太祖
minjŏn　民田
minmyŏnŭri　민며느리
Miryang Pak-ssi　密陽朴氏
mobyŏn　母邊
mobyŏn chŏllae　母邊傳來
Mokchong　穆宗
mokk'al　목칼
mu　穆
muban　武班
mugyŏk　巫覡
muhu　無後
muja　無子
mulgŭp sonoe　勿給孫外
Mun Ik-chŏm　文益漸
Mun Kong-in　文公仁
Mun Kong-yu　文公裕
Mun Kŭk-kyŏm　文克謙
munban　文班
Mundŏk wanghu　文德王后
mun'gye　文契
munjang　門長
munjip　文集
Munjong　文宗
munjung　門中
munkwa　文科
munmyŏng　問名
muryŏt'a　勿與他
Musan-gun　茂山君
myogyŏn　廟見
myoje　墓祭

myojik　墓直
myojŏn　墓田
myŏng　明
myŏngbu　命婦
myŏngbu pongjak　命婦封爵
myŏngbun　名分
myŏngjok　明族
Myŏngjong　明宗
myŏngmaek　命脈
myono　墓奴
myŏnyak　面約

Na Ik-hŭi　羅益禧
nae　內
nae-oe　內外
nae-oe chi ch'e　內外之體
nae-oe son　內外孫
naehyang　內鄉
Nam Hae　南鮃
Nam Kyŏng-u　南景佑
namhyang taeri　南向大利
namnyŏ chi pyŏl　男女之別
napch'ae　納采
napching　納徵
napkil　納吉
nappi　納妃
napp'ye　納幣
ni-tsung　禰宗
nobi　奴婢
"Nobi kyŏlsong chŏnghan"　奴婢決訟定限
Nobi pyŏnjŏng togam　奴婢辨正都監, 奴婢辨定都監
nongjang　農場
nŭngmun nŭngni　能文能吏

obok　五服
obok tosik　五服圖式
oe　外
oe chobumo　外祖父母
oehyang　外鄉
oejok　外族

oesil 外室
oeson 外孫
Ogyŏng ch'ŏn'gyŏllok
　五經淺見錄
ohaeng 五行
ojong 五宗
Omyo 五廟
ongju 翁主
orye 五禮
Oryeŭi chu 五禮儀註
oryun 五倫
osejo 五世祖
osi 娛尸

p'a 派
pae 配
paek 魄
Paek I-jŏng 白頤正
Paek Mun-bo 白文寶
Paekche 百濟
paekse pulch'ŏn 百世不遷
p'agye 罷繼
Pak 朴
Pak Ch'o 朴礎
Pak Sang-ch'ung 朴尚衷
Pak Se-dang 朴世堂
Pak Sŭng-jong 朴承宗
Pak Yŏng-gyu 朴英規
Pak Yu 朴楡
pakchang 薄葬
p'alcha 八字
p'alcho 八條 (Eight Rules)
p'alcho 八祖 (eight ancestral lines)
p'alcho hogu 八祖戶口
P'aryŏkchi 八域志
pan 班
pan ch'inyŏng 半親迎
panbujo 班祔(附)條
pangmae 放賣
P'ap'yŏng Yun-ssi 坡平尹氏
p'arhyang 八鄉
pi 妃 (queen)

pi 卑 (despised)
pich'ŏp 婢妾
pieh-tzu 別子
pijo 鼻祖
pillye 賓禮
pin 嬪
pinjogyŏn 嬪朝見
po 譜
Pŏboe kyehu tŭngnok
　法外繼後謄錄
pobok 報服
pobon 報本
pogyŏng 卜塋
pok 服
pokhap 復合
pokko 復古
pok t'aekcho 卜宅兆
pon 本
Pong Yŏ 奉礪
pon'ga 本家
Ponghwa Chŏng-ssi 奉化鄭氏
pongsa 奉祀
pongsa chŏnt'aek nobi
　奉祀田宅奴婢
pongsa ŭija 奉祀義子
pongsajo 奉祀條
Pongsŏn chabŭi 奉先雜儀
"Pongsŏn chegyu" 奉先祭規
pon'gwan 本貫
pongyŏng wangbi 奉迎王妃
ponjok 本族
ponjŏk 本籍
ponson 本孫
pŏp 法
pŏpche 法制
"P'oŭn pongsago sŏ"
　圃隱奉使藁序
pu 夫
pubyŏn 父邊
pubyŏn chŏllae 父邊傳來
pugyŏn kugo 婦見舅姑
pugyori 副校理

pujang 附葬
pujojŏn 父祖田
pujok 父族
pulbŏp 佛法
pulch'ŏnwi 不遷位
Pulssi chappyŏn 佛氏雜辨
p'ung 風
pun'ga 分家
P'ungsan Yu-ssi 豊山柳氏
p'ungsok 風俗
p'ungsu 風水
pun'gŭp mun'gi 分給文記
punjae 分財
punmyo 墳墓
puong 婦翁
p'yebaek 幣帛
p'yehaeng 嬖幸
p'yejŏkcha 廢嫡子
pyŏl 別
pyŏlcha 別子
pyŏlgŭp mun'gi 別給文記
pyŏllye 變禮
pyŏlmyo 別廟
pyŏlsajŏn 別賜田
Pyŏn Hyo-mun 卞孝文
P'yŏngan 平安
p'yŏngbun 平分
pyŏngch'uk 並畜
p'yŏngmin 平民
P'yŏngyang Cho-ssi 平壤趙氏
Pyŏngjŏng togam 辨正都監
p'yosŏk 標石

sa 士 (scholar; common officer)
sa 嗣 (direct heir)
sa 私 (private; to have an affair)
sach'on 四寸
sach'ŏn 私賤
sadaebu 士大夫
sadaebu changbun chi che
　士大夫葬墳之制
sadaebuga cheŭi 士大夫家祭儀

sadang 祀堂
sado 斯道
saeng 甥
Saganwŏn 司諫院
Sahŏnbu 司憲府
sajo 四祖
sajok 士族
sajŏn 私田
saju 四柱
sambu p'almo 三父八母
sambulgŏ 三不去
samch'on 三寸
samga 三加
samgang 三綱
Samgang haengsil yŏllyŏdo
　三綱行實烈女圖
Samgang haengsilto 三綱行實圖
samgang yukki 三綱六紀
Samguk yusa 三國遺事
samhaeng 三行
samin 士民
samjok 三族
samo kwandae 紗帽冠帶
san-tai 三代
san-tsu 三族
"Sang-fu hsiao-chi" 喪服小記
sangbokpŏp 喪服法
Sangch'on-jip 象村集
sanggaek 上客
sangjang chi ye 喪葬之禮
sangje chi ŭi 喪祭之儀
Sangjŏl karye 詳節家禮
Sangju Pak-ssi 尚州朴氏
sangmin 常民
Sangnye piyo 喪禮備要
sangp'i 相避
sangsok 相續
sangsok yŏllip 相續連立
sangt'u 상투
sap'ung 士風
sarang 사랑
sarye 四禮

Sasŏ chŏryo 四書節要
"Sasŏ ogyŏng sŏngni taejŏn
  pal" 四書五經性理大全跋
sasŏl 雅説
sason 使孫
sasondo 使孫圖
sasŏng 四星 ("four stars")
sasŏng 賜姓 (gift of surname)
sebo 世譜
segyedo 世系圖
Sejo 世祖
Sejong 世宗
sesin 世臣
sesok 世俗
Shang 商
Shao Yung 邵雍
shih 士
shih-ch'en 世臣
Shih-tsu 世祖
Shih-tsu chih 氏族志
shu 庶
Shu-ching 書經
Shun 舜
Shuo-fu 説郛
sije 時祭
sijip kada 시집가다
sijo 始祖
sijomyo 始祖廟
silcha 實子
Silla 新羅
Sillŭksa 神勒寺
sillyŏ 室女
sima 緦麻
Simgirip'yŏn 心氣理篇
simhak 心学
simsang 心喪
sin 信 (faithfulness)
sin 慎 (watchfulness)
Sin Cha-gŭn 申自謹
Sin Cha-gyŏng 申自敬
Sin Cha-su 申自守
Sin Ch'ŏn 辛蕆

Sin Chong-nyŏn 申從年
Sin Hŭm 申欽
Sin Hyo-ch'ang 申孝昌
Sin Kye-dong 申繼童
Sin Sik 申湜
Sin-ssi 申氏
Sin Su-gŭn 慎守勤
Sin Sŭng-in 申承寅
Sin Sŭng-min 申承閔
Sin Ton 辛旽
Sin Ŭi-gyŏng 申義慶
Sin Yun-dong 申允童
Sin Yun-gwan 申允寬
sinhaeng 新行
sinhŭng sadaebu 新興士大夫
Sinjong 神宗
sinju 神主
sinmin 新民
sinsim chi hak 身心之学
sirhaengja 失行者
sirhak 實学
siyangja 侍養子
so 疏
sŏ 壻(婿)(son-in-law)
sŏ 庶 (secondary; commoner)
sŏ 敍 (family member's contact)
sŏ 序 (proper sequence of birth)
Sŏ Kŏ-jŏng 徐居正
Sŏ Kyŏng-dŏk 徐敬德
sŏban 西班
sŏbang 書房
Sobi 小比
sŏbu kyobae 壻婦交拜
sŏch'ŏ 庶妻
sŏgan 石案
sŏgin 石人
sogong 小功
sogŭi 俗儀
sŏgyŏn puji pumo 壻見婦之父母
Sohak 小学
Sohye wanghu 昭惠王后
sŏin 庶人

sŏja　庶子
sojong　小宗
sojongja　小宗子
sok　俗
Sŏk　昔
sŏk　石
Sŏk-su　碩壽
Sok yukchŏn　續六典
sokchŏl　俗節
sŏksang　石床
sŏksil　石室
sŏmin　庶民
sŏmo　庶母
somok　昭穆
sŏn　善
Son Pyŏn　孫抃
sŏng　姓
Song Si-yŏl　宋時烈
Song-ssi　宋氏
Sŏng Ŏk　成抑
sŏngbu　成婦
Sŏnggyun'gwan　成均館
sŏnghak　聖学
"Sŏnghak chibyo"　聖学輯要
Sŏngjong　成宗
Sŏngni taejŏnsŏ chŏryo
　性理大全書節要
songnye　俗禮
Sŏngnyŏng taegun　誠寧大君
sŏn'gŏ　選擧
Sŏnjo　宣祖
Sŏnjong　宣宗
Sŏnsan Kim- ssi　善山金氏
sŏnwang　先王
sŏnyŏ　庶女
sŏnyŏng　先塋
sŏp'a　庶派
sosa　召史
sŏson　庶孫
Sŏun'gwan　書雲觀
sŏwŏn　書院
ssi　氏

ssijok　氏族
ssu-li　四禮
Ssu-ma Kuang　司馬光
Ssu-shu t'ung　四書通
sujŏl　守節
Sukchong　肅宗
Suksun　叔順
Sun-bin　純嬪
Sun Mu　孫穆
Sung　宋
sŭngjung minjŏn　承重民田
sŭngjung nobi　承重奴婢
sŭngjungja　承重子
Sunjong　順宗
sŭp　習
Suro　首露王
susin　修身
susinbang　守新房
susinjŏn　守信田
suyang　收養
suyangja　收養子
Suyang-siyang tŭngnok
　收養侍養謄錄
szu-li　四禮

"Ta-chuan"　大傳
Ta-hsüeh　大学
Ta-hsüeh yen-i　大学衍義
Ta-T'ang k'ai-yüan li
　大唐開元禮
ta-tsung　大宗
Ta-tsung hsiao-tsung t'u
　大宗小宗圖
ta-tsung-tzu　大宗子
taebang　大防
taebu　大夫
taech'ŏng　大廳
t'aegil　擇日
taegong　大功
"Taehak yŏnŭi chuja pal"
　大学衍義鑄字跋
t'aehu　太后

T'aejo 太祖
T'aejo hunyo 太祖訓要
taejok 大族
Taejŏn chuhae 大典註解
Taejŏn hoet'ong 大典會通
Taejŏn husongnok 大典後續錄
taejong 大宗
T'aejong 太宗
taejongga 大宗家
taejongja 大宗子
taek 宅
taemun 大門
t'alchŏkcha 奪嫡子
t'alchong 奪宗
t'alchŏng kibok 奪情起復
tallyŏng 團領
Tamyang-gun 潭陽君
T'ang 唐
tangnae 堂內
Tan'gun 檀君
tangyŏ 黨與
tanmun 祖免
te 德
teril sawi 데릴사위
t'ien-pao 天寶
todŏk 道德
"T'oegye sŏnsaeng ŏnhaengnok"
　退溪先生言行錄
tohak 道学
t'oho 土豪
t'ojang 土葬
tokcha 獨子
Tŏkchong 德宗
tŏkhwa 德化
t'ong 通
tongban 東班
tongbok hwahoe mun'gi
　同服和會文記
tongjok purak 同族部落
tongjong 同宗
tongjong chija 同宗支子
tongjong kŭnsok 同宗近屬

tongnoe 同牢
tongsaeng hwahoe mun'gi
　同生和會文記
tongsaengje 同生弟
tongsangnye 同床禮
tongsŏ 同壻(婿)
tongsŏng 同姓
t'op'ung 土風
t'osok 土俗
tot'ong 道統
tsa-lü 雜律
tseng-tsu-tsung 曾祖宗
Tseng Tzu 曾子
"Tseng Tzu wen" 曾子問
tsu 族
tsu-tsung 祖宗
tsun 尊
tsung 宗
tsung-fa 宗法
tsung-tzu 宗子
T'ung-chien kang-mu 通鑑綱目
Tzu-chih t'ung-chien 資治通鑑

U 禑王
U T'ak 禹倬
Uban 愚磻
ugwi 于歸
ŭi 義 (righteousness; moral
　responsibility)
ŭi 儀 (etiquette)
ŭibŏp 依法
ŭich'ŏp 依牒
ŭihon 議婚
ŭija 義子
ŭijang 義莊
Ŭijong 毅宗
Ŭirye sangjŏngso 儀禮詳定所
uje 虞祭
Uk 旭
ŭm 蔭
ŭmjik 蔭職
ŭmsa 淫祀

ŭmsŏ 蔭敍

ŭn 恩

urye 于禮

Wakō 倭寇

wanch'wi 完聚

Wang An-shih 王安石

"Wang-chih" 王制

Wang Kŏn 王建

Wang Kyu 王規

wangbi 王妃

wangbijo 王妃朝

wanghwa 王化

Wangt'aeja nappiŭi 王太子納妃儀

Wei Kung-su 韋公肅

Wen-hsien t'ung-k'ao 文獻通考

wiho 衛護

wit'o 位土

Wŏlsŏng Son-ssi 月城孫氏

wŏnja 元子

Wŏnjong 元宗

wŏnjong kongsin 原從功臣

Wu Ch'eng 吳澄

wu-fu 五服

wu-tsung 五宗

Wu wang 武王

yang 陽

yangban 兩班

yangbu 養父

yangbumo 養父母

yangch'ŏp 良妾

yangch'ŏpcha 良妾子

Yangdong 良洞

yangganyŏ 良家女

yangin 良人

yangmin 良民

yangmo 養母

Yangnyŏng taegun 讓寧大君

Yao 堯

Yao Shu 姚樞

Yao Sui 姚燧

ye 禮

yebu 豫婦

Yegi ch'ŏn'gyŏllok 禮記淺見錄

yegyŏng 禮經

yehak 禮学

yejang 禮葬

yejŏn 禮典

Yejong 睿宗

yesa 禮事

yesŏ 豫婿

Yeŭich'ujŏng togam 禮儀推正都監

Yi Cha 李籽

Yi Cha-gyŏm 李資謙

Yi Cha-ŭi 李資義

Yi Cha-yŏn 李子淵

Yi Chang-saeng 李長生

Yi Chi-bang 李之芳

Yi Chi-jŏ 李之氏

Yi Chik 李稷

Yi Chin 李瑱

Yi Cho 李慥

Yi Cho-nyŏn 李兆年

Yi Chung-hwan 李重煥

Yi Haeng 李行

Yi Hwa 李和

Yi-Hŏ Ki 李·許奇

Yi Hyŏn 李峴

Yi In-im 李仁任

Yi In-in 李仁人

Yi Kok 李穀

Yi Kye-maeng 李繼孟

Yi Maeng-gyun 李孟畇

Yi Pang-sŏk 李芳碩

Yi Pang-wŏn 李芳遠

Yi Sa-hu 李師厚

Yi Se-ch'ang 李世昌

Yi Sŏng-gye 李成桂

Yi Su-gwang 李睟光

Yi Suk-pŏn 李叔蕃

Yi Sung-in 李崇仁

Yi-ssi 李氏

Yi-ssi karok 李氏家錄
Yi T'aejo 李太祖
Yi T'aejo hojŏk wŏnbon
　李太祖戶籍原本
Yi Tŏk-su 李德壽
Yi Ŭi-bang 李義方
Yi Ŭi-jo 李宜朝
Yi Ŭi-min 李義旼
Yi Wŏn 李原
yin 陰
yŏ 女
Yŏgang Yi- ssi 驪江李氏
yŏ'gun 女君
yŏkch'ŏ 易妻
yŏllip 連立
yŏmmo 簾帽
yŏmyo 廬墓
yŏnbo 年譜
yŏng 令
yŏngch'ŏrya 靈撤夜
Yŏnghŭng 永興
"Yŏnghŭngbu hakkyogi"
　永興府学校記
yŏn'gil 涓吉
Yŏnsan'gun 燕山君
Yŏriga 於里加
yŏsŏ 女婿

yŏson 女孫
yu 儒 (Confucian)
yu 幽 (the world of the dead)
Yu In-jŏ 柳仁著
Yu Yŏng 柳穎
Yü Chi 虞集
Yüan 元
Yüan Ming-shan 元明善
yuch'ŏ ch'wich'ŏ 有妻娶妻
yugol 遺骨
Yukchŏn tŭngnok 六典謄錄
yuktup'um 六頭品
yumilkwa 油蜜菓
yumo 乳母
Yun P'yŏng 尹泙
Yun So-jong 尹紹宗
Yun Sŏn-jwa 尹宣佐
Yun T'aek 尹澤
yung-Hsia pien-i 用夏變夷
yung-ju 榮辱
yunhaeng 輪行
yuŏn 遺言
yuŏp 遺業
yusa 有司
yusin 維新
yusŏ 遺書

Index

Academy, Confucian, 94; in Koguryŏ, 14; in Silla, 14; officials of, sent to China, 18; reconstruction of, in Koryŏ, 18, 22, 99; role of, in early Chosŏn, 100; against Buddhism, 105, 180

Acculturation, 232

"Adopted son" (suyangja), 196, 215, 218, 220. See also Foster son

Adoption, 10, 48–49, 165, 196, 212–213; economic, 212; by widow, 221; replacing secondary son, 272

Adoption, non-agnatic, 214, 357n23; in Koryŏ, 48; prohibited in China, 214

Affinal ties, 341, 343

Adultery, 63, 192, 259, 276, 278

Agnates, collateral, 47

Agnatic descendants, 225, 230

Agnatic ideology, 133

Agnatic kin, 180

"Agnatic principle" (chongppŏp), 129, 130, 136, 139, 143, 191, 216, 268; and succession, 150; and ancestor worship, 164; as genealogical rule, 164; and ritual primogeniture, 176; and inheritance, 206. See also Lineal principle; Son, eldest

Agricultural techniques, improvement of, 224

"Altered rites" (pyŏllye), 163

An Chin, 20

An Hyang, 17, 18, 23

Ancestor, distinguished (hyŏnjo), 12. See also "Four ancestors"

"Ancestor Ceremonies for sadaebu Households" (sadaebuga cheŭi), 134

Ancestor worship, 25, 112, 176, 209, 285; of groups, 182

Ancestral cult, as starting point of transformatory process, 285

Ancestral fields and slaves (pongsa chŏnt'aek nobi), 168

Ancestral hall (sadang), 8, 9, 134, 138, 171, 197, 225, 236; establishment of, 135–136; and ritual heir, 168, 229; as center of ritual, 169, 176; fostering descent consciousness, 285. See also Domestic shrine

Ancestral home (chongga), 229

Ancestral land, 168, 205–206; sale of, prohibited, 211; inviolability of, 228. See also Patrimony

Ancestral prestige, 7

"Ancestral property" (choŏp), 218, 230; in Koryŏ, 43. See also Patrimony

Ancestral ritual (chesa), 175

Ancestral seat (pon'gwan), 6, 85, 308n4; and surname, 238–239; recorded of women, 264

Ancestral services: rotation of (yunhaeng), 168, 171, 227; seasonal (sije), 170; disappearance of, 226, 228–229

Ancient Chinese institutions, 107

"Ancient institutions" (koje), 107–108, 112, 118, 120, 122, 124, 125, 185

Andong Cho, 61

Andong Kim, 61, 333n15

Andong Kwŏn, 61, 96; genealogy of, 165

Ansan, Kim, 34, 58, 86

Apical ancestor (sijo), 6, 164, 172, 230

Aristocratic status, 47, 58, 294, 297. See also

428 *Index*